BOLLINGEN SERIES XCVII

C. G. JUNG
SPEAKING

Interviews and Encounters

EDITED BY

WILLIAM McGUIRE AND

R. F. C. HULL

BOLLINGEN SERIES XCVII

PRINCETON UNIVERSITY PRESS

"Doctor Jung: A Portrait in 1931," from *Harper's*, May 1931, copyright © 1931 by Harper's Magazine; copyright © renewed 1958 by Harper's Magazine. "The 2,000,000-Year-Old Man," from *The New York Times*, Oct. 4, 1936, © 1936 by The New York Times Company, and renewed 1964; reprinted by permission. "On the Frontiers of Knowledge" (the interview by Georges Duplain), from *Spring*, 1960, copyright 1960 by the Analytical Psychology Club of New York, Inc. The two "Talks with Miguel Serrano," from *C. G. Jung and Hermann Hesse*, copyright © 1966 by Miguel Serrano. Albert Oeri's memoir and "A Talk with Students at the Institute," from *Spring*, 1970, copyright © 1970 by the Analytical Psychology Club of New York, Inc. "Is Analytical Psychology a Religion?" from *Spring*, 1972, copyright © 1972 by the Analytical Psychology Club of New York, Inc. "The Hell of Initiation," from J. P. Hodin, *Modern Art and the Modern Mind*, copyright © 1972 by the Press of Case Western Reserve University. Passages from Esther Harding's notebooks, from *Quadrant*, winter 1975, copyright © 1975 by C. G. Jung Foundation for Analytical Psychology, Inc. "The Houston Films," from *Jung on Elementary Psychology*, copyright © 1964 and 1976 by Richard I. Evans.

To

Aniela Jaffé

TABLE OF CONTENTS

Contents

Contents

Contents

Contents

PREFACE

++++++++++++++++++++++++

Jung's psychological type, according to his own statement late in life, was that of the intuitive-intellectual introvert. This category of personality seems scarcely proper to an articulate, expressive, humorous, friendly man, ready, even eager, to talk not only with countless friends and acquaintances, but with visitors who were total strangers, sometimes telephoning him without introduction, and dozens of journalists, ranging widely in national origin and professional competence, bringing a barrage of questions ranging from the obvious to the learned. Would an intuitive-intellectual introvert sit for many hours under bright, uncomfortably hot lights while cameras filmed a lengthy interview dwelling on nearly every aspect of his psychological system and intellectual development? Jung did, and in his eighties. And, beyond all these callers and interviewers, Jung's professional role was talking as well as listening, and his hours spent in analysis and consultation, his seminars and lectures, involved him in far more of the behavior we call outgoing than most self-styled, or so-called, extroverts go in for.

This collection of interviews and encounters, selected from a large number of such documents, includes several kinds of testimony from and about Jung. The "purest," nearest to faithful records of Jung's spoken words are the transcripts from electronic recordings of the radio, film, and television interviews conducted by Weizsäcker, Black, Evans, Freeman, and Gerster, and the tape recording of Jung's talk to the Basel Psychology Club in 1958.[1] With

---

[1] The "oral history" era barely overlapped with Jung's lifetime. Some of his talks to groups in the last years of his life were taped, but there was only one interview with tape-recorder, so far as is known: by K. R. Eissler, for the Sigmund Freud Archives. The transcript is deposited in the Library of Congress, Washington, D. C., under restriction until the year 2002.

such transcripts, a great deal depends upon the expertise of the transcriber, and much can go wrong. The original version of the Houston filmed interview, published in 1964, was confounded by mishearings, misunderstandings, and bad guesses, inevitable when a typist in Texas listened to a rather hoarse Swiss-German voice discussing recondite matters in English. The exertions of four or five auditors familiar with Jung's manner of speaking, subject-matter, and favorite *exempla* put the transcript right, or nearly so, and a revised version of Professor Evans's notably comprehensive interview is closer to faithful. An even "purer" document would be a transcript of this sort that Jung himself had read, corrected, and approved, but he is not known to have worked over such a transcript. Going slightly down a scale, let us consider the transcript of a stenographic record, such as Derek Kitchin's stenogram of the question-and-answer session at Oxford in 1938. Another of Kitchin's skillful stenograms, of Jung's so-called seminar, "The Symbolic Life," given to members of the Guild for Pastoral Psychology in London in 1939, was indeed read and approved by Jung and therefore has merited a place in the Collected Works (in volume 18, which has been given the collective title *The Symbolic Life*). Jung's "Tavistock Lectures," delivered extemporaneously to a medical audience in London in 1935 and taken down by an anonymous shorthand writer, had a similar history. The editors of the Lectures thanked Jung for "passing the report in its final form," though Barbara Hannah tells us that she and Toni Wolff attended the lectures and corrected the transcript.[2] The "Tavistock Lectures" transcript, further corrected by R. F. C. Hull, is also in volume 18.

Undoubtedly, some of the journalists who interviewed Jung over many years took good shorthand notes. And

[2] Barbara Hannah, *Jung: His Life and Work* (New York, 1976), p. 234, where Miss Hannah (who became Jung's pupil in 1929) describes the occasion.

certainly, in the profession, trustworthy interviews have been conducted by reporters with sketchy or peculiar note-taking methods or with nothing but excellent memories. The fidelity of the journalistic interviews in this collection must be accepted on trust, on the reporter's reputation, or on the verisimilitude of the product. The interviewers range in time from the self-effacing anonymous *New York Times* reporter of 1912 (his or her name lost in the morgue of the *Times*) to the strictly pro Gordon Young of the London *Sunday Times* in 1960, and they include the veterans Whit Burnett, Elizabeth Shepley Sergeant (the only one with *echt* Jungian credentials), the archetypal foreign correspondent H. R. Knickerbocker, adroit Frederick Sands of the *Daily Mail*, and Georg Gerster, a gifted Swiss journalist-photographer.

The Viennese reporters, all unidentified, who flocked to interview Jung when he came to lecture at the Kulturbund in the late 1920's and early 1930's, liked to cast their articles in the form of first-person accounts. The similarity, usually, of several news stories printed on the same day suggests that Jung held press conferences. Actually, Jung was not a greatly celebrated figure in those days, and the attention paid him by the working press of Vienna had undoubtedly been promoted by a dynamic woman, Jolande Jacobi, who directed the Kulturbund's lecture program and in the mid 1930's, a Catholic born a Jew, fled to Zurich and became one of Jung's leading exponents.

Jung may have given more newspaper interviews on his travels than the clipping bureaus have supplied. An item from the Tunis press in 1923, the New Orleans *Times-Picayune* in January 1925, or the papers of Rhodes, Jerusalem, or Alexandria in 1933 would be worth unearthing. According to Fowler McCormick, who was Jung's companion when he visited India in 1938 as an honorary delegate to the Silver Jubilee of the Indian Science Congress in Calcutta, reporters swarmed around Jung in the cities—but

no news stories have come to light. As for Jung's unpubli-
cized trip to the United States in December 1924–January
1925, when he also traveled with Fowler McCormick, no
interviews have been traced, and only a couple of brief news
stories have been unearthed.[3] Still, friendly and articulate
introvert as Jung was, he may have granted interviews on
his travels, not only in exotic places like Texas (driving
through in a Chevrolet) and Khartoum (where, in 1926, he
gave a talk at Gordon College) but in the European cities
he constantly visited—these could be embedded like rhi-
zomes in crumbling bound copies and coils of microfilm.

A sub-category of journalist is the literary personage or
savant who, for one reason or another, ventures into journalistic territory. Victoria Ocampo, the celebrated Argentine
woman of letters, often turned her travels and adventures
into *feuilletons* for Buenos Aires papers. Her account of a
visit to Jung in 1934 reads as if she had never known him
before; in any case, through Count Keyserling's epistolary
analysis with Jung, Jung knew her. The Rev. Dr. Howard
L. Philp, psychologist and Anglican priest, drew some fresh
quotables out of Jung in an ostensibly political interview.
An art historian and international civil servant, Pierre
Courthion, took on an interview assignment in the darkest
days of the Second World War, and we hear something
about the furniture in Jung's house along with sober com-

[3] For example, from the *Taos Valley News* (Taos, New Mexico),
Sat., Jan. 10, 1925, headed "Illustrious Visitors to Taos": "Dr. Carl
Jung, world famed psychologist and contemporary of Freud, in
company with Fowler McCormick, son of the famous harvester
machinery magnate and grandson of John D. Rockefeller, Sr. visited
Taos Monday of this week. The party is touring the United States
and came up from Santa Fe to see the ancient village. While here
they registered at the Columbian Hotel." In the same issue, headed
"Visits Taos Again": "James Angelo [Jaime de Angulo], professor
of anthropology in Berkeley University, Calif., visited Taos and attended the Buffalo Dance at the pueblo Tuesday. Mr. Angelo has
been a frequent visitor to Taos, this time accompanying Dr. Jung
and Mr. McCormick. The gentlemen are traveling across the country
in a Chevrolet."

ment appropriate to the time. The novelist Alberto Moravia went to Zurich for a Milan paper and, in the course of walking up the Seestrasse to interview this rather odd Swiss psychiatrist, ruminated on F. Scott Fitzgerald, oblivious that there might have been a real connection. A famous geographer, Hans Carol, who reached the peak of his career after he emigrated to Canada, recalled a conversation in which Jung talked like a social thinker. J. P. Hodin and Patricia Hutchins were each seeking to sound Jung out on an explicit subject, for the book each was writing, and each one got a little more than he was after. Miguel Serrano, who must have been one of the few mystics in any diplomatic corps, appeared to draw out the Jung that he wanted; his accounts are, in any case, impressive and unsettling. Mircea Eliade had already joined Jung at the Eranos Tagung when he undertook an interpretative article aimed at a French public ignorant of Jung (and only slightly aware, at that time, of Freud); the copious direct quotations, heard and set down in the numinous precincts of Eranos, have the authentic ring.

The observations of people who encountered C. G. Jung without having a preconceived interest, or an assignment, are relatively rare. Francis Daniel Hislop, a retired British colonial official, happened to recall an encounter with an obscure, rather wrong-headed, but plainly unforgettable doctor thirty-five years before. Charles Lindbergh went along with his wife's publishers to meet Jung, got involved in the "flying saucers" puzzle (or nonsense, if one was a retired Air Force officer), and fortunately wrote up a vivid account of the visit nearly ten years later. One hopes for more reports of this kind. Did any of the British Army officers interned at Chateau d'Oex, under Jung's command, in the First World War, keep a journal or write descriptive letters home? That was the time when Jung drew a mandala every morning upon rising.

The memories of Jung's boyhood playmate and lifelong

friend Albert Oeri—a professional writer and editor, here writing extra-professionally—though set down nearly fifty years after the occasion, are sharp and amusing. One wants to believe what Oeri wrote: its irreverence validates it. A different sort of document came from Ximena de Angulo, who—the daughter of Cary F. Baynes, translator of Richard Wilhelm's version of the *I Ching*, and of Jaime de Angulo, student of Indian languages, who took Jung to Taos in 1925, and step-daughter of H. G. Baynes, the most prominent Jungian analyst in England—grew up close to the Jung family. She interviewed Jung, in professional style, as a friendly service to a young student, Ira Progoff, concerning his manuscript about Jung. The talk ranged wide, and Ximena de Angulo's report is one of the most incisive and intellectually solid interviews we have.

The memoirs of Jung's devoted followers are suspect as being furthest from objectivity. And yet, who would misquote Dr. Jung? There must be many private records and journals in Jungian cupboards. Passages from Esther Harding's journal were published only after her death, and the material she wrote up is unexpected, at least in the entries for the earlier years, when Jung's attitude toward religion had not been well defined in his writings. Charles Baudouin's journal entries are more subjective and more poetic; he willingly published them, in a book that was posthumous. The recollections of Amy Allenby, Kenneth Lambert, Renée Brand, Elizabeth Osterman, George Hogle, and Margaret Tilly were set down expressly for memorial publications after Jung's death. Each is distinctive and immediate and lights up different facets of Jung. Eleanor Bertine's and Carol Baumann's accounts were prepared to enlighten the Club members back in New York. The Bertine article has a fresh, naïve quality, like a letter home from summer camp. Mrs. Baumann's factual testimony was aimed at correcting the misunderstandings arising from the Ezra Pound/Bollingen Prize controversy, but its readers surely included no doubters, and it deserved to be circulated far more widely.

The most considerable body of "Jung speaking" is not drawn upon for the present book: the "notes" of Jung's Seminars, which he led, mostly in Zurich, from the early 1920's (perhaps earlier, but not recorded) up to the late 1930's. These lively, erudite, and probably rapid-fire sessions were recorded by members and later by professional stenographers. It is unlikely that Jung passed many of the transcripts, and yet, in earlier days, his personal permission (plus a hundred hours of analysis) was requisite to reading them. The real moving force behind the Seminar Notes was a remarkable American woman painter, Mary Foote, whose search for meaning had led her around Europe and then to China. She wrote Jung for an appointment, was given one, and took a long, slow ocean voyage westward in order to keep it. Once in Zurich, she stayed for nearly twenty years—through the war years—and devoted herself to editing the Seminar Notes. The transcripts are mostly still under restriction, but gradually some are being published. For the most part, they give an unvarnished record of what Jung said both in his set lectures and in the roundtable discussions that followed.

The present collection was begun in the mid 1960's, when a profusion of Jung's posthumata was being compiled and studied. Much of that material, actually written by Jung or in the form of transcripts that he approved, is included in volume 18 of the Collected Works. The present volume, outside the Collected Works, was set aside for interviews, and R.F.C. Hull translated, edited, and partially annotated several of these. After his death, in 1974, a great deal more material was added, much of it discovered lately; some thirty items were added when it was decided to broaden the collection to include encounters with Jung as well as interviews, and the headnotes and most of the footnotes were composed. The Editors of the Collected Works—Gerhard Adler, Michael Fordham, and Herbert Read—advised at the early stages of selection, and advice and help were also given by Mr. and Mrs. Franz Jung, Jane A. Pratt, and in particular Aniela Jaffé. The translators who participated, mainly after R.F.C. Hull's death, are named at the end of the articles they prepared: Mrs. Pratt, Ruth Horine, Lisa Ress, Helen Temple, Martin Nozick, Robert and Rita Kimber, Elined Prys Kotschnig, and Frank MacShane. The translations otherwise are Hull's.

The articles have been edited in different ways. Some are given in full, some are abridged more or less, some are recast in dialogue style when this is appropriate. Some, of course, were originally in dialogue style. The headnote to each article indicates what modifications were made. Three dots in the middle of a line indicate an omission. Spellings, etc., have been conformed.

W. M.

NOTE FOR THE 1986 PRINTING

Because of an error in the *Spring 1972* publication of Jung's talk, "Is Analytical Psychology a Religion?" it was incorrectly dated 1937 in this volume (p. 94). The date is now corrected to 1936 and the editorial preface also corrected. This printing contains a few other corrections of factual details.

W. M.

ACKNOWLEDGMENTS

++++++++++++++++++++++++++

Gerhard Adler, for guidance, advice, and information;

Doris Albrecht, Librarian of the Kristine Mann Library, for help with many research problems;

Ruth Bailey, for information and advice;

Stephen Black, for his 1955 BBC interviews;

Dietrich von Bothmer, of the Metropolitan Museum of Art, for information;

British Broadcasting Corporation, for the interviews by Stephen Black and John Freeman;

Joseph Campbell, for information;

Case Western Reserve University, for extracts from J. P. Hodin's *Modern Art and the Modern Mind*;

Dorothy Curzon, for information on Margaret Tilly;

Hans Dieckmann, for help;

Joyce M. Dongray, of BBC, for help in locating Dr. Black;

Mircea Eliade, for his interview in *Combat*, 1952;

Richard I. Evans, for his interviews constituting the "Houston Films" (fully acknowledged on p. 276);

Michael Fordham, for extracts from *Contact with Jung*, and his guidance and advice;

Marie-Louise von Franz, for auditing the "Houston Films" transcript;

John Freeman, for his "Face to Face" interview for the BBC;

Georg Gerster, for his interviews of 1957 and 1960 and for information;

Manfred Halpern, for advice;

Barbara Hannah, for auditing the "Houston Films" transcript;

Harper's Magazine, for E. S. Sergeant's 1931 portrait of Jung;

Hearst Magazines, for extracts from Jung's 1934 article and H. R. Knickerbocker's 1939 interview, both in *Hearst's International–Cosmopolitan*;

Joseph Henderson, M.D., for information on Margaret Tilly;

Her Majesty's Stationery Office, London, for F. D. Hislop's article "Doctor Jung, I Presume," in *Corona*, June 1960;

xix

Acknowledgments

Jasna P. Heurtley, for finding several interviews;

Dr. James Hillman, editor of *Spring*, for permission to use Albert Oeri, "Some Youthful Memories," and Marian Bayes' transcript of a talk with students, from *Spring* 1970, and "Is Analytical Psychology a Religion?", from *Spring* 1972, and for his advice and help;

George H. Hogle, M.D., for reminiscences of his 1947 visit with Jung;

Patricia Hutchins (Graecen), for extracts from her book *James Joyce's World*;

Aniela Jaffé, for her advice and help on countless details;

the Heirs of C. G. Jung, for Jung's spoken words in the interviews recorded for radio, television, and film, and by tape recorder, and their help in general;

the C. G. Jung Foundation for Analytical Psychology, Inc., New York, for extracts from Esther Harding's journal, edited by E. A. Edinger, M.D., and published in *Quadrant*;

Major Donald E. Keyhoe, USMC (Ret.), for advice concerning Lindbergh's 1968 letter about his visit with Jung;

James Kirsch, M.D., for advice and information;

Elined Prys Kotschnig, for her translation of Charles Baudouin's journal extracts in *Inward Light*;

Pamela Long, for research and much other help;

William McCleery, for information about *PM* in 1945;

C. A. Meier, M.D., for advice and information;

The New York Times, for the interview of Oct. 4, 1936;

Gerda Niedieck, for help and advice;

The Observer, London, for extracts from the interviews of Oct. 6, 1935, and Oct. 18, 1936;

Victoria Ocampo, for her 1936 interview in *La Nacion*;

Claire Myers Owens, for her 1954 encounter with Jung, and for information about her work;

Payot (publishers), Paris, for extracts from Charles Baudouin's *L'Oeuvre de Jung*;

Canon Howard L. Philp, for his 1939 interview and for information;

Jane A. Pratt, for advice and help, in addition to her translations;

Acknowledgments

Ira Progoff, for agreeing to the publication of Ximena de Angulo's 1952 interview about his thesis, and for advice;

Dr. I. Reichstein, for the 1958 Basel "seminar";

Lisa Ress, for finding several interviews, in addition to her translation;

Ximena de Angulo Roelli, for her 1952 interview on the Progoff thesis;

Frederick Sands, for extracts from his 1955 interview in the *Daily Mail*;

Schocken Books, Inc., for extracts from Miguel Serrano's *C. G. Jung and Hermann Hesse: A Record of Two Friendships* (United States edn.) translated by Frank MacShane, copyright © 1960 by Miguel Serrano;

Scripps-Howard Newspapers, for Whit Burnett's 1931 interview;

Don L. Stacy, for bringing to the editors' attention Derek Kitchin's transcript of Jung's answers to questions at Oxford, 1938;

The Sunday Times, London, for extracts from Gordon Young's 1960 interview;

Tavistock Publications, for extracts from *Contact with Jung*;

Katharine S. White, for information about her sister, Elizabeth Shepley Sergeant;

Harry Wilmer, M.D., for help with a tape of the Stephen Black interview;

Helen Wolff, for extracts from Charles A. Lindbergh's 1968 letter to her, with the agreement of Anne Morrow Lindbergh.

BIBLIOGRAPHICAL NOTE

CW = *The Collected Works of C. G. Jung*, edited by Herbert Read, Michael Fordham, Gerhard Adler, and William McGuire, and translated by R.F.C. Hull. Princeton and London, 1953–78. 20 vols.

The Freud/Jung Letters, edited by William McGuire, translated by Ralph Manheim and R.F.C. Hull. Princeton and London, 1974.

Letters = *C. G. Jung: Letters*, selected and edited by Gerhard Adler in collaboration with Aniela Jaffé, translations from the German by R.F.C. Hull. Princeton and London, 1973–75.

Memories, Dreams, Reflections by C. G. Jung, recorded and edited by Aniela Jaffé; translated by Richard and Clara Winston. New York and London, 1963. (The editions are differently paginated, therefore double page references are given, first to the New York edn.)

Spring: An Annual of Archetypal Psychology and Jungian Thought. Zurich and New York.

C. G. JUNG SPEAKING

SOME YOUTHFUL MEMORIES

✦✦✦✦✦✦✦✦✦✦✦✦✦✦✦✦✦✦✦✦✦✦✦✦

Albert Oeri (1875–1950), of Basel, was Jung's contemporary, childhood playmate, and fellow student in school and at Basel University. He earned his Ph.D. degree in classical philology and history, and ultimately he became editor-in-chief of the *Basler Nachrichten* and a member of the Swiss National Council. In 1935, Oeri was invited to contribute to a *Festschrift* for Jung's sixtieth birthday,[1] and he wrote these reminiscences. They were translated for publication in *Spring*, 1970.

Though Oeri was writing forty years and more after the events and impressions that he described, his encounters with Jung have the clarity and vividness of recent experiences. This version is slightly abridged.

I suppose I first set eyes on Jung during the time his father was pastor at Dachsen am Rheinfall and we were still quite small. My parents visited his—our fathers were old school friends—and they all wanted their little sons to play together. But nothing could be done. Carl sat in the middle of a room, occupied himself with a little bowling game, and didn't pay the slightest attention to me. How is it that after some fifty-five years I remember this meeting at all? Probably because I had never come across such an asocial monster before. I was born into a well-populated nursery where we played together or fought, but in any case always had contact with people; he into an empty one—his sister had not yet been born.

In the middle years of my boyhood, we sometimes visited the Jung family on Sunday afternoons at the parsonage at Klein-Hüningen, a community near Basel. From the outset,

[1] *Die kulturelle Bedeutung der komplexen Psychologie*, edited by the Psychological Club, Zurich (Berlin: Julius Springer, 1935), pp. 524–528.

Carl displayed a spontaneous friendliness toward me, because he realized that I was no sissy, and he wanted me to join him in teasing a cousin whom he regarded as one. He asked this boy to sit down on a bench in the entrance way. When the boy complied, Carl burst into whoops of wild Indian laughter, an art he retained all his life. The sole reason for his huge satisfaction was that an old souse had been sitting on the bench a short time before and Carl hoped that his sissy cousin would thus stink a little of schnapps. Another time he staged a solemn duel between two fellow students in the parsonage garden, probably so that he could have a good laugh over them later. When one of the boys hurt his hand Carl was truly grieved. Father Jung was even more upset, for he remembered that in his own youth the father of the injured boy, seriously hurt during duelling practice, was carried into his own father's house. We were especially afraid that there would be trouble at school. But when our old headmaster, Fritz Burckhardt, heard of the accident, he merely asked the "duellists" with a mild smile, "Have you been playing at fencing?"

I got somewhat better acquainted with Jung behind his back by secretly reading his school compositions awaiting correction in my father's study. Since my father generally allowed a free choice of topics, one could cheerfully bring up whatever one liked, provided one had any ideas at all. And Jung had plenty of ideas even then, along with the ability to present them. Nevertheless, he would not have received his diploma if the demand for a definite statement of proficiency in all subjects had been rigorously enforced at that time. He was, frankly, an idiot in mathematics. But in those days, happily and sensibly, failing marks were ignored when the partially untalented student was known to be otherwise intelligent.

Jung really wasn't responsible for his defect in mathematics. It was a hereditary failing that went back at least

4

three generations. On October 26, 1859, his grandfather wrote in his diary, after hearing a lecture by Zöllner about a photometrical instrument: "I understood just about nothing at all. As soon as anything in the world has the slightest connection with mathematics, my mind clouds over. I haven't blamed my boys for their stupidity in this respect. It's their inheritance."[2]

Apropos of this quotation, I will take the opportunity to say a few words about Jung's family history. His father was, as already mentioned, the pastor Paul Jung, born December 21, 1842, and died January 28, 1896. He was the youngest son of the diary keeper quoted above, Dr. Carl Gustav Jung, Senior, doctor and professor of medicine at Basel, born September 7, 1795, in Mannheim, where his father was medical advisor and court doctor; he died June 12, 1864, in Basel. Carl Gustav senior had a strange fate. As a young doctor and chemistry teacher at the military school, a great career seemed to lie before him in Berlin. But through his activities as a fraternity member and his participation in the Wartburg Festival, he became involved in the whirl of demagogic persecution, and spent thirteen (according to other versions, nineteen) months in the Hausvogtei prison, finally being set free without ever having been sentenced. He then went to Paris, where Alexander von Humboldt helped him to obtain a position at the University of Basel. He had thirteen children from three marriages. His third wife, mother of the pastor at Klein-Hüningen, was descended from the Freys, an old Basel family. Although he was not a psychiatrist but, in order, professor first of anatomy and then of internal medicine, he founded the "Institute of Hope" for retarded children, and lavished upon the inmates year after year the most personal love and care. His student, the Leipzig anatomist Wilhelm His, wrote: "In Jung, Basel possessed an unusually fine and rich human

[2] Ernst Jung, *Aus den Tagebüchern meines Vaters* (Winterthur, 1910).—A.O.

5

nature. Through the wealth of his spirit, Jung gladdened and heartened his fellow man for decades; his creative powers and the ability to give warmly of himself bore fruit to the benefit of the University, the city, and above all, the sick and needy."[3]

Now for the other side. Carl Gustav Jung's mother, the Klein-Hüningen pastor's wife, was born Emilie Preiswerk, the youngest child of Basler churchwarden Samuel Preiswerk (September 19, 1799—January 13, 1871) and his second wife, a pastor's daughter named Faber from Ober-Ensingen in Württemberg. C. G. Jung's maternal grandfather, like his father's father, had thirteen children. Jung has himself given some information about the psychic constitution of his mother's family in his first paper, "On the Psychology and Pathology of So-Called Occult Phenomena."[4] Churchwarden Preiswerk, administrator of the Basel church, was a visionary who often experienced entire dramatic scenes complete with ghost conversations. He was, however, also a very intelligent and learned gentleman, specifically in the area of Hebrew philology. His grammar book was held in such high esteem by the Jews that in America one of them changed his name to "Preiswerk."

Otherwise the Preiswerks are a patrician family of Basel, and thoroughly Aryan. Pastor Paul Jung, by the way, had an interest in Semitic philology in common with his father-in-law. In Göttingen he had studied under Ewald, and was not only a theologian but also a Doctor of Philosophy. To sum up: scientific abilities and interests are well represented in Jung's paternal as well as maternal ancestry, but those who possessed them were quite dry, scholarly types.

As far as I know, Jung never considered studying anything but medicine. And he applied himself vigorously to its study from the summer semester of 1895 on. That very

[3] Memorial Publication Commemorating the Opening of the Vesalianum, Leipzig, 1885.—A.O.
[4] Orig. 1902; in CW 1, pars. 63ff.

winter his father died. I remember how, shortly before his death, he who had once been so strong and erect complained that Carl had to carry him around like a heap of bones in an anatomy class. Carl's mother together with both children moved into a house near the "Bottminger Mill" in the Basel suburban community of Binningen. She was a wise and courageous woman. When her son once happened to sit in the Zofinger pub until dawn, he thought of her on the way home, and picked her a bouquet of wild flowers by way of appeasement.

Carl—or "the Barrel" as he is still known to his old school and drinking companions—was a very merry member of the Zofingia student club, always prepared to revolt against the "League of Virtue," as he called the organized fraternity brothers. He was rarely drunk, but when so, noisy. He didn't think much of school dances, romancing the house-maids, and similar gallantries. He told me once that it was absolutely senseless to hop around a ballroom with some female until one was covered with sweat. But then he discovered that, although he had never taken lessons, he could dance quite well. At a festival in Zofingen, while dancing in the grand Heitern Platz, he fell seemingly hopelessly in love with a young lady from French Switzerland. One morning soon after, he entered a shop, asked for and received two wedding rings, put twenty centimes on the counter, and started for the door. But the owner stammered something about the cost of the rings being a certain number of francs. So Jung gave them back, retrieved the twenty centimes, and left the store cursing the owner, who, just because Carl happened to possess absolutely nothing but twenty centimes, dared to interfere with his engagement. Carl was very depressed, but never tackled the matter again, and so "the Barrel" remained unaffianced for quite a number of years.

From the first, Jung very actively participated in the Zofingia club meetings, where scholarly reports were read and discussed. In the minutes of the Zofingia, of which, by the way, he was president during the winter semester 1897/98, I find mention of the following papers given by him: "On the Limits of Exact Science," "Some Reflections on the Nature and Value of Speculative Research," "Thoughts on the Concept of Christianity with Reference to the Teachings of Albert Ritschl."[5] Once, when we couldn't get a speaker, Jung suggested that we might hold a discussion without specifying the topic. The minutes read, "Jung *vulgo* 'Barrel,' the pure spirit having gone to his head, urged that we debate hitherto unresolved philosophical questions. This was agreeable to all, more agreeable than might have been expected under our usual 'prevailing circumstances.' But 'Barrel' blithered endlessly, and that was dumb. Oeri, *vulgo* 'It,' likewise spiritually oiled, distorted, in so far as such was still possible, these barreling thoughts . . ." At the next meeting, Jung succeeded in having the word "blithered," which he held to be too subjective, struck from the minutes and replaced by the word "talked."

In this single instance, Jung failed in what he was otherwise generally successful in doing, that is, in intellectually dominating an unruly chorus of fifty or sixty students from different branches of learning, and luring them into highly speculative areas of thought, which to the majority of us were an alien wonderland. When he gave his paper "Some Thoughts on Psychology," as club secretary I could have recorded some thirty discussion topics. It must be remembered that we were studying in the second half of the nineteenth century, a time when an attitude of open materialism was firmly entrenched among doctors and natural scientists, and when so-called scholars of the humanities expressed a kind of total and arrogant critique of the human spirit. Yet despite this, Jung, by choice an outsider, was able to keep everyone under his intellectual thumb.

This was possible—and I would not wish to conceal it—because he had courageously schooled himself, intensively studying occult literature, conducting parapsychological ex-

[5] The publication of Jung's "Zofingia Lectures" is projected.

periments, and finally standing by the convictions he derived therefrom, except where corrected by the result of more careful and detailed psychological studies. He was appalled that the official scientific position of the day toward occult phenomena was simply to deny their existence, rather than to investigate and explain them. For this reason, spiritualists such as Zöllner and Crookes, about whose teachings he could speak for hours, became for him heroic martyrs of science. Among his friends and relatives he found participants for séances. I cannot say anything more detailed about them, for I was at the time so deeply involved in Kantian critique that I could not be drawn in myself. My psychic opposition would have neutralized the atmosphere. But in any case, I was open-minded enough to merit Jung's honest zeal. It was really wonderful to let oneself be lectured to, as one sat with him in his room. His dear little dachshund would look at me so earnestly, just as though he understood every word, and Jung did not fail to tell me how the sensitive animal would sometimes whimper piteously when occult forces were active in the house.

Sometimes too Jung would sit late into the night with his closer friends at the "Breo," an old Zofinger pub in the Steinen district. Afterwards, he didn't like walking home alone through the sinister Nightingale Woods all the way to the Bottminger Mill. As we were leaving the tavern, therefore, he would simply begin talking to one of us about something especially interesting, and so one would accompany him, without noticing it, right to his front door. Along the way he might interrupt himself by noting, "On this spot Doctor Götz was murdered," or something like that. In parting, he would offer his revolver for the trip back. I was not afraid of Dr. Götz's ghost, nor of living evil spirits, but I was afraid of Jung's revolver in my pocket. I have no talent for mechanical things at all, and never knew whether the safety catch was on or whether, due to some careless motion, the gun might not suddenly go off.

At the end of his University years, Jung went into psychiatry. Because I was out of the country for some time, I don't remember the transition period. He had simply found his destined way. That I could not doubt when I visited him once during his residency at Burghölzli and he told me of his lively enthusiasm for his work. It was somewhat painful, though, for this old sinner to see that he had begun to follow his master, Bleuler, on the path of total abstinence as well. At that time he would look so sourly at a glass on the table that the wine would turn to vinegar. Jung very kindly showed me around the institution, accompanying the tour with informative comments. In the wards, restless patients stood around or lay on their beds. Jung engaged some of them in conversation from time to time, wherein their delusions became perceptible. One patient spoke eagerly to me, and I was listening just as eagerly, when suddenly a heavy fist whizzed through the air right next to me. Behind my back an irritated patient who had been lying in bed had sat up and tried to punch me. Jung did not contest my fright at all; instead, he told me that the man could hit with great force if one didn't keep a certain distance from his bed. And at the same time he laughed so hard that I felt like that beleaguered sissy at the Klein-Hüningen parsonage.

[*Translated by Lisa Ress*]

AMERICA FACING ITS MOST
TRAGIC MOMENT

◆◆◆◆◆◆◆◆◆◆◆◆◆◆◆◆◆◆◆◆◆◆◆◆◆

Jung made his third visit to the United States in September
1912, at the invitation of Fordham University, in the Bronx,
New York, to lecture on psychoanalysis. His previous visits
had been in September 1909, for a month, when he and Freud
were invited to lecture at Clark University, in Worcester, Mass.,
and had afterwards traveled as far west as Niagara Falls; and
in March 1910, for a week, when he was summoned to Chicago
for a psychiatric consultation. When Jung received the Fordham
invitation, in March 1912, he and Freud were ostensibly on
friendly terms—their correspondence, at least, still seemed
to be cordial—but in the months following, their differences
flared up. Jung's Fordham lectures, entitled "The Theory of
Psychoanalysis," proved to be more of a critique than an exposition of Freudian theory. While he was in New York, Jung
not only delivered the lectures at Fordham—nine of them, to
an audience of about ninety psychiatrists and neurologists—but
held a two-hour seminar every day for a fortnight, gave clinical lectures at Bellevue Hospital and the New York Psychiatric
Institute on Ward's Island, and addressed the New York
Academy of Medicine. It is not surprising that he attracted
the attention of *The New York Times*, so that an interview
was conducted and the resulting article published, at exceptional length, in the magazine section of the *Times* on Sunday,
September 29. There was a three-quarter photo-portrait, by the
Campbell Studio, a stylish establishment in the Waldorf-Astoria
Hotel, and at the head of the article, framed in a box, was a
selection of aphorisms drawn from Jung's own words (see
below). The anonymous interviewer's own explanatory remarks,
which were interpolated midway, are mostly given here (in
italics) as introduction.

*(Dr. Carl Jung is the Professor of Psychiatry and Psychol-
ogy at the University of Zurich, where for years he has been*

doing work in psychoanalysis.[1] *He is well known in Europe through this work and through his writings. It was he who brought Dr. Sigmund Freud to the recognition of the older school of psychology, and together these two men stand at the head of a school of thought which is considered by many students of the subject to give the most radical explanation of the human mind, and the most fundamental, since the beginning of its study. Dr. Jung lays emphasis upon the fact that psychoanalysis brings to the surface of the conscious mind all the hidden memories and factors of the unconscious mind—which has so long been called the subconscious. He believes that, if a man can understand his hidden motives and impulses, he comes into a new power.*

It is the search for this power as it is to be found in the individual, in the Nation, or in the race which makes psychoanalysis—in the eyes of its followers—the greatest human study being carried on today. Everything that science has discovered is used by these new psychologists. All the fruits of literature, all the myths of the ancients, serve to reveal the hidden influences of man and society.

Psychoanalysis came into maturity in the materialistic age when the followers of Darwin and Spencer believed that they had the whole truth and the full wisdom. All the explanations that were being given were "scientific" and based upon what seemed to the scientist tangible proofs. The schools of neurologists and physiological psychologists all insisted that they, too, were scientific; but there were, nevertheless, many things still in the dark which seemed to be of equal value with all that was known of the mind and its mechanism.

Dr. Sigmund Freud of Vienna, in his study of the hysteria and insanity which came under his attention as a physician, was the first psychologist to persist in searching for the cause which science says must in every case precede

---

[1] In the *Times* article, the older spelling "psychanalysis" is used throughout. It has been edited here to "psychoanalysis," but in general the editing is merely stylistic.

the effect. Other psychologists had ascribed all mental derangements to physical causes, and yet had attained comparatively small results in the treatment of certain cases. This led Freud to believe that there was something besides a physical cause, and he went upon the theory that a mental effect might well have a mental cause in combination with a physical. This made him, in the eyes of his colleagues, a revolutionist, even though his method of study was more thoroughly scientific than that of his predecessors. The great number of cures that he can point to as a result of his method—psychoanalysis—has forced his antagonists to accept much of what he has done, but the war between the new and the old method is still on in Europe, and its echoes are heard here in this country wherever physicians meet together to discuss hysteria, neurosis, and other manifestations of psychic derangement.

Dr. Carl Jung has proceeded upon this same theory, and has added to it other scientific processes. His classrooms are crowded with students, who are eager to understand what seems to many to be an almost miraculous treatment. His clinics are crowded with medical cases which have baffled other doctors, and he is here in America to lecture upon his subject. There is antagonism here, too, but Dr. Jung finds a growing interest in psychoanalysis.)

When I see so much refinement and sentiment as I see in America,[2] I look always for an equal amount of brutality. The pair of opposites—you find them everywhere.

[2] Jung's first analysis of American society took the form of a "Report on America" which he delivered to the Second International Psychoanalytic Congress, at Nuremberg in March 1910, immediately after returning from his second visit. It survives only as a brief abstract (in CW 18, par. 1284; also see par. 1285). For more on his American visits, see *The Freud/Jung Letters*, pp. 245–46 (1909), 301–4 (1910), and 513–16 (1912). For Jung's later observations on the psychology of Americans, particularly his theory of a "Negro complex," see "Mind and Earth" (1927), CW 10, pars. 95ff., and "The Complications of American Psychology" (1930), CW 10. His Fordham lectures, "The Theory of Psychoanalysis," are in CW 4.

1912

America is the most tragic country in the world today.

Prudery is always the cover for brutality.

The chivalry of the South is a reaction against its instinctive desire to imitate the Negro.

The American women have to work harder than any other women to attract the men of their country.

The reason American girls like to marry foreigners is not love of titles, but love of men who are a little dangerous.

America is the most emotional country, and the country of the greatest self-control.

The effort to maintain self-control in the face of brutal instinct makes us a land of neurasthenics.

In America you distrust a man if he has more than one idea.

American wives have thrown themselves into social activity because they are not happy with their husbands. Neither the men nor the women know this.

The regeneration of America depends on whether it has the courage to face itself.

Eliminate prudery and America may become the greatest country the world has ever known.

American women rule the home because the American men have not yet learned to love them.

I find the greatest self-control in the world among the Americans—and I search for its cause. Why should there be so much self-control, I ask myself, in America, and I find for an answer brutality. I find a great deal of prudery. What is the cause, I ask, and I discover brutality. Prudery is always the cover for brutality. It is necessary—it makes life possible until you discover the brute and take real control of it. When you do that in America, then you will be the most emotional, the most temperamental, the most fully developed people in the world.

It seems to me that you are about to discover yourselves.

You have discovered everything else—all the land of this continent, all the resources, all the hidden things of Nature which can serve you in the building of your Nation. You have built your big cities and crowded your cities with theatres and clubs and cathedrals and schoolhouses. It is all ready and waiting for you to use to some great end when you shall discover yourselves. To do that you will have to study your own self-control, you will have to analyze your own consciousness, you will have to admit that you have been hiding from yourselves ever since the Puritans and Huguenots came to this country.

You will not be ashamed of the brutality when you understand it, and as soon as you understand it, it will be transformed into great emotions which shall give impetus to your National development far beyond what you now hope for. Your success in all the big things of art and literature will astound Europe, as today it is astounded by your great systems of business and philanthropy.

In America, as in all countries entered by a conquering race, the conquerors always drop toward the level of the conquered, for it is much easier to go down ten feet than to climb up one. The whole effort toward human development is to push us up that one foot, and if we let go any of the things which we have gained by civilization, we slip quickly. In South Africa the Dutch, who were at the time of their colonizing a developed and civilized people, dropped to a much lower level because of their contact with the savage races. The savage inhabitants of a country have to be mastered. In the attempt to master, brutality rises in the master. He must be ruthless. He must sacrifice everything soft and fine for the sake of mastering savages. Their influence is very great; the more surely they are dominated, the more savage the master must become. The slave has the greatest influence of all, because he is kept close to the one who rules him.

In America the Indians do not influence you now; they

have fallen back before your power, and they are very few. They influenced your ancestors. You, today, are influenced by the Negro race, which not so long ago had to call you master. In the North the Negro's present influence is not great. In the South, where they are not given opportunities equal to the white race, their influence is very great. They are really in control.

I notice that your Southerners speak with the Negro accent; your women are coming to walk more and more like the Negro. In the South I find what they call sentiment and chivalry and romance to be the covering of cruelty. Cruelty and chivalry are another pair of opposites. The Southerners treat one another very courteously, but they treat the Negro as they would treat their own unconscious mind if they knew what was in it. When I see a man in a savage rage with something outside himself, I know that he is, in reality, wanting to be savage toward his own unconscious self.[3]

Your American mind is very direct. It is very logical. It deals so much of the time with what we call reality, that is, with the raw materials of life, in order to bring forth your great enterprises, your great buildings, that you have learned to think, to reason, upon abstractions. If a man in America sees there is some small gap in his business which must be filled to make the business effective, he does not think merely of his own peculiar enterprise, but he thinks

[3] Interviewer's interpolation: "This word 'unconscious,' which Dr. Jung uses constantly, signifies to him all that lies below the threshold of that part of the mind which we recognize as conscious. He believes that in our growth, in childhood and youth, we are storing this unconsciousness of ours with fears and hopes, likes and dislikes; that we push down instinctively into this forgetfulness all the facts which we refuse to face, or which we do not understand. In our maturity, these facts and memories, prejudices, and passionate elements have the same vitality as at the moment of repression, and because they are hidden we do not recognize the part they play in our lives. They are likely in certain cases to dominate the conscious mind and to affect the health of the individual." The foregoing introductory paragraphs followed.

of the gap in relation to all business enterprises like his, and he works out a method and is even likely to organize some great business as a result of having seen a small defect in his own private enterprise.

That is what I call thinking in abstraction, and it is something which the human race is only now learning to do. In antiquity they knew the principles of machinery, but their minds were not equal to making the machines which should express these principles. In some way, when they saw the stuff before them out of which the machine was to be made, they began to think of its form and to delight in it, and they decorated it, and they lost sight of its end, and, hence, never brought it into existence as an effective machine. In America you never lose sight of the end for which you are designing your great machinery of American life. Your end is effective business, the dealing with the raw material of life, and you have built up a great system.

It is expected, because I am a European, that I will criticize America, and it is expected of me as a student of psychology that I should find fault with the way you think, with the way the American mind realizes itself, but I am not a critic; I am a psychoanalyst. It is for me to try to understand, and where one understands one cannot judge; for if every effect has its cause, there must have been sufficient cause for the great effects that I find in your country, and I must search for the cause and not blame the effect.

There is no question but that you have sacrificed many beautiful things to achieve your great cities and the domination of your wildernesses. To build so great a mechanism you must have smothered many growing things, but there must be somewhere a cause, and when you have discovered that, your mechanism will not have its danger for you that it has today. Whatever a man builds is likely to devour him, and the builder in America is in danger of being destroyed—but why should I call him names for that reason? He has to express himself in big buildings, in trusts, in systems, of which we in Europe have as yet only the beginnings. We envy you. We have not learned to think in such great abstractions—and we are not in as great danger as you Americans.

I believe much of this ability to build on a large scale, to crush everything which is in the way of that building, to destroy everything which hinders your processes and systems, grows out of your Puritan ancestry. They had learned to think abstractly before they came here. The biggest problem of the Middle Ages was to learn to think. They chose the greatest abstraction of all, the idea of God, and they sacrificed everything to that idea. Countries went down before it, families were broken up by it, armies were slaughtered in the attempt to learn to think of God, and your Puritans, the Huguenots, and all those to whom the idea of God was greater than anything else, learned to think so well that they left their own homes, and you are the descendants of these people. An abstract thought is always ruthless. It is the most dangerous one to think, and it is the most marvelous.

So you must believe that I am not a critic, but that I am trying to understand. Many things which might displease me will no longer displease me when I understand what their cause is. A people is like an individual. If it suffers, it must not be hurt by a physician unless he is quite sure that in that hurt lies part of the cure.

America does not see that it is in any danger. It does not understand that it is facing its most tragic moment: a moment in which it must make a choice to master its machines or to be devoured by them—and since it does not know this I would not want to hurt it.

America is the country of the nervous disease, and in every nervous disease there is the psychic element. It is the painful witness of some conflict in both soul and body. I try to find out from my patients what they are hiding from themselves, and so, when they come to me, I am only a listener. I make my own mind a blank—receptive. I must have no prejudices, I must be making no judgments upon the moral or spiritual state which they disclose.

After a while in our interviews they speak of something with difficulty, and then it becomes evident where the conflict is. Sometimes it is very childlike—some mistaken idea they have of life which holds them fast and keeps them from true living, and has even set up a nervous ailment as a sign of its existence. If my patient comes to realize that this conflict is real, and is tragic, and that all of his efforts to get away from it are useless as well as unworthy of him, then I can help him. Then what I have learned can be put at his service.

I study the individual to understand the race, and the race to understand the individual. I ask myself, What influence has the building of America had upon the American man and the American woman of today? I find that it is a good subject for the student of psychoanalysis.

There is only so much vital energy in any human being. We call that in our work the Libido. And I would say that the Libido of the American man is focused almost entirely upon his business, so that as a husband he is glad to have no responsibilities. He gives the complete direction of his family life over to his wife. This is what you call giving independence to the American woman. It is what I call the laziness of the American man. That is why he is so kind and polite in his home, and why he can fight so hard in his business. His real life is where his fight is. The lazy part of his life is where his family is.

When men are still in the barbaric stage they make women their slaves. If, while they are still barbaric by nature, some influence makes them see that they dare not treat women as slaves, then what do they do? They do not know yet how to love something which is equal to themselves. They do not know what real independence is, so they must kneel down before this slave and change her into the one thing which they instinctively (even when they are barbarians) respect: they change the slave idea into the mother idea. And then they marry the mother-woman. And they respect her very much, they can depend upon her. They need not be her master. In America your women rule their homes because the men have not yet learned to love them.

I made many observations on shipboard. I notice that whenever the American husband spoke to his wife there was always a little melancholy note in his voice, as though he were not quite free; as though he were a boy talking to an older woman. He was always very polite and very kind, and paid her every respect. You could see that in her eyes he was not at all dangerous, and that she was not afraid of being mastered by him. But when any one told him that there was betting going on he would leave her, and his face became eager and full of desire, and his eyes would get very bright and his voice would get strong, and hard, and brutal. That is why I say his Libido, his vital energy, is in the game. He loves to gamble. That is business today.

It takes much vital energy to be in love. In America you give so many opportunities both to your men and women that they do not save any of their vital force for loving. This is a wonderful country for opportunity. It is everywhere. It spreads out. It runs all over the surface of everything. And so the American mind runs out and spreads over the whole country. But there is a dark side of this. The people of America do not have to dig deep for their own life. In Europe we do.

In Europe we have many divisions. Take my own little country of Switzerland. In Switzerland we must be Swiss, because we won't be German, and we won't be French, and we won't be Italian. And the people of Germany feel the same way. But in America you can be anything. In my country I have not as many opportunities given to me. Therefore I dig deeper and deeper in order to find my own life. In America you think you are concentrated because you are so direct, because you like your men who have only one idea at a time. I find that you distrust a man if he has two ideas. But if he has only one, you give him every chance to launch his enterprise. I do not feel that you care for those things which are profound. You can so easily distract yourself. And anything that you find unpleasant you bury so quickly at once in your unconscious mind.

The American husband is very indignant when he comes to me for treatment for neurasthenia or nervous breakdown, and I tell him it's because he is brutal on one hand and prudish on the other. You have in America the wooden face, just as they have it in England, because you're trying so hard to hide your emotions and your instincts. In Europe we have many little outlets for our emotions. We have an old civilization, which gives us a chance to live like men and women. But in England, even a hundred years ago, the people were still the conquering race that had been colored by the savage instincts of the original inhabitants of the British Isles. The English had to conquer the Celt, and the Celt lived a few hundred years ago in almost savage conditions.

In America you are still pioneers, and you have the great emotions of all adventurous pioneers, but if you should give way to them you would lose in the game of business, and so you practice the greatest self-control. And then this self-control—which holds you together and keeps you from disolution, from going to pieces—reacts upon you and you break down under the effort to maintain it.

That is what I mean by psychoanalysis. The search back into the soul for the hidden psychological factors which, in combination with physical nerves, have brought about a false adjustment to life. In America just such a tragic moment has arrived. But you do not know it is tragic. All you know is that you are nervous, or, as we physicians say, neurotic. You are uncomfortable. But you do not know that you are unhappy.

You believe, for instance, that American marriages are the happiest in the world. I say they are the most tragic. I know this not only from my study of the people as a whole, but from my study of the individuals who come to me. I find that the men and women are giving their vital energy to everything except to the relation between themselves. In that relation all is confusion. The women are the mothers of their husbands as well as of their children, yet at the same time there is in them the old, old primitive desire to be possessed, to yield, to surrender. And there is nothing in the man for her to surrender to except his kindness, his courtesy, his generosity, his chivalry. His competitor, his rival in business, must yield but she need not.

There is no country in the world where women have to work so hard to attract men's attention. There is in your Metropolitan Museum a bas-relief which shows the girls of Crete in one of their religious dances about their god in the form of a bull.[4] These girls of 2000 B.C. wear their hair in chignons; they have puffed sleeves; their corseted waists are very slender; they are dressed to show every line of their figures, just as your women are dressing today.

At that time the reasons which made it necessary to attract men to themselves in this way had to do with the morals of their country. The women were desperate just as they are today, without knowing it. In Athens four or five hundred years before Christ there was even an epidemic of suicide among young girls, which was only brought to an end by the decision of the Areopagus that the next girl who did away with herself would be exhibited nude upon the

---

[4] What Jung saw was apparently a copy of a fresco from Knossos, a new acquisition in the Hall of Reproductions. It is no longer on exhibition. The original fresco is reproduced in Arthur Evans, *The Palace of Minos at Knossos*, vol. 3 (1930), pl. xviii.

streets of Athens. There were no more suicides. The judges of Athens understood sex psychology.

On Fifth Avenue I am constantly reminded of that bas-relief. All the women, by their dress, by the eagerness of their faces, by their walk, are trying to attract the tired men of their country. What they will do when they fail I can't tell. It may be that then they will face themselves instead of running away from themselves, as they do now. Usually men are more honest with themselves than women. But in this country your women have more leisure than the men. Ideas run easily among them, are discussed in clubs, and so here it may be that they will be the first ones to ask if you are a happy country or unhappy.

It may be that you are going to produce a race which are human beings first, and men and women secondarily. It may be that you are going to create the real independent woman who knows she is independent, who feels the responsibility of her independence and, in time, will come to see that she must give spontaneously those things which up to now she only allows to be taken from her when she pretends to be passive. Today the American woman is still confused. She wants independence, she wants to be free to do everything, to have all the opportunities which men have, and, at the same time, she wants to be mastered by man and to be possessed in the archaic way of Europe.

You think your young girls marry European husbands because they are ambitious for titles. I say it is because, after all, they are not different from the European girls; they like the way European men make love, and they like to feel we are a little dangerous. They are not happy with their American husbands because they are not afraid of them. It is natural, even though it is archaic, for women to want to be afraid when they love. If they don't want to be afraid then perhaps they are becoming truly independent, and you may be producing the real "new woman." But up

23

to this time your American man isn't ready for real independence in woman. He only wants to be the obedient son of his mother-wife. There is a great obligation laid upon the American people—that it shall face itself—that it shall admit its moment of tragedy in the present—admit that it has a great future only if it has courage to face itself.

FROM ESTHER HARDING'S
NOTEBOOKS: 1922, 1925

••••••••••••••••••••••••••

M. Esther Harding was born in England in 1888, took her M.D. degree at the University of London in 1914, and began her personal analysis with Jung in the early 1920's. In 1923, she established her practice as an analytical psychologist in New York, and in the years that followed she became the outstanding exponent of Jung's psychology in America. After her death in 1971, her notes of conversations with Jung were found among her papers, and her literary executor, Edward F. Edinger, M.D., selected and edited these for publication.[1] In the summer of 1922, Esther Harding had gone to Küsnacht, near Zurich, to work with Jung.

Küsnacht, 3 July [1922]

Dr. Jung spoke of the inferior function being united to the collective: it is just a bit of nature and, as such, must first be accepted and adapted to. . . . The superior function is in your hands, and you can put it to your uses. The inferior is your master, and you must adapt yourself to it. Yet it is nature; there is life there. The thing that wants to be born must first be found. The form it is to grow into shall later be the object of search, and the search may be a long one. . . .

4 July

I began by describing how I always had so much to say before I got into the room, so that I had to edit my thoughts because of the many undertones of meaning. Jung agreed

---

[1] In *Quadrant* (New York), VIII:2 (winter 1975), a Jung Centennial Issue. For other extracts from Esther Harding's notebooks, see pp. 180, 367, and 440. The texts were taken verbatim from Dr. Harding's papers, except for minor grammatical corrections.

that my language was scanty, and yet he felt it to be full of allusion. Extraverts' language is thin and poor, but profuse, so that although what they want to say may be very slight, at least when they have finished they have said what they set out to say. He went on to say that when speaking to an extravert he has to cut down his thought; also when he is speaking to an introvert he has to cut down, for the thought of an introvert, even if expanded into a book, would not be fully expressed. . . .

I had been trying to find out the meaning of my [slip of the tongue] and thought it was in protest against the extra difficulty of the feminine position regarding searching for the anima. This he denied. He said a man must take up a feminine attitude, while a woman must fight her animus, a masculine attitude. I asked, "Is this why I always want to fight you?" And he replied, "In so far as I am your animus. As far as you are identified to your animus, so far will you project him to me. And then, if you battle me with him who is demonic, I call *my* demon, my anima, to my aid, and it is two married couples fighting. Then you have a hell of a row." He said this is what happens when you get a reciprocal transference. But that as he is not [word illegible], I need not fear that would happen to him.

Then he began talking about how it happens that a professional woman lives her animus. The professional situation is new for woman and needs a new adaptation, and this, as always, is readily supplied by the animus. On the other hand, analysis requires a new adaptation from a man, for to sit still and patiently try to understand a woman's mind is far from a masculine attitude. The only time he does it is as lover to his mistress; he will not do so for his wife, for she is only his wife. In love, his anima shows him how. He then takes on a feminine tenderness and uses the baby talk he learned from his mother; he calls on the eternal image of the feminine in himself. But [in analysis] that won't do. [The male analyst] has got to learn the feminine-ness of a man, which is not the anima. He must not let his masculinity be overwhelmed, or his weakness calls out the animus in the woman patient.

Similarly, the professional woman takes on the animus, the prototype of the father, and develops a god-almightiness, [an imitation of] the hero, instead of developing the masculinity of the female. This animus is *primitive* man, and men want to react to it with their fists. But, as this is a woman, that way is barred to them; so they shun her—just as a man who lives his anima is shunned by all really womanly women.

Dr. Jung went on to speak of the strength of womanhood, how it is stronger than any [imitation of the] male adaptation, and how a woman who is woman from the crown of her head to the tip of her toe can afford to be masculine, just as a man who is sure of his masculinity can afford to be tender and patient like a woman. . . .

Next he spoke of the Self and how it can be separated off from the demons. He reiterated that words in the realm of the spirit are creative and full of power. I said, "You mean as *Logos?*" He replied, "Yes. God spake and created from the chaos—and here we are all gods for ourselves. But use few words here, words that you are sure of. Do not make a long theory or you will entangle yourself in a net, in a trap."

Next he spoke of fear. He said, "Be afraid of the world, for it is big and strong; and fear the demons within, for they are many and brutal; but do not fear yourself, for that is your Self." I said I feared to open the door for fear the demons would come out and destroy. He said, "If you lock them up they will as surely destroy. The only way of delimiting the Self is by experiment. Go as far as your desire goes, and you will presently find that you have gone as far as your own laws allow. If you feel afraid, be brave enough to run away. Find a hole to hide in, for this is the action of a brave man, and by so doing you are exercising courage.

Presently the swing of cowardice will be over, and courage will take its place." I said, "But how hopelessly unstable and changeable you will appear!" He replied, "Then be unstable. A new stability will reassert itself. Does one live for other people or for oneself? Here is the place where one must learn true unselfishness."

The law was made by man. We made it. It is therefore below us, and we can be above it. As St. Paul said, "I am redeemed and am freed from the law." He realized that, as man, he had made it. So also a contract cannot bind us, for we who made it can break it.

Thus, vice too, if entered into sincerely as a means of finding and expressing the Self, is not vice, for the fearless honesty cuts that out. But when we are bound by an artificial barrier, or by laws and moralities that have entered into us, then we are prevented from finding, or even from seeing, that there is a real barrier of the Self outside this artificial barrier. We fear that if we break through this artificial barrier we shall find ourselves in limitless space. But within each of us is the *self-regulating Self*.

5 July

I began the hour by telling Jung how something wonderful had happened to me yesterday, that his talk on the animus relationship had cleared things up, so that much had clicked into place, and that now I felt quite different. I said that yesterday we were dealing with the negative relationship to the animus, but there must also be a positive relationship. He replied that there certainly must—but that the important part of analysis was to get that negative point cleared, for that is the growing point of differentiation from the unconscious. Until that is clear, the voice of the animus is as the voice of God within us; in any case, we respond to it as if it were. When we are not aware of the negative aspect of the animus, we are still animal, still connected to nature, therefore unconscious and less than human. We need to reach a higher degree of consciousness, which must be sought at *that* point. Then we discover a new country. And it is our responsibility to cultivate it. ("To him that knoweth to do good and doeth it not, to him it is sin.") Also the legend of Christ and the man working on the Sabbath, to whom he said, "If thou knowest what thou doest, blessed art thou! But if thou knowest not what thou doest, cursed art thou!" If we are conscious, morality no longer exists. If we are not conscious, we are still slaves, and we are accursed if we obey not the law. He said that if we belong to the secret church, then we belong, and we need not worry about it, but can go our own way. If we do not belong, no amount of teaching or organization can bring us there.

Then I asked him about a single animus figure, and he said, "Many souls are young; they are promiscuous; they are prostitutes in the unconscious and sell themselves cheaply. They are like flowers that bloom and die and come again. Other souls are older, like trees or palms. They find, or must seek, one complete animus, who shall perhaps be many in one. And when they find him, it is like the closing of an electric circuit. Then they know the meaning of life.

"But to have an animus like an archimandrite[2] is as if to say, You are a priest of the Mysteries. And this needs a great humility to counterbalance it. You need to go down to the level of the mice. And as a tree, so great as the height of its branches, so deep must be the depths of its roots. And the meaning of the tree is neither in the roots, nor in the up-lifted crown, but in the life in between them."

Then I asked him how to get the mean between the two worlds, between the world of the unconscious and that of reality. He replied, "You are the mediator. It is in your immediate life that they meet. In the pleroma they are merged—in nature they are one—and the primitive is al-

_____
[2] Dr. Harding had dreamed of an abbot, an archimandrite.—E.F.E.

ways striving up against its oneness. The glacier is always there. Our civilization finds an adaptation that will satisfy these things for a while, and they are quiet. Then they begin to come up again, and again we find a new adaptation, and they are quiet once more. Today we are in a period of great transition, and they come up again. Eventually they will swallow man, but it will not be the same again, for he has attained the union of the opposites through their separation. Possibly, after man will come a period of the animal and then again the plant—who knows?—and who or what will carry on the lamp of consciousness? Who knows?"

❖

In December 1924 Jung came to the United States—his first visit since before the War—and journeyed to the Southwest. With American friends he visited the Grand Canyon on New Year's Day 1925, and then the party motored across Arizona and New Mexico to Taos, where Jung spent a day or two with the Pueblo Indians. He traveled back to New York through the South, and sailed for Europe on January 14.

New York, 13 January [1925]

Dr. Jung gave a talk to a group at Dr. Mann's apartment on 59th Street.[3] He spoke on racial psychology and said many interesting things about the ancestors, how they seem to be in the land. As evidence of this, he spoke about the morphological changes in the skulls of people here in the U.S.A. and in Australia.

He said that in America there is a certain lack of reverence, a certain ruthlessness. The ancestors are not considered here, their values not respected. He spoke of the "single-mindedness" of Americans, which would be impossible to

[3] Kristine Mann (1873–1945), M.D., a founder of the Analytical Psychology Club of New York and of its library, which is now named in memory of her.

Europeans because of all the many considerations to which they must pay due regard. The American disregards these completely, is, indeed, utterly unconscious of them.

❖

In the spring, Dr. Harding again went to Küsnacht to work with Jung.

Küsnacht, 13 May

Dr. Jung talked about the various forms of relationship, about sexuality, about friendship (which is mitigated desire, with its obligations to write frequently and so on). There is a third kind of relationship, the only lasting one, in which it is as though there were an invisible telegraph wire between two human beings. He said, "I call it, to myself, the Golden Thread." This may be masked by other forms of relationship. And other forms may be present without any such thread in them. It is only when the veil of *maya*, of illusion, is rent for us that we can begin to recognize the Golden Thread.

He went on to speak of the three realities that make up the individuated state: God; the Self; and Relatedness. Or in Christian terms: God, Father, and Son; the Spirit, or Self; and the Kingdom of Heaven.

And just as it is impossible to individuate without relatedness, so it is impossible to have real relationships without individuation. For otherwise illusion comes in continually, and you don't know where you are.

"DOCTOR JUNG, I PRESUME"

•••••••••••••••••••••••••••••

In October 1925, Jung embarked on an expedition to East Africa with two friends. Their safari—with the sanction of the Foreign Office in London, it was called the "Bugishu Psychological Expedition"—traveled through Kenya and Uganda during November and December, and in January 1926 the party voyaged down the Nile to Khartoum, thence to Egypt and home. Jung has given vivid accounts in his *Memories, Dreams, Reflections*, chapter 9, "Travels," and in a letter to a sixteen-year-old neighbor boy, Hans Kuhn, which he wrote in Uganda on New Year's Day 1926 (see *Letters*, vol. 1).

The following article, by Francis Daniel Hislop, a retired British foreign officer, appeared in *Corona: The Journal of Her Majesty's Overseas Service* (London), June 1960.

Despite the increased facilities for travel nowadays, I fancy it must still be unusual for a junior Government officer in an up-country station to find himself entertaining a great European thinker of the calibre of Carl Gustav Jung of Zurich. Nevertheless, I had this memorable experience a long time ago, and it occurred because Jung, oddly enough, was wandering about in a safari car, more or less lost.

It happened in 1925 when I was the Assistant District Commissioner at Kapsabet, the Government station for Nandi District in Kenya, an out-of-the-way place in those days. One afternoon I was returning to my bungalow, which lay just off the main road behind a screen of trees, when I saw a large safari box-body car pulled into the side. Now this main road was magnificently broad, bordered and shaded by enormous blue gums, and looking as if it led to some important place. But, alas, just beyond my house it changed abruptly into a neglected earth track. This was, in

fact, part of the old Sclater Road to Uganda for foot cara-
vans in the 1890's. It had become literally side-tracked when
the railway reached Kisumu by a more southern route in
1901 and an easier connection with Uganda was made
across Lake Victoria.

All this explains why the safari car had stopped: the three
Europeans in it had seen where the broad road ended at the
township boundary. They had got out of the car and were
looking at me speculatively as I approached.

I said, "Good afternoon. Can I help you in any way? I'm
the A.D.C. here."

The tallest of the three, a reddish-faced man, replied.
"We're trying to get to Mount Elgon and would like to
know the best road to take." I told them there was no direct
road to Elgon from Kapsabet and they could not possibly
get there in daylight. I went on to explain that Elgon, where
I had recently spent several weeks on a boundary job, was
a sprawling land mass with extensive foothills, and it would
be about seventy miles on earth roads, either by Kakamega
or Eldoret, to get to them. Then it would be over twenty
miles to the summit.

"We aren't interested in the summit," said the spokesman.
"We just want to get to the foothills."

From where we were standing we could see the blue-gray
shape of Elgon away to the north west receding into the
usual mist. As we all gazed at it, thinking, I suppose, how
close it might be as the vulture flew, I again stressed that
they could not get there in daylight and suggested they had
some tea with me, pushed on to the hotel at Eldoret, thirty
miles distant, and made a fair start in the morning.

The tall man then said, "I am Dr. X." (the name escaped
me and I have never discovered who he was).[1] "This is Dr.

---

[1] Helton Godwin Baynes (1882–1943), M.D., English psychotherapist and one of Jung's leading pupils and interpreters. He
translated *Psychological Types* (1923) and other works by Jung.
Baynes made a film of the African expedition which survives and is

33

Jung." He indicated a burly man, middle-aged, with a red-
dish-brown country face. "And this is Mr. Douglas, our secretary, an American."[2] Douglas was a young man, about
twenty-five, athletic looking and darkly handsome. He appeared bored by the proceedings and I do not recollect that
he ever uttered a single word—perhaps the perfect secretary.
On the other hand I noticed that they had no African ser-
vants with them and it occurred to me later that perhaps
this explained young Douglas's gloom.[3]

I led the way to my bungalow, and over tea Dr. X again
took up the batting.

"It may seem odd to you," he said, "but we are in fact
psychologists intending to do some field work."

I started mentally. "Did you say Dr. Jung?"

The burly man smiled and said, "Yes, I am Dr. Jung."

"Of Zurich?"

"Yes, of Zurich." He looked surprised and pleased.

"I cannot help wondering," I said, "what kind of field
work you will find to do on Elgon?"

Dr. X. explained. "Dr. Jung," he said, "is interested in
dreams and their interpretation, and as a change from
studying them among the highly civilized people of Europe,
he wants to get further back and see if he can learn anything from a fairly primitive people. After considering the
possibilities everywhere we decided that the tribes on Mount
Elgon would suit us best for this purpose. And so," he concluded, "we are devoting our summer vacation to this
work."

They were thinking, it seemed, of contacting the Kara-

---

sometimes shown. For photographs of the expedition, see *Letters*,
vol. I, pl. IV.

[2] George Beckwith, a young American friend of Jung's. He died in
an accident soon after returning home from the trip to Africa.

[3] According to Jung's accounts, the safari later included five ser-
vants, a column of bearers, and two automobiles. The expedition,
which had semi-official status, was also given a military escort of
three soldiers for the trek into the Mount Elgon area.

mojong or the Sabei and I told them that these tribes were in Uganda—so far as I knew, in a Closed District, which meant that they would have to get a permit to enter it from the Provincial Commissioner at Mbale. They seemed rather disconcerted, and I hurried on to another obvious weakness in this psychological expedition.

"How," I asked, "do you propose to communicate with these people?"

"We have thought of that," said Dr. X, "and Dr. Jung has learned Swahili for the purpose."

"Yes," said Dr. Jung. "I have spent six weeks learning Swahili."

Somewhat diffidently I pointed out that the Karamojong and the Sabei had their own languages and did not speak Swahili. Dr. Jung said he understood Swahili was the *lingua franca* and everyone spoke it. I explained that though Swahili was indeed the *lingua franca* of East Africa, this only meant that people could be found everywhere who spoke and understood it, but that in fact the majority of the Africans, including the vast majority of the women, did not speak Swahili. Further, the more primitive the tribe the fewer Swahili speakers would there be. I said they would have to use interpreters and probably the Administration would be able to help them in this way. I carefully avoided suggesting that it might be necessary for them to have interpreters who could speak English, as this would have been to cast doubts on Dr. Jung's command of Swahili, and for all I knew a man of his intellectual capacity might have been able to learn more Swahili in six weeks than I could in six years. Like a prophet of doom I went on to say that even with good interpretation, they would run into considerable difficulty, because the more primitive the tribe the more purely materialistic was their language. Swahili was a poor medium for expressing any abstract ideas or emotions, and I was pretty sure that the Karamojong and Sabei languages would be even worse. At this point Dr. X. observed that this

35

situation was not unexpected and they had their own methods of getting results. That, of course, immediately shut me up, and Dr. Jung took up the running, asking me about camping conditions on Elgon.

Eventually he came to the subject of the Elgon caves. "Have you been inside them?" he asked.

"I have been inside one," I replied.

"What did you find inside?"

"Fleas," I answered.

Dr. Jung gave a great bellow of laughter, and Dr. X. joined in a little more moderately, but young Douglas only gave me a sort of sour smile as if I had taken an undue liberty with the great man. I went on to explain that the people who lived on Elgon had always used the caves as cattle shelters, so far as I knew, and the floors were covered with dung and sheep and goat droppings to a great depth. In these rich layers flourished countless millions of fleas. Visiting one with gum boots on and an electric torch had been enough for me.

"Of course," I said, "I know what you have in mind— paintings or such-like by primitive or even prehistoric man. In fact, that's what I was looking for in the cave I visited, but I did not see anything. However, there are many caves. I have never heard of any relics of that kind in any of them, but I don't know if all the caves have ever been visited, more especially by trained observers. You might be lucky and find something that has hitherto been missed. The fleas are rather a deterrent." Shortly afterwards they thanked me warmly and I put them on the road to Eldoret.

It was a queer thing that I never heard any more about this psychological expedition, though I was on the look-out for news. Unless they had resources and prepared lines of work about which they did not tell me, I cannot help thinking that their safari could hardly have produced any useful results. On the other hand I have just looked up the current *Who's Who*, and under the name, "Jung, Carl Gustav,"

(who is still alive—I saw him on television not long ago),[4]
I see "Recreations: sailing, researches about primitive psychology in North Kenya, 1925–26, and other voyages."
The last word is presumably a slip into French for "travels";
I am more intrigued by the dates "1925–26," because either
Dr. Jung and his friends stopped longer than I gathered
was their intention, or they came back the following year,
in which case I can only suppose that they would have been
rather better prepared than on their initial effort.

And what was the result of Dr. Jung's "Researches about
primitive psychology in North Kenya"? Truth compels me
to state that I don't know. It is not my line of country.

[4] See below, the BBC interview with John Freeman, pp. 424ff.

THREE VERSIONS OF A
PRESS CONFERENCE
IN VIENNA

✦✦✦✦✦✦✦✦✦✦✦✦✦✦✦✦✦✦✦✦✦✦✦✦✦

Jung was invited to lecture at the prestigious Kulturbund, in Vienna, on February 22, 1928, and a day or two earlier he was interviewed—simultaneously, it appears—by several representatives of the Vienna press. On February 21, different reports appeared in as many newspapers, and three of them are given here. Though certain themes recur in each article, the reporters seized on different aspects of Jung's comments and expressed them in different terms. The reports are complementary, each supplying details the others lack, but it is doubtful whether any of them reproduced Jung's actual words.

The Kulturbund was a cultural society that sponsored lectures by many European writers, scientists, and political figures, and the invitation to lecture had come from its executive vice-president, Jolande Jacobi (1890–1973). In 1938, after the Nazi occupation of Austria, Dr. Jacobi emigrated to Zurich, became a leading pupil of Jung, and was one of the founders of the C. G. Jung Institute.

1. The Realm of the Unconscious[1]

Coming back to Vienna again after some eighteen years' absence[2] is coming back to the city from which the fame of Sigmund Freud has radiated into the world. Even though

[1] "Das Reich des Unbewussten," *Neue Freie Presse*, Feb. 21, 1928; published as by Jung.
[2] Jung's last visit to Vienna had probably been on March 25–30, 1909, when he and his wife visited Freud. See *The Freud/Jung Letters*, 137J–139F; also 187F n. 1, concerning Ernest Jones's statement, evidently mistaken, in *Sigmund Freud: Life and Work* (II, p. 158), that Jung visited Vienna on April 19, 1910.

differences of scientific opinion have brought about a certain estrangement between Professor Freud and myself, a debt of gratitude nevertheless impels me to honor Freud and Janet[3] as the men who have guided me in my scientific career. Vienna also means for me re-encountering a doctor whose theories have very close and important connections and affinities with my own system. I mean Dr. Bernhard Aschner, whose *Konstitutionslehre* and *Humoralpathologie*[4] have a psychic analogue in my system of psychoanalysis. In the nineteenth century, the century of technology and exact science, we strayed very far from the intuition of earlier periods in history. Purely intellectualistic, analytical, atomistic, and mechanistic thinking has, in my opinion, landed us in a *cul de sac*, since analysis also requires synthesis and intuition. The humoral pathology of Aschner, who, incidentally, has rediscovered medical techniques based predominantly on intuition through his translation of Paracelsus,[5] is for me a proof that the most important insights into body and mind can be gained by ways that are not purely rationalistic.

It is difficult for me to outline the special features of my teachings in a few words. For me the essential thing is the investigation of the unconscious. Whereas Freud holds that in order to cure the neuroses, all of which as you know he derives from sexual roots, it is sufficient to make the unconscious conscious, I maintain that it is necessary to coordinate with consciousness the activities streaming out of the matrix of the unconscious. I try to funnel the fantasies of the un-

[3] Pierre Janet (1859–1947), French neurologist and psychologist, one of the first to recognize the unconscious, though he was hostile to psychoanalysis. Jung studied with him in Paris 1902–3.

[4] These concepts could not be traced.

[5] Jung wrote three essays (in CW 13 and 15) about the Swiss physician and philosopher Philippus Aureolus Theophrastus Bombastus von Hohenheim, known as Paracelsus (1493–1541), founder of a new school of medicine. A ten-volume edition of Paracelsus published in 1589–91 was translated into modern German by Aschner.

conscious into the conscious mind, not in order to destroy them but to develop them. In the case of a neurotic business-man, for example, I might be able to show that his neurosis is due to his unfulfilled artistic inclinations. By examining his dreams, I shall now find out what his special gift is, and the most satisfying cures can be obtained if you can get the neurotic businessman—to stick to this example—to write poems, paint pictures, or compose songs. It may be that artistically speaking these works are completely worthless, but for their creator they have an immense subjective value. Developing fantasy means perfecting our humanity.

In this connection I regard religious ideas as of the utmost importance, by which I do not, of course, mean any particular creed. Even so, as a Protestant, it is quite clear to me that, in its healing effects, no creed is as closely akin to psychoanalysis as Catholicism. The symbols of the Catholic liturgy offer the unconscious such a wealth of possibilities for expression that they act as an incomparable diet for the psyche.

My travels into the interior of Africa and to New Mexico gave me an opportunity to make a thorough study of the manifestations of the unconsious among primitive peoples. I was able to convince myself that religious ideas are inborn in them, and that religions should not be regarded in any sense as neurotic products, as is now asserted in certain quarters. I still remember two natives with whom I climbed a mountain ten thousand feet high in East Africa. During the night they were trembling with fear, and when I asked the cause of their agitation, one of them answered: "Everything is full of spirits."

On Wednesday evening I am going to speak in the Kulturbund on "The Structure of the Psyche."[6] I shall discuss

[6] "Die Struktur der Seele," which had previously appeared in print as the first half of "Die Erdbedingtheit der Seele" in a symposium, *Mensch und Erde*, edited by Count Hermann Keyserling (Darmstadt, 1927); afterwards republished in the *Europäische Revue* (Ber-

the nature of thinking, feeling, of sensation and intuition, of the will, of instinct, and of the fantasies arising out of the unconscious. I hope this will lead to some conclusions about the cure of neurosis. When you consider that various forms of neurosis, especially fatigue neuroses in big cities, are steadily increasing, and remember what a burden of painful feelings, how much unhappiness, how many suicides the neuroses have on their conscience, you will begin to appreciate the value of combatting them.

2. In Quest of the Second Ego[7]

It is my opinion that sex does not play the all-powerful role in psychic life that Freud and his followers attribute to it. Sex is after all only a glandular product, and it would be wrong to describe the brain as a mere appendage of the sex glands. In my conception of dreams and their significance for the sick psyche I am not at one with Freud, either. As you know, the great Viennese investigator calls the dream a wish-fulfilment. Wishes that in the waking state were for some reason or other repressed into the pit of the subconscious are supposed, in his view, to find their way back into consciousness in the dream and to determine the content of the dream-images. In my view the dream is a compensation, a completion of the waking state. Suppose I am in a disagreeable situation and ought to worry about it. In the waking state for some reason or other I don't, and then I will worry about it in the sleeping state. My dream will be this worrying I didn't do. The doctor curing a neurosis according to Freud's method tries to dig up the wishes and

lin), IV (1920). It was later revised and expanded in *Seelenprobleme der Gegenwart* (Zurich, 1931), and this version is translated as "The Structure of the Psyche" in CW 8.

[7] "Die Suche nach dem zweiten Ich," *Neues Wiener Journal*, 21 Feb. 1928; published as an interview with Jung, whose quoted words are translated here without the reporter's comments.

tendencies buried in the subconscious of the patient and to bring them into the clear light of consciousness in order to destroy them. My method is different. The repressed tendencies that are made conscious should not be destroyed but, on the contrary, should be developed further. An example will make this clear. In everyone some kind of artist is hiding. Among savage peoples this is evident from the fact that the warrior decks his spear with feathers or paints his shield. In our mechanized world this urge for artistic creation is repressed by the one-sided work of the day and is very often the cause of psychic disturbances. The forgotten artist must be fetched up again from the darkness of the subconscious, and a path cleared for the urge for artistic expression—no matter how worthless the paintings and poems may be that are produced in this way.

My friend the great English writer H. G. Wells has drawn a wonderful picture of this state of affairs in a novel. The hero of his story *Christina Alberta's Father*[8] is a petty businessman, completely imprisoned in his prosaic surroundings and his business. But in his few leisure hours another ego gradually emerges from his subconscious. He fancies he is the re-embodiment of the Babylonian ruler Sargon I, the reincarnation of the king of kings. Some kind of Sargon, in various disguises, is hiding in everyone of us. The fact that he cannot get out of the subconscious and is unable to develop himself is often the cause of severe psychic disturbances.

The unconscious search, by people who are imprisoned in our narrow machine-world, for the other ego, for completion, is also the reason for their flight back to the primitive. One need only remember the tremendous enthusiasm for ancient Egypt at the time when the tomb of Tutankhamen was discovered. Thirty or forty years ago the tomb

---

[8] Concerning the genesis of this novel (1925) in a conversation between Wells and Jung, see E. A. Bennet, *What Jung Really Said* (1966), p. 93.

would have been a matter of interest only for a few hundred scholars, and would have left the public at large, who still found everything Egyptian distasteful, completely indifferent. Again, one has only to think of the craze for Negro dances, for the Charleston and jazz—they are all symptoms of the great longing of the mass psyche for this more complete development of the powers immanent within us, which primitives possess to a higher degree than we do. All this is still more evident in America. There American millionairesses marry Indian chieftains. That's just it. We are, in a sense, cultural cripples.

3. Back to the Joys of the Golden Age![9]

The world had become impoverished in beauty, and people harked back to the Romans, to their nature-bound thinking, reminding themselves of those distant ages when every bush harbored a shrine, when those most marvellous figures of fantasy, the gods, were nothing other than perfect human beings. After this epoch, the Renaissance, they began remembering the ancient Greeks, Rousseau preached the return to Nature, and the classicists (among them Schiller) the return to the sun of Homer. And in our century we want to go still further back into the past, in our hounded age there rise up before our wistful eyes epochs when man communed with clouds and sun, wind and tempest, the Golden Age of humanity, as it is still sporadically reflected in the primitive, becoming more radiant the further we climb exploringly the genealogical tree of the present races, back to the ancient Egyptians and Babylonians, to the Biblical tribes and their forebears. It is not for nothing that the recent excavations in Egypt and Mesopotamia have aroused such interest, it is not by chance that our civilization was so ready for Negro songs and dances. We all long to go

[9] "Zurück zum Urweltglück!", *Volkszeitung*, 21 Feb. 1928; published as by Jung, from an interview.

home to the joys of the Golden Age, which let us be natural, graceful, and conscious of our strength, delivered from the bane of our time, the neuroses.

The aetiology of the neuroses is the great divide between my theory and that of Sigmund Freud, from whom I parted company some fifteen years ago because of this opposition. My sojourns among the natives of East Africa and the Pueblo Indians of New Mexico proved to me that the causes of neurosis do not necessarily lie in the repression of the sexual instinct; the repression of any other primary instinct, say of hunger, can produce it just as well. Freud's way and mine also diverge very widely in the matter of dream interpretation. Whereas he will always look for sexual causes, I trace the origin of dreams back to age-old mythological influences. Deriving from our remotest ancestors, there slumber in all of us subconscious memories which awaken at night and seek to compensate the false attitude modern man has towards nature. A schizophrenic in my clinic once explained to me that there was a tube in the sun from which it blew out the wind. Many years later a papyrus was discovered that told the scientific world for the first time of an age-old myth about the wind from the sun-tube,[10] a myth that had not only been recorded in the ancient papyrus but also inherited from generation to generation in the deepest layers of the conscious mind. Then, in a single case, the enchained fantasy was allowed to burst forth, at first in inexplicable form. What fell below the threshold of consciousness during the day both in our own lives and those of our ancestors awakens in dreams to posthumous reality.

Proper education is the best safeguard against psychic illness in its manifold forms, which we call neuroses. A schooling that is not too strict, and is actually what many people would call a bad one, is in my experience the best.

[10] See "The 'Face to Face' Interview," below, pp. 434f.

If that doesn't help, try to awaken the hidden artist who slumbers in every man. Give him a chance to bring to light the pictures he carries unpainted within himself, to free the unwritten poems he has shut up inside him, and yet another source of psychic disturbances is removed. Even though the work he produces will hardly ever amount to anything technically and artistically, it has helped to cleanse and release his psyche.

The play of fantasy is also helped by religion, an indispensable auxiliary for the psychologist. Catholicism in particular, with its ceremonial and liturgy, gives fantasy a priceless support, for which reason I have found in my practice that believing Catholics suffer less from neurosis and are easier to cure than Protestants and Jews. For the need of religion, for its validity as a primary instinct of mankind, there are abundant proofs reaching back to the dawn of time. Then it was part of man's unconscious, now it is part of his conscious, psychic diet; to it the doctor must turn when he tries to lead the patient back to himself, to rid him of all the psychic trash that has been pumped into him, to leave more room for the free play of fantasy, to cultivate his open and hidden talents, to make him more balanced, to guide him by the great saying of the Greek poet: Become what you are.

How great the importance of psychic hygiene, how great the danger of psychic sickness, is evident from the fact that just as all sickness is a watered-down death, neurosis is nothing less than a watered-down suicide, which left to run its malignant course all too often leads to a lethal end. Out of the many cultural cripples one-sided cerebral thinking has produced, the psychoanalyst who approaches them not merely as medical specimens but as human beings should be able to bring them closer to nature, make them more natural, as nature wanted them to be and as they faced life thousands of years ago. If the gifts we are endowed with break down before the tasks of life, if they wither away or run riot, we have only our flight from nature to blame, from the Golden Age of our furthest ancestors that returns to us only in dreams, a flight that leads to suppressed naturalness and to oppressive over-civilization of the psyche.

AMERICANS MUST SAY "NO"

++++++++++++++++++++++++++

The Vienna Kulturbund invited Jung to lecture again on January 29, 1931, and his theme was "The Unveiling of the Soul"; the lecture was eventually translated as "Basic Postulates of Analytical Psychology" (CW 8). Again Jung was the subject of several interviews in the Vienna press, brief ones dealing chiefly with his views of primitive people in East Africa and the United States. The publicity evidently caught the eye of the New York *Sun*'s foreign correspondent in Vienna, Whit Burnett, who went to Zurich and interviewed Jung on February 11. Burnett (1899–1973) had been an expatriate writer for several years, first on the Paris *Herald Tribune*. Later in 1931, he and his wife Martha Foley founded the magazine *Story*, which they edited in Vienna, in Palma de Mallorca, and after 1933 in New York. In 1957, in a collection entitled *This Is My Philosophy*, Burnett included Jung's essay "The Spirit of Psychology" (in CW 8 as "On the Nature of the Psyche").

Burnett's interview was published in the *Sun* for February 27, 1931. Except for his opening paragraphs, his comments are omitted here.

(The trouble with the United States is a wholesale misdirecting of lives, according to Dr. Carl Jung, founder of the Zurich school of psychoanalysis and chief opponent in psychology to the Freudian school of psychological thought of Vienna.

The old criticisms that America is too uniform, too speedy, and too "external" are all true, the Zurich scientist believes. What is more devastating is that these "evils" are being taken by the inhabitants of the United States as good standards to be imitated. What is good for some is a poison for most others. The result is that in such centers of speed and uniformity as New York State, there are today, Jung's

*statistical examination shows, as many beds in asylums as
there are in all the other capitals combined.)*

The tempo of America is being taken as a norm to which
life should be directed. In the world today America stands
on one side, with its often enviable "standard of living"
slogan before its eyes, and Russia on the other side, also
uniformly conscious of a present "standard of poverty."
Both countries are today's great forces.

It is, of course, quite impossible to think that these two
diverse natures of America and Russia could merge, or
would merge: they would fight out their differences to the
death. Europe stands between Russia and America as a
refuge of that individualism which is necessary to the
leading of a happy life, an individualism more or less different in each case, but an individualism opposed to the
uniformity of both Russia and America, and an individualism necessary if we are to satisfy our great unconscious and
primary mind which warns us of our misdirections and,
finally, to save us, fosters neuroses.

New York is only one glaring example of what the prevailing notions in America do to the general nature of
people. In other States, like California, where not so much
attention is paid to people's foolishness, the insane are not
so easily separated, and throughout America there are thousands suffering from sick souls who are never quite hospital
cases.

What America needs in the face of the tremendous urge
toward uniformity, desire of things, the desire for complications in life, for being like one's neighbors, for making
records, et cetera, is one great healthy ability to say "No."
To rest a minute and realize that many of the things being
sought are unnecessary to a happy life, and that trying to
live exactly like one's successful neighbor is not following
the essentially different dictates, possibly, of a widely different underlying personality which a person may possess and
yet consciously try to rid himself of, the conflict always

resulting in some form, sooner or later, of a neurosis, sickness, or insanity.

We are awakening a little to the feeling that something is wrong in the world, that our modern prejudice of everestimating the importance of the intellect and the conscious mind might be false. We want simplicity. We are suffering, in our cities, from a need of simple things. We would like to see our great railroad terminals deserted, the streets deserted, a great peace descend upon us.

These things are being expressed in thousands of dreams. Women's dreams, men's dreams, the dreams of human beings, all having much the same collective primal unconscious mind—the same in the central African Negro I have lived among and the New York stockbroker—and it is in our dreams that the body makes itself aware to our mind. The dream is in large part a warning of something to come. The dream is the body's best expression, in the best possible symbol it can express, that something is going wrong. The dream calls our mind's attention to the body's instinctive feeling.

If man doesn't pay attention to these symbolic warnings of his body he pays in other ways. A neurosis is merely the body's taking control, regardless of the conscious mind. We have a splitting headache, we say, when a boring society forces us to quit it and we haven't the courage to do so with full freedom. Our head actually aches. We leave.

When whole countries avoid these warnings, and fill their asylums, become uniformly neurotic, we are in great danger. The last war, I thought, had taught us something. Seemingly not. Our unconscious wish for deserted places, quiet, inactivity, which now and then is being expressed in the heart of our great cities by a lyrical outbreak of some poet or madman, may project us, against our conscious wills, into another catastrophe from which we may never recover. We may gas our lives out, and then will we have deserted refuges and none of us left to sit, and dream, in the sun.

DOCTOR JUNG: A PORTRAIT
IN 1931

♦♦♦♦♦♦♦♦♦♦♦♦♦♦♦♦♦♦♦♦♦♦♦♦♦♦♦♦

The American writer Elizabeth Shepley Sergeant (1881–1965) had analyzed and studied with Jung in Zurich before the first world war, and throughout her life she maintained a devoted interest in analytical psychology. During an extended stay in Zurich, from autumn 1930 to spring 1931, she was a member of Jung's Seminar on "Interpretation of Visions."[1] Her article "Doctor Jung: A Portrait," in *Harper's*, May 1931, abridged here, gives a vivid picture of how Jung conducted his seminars.

Besides novels and stories, E. S. Sergeant's books included *Shadow-Shapes: The Journal of a Wounded Woman* (1919), her experiences as correspondent in France for the *New Republic*, with an account of being wounded when she visited a battlefield; *Fire Under the Andes* (1927); and memoirs of Willa Cather (1953) and Robert Frost (1960).

I had seen him often as a highly civilized modernist, driving a red Chrysler through the twisting streets of Zurich; pondering the problems of the psyche in his sober, book-lined study, with its Oriental paintings and Christian stained glass, before I came upon the primitive Jung, one rainy summer day, outside his favorite dwelling place[2]—a gray stronghold, of medieval outline, standing alone and apart, surrounded by hills and water—where, when his work as a doctor is over, he retires to become for a season the detached scholar and writer who turns experience into theory. Ensconced there in the shelter of the round stone

---

[1] *Interpretation of Visions*, 1930–1934, 9 vols., recorded by Mary Foote and privately issued. Abridged edition: *The Visions Seminars*, ed. Jane A. Pratt and Patricia Berry, 2 vols. (Zurich, 1976).

[2] Jung's "tower" retreat at Bollingen, on the upper lake of Zurich.

tower which he had built with his own hands, dressed in a bright blue linen overall, with his powerful arms in a tub of water, I beheld Doctor Jung earnestly engaged in washing his blue jeans.

His sagacious face was ruddy and shining, and his keen brown eyes, which see so deep into the minds of men, were quietly absorbed in his rancher's task. Doctor Jung never does anything by halves. When he walks up and down the floor at the Psychological Club, expounding a dream to his advanced students, every cell and fiber of his physical being seems to participate; every resource of his great learning, his medical and scientific knowledge, his psychological insight, and his native wisdom is turned in a single living stream upon the question in hand. This massive, peaceful man in blue was putting the same zest and interest into washing. No part of Jung was left in Küsnacht giving consultations.

. . .

Doctor Jung's patients must take a little steamboat at a landing haunted by gulls and wild ducks, and then walk a good ten minutes to a yellow country house standing well within walls and gardens on the edge of the lake of Zurich.[3] They must pull a shining brass bell, of old-fashioned mold, and while its fateful ring resounds through the house—as obviously a hospitable, family mansion as the other is the isolated domain of the creator-scholar—meet the inspection of a group of skirmishing dogs.

Yoggi, the Doctor's special intimate, always manages to slide into the upstairs study behind the visitor, to take his silent, attentive share in the conversation. I noticed at my first interview that Jung's hand—the sensitive, strong hand, with the Gnostic ring—reached down now and then to the shaggy back. And it came to me that this touch with an instinctive hairy being was somehow the riposte to the

[3] At Küsnacht, near Zurich.

51

psychologist's uncanny intuition, his probing mind, his acute awareness—a reassurance to the visitor and to himself. For what is one to think of a doctor who, in a hunch of the shoulders, a half-glance, a witty phrase casually spoken— "you are like an egg without a shell"—can say enough to keep one guessing for a week?

It was comfortable, too, that as he discussed intimate problems, his face now very sober and concerned, Jung tramped the floor, fed the fire, lighted a meditative pipe: common clay and spirit were all one. When he sat stiffly in his chair for a moment and gulped down his tea, he suddenly turned into a German professor. But when his eyes began to twinkle merrily behind their gold-rimmed spectacles, when he moved about again, his driving energy strongly held in leash, I thought of Theodore Roosevelt. "You look more like a stockbroker than a prophet," exclaimed a startled American who had expected to find the "mystic" of Freudian report. The actual Jung, solid and vital in his middle fifties, humorous and skeptical, refuses to stand on a pedestal or to take on any white-bearded Old Testament air. "Yes," he agrees with a young lady, "all men are liars, certainly. I just let them sit in that chair and lie till they get tired of lying. Then they begin to tell the truth." One leaves Jung's presence feeling enriched and appeased, as by contact with a pine tree in the forest—a life as much below ground as above.

*   *   *

When, on Wednesday morning at eleven, at certain seasons of the Zurich year, Doctor Jung enters the long room at the Psychological Club[4] where his Seminar is held, smiling with a deep friendliness at this or that face, the brown portfolio which he hugs to his side seems to be the repository of this joint account—the collective analytical account of a small international group whose common interest is the psyche.

[4] In the town of Zurich.

An involuntary hush falls on the room as Jung himself stands quiet and grave for a moment, looking down at his manuscript as a sailor might look at his compass, relating it to the psychological winds and waves whose impact he has felt on his passage from the door. The hush in the assembly means not only reverence but intense expectation. What world adventure shall we have to-day with this creative thinker? What question, like the stroke of a bronze bell, will he leave ringing in our minds? What drastic vision of our age will he give us that will help us to lose our sense of problems, subjective and oppressive, and move into a more universal and objective realm?

By some mystery yet to be explained Doctor Jung manages within the first five minutes to get vitally on the wire of everyone present—American, British, Dutch, German, Swiss. He lectures in English or rather in American—a language somewhat his own, as American is entitled to be, a pungent, witty tongue. Jung is expounding, with few references to his notes, the dreams of a cultivated business man—a nice, conventional gentleman such as we all know. Soon there appears out of the unconscious an "ape man" bent on rape and violence. This, or some other hellish "opposite" of the conventional human being, which must be recognized and assimilated into the personality before any true release of the spirit can be found. After all, perhaps the philosophic teacher in the gray suit, who is striding up and down (he has no platform, nothing outward to separate him from his students) writing Greek or Norse roots on the blackboard, drawing diagrams of the heavens, symbols from ancient monuments, has a formula. But it is the very old one, familiar to the Greek agora: *Know thyself*. Know the laws of your own being. Accept them, even if they seem paradoxical and incompatible with the views you have grown up with. Live them, instead of living the lives of your parents and grandparents, your neighbors and professional associates.

This may sound simple. But it is not easy for our friend, the business man—whose dreams go on like a detective story, full of surprises, discoveries, and unsolved clues, later to be worked through—nor for any of this company, though it consists of advanced students, medical men and women, philosophers, anthropologists, to accept the fierce, instinctive elements of the unconscious, the howling savages, the "shadow," the evil, that every refined surface conceals. Work with Jung is not easy, either in a private interview or in the Seminar. It is a challenge, a test, a profound creative effort. All that an artist can give an earnest student is a technic—a method of work and a vision of what the life of the artist is, what it demands of sacrifice and concentration. That, it seems to me, is precisely what Doctor Jung gives his students: a technic of living and dealing with practical and unconscious problems; and a vision of the modern conscious man.

The technic, in the Seminar, is illustrated through dream analysis, which with Jung is a very inclusive thing, that ties up mythology and history, Einstein and astrology, modern psychology and Chinese wisdom, the Gnostics, Christian and Jewish theology, and primitive rites. It includes journeys with age-old seers into the fearful reaches of the collective unconscious and concrete, very human questions such as how to make a success of marriage,[5] how to adjust those abiding relationships that Doctor Jung believes to be quintessential in every life. Like all great speakers, Jung seems to draw his inspiration from the moment; if the planes of his face are always changing, as my artist friend declares, so that he never looks twice alike, in the same way his mind changes its weather, its tempo, producing that unexpected nugget of humor or wisdom, or spicy tale of

[5] Sergeant published an "interview" with Jung, entitled "Marriage Is a Problem—not a Solution," in *Hearst's International–Cosmopolitan*, July 1937. It was in fact an "imagined conversation" between a hypothetical patient and Jung, in which he discussed his views on marriage and divorce.

experience, or new psychic vision most calculated to stimulate and enrich his auditors. But he never ceases to be the patient and versatile teacher, the discoverer who is always sniffing the wind, the leader fully aware of his power and responsibility to the little band who are following him into unknown country.

Sometimes with a canny, fiery glance, which one remembers seeing under African helmets, Jung turns and says: "Here is new terrain. Your guess is as good as mine. What have you to suggest?" But it is an unwary student who gives a slipshod or too rational reply. Purely rational thinking has been discarded in this room, but there is a natural scientist in the leader who scans every hasty assumption with skepticism. Science to Jung is not a god; it is a tool that must be used. Analytical Psychology, though it has, like the new painting and the new music, a language of its own, new rhythms, new colors, has a very ancient base. It is only the student who is beginning to think with both an old and a new mind who draws forth from his guide a keen, swift look, like a pat on the back: "That's good! You're absolutely on the right track! Go ahead!"

.   .   .

"There was a moment," Doctor Jung said to me, in discussing this period of his life,[6] "at the end of *Psychology of the Unconscious* when I put down my pen and thought awhile. This book I have written, I said to myself, is the hero myth in different form. All peoples and all times had their hero, but who is our hero? To whom is Christ living? Not to me. Then the question almost formulated itself: 'What is your myth?' There was no answer to this question. I repressed it at once, trampled it under.

[6] His period of collaboration with Freud, 1906–1912. In the latter year he published *Wandlungen und Symbole der Libido*, the book that marked his break with Freud; tr. Beatrice M. Hinkle as *Psychology of the Unconscious* (1916).

"But it was not for a year and six months after the publication of *Psychology of the Unconscious*," he continued, "that I began to be acquainted with my own unconscious. The interval was a sort of incubation period, a preparation for a whole new period of life. A new wind was blowing, for—a very important fact—a new period of life was coming on. In the early forties melancholia in men is statistically increased. I was obliged, as all men are at this point, to get a new orientation in life."

. . .

Jung's books, though "hard reading" for the layman, have, like the doctor, some magical incalculability, some gift to probe a wound and assuage it in the same breath, some power to move us beyond the meaning of the abstract word. I can say for myself that, though I read them years before I knew the author in Zurich, I divined in them the same two Jungs that I now so clearly see. In the forefront of every page a dynamic, thinking, modern man, in whom life, with all its diversity, runs clear and strong like a spring; and in the background a wise, redeeming figure, a very ancient and intuitive man—a sort of gardener, I think, who walks along conversing softly with his dog, his hands full of new shoots to graft on the tree of life.

EVERYONE HAS TWO SOULS

••••••••••••••••••••••••••••

Again Jung was invited to lecture at the Kulturbund in Vienna in early November 1932, on a subject that is no longer recorded. The following interview, "Jeder Mensch hat zwei Seelen," appeared in the *Neues Wiener Journal* on November 9, 1932, entirely in Jung's words.

My contention that man is born equipped with a highly differentiated and fully developed brain with innumerable attributes has often met with antagonism. Most people continue to believe that everything they have become, every reaction of their psychic ego to everyday occurrences, is determined by their education and their environment.

Few people know anything about the ancestral soul and even fewer believe in it. Aren't we all the carriers of the entire history of mankind? Why is it so difficult to believe that each of us has two souls? When a man is fifty years old, only one part of his being has existed for half a century. The other part, which also lives in his psyche, may be millions of years old. Every newborn child has come into this world with a fully equipped brain. Although in the early stages of life the mind has not gained complete mastery over the body, it is clearly preconditioned for reacting to the outer world—that is, it has the capacity to do so. Such mental patterns exert their influence throughout life and remain decisive for a person's thinking. The newborn does not begin to develop his mental faculties on the first day of his life. His mind, a finished structure, is the result of innumerable lives before his and is far from being devoid of content. It is unlikely that we shall ever discover the remote past, into which the impersonal psyche of the individual reaches.

There is no doubt that man's personal psyche develops only during his lifetime, and that environment and education are decisive influences in this process. These influences become effective from the first days of a child's life. On the whole, the receptivity of a small child's brain tends to be widely underestimated, but the practicing psychologist has frequent evidence to the contrary. With neurotics, one constantly comes up against psychic defects that date back to very early childhood experiences. It is not a rare occurrence for a somewhat severe reprimand administered to a child in his playpen or his bed to affect him during his entire life.

The two souls give rise to frequent contradictions in a person's thinking and feeling. Quite often the impersonal and the personal psyche are even in direct opposition. There are hundreds of examples which demonstrate to the psychologist that two souls live in every man. Exercising their imagination—which I call the mother of human consciousness—many of my patients painted pictures and described dreams which displayed a strange conformity with definite laws and showed peculiar parallels to Indian and Chinese temple images. Where were these people supposed to have obtained knowledge about the ancient temple cultures of the Far East? I have treated patients who had visions about events which happened hundreds of years ago. All this can come only from the unconscious, the impersonal soul, the finished brain of the newborn. Contemporary man is but the latest ripe fruit on the tree of the human race. None of us knows what we know.

[*Translated by Ruth Horine*]

AN INTERVIEW ON
RADIO BERLIN

++++++++++++++++++++++++

On June 21, 1933, Jung accepted the presidency of the Über-
staatliche Ärztliche Gesellschaft für Psychotherapie (International Medical Society for Psychotherapy), which united national societies in Denmark, Germany, Great Britain, Holland,
Sweden, and Switzerland and had its headquarters in Zurich.
Though Jewish and other anti-Nazi members had been expelled
from the German national society, Jung as president enabled
them to become members of the International Society. Thus
has Jung's leadership been defended by his followers, while his
adversaries have attacked his participation in a Society that had
links with Nazi Germany. The issue has been, and still is,
warmly debated.[1] A document of the time is an interview with
Jung by Dr. Adolf Weizsäcker, a German neurologist and psychiatrist who had previously been his pupil. It was recorded
and broadcast by Radio Berlin on June 26, 1933. On the same
date Jung began a seminar on dreams, given to a group of
analytical psychologists in Berlin, which continued for five
days. Its members included at least four analysts who subsequently left Nazi Germany; Gerhard Adler, who settled in
London; and James Kirsch, Hilde Silber (Kirsch), and Max
Zeller, who settled in Los Angeles, California.[2] A transcript of

[1] Jung's statements and speeches as president of the Society and its
various international congresses and editor of its organ, *Zentralblatt
für Psychotherapie und ihre Grenzgebiete* (Leipzig), are printed in
an appendix to CW 10. For historical accounts, see Ernest Harms,
"Carl Gustav Jung—Defender of Freud and the Jews," *Psychiatric
Quarterly* (Utica, N. Y.), April 1946, and Aniela Jaffé, "C. G. Jung
and National Socialism," in her *From the Life and Work of C. G.
Jung*, tr. R.F.C. Hull (New York, 1971). Also see Jung's letter to
James Kirsch, 26 May 1934, in *Letters*, ed. Adler, vol. 1, and below,
"On the Attack in the *Saturday Review of Literature*," pp. 192ff.
[2] For a firsthand account of the seminar by another of its mem-
bers and a discussion of Jung's "dim view of the new government
and the prospects for Germany" during that visit to Berlin, see

the lectures that Jung gave in the seminar and of the radio interview has long been extant in mimeographed form.

Today we have particular pleasure in welcoming to our studio the most progressive psychologist of modern times, Dr. Carl Gustav Jung of Zurich. Dr. Jung is at present in Berlin giving a course of lectures, and he has kindly expressed his willingness to answer a number of questions bearing on contemporary problems. From this you will see that there is a school of modern psychology which is fundamentally constructive. We all know very well that psychology and analysis for their own sakes have rightly become suspect nowadays. We are tired of this continual probing and breaking down along intellectual lines, and it is fortunate for us that there is one psychologist who approaches the human psyche in an entirely different way from the other well known psychologies or psychotherapies, especially Freudian psychoanalysis. Dr. Jung comes from a Protestant parsonage in Basel. That is important. It puts his whole approach to man on a different footing from that of Freud and Adler. The crucial thing about this psychology is that Dr. Jung does not tear to pieces and destroy the immediacy of our psychic life, the creative element which has always played the decisive role in the history of the German mind, but approaches it with deep reverence and does not devalue it, letting himself be guided in the practical treatment of conflicts or neuroses by the positive and constructive forces which lie dormant in the unconscious psychic life of every man and can be awakened. Hence his psychology is not intellectual but is imbued with vision; it seeks to strengthen the positive forces in man and does not stop at triumphantly laying bare the negative elements, since that brings nothing

Barbara Hannah, *Jung: His Life and Work* (New York, 1976), pp. 209–213.

*really new into the life of the individual or of the com-
munity. Permit me now, Dr. Jung, to put a number of
questions to you and to ask you to answer them, which you
can as a Swiss, with a certain detachment, and as a psychologist, with great experience of the human psyche. I would
like to ask you, first, whether there is in your psychological
experience a decisive difference between the psychic situation of the Germans and that of Western Europeans, and
wherein this difference consists? The fact of the matter is
that we are at the moment surrounded by the deepest misunderstandings, and it would interest us to hear, quite
briefly, what you think might be the cause of these misunderstandings, and whether the differences between our
nature and theirs are so great as to make these misunderstandings comprehensible to us.*

There is indeed an enormous difference between the
psychic attitude of the Germans and that of Western Europeans. The nationalism that Western Europeans know
seems to them a kind of chauvinism, and they cannot
understand how it is that in Germany it has become a
nation-building force, because nationalism for them still
means their own brand of chauvinism. This peculiarity of
the Germans can be explained only by the youthfulness of
the German nation. Their enthusiasm for the reconstruction
of the German community remains incomprehensible to
Western Europeans because this necessity no longer exists
for them in the same degree, since they achieved national
unity in earlier centuries and in other forms.

*Yes, and now I would like to ask a second question which
is extraordinarily important for us, because the new turn of
events in Germany is being led by the younger generation.
How do you explain the assurance of German youth in
pursuit of their visionary goal, and what is the significance
of the fact that the older generation cannot quite rid themselves of a kind of reserve even though they would very*

much like simply to affirm what is happening? What in your view should be done in order to bridge over this hopeless gulf between the generations, which deepens still further the cleavage in our German nationhood? What is the cause of it all?

The assurance of German youth in pursuit of their goal seems something quite natural to me. In times of tremendous movement and change it is only to be expected that youth will seize the helm, because they alone have the daring and drive and sense of adventure. After all, it's their future that's at stake. It is their venture and their experiment. The older generation naturally takes a back place and they should possess enough experience of life to be able to go along with this necessary course of events. They too had their time, once. The gulf between the older and younger generation is due precisely to the fact that the older generation did not go along with the times and, instead of foreseeing it, was overtaken by the storm of a new epoch. But that is not by any means specific of the Germans. It is something you can observe in all countries at the present time. The older generation have immense difficulty in finding their way about in a new world. Political changes go hand in hand with all sorts of other changes in art, philosophy, in our religious views. Everywhere the wind of change is blowing. And I come very much into contact with people of the older generation who have confessed to me that they have little real understanding of the new time and the utmost difficulty in finding their way about. Many of them even turn directly to me for advice, for with a little psychology one can understand these things. With a little psychological knowledge, too, it would have been possible to foresee the changes. But the older generation has, I am bound to say, committed the unforgivable mistake of overlooking the real man in favor of an abstract idea of man. This error hangs together with the false intellectualism that characterized the whole nineteenth century.

An Interview on Radio Berlin

Thank you, Dr. Jung. We have now heard something of your attitude to the more general problems of the situation as a whole. I would like now to ask some more specific questions about your psychology. What in your view is the position of psychology in general at the present day? What is its task in such a time of activity?

It is just because we live in an active and responsible time that we need more consciousness and self-reflection. In a time like ours, when tremendous political and social movements are afoot, I as a psychologist am very often turned to, as I have said, by people who feel the need for psychic orientation. This need reflects a sound instinct. When general confusion reigns, as it does in Europe today, when there is a widespread splintering of opinions, there instinctively arises in us a need for a common *Weltanschauung*, I would say, which allows us to take a unitary view of things and discern the inner meaning of the whole movement. If we do not succeed in getting this view, it may easily happen that we are as it were unconsciously swept along by events. For mass movements have the peculiarity of overpowering the individual by mass suggestion and making him unconscious. The political or social movement gains nothing by this when it has swarms of hypnotized camp followers. On the contrary there is the danger of equally great disillusion on awaking from the hypnosis. It is therefore of the greatest value for mass movements to possess adherents who follow not from unconscious compulsion but from conscious conviction. But this conscious conviction can be based only on a *Weltanschauung*.

And you think, if I understand you correctly, that such a Weltanschauung *can in certain cases best be acquired with the help of psychology—your psychology—so that people can stand firm inwardly in order to work successfully and surely in the outer world, because otherwise their unconscious impulses, moods, and I don't know what, can obtrude*

63

themselves in their outward activities. You see, the fact is that in Germany today psychology is suspect in many quarters precisely because it is concerned with the self-development of the so-called individual, and so they suspect this famous parlor individualism or individualism de luxe of belonging to an age which is now really over for us. So I would like to ask you: How, just at the present time, when the collective forces of the whole community have taken the lead in molding our way of life, how are we to assess the efforts of psychology in the practical role it would have to play for the whole of life and the whole community?

The self-development of the individual is especially necessary in our time. When the individual is unconscious of himself, the collective movement too lacks a clear sense of purpose. Only the self-development of the individual, which I consider to be the supreme goal of all psychological endeavor, can produce consciously responsible spokesmen and leaders of the collective movement. As Hitler said recently, the leader must be able to be alone and must have the courage to go his own way. But if he doesn't know himself, how is he to lead others? That is why the true leader is always one who has the courage to be himself, and can look not only others in the eye but above all himself.

Now I come to something quite specific. What difference—though I have already stressed this a little at the beginning—what difference is there between a psychology like yours, imbued with vision, and the psychologies of Freud and Adler, which are built entirely on an intellectual basis?

It is, you see, one of the finest privileges of the German mind to let the whole of creation, in all its inexhaustible diversity, work upon it without preconceptions. But with Freud as well as with Adler a particular individual standpoint—for instance, sexuality or the striving for power—is set up as a critique against the totality of the phenomenal world. In this way a part of the phenomenon is isolated from the whole and broken down into smaller and smaller fragments, until the sense that dwells only in the whole is distorted into nonsense, and the beauty that is proper only to the whole is reduced to absurdity. I could never take kindly to this hostility to life.

I am particularly grateful to you, Dr. Jung, for that answer. I think it will act on many of us like a liberation. In conclusion, I still have a question that is of particular concern to us today, and that is the question of leadership. From your psychological experience, have you anything to say about the idea of personal leadership and of a leading élite that is now acknowledged in Germany, in contradistinction to an elected government dependent on the opinion of the masses as evolved in Western Europe?

Today we are living in a time of barbarian invasions, but they take place inwardly in the psyche of the people. It is a breaking of the nations. Times of mass movement are always times of leadership. Every movement culminates organically in a leader, who embodies in his whole being the meaning and purpose of the popular movement. He is an incarnation of the nation's psyche and its mouthpiece. He is the spearhead of the phalanx of the whole people in motion. The need of the whole always calls forth a leader, regardless of the form a state may take. Only in times of aimless quiescence does the aimless conversation of parliamentary deliberations drone on, which always demonstrates the absence of a stirring in the depths or of a definite emergency; even the most peaceable government in Europe, the Swiss Bundesrat, is in times of emergency invested with extraordinary powers, democracy or no democracy. It is perfectly natural that a leader should stand at the head of an élite, which in earlier centuries was formed by the nobility. The nobility believe by the law of the nature in the blood and exclusiveness of the race. Western Europe doesn't understand the special psychic emergency of the young

German nation because it does not find itself in the same situation either historically or psychologically.

Thank you, Dr. Jung, for answering these questions so readily, and also for the gist of your answers, which will surely be of the greatest import for many of our listeners. The fact is that we are living today in a phase of reconstruction where everything depends on inwardly consolidating what has been achieved and building it into the psyche of the individual. For this purpose we need, if I may express my personal opinion, leaders like you, who really know something about the psyche, the German psyche, and whose psychology is not just intellectual chatter but a living knowledge of human beings.

DOES THE WORLD STAND ON
THE VERGE OF
SPIRITUAL REBIRTH?

++++++++++++++++++++++++++++

Hearst's International–Cosmopolitan for April 1934 carried this article "by C. G. Jung," with the subheading, "A famous ultra-modern psychologist finds that the supreme need of man's spirit is met by the ancient spirit of Easter." It was illustrated with drawings of an inspirational character by Harold von Schmidt. Jung, however, wrote to an American correspondent on April 21, 1934: "By the way, my so-called article in the *Cosmopolitan Magazine* was an interview with a reporter and not an article written by myself. I have not even seen a copy of it." The name of the reporter and the occasion of the interview have not been discovered. The same article, with minor variations (and an additional paragraph, marked with an asterisk, on p. 74), was published under the title "The Soul of Modern Man" in a digest-type magazine, *The Modern Thinker* (New York), August 1934. In the present version, excessive emphatic italics have been eliminated.

This is what theologians for several centuries have been crying for; what many of them have professed to see through the fog of doubts, disillusion and despair, like a star glowing in the high heavens.

I am not a theologian; I am a doctor, a psychologist. But as a doctor, I have had experience with thousands of persons from all parts of the world—those who came to tell me the stories of their lives, their hopes, their fears, their achievements, their failures. I have studied carefully their psychology, which is, and which must be, my guide.

Out of my experience with those thousands of patients, I have become convinced that *the psychological problem of today is a spiritual problem, a religious problem.* Man today hungers and thirsts for a safe relationship to the psychic forces within himself. His consciousness, recoiling from the difficulties of the modern world, lacks a relationship to safe spiritual conditions. This makes him neurotic, ill, frightened. Science has told him that there is no God, and that matter is all there is. This has deprived humanity of its blossom, its feeling of well-being and of safety in a safe world.

As modern man is driven back upon himself by doubt and fear, he looks inward to his own psychic life to give him something of which his outer life has deprived him. In view of the present widespread interest in all sorts of psychic phenomena—an interest such as the world has not experienced since the last half of the seventeenth century—it does not seem beyond the range of possibility to believe that we stand on the threshold of a new spiritual epoch; and that from the depths of man's own psychic life new spiritual forms will be born.

Look at the world about us, and what do we see? The disintegration of many religions. It is generally admitted that the churches are not holding the people as they did, particularly educated people, who do not feel any longer that they are redeemed by a system of theology. The same thing is seen in the old established religions of the East— Confucianism and Buddhism. Half the temples in Peking are empty. In our Western world millions of people do not go to church. Protestantism alone is broken up into four hundred denominations.

Contrast this state of life and thought with that of the Middle Ages. In those centuries almost everyone went to Mass every morning. The whole life was lived within the church, which became a tremendous outlet of psychic energy.

Instead, we have today an intricate and complicated life full of mechanical devices for living. A life crowded with motor cars and radios and motion pictures. But none of these things is a substitute for what we have lost. Religion gives us a rich application for our feelings. It gives meaning to life.

Man in the Middle Ages lived in a meaningful world. He knew that God had made the world for a definite purpose; had made *him* for a definite purpose—to get to heaven, or to get to hell. It made sense. Today the world in which all of us live is a madhouse. This is what many people are feeling. Some of those people come to me to tell me so.

All that energy which was the origin of the rich blossom of man's emotional life during the Middle Ages, and which found expression in the painting of great religious pictures, the carving of great religious statues, the building of the great cathedrals, has gone flat. It is not lost, because it is a law that energy cannot be lost.

Then what has become of it? Where has it gone? The answer is that it is in man's unconscious. It may be said to have fallen down into a lower storey.

Take the example of a business man—successful, rich, not yet old. He is perhaps forty-five. He says, "I have made my fortune; I have sons who are old enough to carry on the business which I founded. I will retire. I will build a fine house in the country and live there without any cares and worries." So he retires. He builds his house and goes to live in it. He says to himself, "Now my life will begin."

But nothing happens.

One morning he is in his bath. He is conscious of a pain in his side. All day he worries about it; wonders what it can be. When he goes to the table he does not eat. In a few days his digestion is out of order. In a fortnight he is very ill. The doctors he has called in do not know what is the matter with him. Finally one of them says to him: "Your life lacks interest. Go back to your business. Take it up again."

The man is intelligent, and this advice seems to him sound. He decides to follow it. He goes back to his office and sits down at his old desk and declares that now he will help his sons in the management. But when the first business letter is brought to him, he cannot concentrate on it. He cannot make the decisions it calls for. Now he is terribly frightened about his condition.

You see what happened. He couldn't go back. It was already too late. But his energy is still there, and it must be used.

This man comes to me with his problem. I say to him: "You were quite right to retire from business. But not into nothingness. You must have something you can stand on. In all the years in which you devoted your energy to building up your business you never built up any interests outside of it. You had nothing to retire on."

This is a picture of the condition of man today. This is why we feel that there is something wrong with the world. All the material interests, the automobiles and radios and skyscrapers we have, don't fill the hungry soul. We try to retire from the world, but to what? Some try to go back to the churches. A few are able to do this. But many are not finding this entirely satisfactory. They are like the business man who tried to go back to his desk.

And these people come to me, asking me to help them to find a meaning in their lives. What shall I tell them?

Among them comes a man who is only slightly neurotic. He says to me: "I am not really very sick. Perhaps I should not be here at all taking up your time. But I know you are busy with the human mind. I thought, therefore, that you might be able to tell me on what terms I may live. I have the feeling of being forlorn and lonely in a world that makes no sense."

I say to him: "My dear man, I don't know any more than you do the meaning of the world or the meaning of your life. But you—all men—were born with a brain ready-made. It took millions of years to build the brain and the body we now have. Your brain embodies all the experience of life. The psyche, which may be called the life of the brain, existed before consciousness existed in the little child.

"Now, suppose that I am in need of advice about living, and I know of a man who is already thousands of years old. I go to him and say, 'You have seen many changes; you have observed and experienced life under many aspects. My life is short—perhaps seventy years, perhaps less—and you have lived for thousands of years. Tell me the meaning of life for me.'"

When I say this to my patient, he cocks his ears and looks at me.

"No," I say, "I am not that man. But that man speaks to you every night. How? In your dreams."

I go on: "You are in trouble. You feel that your life has no orientation. I cannot tell you what to do. But let us ask the Great Old Man. He will tell you. Go away for a few days, and you will have a dream. Come back and tell me about it."

He goes away; he comes back and brings me a dream. It is difficult to work out. But we do work it out together, and it tells us something about him.

Certain people lose connection with life because they have made mistakes, or because they are living the wrong way, in a life that is intellectual only. The dreams they bring to a psychologist will take up these things first.

All dreams reveal spiritual experiences, provided one does not apply one's own point of view to the interpretation of them. Freud says that all man's longings expressed in his dreams relate to sexuality. It is true that man is a being with sex. But he is also a being with a stomach and a liver. As well say that because he has a liver all his troubles come from that one organ.

Primitive man has little difficulty with sex. The fulfillment of his sexual desires is too easy to constitute a problem.

What concerns primitive man—and I have lived among primitives, and Freud has not—is his *food*: where he is to get it, and enough of it.

Civilized man in his dreams reveals his spiritual need.

When modern science disinfected heaven it did not find God. Some scientists say that the resurrection of Jesus, the virgin birth, the miracles—all those things which fed Christian thought through ages, are pretty stories, but none the less untrue. But what I say is, Do not overlook the fact that these ideas which millions of men carried with them through generations are great eternal psychological truths.

Let us look at this truth as the psychologist sees it. Here is the mind of man, without prejudice, spotless, untainted, symbolized by a virgin. And that virgin mind of man can give birth to God himself.

"The kingdom of heaven is within you." This is a great psychological truth. Christianity is a beautiful system of psychotherapy. It heals the suffering of the soul.

This is the truth which man has clung to through the ages. Even after his consciousness has listened too long at the door of modern materialistic science, he clings to it in his unconscious. The old symbols are good today. They fit our minds as well as they fitted the minds that conceived them.

Deep in the unconscious of each one of us are all the attempts of that Great Old Man to express his spiritual experiences.

Suppose I ask you to stay in my house. I tell you that it is well built, comfortable; that our life is pleasant; that you will have good food. You can swim in the lake and walk in the garden. With these beliefs in your mind you decide to come, and you enjoy your stay. But suppose, when I ask you, I say to you: "This house is unsafe. The foundations are not secure. We have many earthquakes in this region. Besides all that, we have had illness here. Someone recently died of tuberculosis in this room." Under those conditions and with these ideas in your mind, do you enjoy your stay in that house?

That medieval man we have talked of had a beautiful relationship with God. He lived in a safe world, or one that he believed to be safe. God looked out for everyone in it; he rewarded the good and punished the bad. There was the church where the man could always get forgiveness and grace. He had only to walk there to receive it. His prayers were heard. He was spiritually taken care of.

But what is modern man told? Science has told him that there is no one taking care of him. And so he is full of fear.

For a time, after we gave up that medieval God, we had gold for a deity. But now that, too, has been declared incompetent. We trusted in armies, but the threat of poison gas defeated them. Already people talk about the next war. In Berlin they have built dugouts under the streets for retreat from poison gas attacks. If they go on talking in this way, thinking this way, the next war will explode of itself.

Naturally enough, in a world of this sort, everybody gets neurotic. Even if the house you live in is really safe, if you have the idea that it is not, you will suffer. Your reaction depends entirely on what you think.

In making this point to my students, I say: "How do you measure a thing? By its effects. And usually by its terrible effects. An avalanche occurs which wipes away a dozen farms, kills scores of cows, and you say, 'An elephant of an avalanche!' Now, tell me, what is the most destructive thing you know of?"

In turn we consider fire, earthquakes, volcanic eruptions, floods, diseases.

Then I say, "Can you think of nothing more terrible than any of these things? What about the World War?"

Ah, yes! High explosives.

"But," I say, "do high explosives make themselves? Do they declare war and march to war? Do they bring the men with them?"

73

It is the psyche of man that makes wars. Not his consciousness. His consciousness is afraid, but his unconscious, which contains the inherited savagery as well as the spiritual strivings of the race, says to him, "Now it is time to make war. Now is the time to kill and destroy." And he does it.

The most tremendous danger that man has to face is the power of his ideas. No cosmic power on earth ever destroyed ten million men in four years. But man's psyche did it. And it can do it again.

I am afraid of one thing only—the thoughts of people. I have means of defence against things.

I live here in my house happily with my family. But suppose they get the illusion that I am a devil. Can I be happy with them then? Can I be safe? All of us are subject to mass infections.

Mass infections are greater than man. And man is their victim. He shouts and parades and pretends that he is the leader, but really he is their victim. They are the uprush of earthly and spiritual forces from the depth of the psyche.

Turn the eye of consciousness within to see what is there. Let us see what we can do in small ways. If I have planted a cabbage right, then I have served the world in that place. I do not know what more I can do.

Examine the spirits that speak in you. Become critical. The modern man must be fully conscious of the terrific dangers that lie in mass movements. Listen to what the unconscious says. Hearken to the voice of that Great Old Man within you who has lived so long, who has seen and experienced so much. Try to understand the will of God: the remarkably potent force of the psyche.

* It is all there. *The kingdom of heaven is within you.* This is a great psychological truth. Christianity is a beautiful system of psychotherapy. It heals the suffering of the soul.

I say: Go slow. Go slow. With every good there comes a corresponding evil, and with every evil a corresponding good. Don't run too fast into one unless you are prepared to encounter the other.

I am not concerned about the world. I am concerned about the people with whom I live. The other world is all in the newspapers. My family and my neighbors are my life—the only life that I can experience. What lies beyond is newspaper mythology. It is not of vast importance that I make a career or achieve great things for myself. What is important and meaningful to my life is that I shall live as fully as possible to fulfil the divine will within me.

This task gives me so much to do that I have no time for any other. Let me point out that if we were all to live in that way we would need no armies, no police, no diplomacy, no politics, no banks. We would have a meaningful life and not what we have now—madness.

What nature asks of the apple-tree is that it shall bring forth apples, and of the pear-tree that it shall bring forth pears. Nature wants me to be simply man. But a man conscious of what I am, and of what I am doing. God seeks consciousness in man. This is the truth of the birth and the resurrection of Christ within. As more and more thinking men come to it, this is the spiritual rebirth of the world. Christ, the LOGOS—that is to say, the mind, the understanding, shining into the darkness. Christ was a new truth about man.

Mankind has no existence. I exist, you exist. But mankind is only a word. Be what God means you to be; don't worry about mankind. In worrying about mankind, which doesn't exist, you are avoiding looking at what does exist—the self. You are like a man who leans over his neighbor's fence and says to him: "Look, there is a weed. And over there is another one. And why don't you hoe the rows deeper? And why don't you tie up your vines?" And all the while, his own garden, behind him, is full of weeds.

FROM CHARLES BAUDOUIN'S
JOURNAL: 1934

••••••••••••••••••••••••••

Charles Baudouin (1893–1963), professor in the University of Geneva, was founder there of the Institut de Psychagogie, whose patrons were Freud, Adler, and Jung and whose program was correspondingly catholic. Eventually, Baudouin associated himself with the school of analytical psychology as an analyst, teacher, and writer. His posthumous book *L'Oeuvre de Jung* (1963) contains, in a chapter entitled "Jung, homme concret," a number of passages from Baudouin's journal, reporting his encounters with Jung over more than twenty years. The earliest one was written after Baudouin attended a seminar that Jung gave to the Société de Psychologie in Basel, October 1–6, 1934.[1] That version, slightly abridged, was translated and published as "Jung, the Concrete Man" in the Friends annual *Inward Light* (Washington), fall–winter, 1975–76. It is further abridged here. (For other extracts see pp. 146, 190, 235, 365.)

Basel, Sunday, October 7, 1934

It is time to assemble the impressions which Jung's personality has left upon me during these few days, to bind the sheaf, to present the portrait. A standing portrait, emphatically, for I see him on his feet, talking and teaching. The word "stature" is what springs to mind, or the German word "Gestalt." This is no man of study or office; this is a force.

One of the anecdotes with which he bespangles his lectures stands out for me. I hope I shall not do it an injustice

---

[1] Published, somewhat adapted, in *L'Homme à la découverte de son âme* (Geneva, 1944), edited by Roland Cahen-Salabelle. Jung included much of the same material in his Tavistock Lectures, given in London, Sept. 30–Oct. 4, 1935 (in CW 18).

by repeating it from memory. He had been living with a tribe of Pueblo Indians[2] where, to identify a stranger, they do not ask for his passport, but they ask themselves, "What animal is this?" That is to say, "Of what totem is he?" and they watch him, for to belong to a totem is to be the totem; so strong is the "participation," and the sacred animal has so impregnated the man, that one has but to look at him walk and act and live to recognize him. When the man is from a neighboring tribe, the game is easy enough, apparently; but with a white man, so different from all one knows, it is another matter. Jung knew, from his interpreter, of his hosts' embarrassment at having failed to identify him. However, he won their hearts sufficiently for them to invite him one day—a sign of confidence and welcome—to visit the upper story of the house. This meant climbing a ladder. But while the Indians mount with their backs to the ladder and with the agility of monkeys, he naturally climbed in European fashion, facing the ladder, setting his feet deliberately on the rungs and presenting to the onlookers his square, powerful back. A great clamor broke out then among the Indians, which he later had explained to him. On seeing him mount that way, they had recognized his totem: the bear! the bear!

He had the wit to enter into the spirit of the thing, and his understanding of "primitives" was advanced enough for him to feel all the seriousness of it. Substantially, he told them: "Yes, you have guessed aright; the bear is the totem of my country; it has given its name to our capital, Bern; it figures in the coat of arms of the city." And on his return to Switzerland he sent them, as evidence and as a souvenir, a little wooden bear such as we carve over here. He received in return and as a pledge of friendship, if I remember rightly, a pair of leather breeches.

· · ·

[2] See above, p. xiv. Jung was at the Taos Pueblo for a day or two in 1925.

These last days, telling us about the tribes, the spirits of the forest, that other world of mystery that comes alive suddenly at nightfall, he has been more like the sorcerer penetrated by the spirits he talks about, skilled at evoking them and making their disquieting presence hover above the suspenseful audience. Then, all of a sudden, a good story will release the tension with a well-placed laugh. His is a compact force that is fed by a substantial sum of human experience and flows back to him as though multiplied by the response of his own tribe, this circle of disciples from both continents who surround and sustain him. Unkind gossip has accused these disciples and auditors of snobbery. To be sure there is some of it, as there was around the courses which Bergson gave at the Collège de France; which is no argument against Bergson, nor yet against Jung. But when someone raised the objection that a majority of his disciples were women, Jung is said to have replied: "What's to be done? Psychology is after all the science of the soul, and it is not my fault if the soul is a woman." A jest; but for anyone who has followed his teaching, a jest which is itself charged with experience, and behind which one sees arising in all its ambiguous splendor the archetype of the anima.

. . .

Observing him, seeing him teach and then relax in a more intimate circle, I registered during this week in Basel many aspects of his being and appearance, many disparate expressions. Under the high forehead of the thinker, the planes of his face are firm and full; the gray eyes seem suddenly curiously small and made for gimlet scrutiny; at other moments they are chiefly mischievous, and the face becomes that of a confessor-accomplice, a priest who enjoys life, suddenly red in the face with a hearty laugh; but the profile then calls one to order—it is much more serious, angular, and marks the top-level intellectual.

But watching him live, one perceives that these disparate expressions are organized into a coherent whole. One feels that he denies none of them, that being and appearance (the self and the persona) have found their *modus vivendi,* that his teaching about "integrating all the functions" to form a totality is not book knowledge but lived, which amounts to affirming that he belongs not only among the scholars but among the sages.

I knew Jung from his books and I had met him personally. But during this week passed in his company I feel I have discovered him. To tell the truth, I have made two discoveries. First of all, I have been struck by the strongly *concrete* character of this man and of his thinking. Secondly, I have realized all he owes to his mingling with the "primitives"; those journeys have not been picturesque accidents in his life; they are among the nutritive substances of his thought. I would add that these two points are intimately connected.

The concreteness stands out every moment from his way of expounding ideas, laying emphasis on the facts, his gestures sober and restrained but felt to be charged with energy and asking only to go ahead uncurbed. This is especially visible when he describes one of his African scenes; in fact he acts it out in abbreviated form, he makes it visible. There was that anecdote to illustrate the fact that primitives do not know will-power in the sense that we understand it; they must first mobilize the needful energy for an action and this is the purpose served by certain precise incantatory rituals. For example, the boy who is charged with carrying the mail to town (who knows how many leagues away!) remains passively sitting when the European quietly asks him to perform this service and offers to reward him; it is as if he did not understand. But the sorcerer passes by, takes the case in hand—and the whip too!—starts dancing the "running dance" around the boy; the tribe joins in, the boy is drawn into the circle and finally, as if shot from a sling, is off; and he runs at that! All was reproduced before us; we *saw* it.

But this play of gesture to demonstrate and explain flourishes yet more freely in familiar conversation. We were speaking one evening of "telepathic" dreams where, between persons who are emotionally close, a mutual unconscious communication and penetration appears to take place. Jung finally, to sum up his thoughts on the matter, acted them out as follows: with brief, firm gestures he touched first my forehead, then his own, and thirdly drew a great circle with his hand in the space between us; the three motions underscored the three clauses of this statement; "In short, one doesn't dream here, and one doesn't dream here, one dreams there." And *there* the hand kept turning, like the above-mentioned sling and the idea, like the messenger, was launched.

I have said that this concreteness is tied up with Jung's African experience. I came to see that he had a feeling of concreteness about the soul; when he entitles a book *Wirklichkeit der Seele*[3] (Reality of the Soul) it is no vain expression. To be sure, he had been convinced by his patients of this concrete aspect of the things of the psyche, but certainly the "primitives" brought him into touch with it in a closer and more convincing way, for this is how they feel. When he was telling me the other day, at Dr. von Sury's,[4] about these "ancestral spirits," which fall upon one on return to one's birthplace, and which he himself feels whenever he returns to Basel, I recognized that these "spirits" had weight, like the atmosphere during a thunderstorm. And when he was led by this reflection to study, on the wall, the genealogical tree of the von Sury family, I realized how he

---

[3] Published in Zurich the same year, 1934. It contained nine papers, later distributed throughout the CW.

[4] Kurt von Sury, M.D., of Basel, who joined with Jung and others to form the Swiss Society for Practical Psychology in January 1934.

felt those roots digging down and holding fast in an earth that was real and solid.

. . .

This concreteness of Jung's was part of his make-up. In his childhood recollections he tells us of the torments he went through over mathematics, especially over algebraic abstractions, which he found incomprehensible. To make sense out of them, he had to put back numbers in place of letters. The simple equation $a = b$ infuriated him and seemed a rank deception: since a is one thing and b is another, it is a lie to say they are equal. If this was an inborn disposition of his mind, it could not but be reinforced and justified in his eyes by his fertilizing contacts with "primitive mentality." The academic mind expected a mapmaker; and it finds itself face to face with an explorer who emerges from the brush armed, weighed down, and solidly swathed in magnificent vines and creepers, trailing with him all the odors of the forest.

. . .

[*Translated by Elined Prys Kotschnig*]

VICTORIA OCAMPO
PAYS JUNG A VISIT

++++++++++++++++++++++++++

The distinguished Argentine writer, publisher, and translator Victoria Ocampo had apparently not met Jung before the encounter with him, in 1934, that she describes in this extract from an article in *La Nacion* (Buenos Aires), March 5, 1936. Earlier, however, she had arranged to have Jung's *Psychological Types* translated into Spanish by Ramón Gomez de la Serna; it was published in Buenos Aires late in 1934, and for it Jung had written a special foreword, dated October 1934 (included in CW 6). Jung, for his part, was acquainted with Victoria Ocampo's personality through numerous references to her in letters written to him by Count Hermann Keyserling, who, in a letter in November 1929, described a "strangely intense and at the same time unreal relationship" that had developed between them during his travels in South America. Some of Jung's letters to Keyserling that discuss the relationship are published in *Letters*, edited by Gerhard Adler, vol. 1, Dec. 20, 1929, April 23, 1931, and August 13, 1931. (The first part of Victoria Ocampo's 1936 article discussed ideas provoked by *Psychological Types*. The entire article was collected in *Domingos en Hyde Park*, 1936, a volume in Ocampo's *Testimonios*.)

In October of 1934, on my return from Rome to Paris, I made a detour and stopped in Zurich to see the author of *Psychological Types*. It was pouring rain that afternoon when in Küsnacht my taxi dropped me, armed with an umbrella, and disarmed by contradictory emotions, before Dr. Jung's door. Was it because of the long hours on the train, the sudden change of temperature, the rain, the proximity of the great man? I don't know. The fact is that I

82

was aware of the growth and development within me of one of those inferiority complexes which make us feel and play the role of the idiot to perfection. It was in this unhappy state that I, my umbrella, and my emotions, entered the house of the famous Swiss psychiatrist. But my umbrella—whose fate I envied at that moment—remained in the vestibule while we (my emotions and I) had to go up a staircase. We were requested to wait in a small study, its walls lined with books. This interval was providential. On several shelves, I suddenly perceived, lined up in a tight row, a regiment of detective novels. The arrival of the dove with the olive branch could not have produced in Noah's heart greater delight than this discovery did in mine. To me it also announced "Land!"

"Homo sum!" I thought. In Dr. Jung's house they (he or his family) also read those completely silly stories that were read in mine or yours, and which relax you like a yawn. I finally recovered my nerve. True, I know through experience the weakness of certain princes of the mind for detective novels; my library, rich in this type of literature, has repeatedly been sacked by such people. But despite this, I did not expect to find Edgar Wallace in the home of the most eminent professor of the University of Zurich.[1] I was enchanted.

Completely comforted, a few minutes later I entered Dr. Jung's office.

I immediately notice that he is tall, very tall. But, strangely, my eyes, which I raise to his, do not learn from his face anything but an expression of power and intelligence which suffuses it; an intelligence which comes at me like an enormous elephant, blotting out all else.

An elephantine intelligence! It is my feeling that that great intelligence which sees everything does not see me,

---

[1] Jung had resigned in 1914 from the medical faculty of the University; in 1934, he was a lecturer at the Federal Technical Institute (ETH).

that it is going to knock me down and flatten me out. Instinctively I tend to avoid him and to throw things at him. He catches them one by one, with that extreme, incredible adroitness of elephants ... (whether it is a matter of tearing up a tree trunk or catching a cube of sugar). And so we start our conversation.

Suddenly he says something which I still ponder and which I believe is, of the entire interview, most worthy of repeating. When I ask him whether he would not like to deliver some lectures in Argentina, he answers: "What for? They could not be interested. They would not understand. Because they are Latins? Because they are Catholics?"

I wished I might have immediately been given a long lecture to explain what he meant; but patients were waiting for him, with God knows what burden of complexes.

Jung accompanied me to the vestibule (where I picked up my umbrella, which I no longer envied). His two dogs did not leave his side, and jostling them, we all went down the stairs. One was an extravert, the other an introvert, the master of the house told me, laughing. I did not have to ask which one was which.

As he himself confessed, *Psychological Types*, which I recommend to my friends both known and unknown, "is the result of almost twenty years' work in the field of practical psychology."

Huxley says that when we read Jung's books, we feel that his intuitive understanding of the human being is as profound as Dostoevski's.

For myself, I confess that a work like *Psychological Types* stirred me as deeply as the *Brothers Karamazov*.

[*Translated by Martin Nozick*]

MAN'S IMMORTAL MIND

✦✦✦✦✦✦✦✦✦✦✦✦✦✦✦✦✦✦✦✦✦✦✦✦✦

Jung was invited by the Tavistock Clinic in London—officially called the Institute of Medical Psychology—to give a series of five lectures, which he delivered September 30 to October 4, 1935, to an audience of some two hundred medical men and women. A mimeographed transcript of the lectures was privately circulated under the title "Fundamental Psychological Conceptions"; not until 1968 was the text published, as *Analytical Psychology: Its Theory and Practice*.[1] The London press took notice of Jung's presence, and during his visit several interviews were published, of which one in the *Observer* for October 6, 1935, is noteworthy. It is abridged here. "The laughter of Dr. C. G. Jung may be heard in London at the moment, after a silence of ten years"—thus the anonymous reporter begins, and he goes on to describe Jung's enormous good humor. "As he talked, the abrupt cleavage between his own psychological theory and practice and those of Freud, with whom he parted company intellectually many years ago, became apparent. How abrupt is the cleavage he revealed in a sentence typical of his sudden, epigrammatic manner of speech—"

Sex is a playground for lonely scientists.

You might as well study the psychology of nutrition as the psychology of sex. Primitive man, of course, had the sex instinct, but he was much more deeply concerned with feeding himself. Besides, why base the psychology of a man on his bad corner?

When I deal with one who is mentally unbalanced I am not concerned only with one function of his mind and body. I look for the ancient man in him. I try to trace the strata of the human mind from its earliest beginnings, just as a

[1] As "The Tavistock Lectures" in CW 18.

geologist might study the stratification of the earth. The fear of ancient man crouching at the ford is in all our unconscious minds, as well as all other fears and speculations born of man's experience through the ages. The mind of mankind is immortal.

For instance, I remember suddenly feeling, during an earthquake in Switzerland, that the earth was alive, that it was an animal. At once I recognized the ancient Japanese belief that a huge salamander lies inside the earth, and that earthquakes happen when he turns in his sleep.[2]

A patient of mine once told me that whenever lightning flashed she saw a great black horse. That is another primitive idea—that lightning was a horse's leg striking downwards, the horse of Odin.[3] If a man or a woman ceases to be able to communicate with us, we say that he or she is insane. But if I can find the ancient man in them, if I can explain the great black horse in the lightning, I may be able to make them communicate with me. I may be able to restore the bridge—more easily if I can discover from their dreams what is in their unconscious minds.

That is why I correspond not only with medical scientists, but with students of religion and mythology in all parts of the world. That is why I am at present studying medieval texts in the British Museum. The medieval stratum in our unconscious mind is nearest to the surface.

The study of medical science is in transition. The relationship between mind and body is being more fully appreciated. Not that there is anything new in that. The medieval doctors studied dreams. Eastern medicine is based on psychotherapy—the treatment of disease by hypnotic influence.

[2] Cf. ibid., par. 67 (where Jung told the same story), n. 17: "According to a Japanese legend, the *namazu*, a kind of catfish of monstrous size, carries on its back most of Japan, and when annoyed it moves its head or tail, thus provoking earthquakes" (editorial note).

[3] See *Symbols of Transformation* (CW 5), p. 277.

Psychology is not yet, of course, a recognized part of the medical curriculum. There is much enthusiasm, but there is also much misunderstanding and misinterpretation. Still, I have four hundred students at Zurich, and the criminal courts call me in as a last resort if they are unable to decide upon the guilt or innocence of a suspect.[3a]

In twenty years you will have your organization of approved medical psychologists, just like your Medical Register.

And your next book?

It is nearly finished. I shall call it "Dream Symbols of the Individuation Process."[4] It's about how man becomes himself. Man is always an individual, but he's not always himself. . . . "Be yourself," as the Americans say.

[3a] Cf. "On the Psychological Diagnosis of Evidence" (orig. 1937), CW 2, pars. 1357ff. Jung had been requested by the Criminal Court of Canton Zurich, in 1934, to submit an expert opinion on an accused murderer, using the association experiment.

[4] Jung's lecture at the Eranos Conference, August 1935, so entitled, was included in *The Integration of the Personality* (1939) and later was revised as Part II of *Psychology and Alchemy* (CW 12).

THE 2,000,000-YEAR-OLD MAN

++++++++++++++++++++++++++

Harvard University invited Jung to its Tercentenary Conference on Arts and Sciences, in September 1936, to participate in a symposium on "Factors Determining Human Behavior."[1] When he disembarked in New York, he had prepared a press release, devoted chiefly to setting forth his political—or, as he insisted, his nonpolitical—position.[2] Upon leaving New York to sail to England, he was interviewed by the *New York Times* at the Hotel Ambassador, and the article, headed "Roosevelt 'Great,' Is Jung's Analysis," appeared in the issue of Sunday, October 4, 1936. The following text omits the reporter's comments, except for the indirect quotations from Jung, given in brackets.

Before I came here I had the impression one might get from Europe that he [Roosevelt] was an opportunist, perhaps even an erratic mind. Now that I have seen him and heard him when he talked at Harvard, however, I am convinced that here is a strong man, a man who is really great. Perhaps that's why many people do not like him.

[Dr. Jung paid his respects to dictators, explaining their rise as due to the effort of peoples to delegate to others the complicated task of managing their collective existence so that individuals might be free to engage in "individuation." He defined the term as the development by each person of his own inherent pattern of existence.]

People have been bewildered by the war, by what has occurred in Russia, Italy, Germany, Spain. These things take

[1] For Jung's contribution, "Psychological Factors Determining Human Behaviour," see CW 8, pars. 232ff.

[2] No publication of the press release has come to light, but the text is printed in CW 18, pars. 1300–1304.

their breath away. They wonder if it is worth while living because they have lost their beliefs, their philosophy. They ask if civilization has made any progress at all.

I would call it progress that in the 2,000,000 years we have existed on earth we have developed a chin and a decent sort of brain. Historically what we call progress is, after all, just a mushroom growth of coal and oil. Otherwise we are not any more intelligent than the old Greeks or Romans. As to the present troubles, it is important simply to remember that mankind has been through such things more than once and has given evidence of a great adaptive system stored away in our unconscious mind.

[It is to this great adaptive system in every individual that he addresses himself, he explained, when a patient comes to him, broken down by his struggles with the problems of his individual existence.]

Together the patient and I address ourselves to the 2,000,-000-year-old man that is in all of us. In the last analysis, most of our difficulties come from losing contact with our instincts, with the age-old unforgotten wisdom stored up in us.[3]

And where do we make contact with this old man in us? In our dreams. They are the clear manifestations of our unconscious mind. They are the rendezvous of the racial history and of our current external problems. In our sleep we consult the 2,000,000-year-old man which each of us represents. We struggle with him in various manifestations of fantasy. That is why I ask a patient to write up his dreams. Usually they point the way for him as an individual.

[Dr. Jung said we dream all the time—it is normal to dream. Those who say they have a dreamless sleep, he insisted, merely forget their dreams immediately on waking. In all languages, he pointed out, there is a proverb record-

[3] Cf. "A Talk with Students at the Institute" (1958), below, pp. 359ff.

ing the wisdom of sleeping on any difficult problem. . . . Even when awake, Dr. Jung concluded, we dream; unbidden fantasies flit through the background of our minds and occasionally come to notice when our attention to immediate external problems is lowered by fatigue or reverie.]

There is hope of repairing a breakdown whenever a patient has neurotic symptoms. They indicate that he is not at one with himself and the neurotic symptoms themselves usually diagnose what is wrong. Those who have no neurotic symptoms are probably beyond help by any one.

THE PSYCHOLOGY OF
DICTATORSHIP

++++++++++++++++++++++++++

On his eastward crossing of the Atlantic in October 1936, after the visit to Harvard, Jung wrote a lecture on "Psychology and National Problems," which he delivered to the Tavistock Clinic (Institute of Medical Psychology), London, on October 14, 1936.[1] Ideas resembling those in the lecture occurred, naturally, in interviews that Jung gave to London newspapers during his visit. One of these, in the *Daily Sketch* for October 15, was headed "Why the World Is in a Mess. Dr. Jung Tells Us How Nature Is Changing Modern Woman." Another, in the *Observer* for October 18, is given here, without the reporter's introductory words. The same text was published partially in *Time*, Nov. 9, 1936, and fully in *The Living Age* (New York), December 1936.

Hitler, Mussolini, Stalin, yes, and Roosevelt, they are tribal rulers. England and Switzerland are still tribal. They preserve their local differences and distinctions. You have your Welsh, Irish, Scottish. You observe your ancient tribal customs—the ceremony with which the Lord Mayor greets the King when he crosses the boundary of the City of London, for instance.

There are people who grow impatient of such customs. That is wrong. They are healthy, because they are good for the unconscious. When the old tribal institutions—the former small duchies and princedoms of Germany and Italy—are broken up, then comes the upheaval, before a new tribal order is created. It is always the same. The tribe has its personal ruler. He surrounds himself with his own par-

_____
[1] Not published until 1976, in CW 18, pars. 1305ff.

ticular followers, who become an oligarchy. Then the "State" takes his place.

The State is a ghost, a mirror-reflex of the personal ruler. The ghost-State creates its own oligarchy. Capitalism is an oligarchy. The American trusts were an oligarchy. But there is always the struggle against the oligarchy. The people look to their State to give them more wages, higher standards of living. The State can only do so by dissipating energy, by tapping resources.

And so the time comes when the State must make fake money. First it is called "inflation." Then, because that is unpopular, "devaluation." Now they are calling it "dilution." But it is all the same thing—fake money. Thus you have insecurity. Savings become illusory. Since nature is aristocratic, the valuable part of the population is reduced to the level of misery.

Communistic or Socialistic democracy is an upheaval of the unfit against attempts at order. Consider the stay-in strikes in France, the former Socialistic upheavals in Germany and Italy. This state of disorder called democratic freedom or liberalism brings its own reactions—enforced order. In as much as the European nations are incapable of living in a chronic state of disorder, they will make attempts at enforced order, or Fascism.

Russia is the typical oligarchy, as it always was. The Communist Party is a privileged ruling caste. They are working toward the same thing in Germany. The S.S. men are being transformed into a caste of knights ruling sixty million natives. So you see, the tribal boundaries may be extended, the smaller tribes may be transformed into a nation, but the tribal idea remains. The dictatorships of Germany, Russia, and Italy may not be the best form of government, but they are the only possible form of government at the moment.

I have just come from America, where I saw Roosevelt. Make no mistake, he is a force—a man of superior and impenetrable mind, but perfectly ruthless, a highly versatile mind which you cannot foresee. He has the most amazing power complex, the Mussolini substance, the stuff of a dictator absolutely.

There are two kinds of dictators—the chieftain type and the medicine man type. Hitler is the latter. He is a medium. German policy is not made; it is revealed through Hitler. He is the mouthpiece of the gods as of old. He says the word which expresses everybody's resentment.

I remember a medicine man in Africa who said to me almost with tears in his eyes: "We have no dreams any more since the British are in the country." When I asked him why, he answered: "The District Commissioner knows everything."

Mussolini, Stalin, and Roosevelt rule like that, but in Germany they still have "dreams." You remember the story of how, when Hitler was being pressed by other Powers not to withdraw Germany from the League of Nations, he shut himself away for three days, and then simply said, without explanation: "Germany must withdraw!" That is rule by revelation.

Hence the sensitiveness of Germans to criticism or abuse of their leader. It is blasphemy to them, for Hitler is the Sybil, the Delphic oracle.

After the dictators? Oligarchy in some form. A decent oligarchy—call it aristocracy if you like—is the most ideal form of government. It depends on the quality of a nation whether they evolve a decent oligarchy or not. I am not sure that Russia will, but Germany and Italy have a chance.

Without the aristocratic ideal there is no stability. You in England owe it to the "gentleman" that you possess the world.

IS ANALYTICAL PSYCHOLOGY
A RELIGION?

••••••••••••••••••••••••••

After speaking at the Harvard Tercentenary Conference, Jung spent a week at Bailey Island, Maine, giving the first half of a seminar on "Dream Symbols of the Individuation Process," based on his 1935 Eranos lecture.[1] Afterward, Jung traveled to New York City for another week of consultations and lecturing, and he sailed for England on October 3. The previous evening, during a farewell supper party, Jung talked extemporaneously. Several members of the audience took notes, which were compiled by Eleanor Bertine, Esther Harding, and Jane A. Pratt for restricted circulation among the members of the group. Finally in *Spring* 1972 the notes were published, as edited by Mrs. Pratt, who included the following introductory comment:

"Few who were there will ever forget the circumstances under which Jung spoke that evening. Immediately preceding the supper with his friends, Jung had given a large public lecture in the ballroom of the Plaza Hotel. This lecture, entitled 'The Concept of the Collective Unconscious,'[2] was difficult, and dealt with controversial ideas crucial to the understanding of his work. All of Jung's most prominent New York supporters and detractors had come to hear it. But the occasion was not propitious. The lecture (at that time) required slides, a lot of them, and an enthusiastic follower had volunteered to project them, but either this man's skills were insufficient, or the slides were possessed. They came on upside down or reversed, and fell on the floor when he attempted to right them. If Jung wanted to see one again, they moved forward, if he said to go on, they went back. So Jung stood, pointer in hand, on a raised platform before his huge audience, either

---

[1] See above, "Man's Immortal Mind," n. 4. Also see p. xviii, Note.
[2] Again given as a lecture to the Abernethian Society at St. Bartholomew's Hospital, London, on Oct. 19, 1936, and revised in CW 9 i.

waiting for the right pictures to appear, or hurrying to comment intelligibly upon them before they passed on. Meanwhile his adherents suffered. Reacting at first with great consideration to the awkwardness of his assistant, his remarks became sharper by shades—since negative feelings will out—and the suffering of the adherents increased. Yet that misfortunate lecture ended without anything basically human being destroyed—not even Jung's relation to the assistant, who admitted the justice of a certain irritation. Only the muddle and all the interruptions had completely destroyed the continuity of Jung's important argument. Later he was reported to have told someone: 'I was analyzed tonight, if never before.' In place of the impressive exposition that he planned, Jung had given a small demonstration. Conceivably this may have influenced the content of what he said later"—as follows:

I hardly know what to say to you tonight. I have talked so much, twice already this evening. I do not know what more there is. I can only hope that something will come to me that I can give you.[3]

Many people have asked me, and doubtless asked you too, whether analytical psychology is not really a religion. Also, in connection with the subject of my Yale lectures, as well as that of the Seminar, I have had to give a great deal of attention lately to the relation of psychology to religion. So now at the end of the Seminar I would like to speak to you about this question.

The activation of the unconscious is a phenomenon peculiar to our day. All through the Middle Ages people's psychology was entirely different from what it is now; they had no realization of anything outside of consciousness. Even the psychological science of the eighteenth century completely identified the psyche with consciousness.

[3] This opening paragraph was added from another version by E. F. Edinger, who contributed one or two other minor changes in the text.

If you had a kind of X-ray by means of which you could observe the state of the unconscious in a man of two or three hundred years ago and compare it with that in a modern man, you would see an enormous difference. In the first man it would be quiescent; in the modern man, tremendously aroused and active. Formerly men did not even feel that they had a psychology as we do now. The unconscious was contained and held dormant in Christian theology. The *Weltanschauung* that resulted was universal, absolutely uniform—without room for doubt. Man had begun at a definite point, with the Creation; everyone knew all about it. But today archetypal contents, formerly taken care of satisfactorily by the explanations of the Church, have come loose from their projections and are troubling modern people. Questions as to where we are going, and why, are asked on every side. The psychic energy associated with these contents is stirring as never before; we cannot remain unconscious of it. Whole layers of the psyche are coming to light for the first time. That is why we have so many flourishing "isms." Much of this energy goes into science, to be sure; but science is new, its tradition is recent and does not satisfy archetypal needs. The present psychological situation is unprecedented; from the point of view of all previous experience, it is abnormal.

As a result, men have begun to be aware that they have a psychology. A man from the past would have no understanding of what we mean when we say that something is going on in our heads. Nothing like that happened to him. Had he felt such a thing he would have thought himself crazy. Men used to say: "I feel something move in my heart"—or, before that, they felt it lower down in the stomach. They were aware only of thoughts that moved the diaphragm or the guts. The Greek word *phren*, meaning "spirit," is the root of the word "diaphragm." When people began to feel things moving in their heads they were afraid, and they went to the doctors, for they knew something was wrong. It was from the doctors that this new kind of psychology came. So it is a somewhat pathological psychology.

Latency is probably the best condition for the unconscious. But life has gone out of the churches, and it will never go back. The gods will not reinvest dwellings that once they have left. The same thing happened before, in the time of the Roman Caesars, when paganism was dying. According to legend,[4] the captain of a ship passing between two Greek islands heard a great sound of lamentation and a loud voice crying: *Pan ho megas tethneken*, Great Pan is dead. When this man reached Rome he demanded an audience with the emperor, so important was his news. Originally Pan was an unimportant nature spirit, chiefly occupied with teasing shepherds; but later, as the Romans became more involved with Greek culture, Pan was confused with *to pan*, meaning "the All." He became the *demiurgos*, the *anima mundi*. Thus the many gods of paganism were concentrated into one God. Then came this message, "Pan is dead." Great Pan, who is God, is dead. Only man remains alive. After that the one God became one man, and this was Christ; one man for all. But now that too is gone, now every man has to carry God. The descent of spirit into matter is complete.

Jesus, you know, was a boy born of an unmarried mother. Such a boy is called illegitimate, and there is a prejudice which puts him at a great disadvantage. He suffers from a terrible feeling of inferiority for which he is certain to have to compensate. Hence the temptation of Jesus in the wilderness, in which the kingdom was offered to him. Here he met his worst enemy, the power devil; but he was able to see that, and to refuse. He said, "My kingdom is not of this world." But "kingdom" it was, all the same. And you remember that strange incident, the triumphal entry into Jerusalem. The utter failure came at the Crucifixion in the

[4] Plutarch, *De defectu oraculorum*, 17. (The Greek quotation has been corrected in accordance with the Loeb edition.)

tragic words, "My God, my God, why hast thou forsaken me?" If you want to understand the full tragedy of those words you must realize what they meant: Christ saw that his whole life, devoted to the truth according to his best conviction, had been a terrible illusion. He had lived it to the full absolutely sincerely, he had made his honest experiment, but it was nevertheless a compensation. On the Cross his mission deserted him. But because he had lived so fully and devotedly he won through to the Resurrection body.

We all must do just what Christ did. We must make our experiment. We must make mistakes. We must live out our own vision of life. And there will be error. If you avoid error you do not live; in a sense even it may be said that every life is a mistake, for no one has found the truth. When we live like this we know Christ as a brother, and God indeed becomes man. This sounds like a terrible blasphemy, but not so. For then only can we understand Christ as he would want to be understood, as a fellow man; then only does God become man in ourselves.

This sounds like religion, but it is not. I am speaking just as a philosopher. People sometimes call me a religious leader. I am not that. I have no message, no mission; I attempt only to understand. We are philosophers in the old sense of the word, lovers of wisdom. That avoids the sometimes questionable company of those who offer a religion.

And so the last thing I would say to each of you, my friends, is: Carry through your life as well as you can, even if it is based on error, because life has to be undone, and one often gets to truth through error. Then, like Christ, you will have accomplished your experiment. So, be human, seek understanding, seek insight, and make your hypothesis, your philosophy of life. Then we may recognize the Spirit alive in the unconscious of every individual. Then we become brothers of Christ.

QUESTIONS AND ANSWERS AT
THE OXFORD CONGRESS, 1938

++++++++++++++++++++++++

The tenth International Medical Congress for Psychotherapy was held at Oxford from July 29 to August 2, 1938. Jung presided, in his capacity as president of the International General Medical Society for Psychotherapy,[1] which sponsored the Congress. On August 1, at the request of a number of doctors at the Congress, Jung participated in a question-and-answer session, which was recorded in shorthand by Derek Kitchin. The transcript has been in private hands and is published here for the first time.

1. *What is your view on the exact nature of psychic causation?*

That sounds very dangerous, but it is not so terrible. It means really the question of causality *versus* finality. It is a simple fact of logic that you can explain a sequence of events either from A to Z or from Z to A. You may say that A is the big *causa prima*, the absolute *causa efficiens* from which depends the sequence as a sequence; or you can consider the Z as the final cause, which has an attractive effect upon the events which precede it. This simply means that we take the sequence of events which we observe as a solid connection. In itself it is not a solid connection at all. The sequence of events has perhaps no connection whatever. If we try to explain the sequence we have got to apply the idea that there is a connection. We cannot help that: the idea of causation is a category of judgment *a priori*, and we cannot look at any sequence of events without applying that cate-

[1] For Jung's presidential address to the Congress, see CW 10, pars. 1069–73. At this time, Oxford University gave him a D.Sc. hon.

gory. It is not quite correct. We might have said: "You cannot look at a sequence of events without applying the *idea* of connection."

The idea of causality itself is a thoroughly magical idea. We assume that this thing here, the *causa prima*, has a virtue, that of producing subsequent events. So we make the same assumption about the final cause: that it has the virtue of attracting a series of events towards itself so that it appears to be the result, the goal, the aim. That is mere assumption. It is the way our mind deals with a sequence of events.

Now, as everywhere in natural science, and also in psychology and psychotherapy, we consider the sequence of psychic events as a connection, a solid sequence, that either begins with a prime cause or follows a final cause. Both ways have been applied: the Freudian point of view is a strict causality point of view, and the Adlerian point of view is as strict a final-cause point of view.

I handle the case more skeptically. I should say that if we have to apply the cause either way, we want to explain either way. Any biological process has two aspects: you can explain it either from the beginning or from the end. You have "Either–or," or rather, "Either–and/or." You have to say that it is surely in a way a causation, but the *causa prima* has a sort of magical effect. At the same time, inasmuch as it is purposive, teleological, it is also directed by the final cause, or by the idea of the goal, or whatever you like to call it. I take the whole question of causation as a problem of the theory of cognition.

2. *How would you define volition? What, in your view, is the relationship of the volitional process to the process of repression and inhibition?*

That also is a very central problem. It is of great interest to me that such questions should be asked at all. I think it is very important. I always hold that psychology is such a complicated chapter of human knowledge that those who deal with it should really have some philosophical preparation. Medical psychology, surely, cannot stand alone. This is a science much too big for our medical preparation. We medical people ought to take loans from other sciences. For instance, we should have some knowledge of primitive psychology, of history, philosophy, and so on. Many things with which we are grappling in our psychology could be simplified and made easier by knowledge that we have gained in other spheres.

Therefore we have a natural tendency to simplify and to create, at least for ourselves, a terminology which is generally understandable. But I am thoroughly convinced that we shall not be able to evolve such a teminology from medical psychology alone. That would always remain a sort of slang, a medical slang, and we have plenty of such slang already; I don't advocate any further increase of that kind of thing. I am also a strong adherent of the idea that our terminology should be correct. We should not use hybrid words, or badly constructed Graeco-Latin terms; words of entirely wrong derivation. You know that the terminology in the field of medical psychology is still in the state of the old Babylonian confusion of tongues. It really is so, as it is said in *Green Pastures*,[2] that when the Lord heard those people cursing while they were building the tower of Babel he turned them all into foreigners and sent them all to Europe. People speak different languages in Europe; they don't do so in America.

This definition of volition: here I can only give you my own point of view, which is quite subjective. It is a mere proposition, which I submit to further discussion. I hold that this question ought to be settled with the help of primi-

[2] A play by Marc Connelly (1930; later filmed), adapted from stories by Roark Bradford based on American Negro folk-themes. Jung mentioned the film in his 1940 Eranos lecture, "On the Psychology of the Idea of the Trinity"; cf. CW 11, par. 266.

tive psychology. Many of our difficulties would vanish if we had a better knowledge of primitive psychology. You know, perhaps, that I have done some work along that line. I have been to primitive countries and I have done actual field work with primitives, in order to gain an immediate impression of the primitive mind. I can assure you that what we call "will" or "volition" is a phenomenon that does not exist with primitives, or only in traces.

I will give you a very simple example.[3] Once I wanted to send a letter to a very distant station, about 120 kilometres from the place where we were. The chief sent me a man, a runner, and I gave him my letter, and said, "Here is the letter, now you go down to the station." The man simply stared at me as if he did not understand a word. I spoke his language—that means, I spoke the pidgin Swahili; he understood it, but it did not reach him somehow. I did not know what the matter was. I repeated, "Here is the letter, and now you go." He went on staring at me as he had before, as if he did not understand a word, but he seemed willing. I said, "That man is idiotic." In the meantime my headman, a Somali, came up and said, "You don't do it in the right way." He took a whip and began to dance up and down in front of that good native, and curse him up and down, and his ancestors and his children; and so that man began to wake up, wondering what great thing was in store for him: he heard that this here is the great white man who wants to send a letter to the other white man at the station, and that he should run in such and such a way; and then the messenger's staff was brought, a cleft stick, and the letter was put into the cleavage, and that was handed to him, and then he was shown how he should run. And during all that procedure that man's face came up like the sun on Sunday morning; a large grin appeared, and he grasped

[3] Jung recounted the same story in more detail, from his visit to East Africa in 1925–26, in "A Radio Talk in Munich" (1930), CW 18, pars. 1288–91.

it; then he went off, and in one stretch he ran that 120 kilometres. That is a very simple example of how it ought to be done in many cases.

Every primitive needs the *rite d'entrée*, which is what some people call the procedure about which I have told you. This means that you must put his mind into the frame of doing, if you want something outside the ordinary. Naturally, if it is something of his every-day, there is a certain adaptation, a certain attitude to it; but if he has to bring a letter somewhere, that is something else. To us it is nothing extraordinary, but to him it is an extraordinary thing, and that thing needs a *rite d'entrée*. Hunting is for many tribes not an ordinary affair, so they have a special *rite d'entrée* for hunting. They work themselves up into the state of doing the special thing. For instance, the Australian aborigines have a special routine for making a man angry, in order to get the idea into him that he should avenge a man who has been killed by another tribe. It is done in a very elaborate way, the waking-up ceremonial. I cannot go into details, but at the very moment when that man is thoroughly awake, you tell him that the man has been killed and that he ought to do something about it; and then the whole tribe wakes up and seeks the enemy. If they find him, there will be a battle about it, but if they don't find him, the excitement subsides, and everyone goes home as if nothing had happened.

This shows that the will was practically non-existent and that it needed all that ceremonial which you observe in primitive tribes to bring up something that is an equivalent of our word "decision." Slowly through the ages we have acquired a certain amount of will power. We could detach so much energy from the energy of nature, from the original unconsciousness, from the original flow of events, an amount of energy we could control. We can say now, "I have made up my mind, I am going to do this and that," with a certain amount of energy. I cannot exceed that amount of energy; I have only a certain amount of will power. So you say, when the task is too difficult or when there are too great inhibitions, "I cannot carry through my decision." There are people who have a lot of will power at their disposal, and others who have very little. Also, as you know, the education of children consists to a great extent of building up that volition, because it is not there to begin with.

We see them in extraordinary situations, these ancient *rites d'entrée*. All rites are in a way *rites d'entrée* or *rites de sortie*, which are meant to get us out of a certain predicament. One of the most striking examples of the *rite de sortie* is when a tribe has been making war on another tribe and a man has succeeded in killing somebody. Then, of course, he is a great warrior; then he is all excited and he comes home. You would expect a wonderful reception. Not at all; they catch him before he enters the village, the great, victorious hero, and they put him in a little hut and they feed him on a vegetarian diet for a few months in order to get him out of his blood-thirst—which is a very recommendable thing!

Now, what we do, or what we decide, is not all willpower or volition, because we are acting a great deal on instinct, and instinct has no merit at all. That is no moral decision; we are simply moved to do something, just as it happens. Instinctive reaction has the quality of "all or none." It happens or it does not happen. With the will it is an entirely different proposition. The will, volition, is a moral action, and naturally it has a direct connection with repression and inhibition. You can repress instincts by your will, easily or, it may be, with great difficulty. You cannot bring about so-called sublimation by means of instinct; that will not happen. But you can bring it about by volition. Inhibition can be an absence of will; for instance, when you want to do something, you really wish it, but you cannot carry it out because your volition is inhibited; the energy is absent, it is taken away. On the primitive level that phenomenon is a very frequent one; it is the loss of the soul; it has that quality. There are many patients who will tell you that today they have no libido at all; or that suddenly, when they woke up in the morning, their libido had gone, or that at a certain moment during the day it had vanished. They have what the people in South America call "lost the *gana*."[4] It is a peculiar concept, and shows exactly what that is, I mean that loss. For instance, Argentine people play tennis; a ball jumps over the fence. There is a little Indian girl outside, and the people inside ask her to throw the ball in. She sadly stares at the people and does nothing. Then naturally they ask her, "Why don't you throw the ball over the fence?" "I have no *gana*," no pleasure in doing it. "I can't do it, because I have no pleasure in it"; and then you can't do it. That, you see, is a primitive concept. *Gana* is what we would call libido, or energy, or volition. When *gana* is absent, that is an excellent motive. For instance, when somebody asks you a favor, and you say, "I'm sorry, it doesn't please me," or that you don't like it, that is very impolite. But in South America it is different. There people understand what it means when you say it doesn't please you; that is enough. You say, "I have no *gana*"; that counts. There is also a social recognition of the extraordinarily important fact whether somebody is pleased to do something or not. With us this apparently does not count at all. I am afraid that is a piece of primitive psychology. That is what we call an inhibition. I should think it would be of a certain importance for our medical psychology if we could consider these primitive conditions a bit more. Many things could then be explained in a way that would allow primitive psychology to come in without medical knowledge.

[4] Jung apparently picked up the idea of *gana* from Count Hermann Keyserling, who discussed it in *South-American Meditations* (1932). Cf. above, p. 82.

3. *In what respect, if any, does the treatment of neurosis in the second half of life—that means after thirty—differ from that in the first half of life?*

This is also a question which you could discuss for several hours. It is quite impossible for me to go into details; I only can give you a few hints. The first half of life, which I reckon lasts for the first 35 or 36 years, is the time when the individual usually expands into the world. It is just like an exploding celestial body, and the fragments travel out into space, covering ever greater distances. So our mental horizon widens out, and our wishes and expectation, our ambition, our will to conquer the world and live, go on expanding, until you come to the middle of life. A man who after forty years has not reached that position in life which he had dreamed of is easily the prey of disappointment. Hence the extraordinary frequency of depressions after the fortieth year. It is the decisive moment; and when you study the productivity of great artists—for instance, Nietzsche[5]—you find that at the beginning of the second half of life their modes of creativeness often change. For instance, Nietzsche began to write *Zarathustra*, which is his outstanding work, quite different from everything he did before and after, when he was between 37 and 38. That is the critical time. In the second part of life you begin to question yourself. Or rather, you don't; you avoid such questions, but something in yourself asks them, and you do not like to hear that voice asking "What is the goal?" And next, "Where are you going now?" When you are young you think, when you get to a certain position, "This is the thing I want." The goal seems to be quite visible. People think, "I am going to marry, and then I shall get into such and such a position, and then I shall make a lot of money, and then I don't know what." Suppose they have reached it; then comes another question: "And now what? Are we

[5] From 1934 to 1939, Jung had been giving a detailed seminar in Zurich on "Psychological Aspects of Nietzsche's *Zarathustra*."

really interested in going on like this forever, for ever doing the same thing, or are we looking for a goal as splendid or as fascinating as we had it before?" Then the answer is: "Well, there is nothing ahead. What is there ahead? Death is ahead." That is disagreeable, you see; that is most disagreeable. So it looks as if the second part of life has no goal whatever. Now you know the answer to that. From time immemorial man has had the answer: "Well, death is a goal; we are looking forward, we are working forward to a definite end." The religions, you see, the great religions, are systems for preparing the second half of life for the end, the goal, of the second part of life.

Once, through the help of friends, I sent a questionnaire to people who did not know that I was the originator of the questionnaire. I had been asked the question, "Why do people prefer to go to the doctor instead of to the priest for confession?" Now I doubted whether it was really true that people prefer a doctor, and I wanted to know what the general public was going to say. By chance that questionnaire came into the hands of a Chinaman, and his answer was, "When I am young I go to the doctor, and when I am old I go to the philosopher." You see, that characterizes the difference: when you are young, you live expansively, you conquer the world; and when you grow old, you begin to reflect. You naturally begin to think of what you have done. There a moment comes, between 36 and 40— certain people take a bit longer—when perhaps, on an uninteresting Sunday morning, instead of going to church, you suddenly think, "Now what have I lived last year?" or something like that; and then it begins to dawn, and usually you catch your breath and don't go on thinking because it is disagreeable.

Now, you see, there is a resistance against the widening out in the first part of life—that great sexual adventure. When young people have resistance against risking their life, or against their social career, because it needs some concentration, some exertion, they are apt to get neurotic. In the second part of life those people who funk the natural development of the mind—reflection, preparation for the end—they get neurotic too. Those are the neuroses of the second part of life. When you speak of a repression of sexuality in the second part of life, you often have a repression of this, and these people are just as neurotic as those who resist life during the first part. As a matter of fact it is the same people: first they don't want to get into life, they are afraid to risk their life, to risk their health, perhaps, or their life for the sake of life, and in the second part of life they have no time. So, you see, when I speak of the goal which marks the end of the second half of life, you get an idea of how far the treatment in the first half of life, and in the second half of life, must needs be different. You get a problem to deal with which has not been talked of before. Therefore I strongly advocate schools for adult people. You know, you were fabulously well prepared for life. We have very decent schools, we have fine universities and that is all preparation for the expansion of life. But where have you got the schools for adult people? for people who are 40, 45, about the second part of life? Nothing. That is taboo; you must not talk of it; it is not healthy. And that is how they get into these nice climacteric neuroses and psychoses.

4. *Would you say that the attitude to be attained in the second half of life should be conceived as one of the objective type rather than as one of sublimation?*

This is a profound and very ticklish question. You see, in the first part of life it seems that sublimation is the thing indicated, and in the second part of life it seems that objectivity is indicated. Now, what is sublimation? This term has been taken from alchemy. It is really an alchemical term, and when you understand it in that sense it does not evoke the psychological fact which we understand as sublimation. Sublimation means that you don't do what you really wish to do, and play the piano instead. That is nice, you see! Or, instead of giving way to your terrible passions, you go to Sunday school. Then you say you have sublimated it—"it"! It is, of course, an act of volition. I don't want to ridicule it at all, only sometimes it has a somewhat humorous aspect. Life, in spite of its misery, sometimes has an exceedingly humorous aspect. And so those people who perform miracles of moral self-restraint occasionally look rather comical. It would be bad if this were not so; there would be no fun in life at all. So even sublimation, which is a very useful and heroic thing, sometimes looks a bit funny; but it is never a serious thing, and it is certainly a way of dealing with the difficulties of life, all those difficulties that are forced upon us by our original nature. We have a very unruly and passionate nature, perhaps, and we simply hurt ourselves if we live it in an uncontrolled way. Try to tell the truth. You would like to tell the truth, I am sure. Nobody likes to lie if he is not forced to. But just tell the truth for twenty-four hours and see what happens! In the end you can't stand yourself any more. So, you see, you can't let go of all your ambitions; you can't beat down every man who gets your goat; you can't express your admiration to every pretty woman you see. You must control yourself, after all, and that is also a considerable piece of sublimation. Take swearing: you must not use this impossible language, and so, instead of saying something disagreeable, you say something agreeable, as you have learnt, and all that continues—ethics, self-repression, and sublimation. And the worse your passions are, the more you must use this sublimation mechanism, otherwise you get into hot water. And you don't like that either.

Now surely the passions are likely to be worse in the first half of life than in the second. There is a certain saying about the virtues of Solomon and David, who grew virtuous on account of their old age. There is also a French saying: "Si jeunesse savait, si vieillesse pouvait!" *Enfin*, in the second half of life people have a chance to be more virtuous, some-how. They don't make enough use of that chance, and that comes from the fact that, unfortunately, they have learned more objectivity than sublimation. They say, for instance, "Oh well, after all, it seems to be human nature that one has certain weaknesses"; so they begin to allow themselves certain weaknesses, and gradually, the more the passions subside, the more you can yourself allow to side-step a little bit, to make little mistakes and to excuse yourself by saying it is not so terribly serious after all. An elderly gentleman, of course, can allow himself to show some tenderness to a nice young girl. Formerly he would have blushed; it would have been shocking; but now he can show his appreciation and everyone will say, "How nice and fatherly that is!" Also, ladies of a certain age can allow themselves to have very liberal views, and to express such views, and among those are things which they never would have said before in younger age, because it would have been too shocking. But when they are older one thinks, "That's nice; that shows a certain experience of life"; and they are very free in the way in which they express themselves. That is great objectivity; that is already the beginning of a certain philos-ophy that deals with facts as they are. It is perhaps a sort of disillusionment, or perhaps it is a sort of superiority gained through experience of life. You know that your virtues are not going to increase very considerably any more. Even your virtues grow gray hair and become bald. And so, what can you do? You say, "Oh, that's fine; you mustn't expect too much." And that is how we deal with ourselves in the second part of life. I do not speak of how the analyst ought to deal with his patients. There is an "ought," but there is a certain wisdom, and that belongs to the secrets of the art, which I shall not reveal here!

5. *Would you give us some hints with regard to religious experience? Is a so-called religious feeling a valid psycho-logical experience?*

Well, I understand this question in the following way. Is the religious experience a valid experience? What is a valid experience? For instance, if a dog bites me, is that a valid experience? It is an experience; and if I have a religious experience, well, that is an experience too, and how shall I say that it is valid? You might say, "Oh, you have an imagination, you have an illusion; you think that you had a religious experience." Well, that does not concern me. Perhaps it is an illusion; how do I know? There is no criterion. I can only say, "I felt it like this." Of course, you can draw conclusions, and so you can ask, "Are the conclusions you draw from it valid?" For instance, you can draw the conclusion that you have an experience of your patron saint, who has appeared to you, or you have seen the Mother of God, or something like that. Then you can ask, "Is that valid? Is that interpretation valid?" You know how divided opinions are. Opinions are geographically rather different. For instance, a vision with us will be interpreted in terms of traditional Christianity; several hundred miles more South, in terms of Islamic mentality, and a little bit more East, it will be something else again; and sometimes there is a considerable difference in the interpretation of such experiences, but the experiences themselves are always valid— because they exist. For instance, is it a valid fact that there are elephants? You cannot even say that elephants are needed; you only can say they exist. And so with such experiences. The moment a man says, "I had a religious experience," you can only say, "Well, you had a religious experience." You can hold all sorts of views about it. You can say, "Oh, that was merely because your stomach was not all right, or you have slept badly." But that is merely explaining away the fact that he had such an experience. Of course you can say, "Well, that may be quite pathological." And in that case you must go to the *Encyclopaedia Britannica* and look up that kind of experience. All human experiences, you know, are registered in the *Encyclopaedia Britannica*! And then you will be taught whether there was that experience, and of what kind. But it may be that it is not contained in the *Encyclopaedia Britannica*, and in that case you can say, "Well, I have never heard of such an experience; I don't know what it is," and you have got to explain it to yourself somehow.

But, generally speaking, religious experience is something we are fairly well acquainted with. We have the history of religions; we have innumerable texts which inform us about the forms of religious experience. So we know it is a universal phenomenon, and if it is absent, then we are confronted with an abnormal case. If somebody should say, "I don't know what a religious experience is," then I say that something is lacking, because the whole world has at times religious experience, and you must have lost it somewhere if you don't know what it is. You are not in a normal frame of mind. There is some trouble. When that is the case, we know that some other type of psychological function is exaggerated through the admixture of the energy which should normally be in a religious experience. When you look at the life of a primitive tribe, as long as its religious life is well organized, things are in order. Now let a missionary come in, who can sense nothing of primitive religions and simply says, "This is all wrong," and then you see how the religious life of the tribe begins to disintegrate. This is one of the most extraordinary phenomena. Then people become greedy, they become fresh; then a mission boy steps up to me and says, "I'm a brother of yours, I'm just as good as you are, I know of those fellows Johnny, Marki, and Luki, all the bunch of them." That's how they talk. For years they sing a hymn in which there is a word meaning "hope," or "confidence." A missionary who listened to that hymn didn't know the accentuation of that word properly: If you put the accent on the last syllable it means "hope," and if you put it on the first, it means "locust." So they sang, "Jesus is our locust," and that went quite well, because the locust is a religious figure in Africa. So it meant something to them: "Jesus is a locust." But it would have meant precious little to them to sing, "Jesus is our hope and confidence." Even the highest people to whom I talked were quite unable to understand the elements of the Christian religion. How could they? I have not found one mission boy in Africa who could have understood the elements of the Christian faith or what it is all about. The Pueblo Indians told me, "Oh, it is very nice what the priest is doing; he comes along every second month, and when we bury our dead he does very interesting things with them, but then we do the Indian medicine afterwards." You see, they always wrap up the dead twice, first according to the Christian rite and afterwards according to the Indian rite, and then it is finished. The same with birth; in Indian families everything is done twice. I said, "That's very nice, but do you know about Jesus?" And they say, "Oh yes, we know about Jesu, and the priest often talks with a man he calls Jesu." And I say, "What about the man?" and they say, "Oh, we don't know; we don't understand what he is all about." And they are highly civilized people, philosophical people, even. The man who talked like that to me was a philosopher. He was very critical, he had an excellent psychology. He said, "Look at the white man's face: sharp lines, disappointed nose; and these Americans are always seeking something. We don't know what they are seeking; we think they are all crazy." He made the right diagnosis! Don't be too triumphant; it isn't only the Americans; it is the white man. And he felt it. It was the first time I got a really objective line on the white man. I saw suddenly with his eyes. Such people understand nothing of the Christian religion, what it really is.

If you break up a tribe, they lose their religious ideas, the treasure of their old tradition, and they feel out of form completely. They lose their *raison d'être*, they grow hopeless. That medicine man, with tears in his eyes, said, "We have no dreams any more." "Since when?" "Oh, since the British are in the country." They are entirely *dépossedés*, all the meaning goes out of their life; it does not make sense any more because we infect them with our insanity. Because it is an insanity: we have lost the religious order of life. That is my idea, and that is the point at which I will come to a conclusion.

DIAGNOSING THE DICTATORS

++++++++++++++++++++++++

H. R. Knickerbocker was one of the great American foreign correspondents, picturesque, intelligent, and tireless. Born in Texas in 1898, he was studying psychiatry in Munich at the time of Hitler's Beerhall Putsch in 1923, switched to journalism, and spent most of his career in Berlin. But he also covered the Soviet Union (Pulitzer Prize, 1931), the Italian-Ethiopian War, the Spanish Civil War, the Sino-Japanese War, Anschluss in Austria, and the Munich Pact. He reported the Battle of Britain and the war in the Pacific; in 1949, he died in a plane crash in Bombay.

Knickerbocker visited Jung in Küsnacht in October 1938, having come directly from Prague, where he had witnessed the breakup of Czechoslovakia. His interview, one of the lengthiest that Jung gave, was published in *Hearst's International–Cosmopolitan* for January 1939, and some of it appeared in a different form in Knickerbocker's book *Is Tomorrow Hitler's?* (1941). The *Cosmopolitan* article is the basis of the interview given here, which has been edited to eliminate material other than the questions and answers. The same issue of the magazine contained a biographical sketch of Jung by Elizabeth Shepley Sergeant (see p. 50). These *Cosmopolitan* articles made Jung's name famous in the United States.

What would happen if you were to lock Hitler, Mussolini, and Stalin in a room together and give them one loaf of bread and one pitcher of water to last them a week? Who would get all the food and water, or would they divide it?

I doubt if they would divide it. Hitler, being a medicine man, would probably hold himself aloof and have nothing to do with the quarrel. He would be helpless because he would be without his German people. Mussolini and Stalin, being both chiefs or strong men in their own right, would probably dispute possession of the food and drink, and Stalin, being the rougher and tougher, would probably get all of it.

There were two types of strong men in primitive society. One was the chief who was physically powerful, stronger than all his competitors, and the other was the medicine man who was not strong in himself but was strong *by reason of the power which the people projected into him.* Thus we had the emperor and the head of the religious community. The emperor was the chief, *physically* strong through his possession of soldiers; the seer was the medicine man, possessing little or no physical power but an actual power sometimes surpassing that of the emperor, because the people agreed that he possessed magic—that is, supernatural ability. He could, for example, assist or obstruct the way to a happy life after death, put a ban upon an individual, a community or a whole nation, and by excommunication cause people great discomfort or pain.

Now, Mussolini is the man of *physical* strength. When you see him you are aware of it at once. His body suggests good muscles. He is the chief by reason of the fact that he is individually stronger than any of his competitors. And it is a fact that Mussolini's mentality corresponds to his classification: he has the mind of a chief.

Stalin belongs in the same category. He is, however, not a creator. Lenin created; Stalin is devouring the brood. He is a conquistador; he simply took what Lenin made and put his teeth into it and devoured it. He is not even creatively destructive. Lenin was that. He tore down the whole structure of feudal and bourgeois society in Russia and replaced it with his own creation. Stalin is destroying that.

Mentally, Stalin is not so interesting as Mussolini, who resembles him in the fundamental pattern of his personality, and he is not anything like so interesting as the medicine man, the myth—Hitler.

Anybody who takes command of one hundred and seventy million people as Stalin has done, is bound to be interesting, whether you like him or not.

No, Stalin is just a brute—a shrewd peasant, an instinctive powerful beast—no doubt in that way far the most powerful of all the dictators. He reminds one of a Siberian saber-toothed tiger with that powerful neck, those sweeping mustaches, and that smile like a cat which has been eating cream. I should imagine that Genghis Khan might have been an early Stalin. I shouldn't wonder if he makes himself Czar.

Hitler is entirely different. His body does not suggest strength. The outstanding characteristic of his physiognomy is its dreamy look. I was especially struck by that when I saw pictures taken of him during the Czechoslovakian crisis; there was in his eyes the look of a seer.

There is no question but that Hitler belongs in the category of the truly mystic medicine man. As somebody commented about him at the last Nürnberg party congress, since the time of Mohammed nothing like it has been seen in this world.

This markedly mystic characteristic of Hitler's is what makes him do things which seem to *us* illogical, inexplicable, curious and unreasonable. But consider—even the nomenclature of the Nazis is plainly mystic. Take the very name of the Nazi State. They call it the Third Reich. Why?

Because the First Reich was the Holy Roman Empire and the second was the one founded by Bismarck and the third is Hitler's.

Of course. But there is a deeper significance. Nobody called Charlemagne's kingdom the First Reich nor Wilhelm's the Second Reich. Only the Nazis call theirs the Third Reich. Because it has a profound *mystical* meaning: to every German the expression "Third Reich" brings echoes in his unconscious of the Biblical hierarchy. Thus Hitler, who more than once has indicated he is aware of his mystic calling, appears to the devotees of the Third Reich as something more than mere man.

Again, you take the widespread revival in the Third Reich of the cult of Wotan. Who was Wotan? God of wind. Take the name *"Sturmabteilung"*—Storm Troops. Storm, you see—the wind. Just as the swastika is a revolving form making a vortex moving ever toward the left—which means in Buddhist symbolism sinister, unfavorable, directed toward the unconscious.

And all these symbols together of a Third Reich led by its prophet under the banners of wind and storm and whirling vortices point to a mass movement which is to sweep the German people in a hurricane of unreasoning emotion on and on to a destiny which perhaps none but the seer, the prophet, the Führer himself can foretell—and perhaps, not even he.

But why is it that Hitler, who makes nearly every German fall down and worship him, produces next to no impression on any foreigner?

Exactly. Few foreigners respond at all, yet apparently every German in Germany does. It is because Hitler is the mirror of every German's unconscious, but of course he mirrors nothing from a non-German. He is the loudspeaker which magnifies the inaudible whispers of the German soul until they can be heard by the German's unconscious ear.

He is the first man to tell every German what he has been thinking and feeling all along in his unconscious about German fate, especially since the defeat in the World War, and the one characteristic which colors every German soul is the typically German inferiority complex—the complex of the younger brother, of the one who is always a bit late to the feast. Hitler's power is not political; it is *magic*.

What do you mean by magic?

To understand this you must understand what the unconscious is. It is that part of our mental constitution over which we have little control and which is stored with all sorts of impressions and sensations; which contains thoughts and even conclusions of which we are not aware.

Besides the conscious impressions which we receive, there are all sorts of impressions constantly impinging upon our sense organs of which we don't become aware because they are too slight to attract our conscious attention. They lie *beneath* the threshold of consciousness. But all these subliminal impressions are recorded; nothing is lost.

Someone may be speaking in a faintly audible voice in the next room while we are talking here. You pay no attention to it, but the conversation next door is being recorded in your unconscious as surely as though the latter were a dictaphone record. While you sit here my unconscious is taking in quantitites of impressions of you, although I am not aware of them and you would be surprised if I should tell you all that I have already learned unconsciously about you in this short space of time.

Now, the secret of Hitler's power is not that Hitler has an unconscious more plentifully stored than yours or mine. Hitler's secret is twofold: first, that his unconscious has exceptional access to his consciousness, and second, that he allows himself to be moved by it. He is like a man who listens intently to a stream of suggestions in a whispered voice from a mysterious source and then *acts upon them*. In our case, even if occasionally our unconscious does reach us as through dreams, we have too much rationality, too much cerebrum to obey it. This is doubtless the case with Chamberlain, but Hitler listens and obeys. The true leader is always *led*.

We can see it work in him. He himself has referred to his Voice. His Voice is nothing other than his own unconscious, into which the German people have projected their own selves; that is, the unconscious of seventy-eight million Germans. That is what makes him powerful. Without the German people, he would not be what he seems to be now.

It is literally true when he says that whatever he is able to do is only because he has the German people behind him—or, as he sometimes says, because he *is* Germany. So, with his unconscious being the receptacle of the souls of seventy-eight million Germans, he is powerful, and with his *unconscious perception* of the true balance of political forces at home and in the world, he has so far been infallible.

That is why he makes political judgments which turn out to be right against the opinions of all his advisers and against the opinions of all foreign observers. When this happens, it means only that the information gathered by his unconscious, and reaching his consciousness by means of his exceptional talent, has been more nearly correct than that of all the others, German or foreign, who attempted to judge the situation and who reached conclusions different from his. And of course, it also means that, having this information at hand, he is willing to *act* upon it.

I suppose that would apply to the three really critical decisions he made, each of which involved the acute danger of war: when he marched into the Rhineland in March, 1936, and into Austria in March, 1938, and when he mobilized and forced the Allies to abandon Czechoslovakia. Because in each one of these cases we know that many of Hitler's highest military advisers warned him against doing it, since they believed the Allies would resist, and also that if war came Germany would be bound to lose.

Precisely! The fact is that Hitler was able to judge his opponents better than anyone else, and although it appeared inevitable that he would be met by force, *he knew* his opponents would give in without fighting. That must have been the case especially when Chamberlain came to Berchtesgaden. There for the first time Hitler met the elder British statesman.

As Chamberlain proved later at Godesberg, he had come to tell him, among other things, not to go too far or Britain would fight. But Hitler's unconscious eye which so far has not failed him, read so deeply the character of the British Prime Minister that all the later ultimatums and warnings from London made no impression whatever on his unconscious: Hitler's unconscious knew—it didn't guess or feel, it *knew*—that Britain would not risk war. Yet Hitler's speech in the Sports Palace when he announced to the world a holy oath that he would march into Czechoslovakia October first, with or without the permission of Britain and France, indicated for the first and only time that Hitler the man, in his supremely critical moment, had fear of following Hitler the prophet.

His Voice told him to go ahead, that everything would be all right. But his human reason told him the dangers were vast and perhaps overwhelming. Hence for the first time Hitler's voice trembled; his breath failed. His speech lacked form and trailed off at the end. What human being would *not* be afraid in such a moment? In making that speech which fixed the destiny of perhaps hundreds of millions of people, he was a man doing something of which he was deathly afraid but forcing himself to do it because it was ordered by his Voice.

His Voice was correct. Now who knows but that his Voice may continue to be correct? If it does, it will be very interesting to observe the history of the next few years because, as he said just after his Czech victory, Germany stands today on the threshold of her future. That means he has just begun and if his Voice tells him that the German people are destined to become the lords of Europe and perhaps of the world, and if his Voice continues always to be right, then we are in for an extremely interesting period, aren't we?

Yes, it seems that the German people are now convinced they have found their Messiah.

In a way, the position of the Germans is remarkably like that of the Jews of old. Since their defeat in the World War they have awaited a Messiah, a Savior. That is characteristic of people with an inferiority complex. The Jews got their inferiority complex from geographical and political factors. They lived in a part of the world which was a parade ground for conquerors from both sides, and after their return from their first exile to Babylon, when they were threatened with extinction by the Romans, they invented the solacing idea of a Messiah who was going to bring all the Jews together into a nation once more and save them.

And the Germans got their inferiority complex from comparable causes. They came up out of the Danube valley too late, and founded the beginnings of their nation long after the French and the English were well on their way to nationhood. They got too late to the scramble for colonies, and for the foundation of empire. Then, when they did get together and made a united nation, they looked around them and saw the British, the French, and others with rich colonies and all the equipment of grown-up nations, and they became jealous, resentful, like a younger brother whose older brothers have taken the lion's share of the inheritance.

This was the *original* source of the German inferiority complex which has determined so much of their political thought and action and which is certainly decisive of their whole policy today. It is impossible, you see, to talk about Hitler without talking about his people, because Hitler is only the German people.

It occurred to me that the last time I was in America that one could make an interesting geographical analogy about Germany. In America I noticed that somewhere on the East Coast there exists a certain class of people called "poor white trash" and I learned that they are largely descendents of early settlers, some of them bearers of fine old English names. The poor white trash were left behind when some of the people with energy and initiative climbed into their covered wagons and drove West.

Then, in the Middle West you meet the people I consider the most stable in America; I mean psychologically the best balanced. Yet in some places farther west you meet some of the least-balanced people.

Now, it seems to me that, taking Europe as a whole, and including the British Isles, you have in Ireland and Wales the equivalent of your West Coast. The Celts possess colorful imaginative faculties. Then, to correspond to your sober Middle West, you have in Europe the English and the French, both of them psychologically stable peoples. But then you come to Germany, and just beyond Germany are the Slav mujiks, the poor white trash of Europe.

Now, the mujiks are people who can't get up in the morning, but sleep all day. And the Germans, their next-door neighbors, are people who could get up, but got up too late. Don't you remember how the Germans even today represent Germany in all their cartoons?

Yes, "Sleepy Michael," a tall, lean fellow in a nightgown and nightcap.

That's right, and Sleepy Michael slept through the division of the world into colonial empires, and so the Germans got their inferiority complex, which made them want to fight the World War, and of course when they lost it their feeling of inferiority grew even worse, and developed a desire for a Messiah, and so they have their Hitler. If he is not their true Messiah, he is like one of the Old Testament prophets: his mission is to unite his people and lead them to the Promised Land. This explains why the Nazis have to combat every form of religion besides their own idolatrous brand. I have no doubt but that the campaign against the Catholic and Protestant churches will be pursued with relentless and unremitting vigor, for the very sound reason, from the Nazi point of view, that they wish to substitute the new faith of Hitlerism.

Do you consider it possible that Hitlerism might become for Germany a permanent religion for the future like Mohammedanism for the Moslems?

I think it highly possible. Hitler's "religion" is the nearest to Mohammedanism, realistic, earthy, promising the maximum of rewards in this life, but with a Moslem-like Valhalla into which worthy Germans may enter and continue to enjoy themselves. Like Mohammedanism, it teaches the *virtue* of the sword. Hitler's first idea is to make his people powerful because the spirit of the Aryan German deserves to be supported by might, by muscle and steel.

Of course, it is not a spiritual religion in the sense in which we ordinarily use the term. But remember that in the early days of Christianity it was the church which made the claim to total power, both spiritual and temporal! Today the church no longer makes this claim, but the claim has been taken over by the totalitarian states which demand not only temporal but spiritual power.

Incidentally, it occurs to me that the "religious" character of Hitlerism is also emphasized by the fact that German communities throughout the world, far from the political power of Berlin, have adopted Hitlerism. Look at the South American German communities, notably in Chile.

(It surprised me that in this analysis of the dictators nothing had been said of the influence of the fathers and mothers of the strong men. Doctor Jung assigned them no major role.)

It is a great mistake to think that a dictator becomes so on account of personal reasons, such as that he had a strong resistance to his father. There are millions of men who resisted their fathers just as strongly as, say, Mussolini or Hitler or Stalin, but who never became dictators or anything like dictators.

The law to remember about dictators is: *"It is the perse-cuted one who persecutes."* The dictators must have suffered from circumstances calculated to bring about dictatorship. Mussolini came at the moment when the country was in chaos, the workmen out of hand and a threat of Bolshevism was terrifying the people.

Hitler came when the economic crisis had reduced the standard of living in Germany and increased unemploy-ment to an intolerable level, and after the great inflation of the currency which, although stabilization had come, had impoverished the whole middle class. Both Hitler and Mussolini received their power from the people and their power cannot be withdrawn. It is interesting that both Hitler and Mussolini base their power chiefly upon the lower middle class, workers and farmers.

But to go on with the circumstances under which dic-tators come to power: Stalin came when the death of Lenin, unique creator of Bolshevism, had left the party and the people leaderless and the country uncertain of its future. Thus the dictators are made from human material which suffers from overwhelming needs. The three dictators in Europe differ from one another tremendously, but it is not so much they who differ as it is their peoples.

Compare the way the German people think and feel about Hitler with the way the Italians think and feel about Mussolini. The Germans are highly impressionable. They go to extremes; are always a bit unbalanced. They are cosmopolitan, world citizens; easily lose their national identity; like to imitate other nations. Every German man would like to dress like an English gentleman.

Not Hitler. He always has dressed in his own way, and nobody could ever accuse him of trying to look as if he got his clothes on Savile Row.

Precisely. Because Hitler is saying to his Germans, "Now, *bei Gott*, you have got to start being *Germans!*"

The Germans are extraordinarily sensitive to new ideas,

and when they hear one which appeals to them they are likely to swallow it uncritically, and for a time to be completely dominated by it; but after a while they are equally likely to throw it violently away and adopt a newer idea, quite probably contradicting the first one entirely. This is the way they have run their political life.

Italians are more stable. Their minds do not roll and wallow and leap and plunge through all the extravagant ecstasies which are the daily exercise of the German mind. So you find in Italy a spirit of balance lacking in Germany. When the Fascists took power in Italy, Mussolini did not even remove the king. Mussolini worked not with ecstasy of spirit, but with a hammer in his hand, beating Italy into the shape he wanted it, much as his blacksmith father used to make horseshoes.

This Mussolini-Italian balance of temperament is borne out by the Fascist treatment of the Jews. At first they did not persecute the Jews at all, and even now, when for various reasons they have begun an anti-Semitic campaign, it has kept a certain proportion. I suppose the chief reason why Mussolini went in for anti-Semitism at all was that he became convinced that world Jewry was probably an incorrigible and effective force against Fascism—Léon Blum in France, especially, I think—and also, he wished to make his ties with Hitler more solid.

So you see, while Hitler is a medicine man, a form of spiritual vessel, a demi-deity or even better, a myth, Mussolini is a man, and therefore everything in Fascist Italy has a more human shape than it has in Nazi Germany, where things are run by revelation. Hitler as a man scarcely exists. At any rate, he disappears behind his rôle. Mussolini, on the contrary, never disappears behind his rôle. His rôle disappears behind Mussolini.

I saw the Duce and the Führer together in Berlin the time Mussolini paid his formal visit; I had the good luck to be placed only a few yards away from them, and could study them well. It was entertaining to see Mussolini's expression when they put on the goose step. If I had not seen it I should have fallen into the popular delusion that his adoption of the German goose step for the Italian army was in imitation of Hitler. And that would have disappointed me, because I had discerned in Mussolini's conduct a certain style, a certain format of an original man with good taste in certain matters.

I mean, for example, that it was good taste of the Duce to keep the King. And his choice of title, "Duce"—not Doge as in old Venice, nor Duca, but Duce, the plain Italian word for leader—was original and in my opinion showed good taste.

Now, as I observed Mussolini watching the first goose step he had ever seen, I could see him enjoying it with the zest of a small boy at a circus. But he enjoyed even more the stunt when the cavalry comes and the mounted drummer gallops ahead and takes his place on one side of the street while the band takes its place on the other. The drummer must gallop around the band and up to the front to take his station there, and this he does without touching the reins, guiding his horse only by pressure of the knees, since both hands are busy with the drums.

On this occasion it was done magnificently and it pleased Mussolini so much he broke out laughing and clapped his hands. When he got back to Rome afterwards, he introduced the goose step and I am convinced he did it solely for his own aesthetic enjoyment. It really is a most impressive step.

In comparison with Mussolini, Hitler made upon me the impression of a sort of scaffolding of wood covered with cloth, an automaton with a mask, like a robot, or a mask of a robot. During the whole performance he never laughed; it was as though he were in a bad humor, sulking.

He showed no human sign. His expression was that of an inhumanly single-minded purposiveness, with no sense of humor. He seemed as if he might be the double of a real person, and that Hitler the man might perhaps be hiding inside like an appendix, and deliberately so hiding in order not to disturb the mechanism.

What an amazing difference there is between Hitler and Mussolini! I couldn't help liking Mussolini. His bodily energy and elasticity are warm, human, and contagious. You have the homely feeling with Mussolini of being with a human being. With Hitler, you are scared. You know you would never be able to talk to that man; because there is nobody there. He is not a man, but a collective. He is not an individual; he is a whole nation.

I take it to be literally true that he has no personal friend. How can you talk intimately with a nation? You can no more explain Hitler by the personal approach than you can explain a great work of art by examining the personality of the artist. The great work of art is a product of the time, of the whole world in which the artist is living, and of the millions of people who surround him, and of the thousands of currents of thought and the myriad streams of activity which flow around him.

Thus it would be easier for Mussolini, who is only a man, to find a successor, than for Hitler. With good luck, I should think Mussolini might find someone to take his place, but I don't see how Hitler can.

What if Hitler were to marry?

He cannot marry. If he married, it would not be Hitler marrying. He would cease to be Hitler. But it is incredible that he should ever do so. I shouldn't wonder if it may be shown that he has sacrificed his sex life entirely to the Cause.

This is not an unusual thing, especially for the type of medicine-man leader, although it is much less usual in the type of the chief. Mussolini and Stalin seem to lead entirely normal sex lives. Hitler's real passion, of course, is Germany.

You could say that he has a tremendous mother complex, which means that he will be under the domination either of a woman or of an idea. Idea is always female. Mind is female, because the head, the brain, is creative; hence like a womb, female. The unconscious of a man is always represented by a woman; that of a woman always by a man.

How important a role does what we call personal ambition play in the makeup of the three dictators?

I should say that it plays a very minor role in Hitler. I don't think Hitler has personal ambition beyond that of the average man. Mussolini has more than average personal ambition, but it is not sufficient to explain his force. He also feels that he coincides with the national need. Hitler does not rule Germany. He is simply the exponent of the trend of things. This makes him uncanny and psychologically fascinating. Mussolini rules Italy to a certain extent, but for the rest he is an instrument of the Italian people.

With Stalin it is different. His dominant characteristic is overwhelming *personal* ambition. He does not identify himself with Russia. He rules Russia like any Czar. Remember, he is a Georgian anyway.

But how do you explain Stalin's having taken the course he has? It seems to me that Stalin, far from being uninteresting, is also enigmatic. Here you have a person who spent the greater part of his life as a revolutionist Bolshevik. His cobbler father and pious mother sent him to a theological school. In his early years he became a revolutionary and from then on for the next twenty-five years he did nothing but fight the Czar and the Czar's police. He was put into a dozen jails and broke out of all of them. Now, how do you explain that a man who had fought the Czar's tyranny all his life should suddenly become a kind of Czar himself?

That is not remarkable. It is because you always become the thing you fight the most. What undermined the armed force of Rome? Christianity did. Because when the Romans conquered the Near East, they were conquered by its religion.

When you fight a thing you have to get very close to it, and it is likely to infect you. You must know Czarism very well in order to defeat it. Then, when you have driven out the Czar, you become a Czar yourself, just as a wild-animal hunter may become bestial.

I know of one fellow who, after many years of big-game hunting in a proper sporting manner, had to be arrested because he took a machine gun to the animals. The man had become as blood-lustful as the panthers and lions he killed.

Stalin fought so much against the Czar's bloody oppression that he is now doing exactly the same as the Czar. In my opinion, there is no difference at all now between Stalin and Ivan the Terrible.

But what about the fact reported by many, and observed by myself, that the standard of living in the Soviet Union has risen considerably and is still rising from the low point of the famine of 1933?

Of course. Stalin can be a good administrator at the same time that he is a Czar. It would be a miracle if anybody could keep so naturally rich a country as Russia from being prosperous. But Stalin is not very original, and it is such bad taste for him to go about turning himself into a Czar so crudely, in front of everybody, without any concealment at all! It is really *proletarian!*

But you still have not explained to me how Stalin, the loyal Communist party man, the underground worker for what was then a highly altruistic ideal, should have changed into a power-grabber.

In my opinion the change came about in Stalin during the 1918 revolution. Up to that time he had labored, unselfishly perhaps, for the good of the Cause, and probably had never thought of personal power for himself, for the very good reason that there never appeared to be the shadow of a chance that he could even aspire to anything like personal power. The question didn't exist for him. But during the revolution Stalin saw for the first time how you *acquire* power. I am sure he said to himself with astonishment, "But it is so easy!" He must have watched Lenin and the others reach the full rank of complete power, and have said to himself, "So that is how it is done! Well, I can go them one better. All you have to do is to do away with the fellow in front of you."

He would certainly have done away with Lenin if Lenin had lived. Nothing could have stopped him, as nothing has stopped him now. Naturally, he wants his country to prosper. The more prosperous and greater his country is, the greater he is. But he cannot devote his full energies to promoting the welfare of his country so long as his *personal* drive for power is not satisfied.

But surely he's got fullest power now.

Yes, but he's got to keep it. He is surrounded by a pack of wolves. He must keep forever on the alert. I must say that I think we owe him a debt of gratitude!

Why?

For the wonderful example he has given the whole world of the axiomatic truth that Communism always leads to dictatorship.

But now let us leave this aside and let me tell you what my therapy is. As a physician, I have not only to analyze and diagnose, but to recommend treatment.

We have been talking nearly all the while about Hitler and the Germans, because they are so incomparably the most important of the dictator phenomena at the moment. It is for this, then, that I must propose a therapy. It is extremely difficult to deal with this type of phenomenon.

It is excessively dangerous. I mean the type of case of a man acting under compulsion.

Now, when I have a patient acting under the command of a higher power, a power within him, such as Hitler's Voice, I dare not tell him to disobey his Voice. He won't do it if I do tell him. He will even act more determinedly than if I did not tell him. All I can do is attempt, by *interpreting* the Voice, to induce the patient to behave in a way which will be less harmful to himself and to society than if he obeyed the Voice immediately without interpretation.

So I say, in this situation, the only way to save Democracy in the West—and by the West I mean America too—is not to try to stop Hitler. You may try to divert him, but to stop him will be impossible without the Great Catastrophe for all. His Voice tells him to unite the German people and to lead them toward a better future, a bigger place on the earth, a position of glory and richness. You cannot stop him from trying to do that. You can only hope to influence the direction of his expansion.

I say let him go East. Turn his attention away from the West, or rather, encourage him to keep it turned away. Let him go to Russia. That is the logical *cure* for Hitler.

I don't think Germany will be satisfied with a bit of Africa, big or small. Germany looks at Britain and at France with their magnificent colonial empires, and even at Italy with her Libya and Ethiopia, and thinks of her own size, seventy-eight million Germans as against forty-five million British in the British Isles and forty-two million French and forty-two million Italians and she is bound to think that she ought to have a place in the world not merely as large as that occupied by any one of the other three Western Great Powers, *but much larger*. How is she going to get that in the West without destroying one or more of the nations which now occupy the West? There is only one field for her to operate in, and that is *Russia*.

Diagnosing the Dictators

And what will happen to Germany when she tries accounts with Russia?

Ah, that's her own business. Our interest in it is simply that it will save the West. Nobody has ever bitten into Russia without regretting it. It's not very palatable food. It might take the Germans a hundred years to finish that meal. Meanwhile we should be safe, and by we, I mean all of Western civilization.

Instinct should tell the Western statesmen not to touch Germany in her present mood. She is much too dangerous. Stalin's instinct was correct when it told him to let the Western nations have a war and destroy one another, while he waited to pick the bones. That would have saved the Soviet Union. I don't believe he ever would have entered the war on the side of Czechoslovakia and France, unless it were at the very end, to profit from the exhaustion of both sides.

So I say, studying Germany as I would a patient, and Europe as I would a patient's family and neighbors, let her go into Russia. There is plenty of land there—one sixth of the surface of the earth. It wouldn't matter to Russia if somebody took a bite, and as I said, nobody has ever prospered who did.

How to save your democratic U.S.A.? It must, of course, be saved, else we all go under. You must keep away from the craze, avoid the infection. Keep your army and navy large, but save them. If war comes, wait.

America must keep big armed forces to help keep the world at peace, or to decide the war if it comes. You are the last resort of Western democracy.

But how is the peace of Western Europe going to be preserved by letting Germany "go East," as you put it, since England and France have now formally guaranteed the frontiers of the new rump state of Czechoslovakia? Won't

133

there then be war anyway if Germany attempts to incor-
porate the rump state in her administrative system?

England and France will not honor their new guarantee
to Czechoslovakia any more than France honored her
previous pledge to Czechoslovakia. No nation keeps its
word. A nation is a big, blind worm, following what? Fate,
perhaps. A nation has no honor; it has no word to keep.
That is the reason why, in the old days, they tried to have
kings who did possess personal honor and a word.

Don't you know that if you choose one hundred of the
most intelligent people in the world and get them all together, they are a stupid mob? Ten thousand of them
together would have the collective intelligence of an alliga-
tor. Haven't you noticed that at a dinner party the more
people you invite the more stupid the conversation? In a
crowd, the qualities which everybody possesses multiply,
pile up, and become the dominant characteristics of the
whole crowd.

Not everybody has virtues, but everybody has the low
animal instincts, the basic primitive caveman suggestibility,
the suspicions and vicious traits of the savage. The result is
that when you get a nation of many millions of people, it
is not even human. It is a lizard or a crocodile or a wolf.
Its statesmen cannot have a higher morality than the animal-
like mass morality of the nation, although individual statesmen of the democratic states may attempt to behave a little
better.

For Hitler, however, more than for any other statesman
in the modern world, it would be impossible to expect that
he should keep the word of Germany against her interest,
in any international bargain, agreement or treaty. Because
Hitler is himself the nation. That, incidentally, is why
Hitler always has to talk so loud, even in private conversation—because he is speaking with seventy-eight million
voices.

That's what a nation is: a monster. Everybody ought to fear a nation. It is a horrible thing. How can such a thing have honor or a word? That's why I am for *small* nations. Small nations mean small catastrophes. Big nations mean big catastrophes.

✧

The telephone rang. In the stillness of the study and a wind-less day without, I could hear a patient cry that a hurricane in his bedroom was about to sweep him off his feet.

"Lie down on the floor and you will be safe," advised the doctor.

It is the same advice the sage physician now gives to Europe and America, as the high wind of Dictatorship rages at the foundations of Democracy.

JUNG DIAGNOSES THE
DICTATORS

••••••••••••••••••••••••

An English clergyman and psychologist, Howard L. Philp, evidently having seen Knickerbocker's interview in the *Cosmopolitan*, arranged to have a talk with Jung at the home of their common friend, Dr. E. A. Bennet, during one of Jung's visits to London. He published the resulting article, entitled "Jung Diagnoses the Dictators," in *The Psychologist* (London), May 1939. Philp continued to pursue an interest in psychology, and after the war he wrote a book on Freud and religion and then embarked on a study of Jung. This resulted in an intensive correspondence, and Philp published Jung's letters of reply in *Jung and the Problem of Evil* (London, 1958); they are reprinted in CW 18, pars. 1584ff. London University awarded Philp a D.Litt. for his work on Freud and Jung. Later he became a Canon of Salisbury Cathedral.

Philp's conversation with Jung in 1939 began with a recollection of the striking prophecy that Jung had made regarding Czechoslovakia, in his interview with Knickerbocker: "England and France will not honor their new guarantee to Czechoslovakia any more than France honored her previous pledge to Czechoslovakia" (above, p. 134), and he went on to quote Jung's entire paragraph.

The line that you forecast in that remark has been remarkably fulfilled. And now, seeing what has happened to Czechoslovakia, have you anything you want to add to that?

What, to Czechoslovakia?

England has now given a guarantee to Poland. What effect is this going to have on Hitler?

That is very difficult to foresee. Hitler has no real *personal*

136

psychology. He is a funny fellow. Hitler cannot give a promise. There is no person there to give the promise! He is the megaphone which voices the mood or the psychology of the eighty million German people. It has been said that more than half the Germans are at the back of him. This is probably true, but it is only part of the truth, for he represents the unconscious mind not only of the people of Germany but of other countries. He voices the unconscious feelings of many English and French people. Some Czechoslovakians are dead against him but they, like many others, may feel a kind of admiration for him at the same time. They say: "Look what he is doing. Isn't he a devil!" In a sense they admire his power.

The same kind of thing often happens when we read detective yarns or gangster stories. There is a part of us which becomes identified even with characters whom we dislike. Hitler voices what he wants and gets it.

Has Hitler a special sensitivity?

Decidedly. It is as if he possesses nervous tentacles stretching out in every direction. This makes him sensitive to all his nation is feeling. Hitler falls into the class of the medicine man, the mystic, the seer. He has about him a dreamy look. In fact all this is the most significant element about him. He is not a leader in the sense that Mussolini is. When Hitler speaks he tells the Germans nothing new, but simply what they want to hear. Especially he is the mirror of that inferiority complex which is so markedly a German characteristic.

One of the reasons for this is that the Germans are comparatively young as a nation. When at last they became a unified nation they found that the British and French had been nations long before them and that they were too late in the scramble for colonies, whereas the British and French possessed rich colonies and all that belongs to a fully matured nation. This made Germany jealous and resentful.

Out of it there came the World War, and when Germany lost this she became even more dominated by an inferiority complex. Just as the Jews of old looked for a Messiah who would deliver them, so the Germans have looked for their savior, and in Hitler they believe they have found him.

Hitler is simply what the Germans have made him. You cannot realize that too clearly. It is the key to understanding him and also the Germans themselves. He is like a mask, but there is nothing behind that mask.

You have written a very important book on psychological types. In what particular type would you place Hitler?

I would not place him as a man, for individually he is quite uninteresting and unimportant. He is simply a great phenomenon. Seeing Hitler and Mussolini together as I have done is an unimaginable experience. Mussolini fills his uniform, but Hitler does not even fit into his clothes! Hitler is all mask. Mussolini has a certain vitality about him. He is a man—natural, warm, rough, and ruthless. If he says "no" he means no. He can speak as a real person. If you said to him: "You promised to do something and you lied," he would probably admit his lie and might even blush. He is more human than Hitler. He would know what he had promised and would know that he had lied.

Another difference between them is in respect of their personal ambition. In Hitler ambition takes quite a small place. It is probably true to say that Hitler does not possess ambition beyond the ordinary man. But Mussolini has more than average ambition although this is insufficient to explain his force. He feels that he corresponds to the national needs of Italy. Hitler does not rule Germany in the same way. He is sensitive to the trend of affairs in his country.

Hitler cannot be understood apart from a consideration of the unconscious factors which play their part in his makeup and in fact in the world. It is certain that Hitler does not understand himself; if he did he would not be lacking in a sense of humor and would not take himself so seriously. There are a number of ways in which unconscious forces play their part. The collective unconscious is a real fact in human affairs. It would need volumes to explain its various ramifications. We all participate in it. In one sense it is the accumulated human wisdom which we unconsciously inherit; in other senses it implies the common human emotions which we all share.

It is understandable, therefore, that there is such a force as the collective unconscious of a nation; in Germany Hitler has an uncanny power of being sensitive to that collective unconscious. It is as if he knows what the nation is really feeling at any given time.

Hitler has sacrified his individuality, or else does not possess one in any real sense, to this almost complete subordination to collective unconscious forces and he is able to draw upon this hidden store. He himself has spoken of being able to hear a voice. To him it is as if he does, and the voice which he hears is that of the collective unconscious, especially of his own race. It is this fact which makes dealing with Hitler such a problem. He is virtually the nation. And the trouble about a nation is that it does not keep its word and has no honor, at least on the level of the collective unconscious. A nation as such, for all the claims of the totalitarian states, is a blind force.

You can take a hundred very intelligent men and when you have them all together they may be nothing more than a silly mob. The crowd does not rise to the level of the highest intelligences in it, but the qualities which everyone has become the dominant characteristics of the whole crowd.

One form under which the unconscious appears to a man is that of a female figure. In a similar way the personified unconscious appears to a woman in the guise of a man. One of the major problems is to gain the right kind of relationship to these figures in ourselves. You can have these figures in all forms. Take a perfectly naïve individual and he will call the female figure "Mother"—meaning his own mother. Then she will die, although as a matter of fact in many men she never dies as a force. Unless a man gains a right relationship to this female figure he becomes possessed by it and it becomes a disturbing distintegrating factor.

Hitler has never gained a healthy relationship to this female figure, which I call the anima. The result is that he is possessed by it. Instead of being truly creative he is consequently destructive. This is one reason why Hitler is dangerous: he does not possess within himself the seeds of true harmony.

Is Hitler likely to change? Is it likely that one day he will lose his impersonal quality and perhaps even marry?

It is not very probable. But you can expect almost anything from him. He will turn around and say something quite different from what he has said before. He will lose his job when he loses his voice. This might happen, but I do not think it will. Nor do I think that he will turn into a normal human being. He will probably die in his job.

Dr. Jung, how do you keep your patience with us and our puny problems, when Europe is falling apart and you have work of world importance?

Because the world problem starts with the individual.

You mean the man in conflict with himself ultimately makes war and revolution?

Certainly. And the man at peace with himself, who accepts himself, contributes an infinitesimal amount to the good of the universe. Attend to your private and personal conflicts and you will be reducing by one millionth millionth the world conflict.[1]

[1] The last two questions and answers were published, in a slightly different form, as part of E. S. Sergeant's article on Jung in *Hearst's International–Cosmopolitan*, January 1939, cited in the headnote to the foregoing interview by Knickerbocker.

A WARTIME INTERVIEW

++++++++++++++++++++++++++

In the summer of 1942, Switzerland was encircled by the Axis powers—on the west, France unoccupied and occupied was under Nazi control. For the Allies it was the darkest time of the war. The Swiss, in their neutrality, carried on an existence as nearly normal as they could. The Eranos Conference, at Ascona, went on with plans for its annual meeting in August, on the theme "The Hermetic Principle in Mythology, Gnosis, and Alchemy." Jung agreed to speak on an alchemical subject, "The Spirit Mercurius,"[1] and when the *Tribune de Genève* sent a journalist to interview him on "the spiritual values of the Swiss" in June, he was deep in research. The interviewer, Pierre Courthion, was a French-Swiss art historian and educator, who had served the League of Nations as chief of the arts section of the International Institute for Intellectual Co-operation and had written and lectured widely on modern art. His article, published on June 19, 1942, is somewhat abridged in this version.

C. G. Jung lives in Küsnacht, at the back of a garden, in a comfortable house full of Biedermeyer furniture and family pictures. His secretary took me to a book-lined room, its tables piled with manuscripts, and I saw a very tall man coming toward me. He was dressed in dark clothes and wore a little black silk skull cap. Pushing aside with an enormous hand the lectern on which a volume of Berthelot's Greek texts[2] lay open, he offered me a seat and sat down himself in an armchair by the window. While he was inquiring if I had had much trouble finding the place (which

[1] In CW 13; originally in *Eranos-Jahrbuch 1942*.
[2] M. Berthelot, *Collection des anciens alchimistes grecs* (Paris, 1887–88), in 3 vols. Jung cited it in "The Spirit Mercurius" and other alchemical writings.

is secluded, at number 228 on the interminable Seestrasse, past the village and the Sonne hotel) I watched him against the light from windows through which the branches of the still-leafless trees could be seen trembling in the mist.

. . .

Jung lighted his copper-stemmed pipe and told me about his life; his travels as an "itinerant psychologist" to India, then Africa,[3] to study the psychology of primitive people. From Kenya and Uganda he went to the Sudan and Khartoum, then down the Nile to investigate the influence of the African mentality on Egypt. "In Egypt," he said, "the external appearance is Asiatic, but there is a religious influence that is entirely African." And, Jung told me humorously, when he got back to Switzerland he realized that he had gone a long way looking for what he could have found close to home, in the Lötschental,[4] for example. "These studies," he said, "are not easy. You have to get people's confidence before they will tell you about themselves. But what surprises! Things you read about in Paracelsus still exist. I've met sorcerers, spell-casters. Did you know that there are still some places in Bern or St. Gall where they make pacts with the devil and sign them with blood? That they practice magic on cows? In the Swiss soul, as all human souls, there are regions we do not know about. . . ."

. . .

"What will individuals of different types tend to do? That's very important to know. The rest is just mechanics. The creative instinct, the will of the creator, that is what matters. In other words: With the devil's grandmother for a mother and the devil for a father, how does one get to be the good Lord's child?"

[3] Jung visited East Africa in 1925, India not until 1938.
[4] A secluded valley in the Bernese Alps of nothern Canton Valais. Its people preserve archaic folk customs.

Jung has a laugh whose sonority is somehow intentionally reassuring. When I asked him about the signs and symbols being studied again today, he said: "The symbol has a very complex meaning because it defies reason; it always presupposes a lot of meanings that can't be comprehended in a single logical concept. The symbol has a future. The past does not suffice to interpret it, because germs of the future are included in every actual situation. That's why, in elucidating a case, the symbolism is spontaneously applicable, for it contains the future; within its zone of mystery, it comprises the individual's defense. For example, a developing disease always has a counter-aspect: together with fever as a germ infection, there is simultaneously fever as a bodily reaction and defense. Why, the dream is even a defense. In explaining dreams from a causal point of view, Freud got to their primary causes. But what interests me is why a person dreams of one thing rather than another. If you look at a dream conscientiously you can see that some of the details in it have been changed from impressions that you had before. Thus the dream invents an accident when it needs one, when it *wants an accident*. In the end, we have to ask what the aim of the dream is from a teleological point of view. Why does this person's unconscious wish to show him an image like that? And here is where I learned a great deal from primitive people: the dream is a product of the imagination, a gallery of images, images of protection from some blow that is threatening; the function of the dream is to compensate the conscious attitude. I believe that what dreams show us in vivid and impressive images are our vulnerable points. That is why the medieval doctors asked about dreams. So we must observe the same rule. A Dutchman said, 'Magic is the science of the jungle,' and the Chinese claim that when we wake up troubled it is because the soul—*kuei*, the body-soul, which is less spiritual than the spirit and causes apparitions (ghosts) after death— is hovering above us. The imagery of alchemy is found all over the world."

Jung's firm strength surprised me, and the modest way he had of expressing his experience of the human soul in a few words (on a scale that ranges from the greatest common sense to extreme intuition). He spoke slowly, distinctly; then, as if perceiving my confusion in traversing this obscure psychological domain where he himself moves so easily, he stopped for a moment and got up to switch on an overhead lamp. Its reflections made the shadows of his face look purple.

Our interview continued between two lights: the fading light of day (thick fog right up to the windows now) and the still tentative light from the lamp, filtered through its yellow shade. In the confined space of the room, fantastic, flickering apparitions came to life.

Still illustrating the premonitions he had mentiond before, Jung said to me, "Take the tendency to commit suicide—right from the beginning. What happens? You don't pay attention on the street. One day you fall down stairs. Then there is a little automobile accident. It doesn't look like anything. Yet these are the preliminaries. Chance? Primitive people never mention chance. That is why I say, 'Be careful when you are not at one with yourself, in your moments of dissociation.'"

Jung sat up in his big green armchair and put down his pipe, by that gesture emphasizing what he was about to say. Weighing each word, he stated, "*One must never give way to fear, but one must admit to oneself that one is afraid.*" Yet knowing about a repression does not always cure it; sometimes one has to confess to it openly. Then the doctor told me an ultra-simple tale about a hotel maid who came to him seeking treatment for the agonies of insomnia. He explained to her about sailing a boat, how one lets oneself go with the wind. "When you want to sleep," he told her, "*go with the wind.*" And in the rhythmic reassurance of being rocked the young woman found sleep again.[5]

[5] Jung describes this case in more detail in his interview with Duplain, "On the Frontiers of Knowledge," below, pp. 417ff.

"You see," he said, "nothing is more thrilling than trying to understand. One comes to see that life is great and beautiful, that nonsense and stupidity do not always triumph."

Carl Gustav Jung stood up, and it seemed to me that I was now facing another man, pale, with an arched nose, almost pointed at the tip. He took off his cap (his forehead is higher than I expected) and led the way to another room, equally encumbered with old books and work tables, where he showed me some remarkable paintings on cloth made by Tibetan monks. The door onto the stairs was partially open and the big house was full of voices and laughter. A burst of sound escaping from a piano somewhere brought us a phrase of Schumann.

My host accompanied me to the garden gate. In the night fog we spoke sadly of the replica of servitude to which many individuals are reduced. But as I grasped Jung's powerful hand in mine, I felt passing into me the vibrant, tenacious, communicative warmth of an immense hope.

[Translated by Jane A. Pratt]

FROM CHARLES BAUDOUIN'S
JOURNAL: 1945

••••••••••••••••••••••••••••

Zurich. Wednesday, January 10, 1945[1]

I am beginning to know the streets: the stairs to the terrace of the Sankt Peter church that have to be climbed down carefully because of the snow; the bridges to be crossed over the swift sea-green Limmat under the excited, discordant cries of the gulls; the slopes going up the right bank.

After I reached the Stadelhofen station, the train got me to Küsnacht in a few minutes. Then a quarter of an hour on foot along the Seestrasse, the big straight road that runs a short distance back of the lake. The snow is still thick and white. The well-to-do villas are widely spaced and withdrawn into gardens and parks full of firs; one hears the sound of a saw felling a tree. Then comes the Jung house, its round tower capped with a cone of gray tile; recognizable by the inscription over the doorway: *Vocatus atque non vocatus Deus aderit.*

The master came down the steps to greet me. He was wearing a skull cap that he did not take off later. For he is still convalescing from a fracture with various complications —embolism and thrombosis—which requires a lot of care. He has not been able to go back to his courses in Basel.[2] But he is progressing; the gray eyes that sometimes look quite small have lost nothing of their malice; the color of the face

[1] From *L'Oeuvre de Jung* (1963); see above, p. 76. This extract also appeared, in French, in *Contact with Jung* (1966).

[2] In 1943 Jung was named professor of medical psychology at Basel University but had to resign soon afterward on account of illness.

is good and when he gives himself up to one of his hearty laughs over some story it becomes frankly red.

We lunched in a great high room, like the hall of a castle, reigned over by a chimney and a series of good reproductions of familiar paintings, notably from the Louvre: Ghirlandaio's *The Old Man and the Child*, an *Adoration*, a *David and Goliath*, and the famous portrait of Galileo which Jung pointed out with special partiality: "That fellow," he said, "is my friend, with his beautiful child's eyes." At the table there were four of us: Mrs. Jung, the secretary, the master, and myself.

After lunch he and I went up to have coffee in his study, where there is a tall green tile stove that he stroked, saying "It's human." The window opens onto the garden, which runs down to the lake, and there is a shed for small boats. The situation is something like that of Spitteler's house on the edge of Lake Lucerne, except that there the slope is much greater and the garden more spacious. Among his abundant books Jung is particularly proud of his collection of unintelligible alchemical texts, which is richer than the collection in the library of Basel. He showed me several of them. Alchemy fascinates him, he said.

I submitted to him some of my subjects' dreams taken from among those that I am now presenting in my lectures at Zurich University. At Madeleine's dream of "the man with serpent feet" he got up, fetched a Gnostic book, and turning without hesitation to the page showed me a reproduction of a gem representing the son of Chaos—"the man with serpent feet."

He thinks that the process of integration into a group and the process of individuation are two aspects of the same phenomenon. In India there are rites of circumambulation in the cults of Shiva and his Shakti.

Jung spoke of the "possession" rampant in Hitler's Germany, upon which rationalistic Anglo-Saxon arguments can get no purchase. In this unhappy time Jung believes only in inner action by the individual. The press, propaganda, meetings, all "come to nothing." After such a calamity to a people, what will become of them? Maybe, when one has lost all, nothing remains but to become a saint. Even now there are immense prayer meetings in Germany: they congregate secretly at night and pray for deliverance from the Antichrist.

At 3 o'clock I left Jung. His pupil, Mrs. Jolande Jacobi, was waiting for me at Stadelhofen. She took me home and gave me tea. She is in mourning, having received news of the death of her husband and several members of her family in Budapest. . . . Concerning the man with serpent feet, she completed the information Jung had provided by telling me that he was also an aspect of Pan, and Pan was, moreover, the god of epilepsy! (The sight of an epileptic had been the starting point of my subject's dream.)

[Translated by Jane A. Pratt]

THE POST-WAR
PSYCHIC PROBLEMS OF
THE GERMANS

♦♦♦♦♦♦♦♦♦♦♦♦♦♦♦♦♦♦♦♦♦♦♦♦♦♦♦♦

Four days after the unconditional surrender of the German
Army at Rheims, this interview by Peter Schmid was published
in *Die Weltwoche* (Zurich) for May 11, 1945, under the title
"Werden die Seelen Frieden finden?" (Will the Souls Find
Peace?). The interview probably took place somewhat earlier.
A partial translation was published by the newspaper *PM* (New
York), May 10, 1945.

*Do you not think that the end of the war will bring about
great changes in the psyche of Europeans, particularly the
Germans, who are now awakening as though from a long
and terrible dream?*

Indeed I do. As to the Germans, we have a psychic problem ahead of us the magnitude of which cannot yet be foreseen, though its outlines can already be discerned in the
cases I am treating. For the psychologist one thing is clear,
and that is that he ought not to make the popular sentimental distinction between Nazis and opponents of the
regime. Two cases I am now treating are both outspoken
anti-Nazis, and yet their dreams show that behind all the
decency the most pronounced Nazi psychology is still alive
with all its violence and savagery. When Field Marshal
von Küchler,[1] questioned by a Swiss reporter about the
German atrocities in Poland, exclaimed indignantly: "Ex-

---

[1] Georg von Küchler (1881–196?), led the Nazi invasion of
western Poland in September 1939. He was tried and sentenced to
prison as a war criminal by the Nuremberg Tribunal.

cuse me, that wasn't the Wehrmacht, it was the Party!" this proved that a division into decent and indecent Germans is thoroughly naïve. All of them, whether consciously or unconsciously, actively or passively, have their share in the horrors; they knew nothing of what was going on and yet they did know, as though party to a secret *contrat génial*. For the psychologist the question of collective guilt, which worries politicians so much and will go on worrying them, is a fact, and it will be one of the most important tasks of therapy to get the Germans to admit this guilt. Even now I am receiving many applications from Germans who want to be treated by me. If they come from those "decent Germans" who want to foist the guilt onto a couple of men in the Gestapo, I regard the case as hopeless. I shall have no alternative but to answer the applications with a questionnaire asking certain crucial questions, like "What do you think about Buchenwald?" Only when a patient sees and admits his own responsibility can individual treatment be considered.

But how was it possible that the Germans, of all people, got themselves into this hopeless psychic mess? Could it have happened to any other nation?

Here you must allow me to go back a bit and to recapitulate my theory as to the general psychic antecedents of this National Socialist war. Let us take a small practical example as a starting point. One day a woman comes to me and breaks out into the wildest accusations against her husband: he is a veritable devil who torments and persecutes her, and so on and so forth. In reality the good man is a perfectly respectable citizen, quite innocent of any such demonic intentions. Where does this crazy idea come from in this woman? It is the devil in her own soul that she is projecting; she has transferred her own wishes and her own rages to her husband. I make this clear to her; she admits it and becomes a contrite little lamb. Everything seems to be in order. And yet that is just the thing I find most disquieting, because I don't know where the devil, who had previously attached himself to the image of the husband, has gone to. Exactly the same thing happened on a large scale in the history of Europe. For primitive man the world is full of demons and mysterious powers which he fears; the whole of Nature is animated by these forces, which are nothing but man's own inner powers projected into the outside world. Christianity and modern science have de-demonized Nature, which means that the European has consistently taken back the demonic powers out of the world into himself, and has steadily loaded his unconscious with them. Out of man himself the demonic powers rise up in revolt against the supposed spiritual constraints of Christianity. The demons begin to break out in Baroque art: the columns writhe, the furniture sprouts satyr's feet. Man is slowly transformed into a uroboros, the "tail-eater" who devours himself, from ancient times a symbol of the demon-ridden man. The first perfect example of this species was Napoleon.

The Germans display a specific weakness in the face of these demons because of their incredible suggestibility. This shows itself in their love of obedience, their supine submission to commands, which are only another form of suggestion. This hangs together with the general psychic inferiority of the Germans, the result of their precarious position between East and West. Of all the Western peoples, they were the ones who, at the general exodus from the Eastern womb of the nations, remained too long with their mother. Finally they did get out, but arrived too late, while the mujïk never broke loose at all. Hence the Germans are profoundly troubled with a national inferiority complex, which they try to compensate by megalomania: "Am deutschen Wesen soll die Welt genesen"[2]—though they are none

---

[2] Roughly, "the German spirit will be the world's salvation." A Nazi slogan derived from a poem by Emanuel Geibel (1815–84),

too comfy in their own skins! It is a typical adolescent psychology, apparent not only in the extraordinary prevalence of homosexuality but in the absence of an anima figure in German literature (the great exception here is Goethe). It is also apparent in German sentimentality and "Gemütlichkeit," which is really nothing but hardness of heart, unfeelingness, and soullessness. All those charges of soullessness and bestiality which German propaganda levelled at the Russians apply to themselves; Goebbels' speeches are nothing but German psychology projected upon the enemy. The immaturity of the personality also displayed itself in a terrifying way in the German General Staff, whose lack of character resembled the squashiness of a mollusc inside a panzer.

Germany has always been the land of psychic catastrophes: the Reformation, peasant wars and wars of religion. Under National Socialism, the pressure of the demons became so great that they got human beings into their power and blew them up into lunatic supermen, first of all Hitler who then infected the rest. All the Nazi leaders were possessed in the truest sense of the word, and it is assuredly no accident that their propaganda minister was branded with the ancient mark of the demonized man—a clubfoot. Ten per cent of the German population today are hopeless psychopaths.

You have been talking of the psychic inferiority and demonic susceptibility of the Germans, but do you think this also applies to us Swiss, so far as we are Germanic in origin?

We are insulated against this susceptibility by the smallness of our country. If eighty million Swiss were piled together the same thing might happen, for the demons hurl

---

"Deutschlands Beruf." Geibel's lines became famous when Wilhelm II quoted them (inaccurately, as above) in a speech at Münster in 1907.

themselves by preference on the mass. In any collectivity man is rootless and then the demons can get him. Hence the technique of the Nazis never to form individuals but only huge masses. Hence, too, the faces of the demonized man of today: lifeless, rigid, blank. We Swiss are protected against these dangers by our federalism and our individualism. Such a mass accumulation would not be possible with us as it was in Germany, and in this isolation lies perhaps the therapy with which one can conquer the demons.

But what will happen if this therapy is carried out by bombs and guns? Won't military subjection of the demonized nation merely intensify the feeling of inferiority and make the disease worse?

The Germans today are like a drunken man who wakes up the next morning with a hangover. They don't know what they've done and don't want to know. The only feeling is one of boundless misery. They will make convulsive efforts to rehabilitate themselves in face of the accusations and hatred of the surrounding world, but that is not the right way. The only redemption lies, as I have already indicated, in a complete admission of guilt. *Mea culpa, mea maxima culpa!* Out of honest contrition for sin comes divine grace. That is not only a religious but also a psychological truth. The American treatment of conducting the civilian population through the concentration camps and letting them see all the abominations committed there is therefore quite right. Only, the object lesson should not be driven home with moral instruction; repentance must come from inside the Germans themselves. It is possible that positive forces will emerge from the catastrophe, that from this introversion prophets will once again arise, for prophets are as characteristic of this strange people as the demons. Anyone who falls so low has depth. In all probability there will be a miraculous haul of souls for the Catholic Church—the Protestant Church is too split up. There are reports that the general misery has reawakened the religious life in Germany; whole communities fall to their knees in the evenings, beseeching God to deliver them from the Antichrist.

Then one can hope that the demons will be banished and that a new and better world will rise on the ruins?

No, the demons are not banished, that is a difficult task that still lies ahead. Now that the angel of history has abandoned the Germans, the demons will seek a new victim. And that won't be difficult. Every man who loses his shadow, every nation that falls into self-righteousness, is their prey. We love the criminal and take a burning interest in him because the devil makes us forget the beam in our own eye when observing the mote in our brother's and in that way outwits us. The Germans will recover when they admit their guilt and accept it; but the others will become victims of possession if, in their horror at the German guilt, they forget their own moral shortcomings. We should not forget that exactly the same fatal tendency to collectivization is present in the victorious nations as in the Germans, that they can just as suddenly become a victim of the demonic powers. "General suggestibility" plays a tremendous role in America today, and how much the Russians are already fascinated by the devil of power can easily be seen from the latest events, which must dampen our peace jubilations a bit. The most sensible in this respect are the English: their individualism saves them from falling for the slogan, and the Swiss share their amazement at the collective unreason.

Then we must anxiously wait and see which way the demons go next?

I have already suggested that the only salvation lies in the piecemeal work of educating the individual. That is not as hopeless as it may appear. The power of the demons is immense, and the most modern media of mass suggestion —press, radio, film, etc.—are at their service. But Christianity, too, was able to hold its own against an overwhelming adversary not by propaganda and mass conversions—that came later and was of little value—but by persuasion from man to man. And that is the way we also must go if we wish to conquer the demons.

I don't envy you your task in writing about these things. I hope you will succeed in presenting my ideas in such a way that people won't find them too strange. Unfortunately it is my fate that other people, especially those who are themselves possessed by demons, think me mad because I believe in these powers. But that is their affair; I know they exist. There are demons all right, as sure as there is a Buchenwald.

FOUR "CONTACTS WITH JUNG"

＊＊＊＊＊＊＊＊＊＊＊＊＊＊＊＊＊＊＊＊＊＊＊＊＊＊＊

Michael Fordham, the leading medical analyst among British Jungians and co-editor of the Collected Works, edited *Contact with Jung* (London, 1966), a collection of "essays on the influence of Jung's work and personality" by forty-two of Jung's pupils in Europe, England, America, and Israel. Excerpts from four vivid and immediate recollections, dating from the late 1930's to the late 1950's, have been chosen. (The selections from Charles Baudouin's journal for 1945 and 1954, in the present volume, were also included, in French, in *Contact with Jung*.)

A. I. ALLENBY (OXFORD)

I first got in touch with Jung after the end of the second world war. I then wrote to him, and told him who I was and what I was doing, which included writing a thesis on the psychology of religion. With his reply Jung sent the manuscript of his article on the Trinity[1]—a new version which had not yet appeared in print. This was generous indeed, and an endearing token of encouragement for the complete stranger that I was to him then. Only about a month before his death I again received a letter from Jung, in reply to one of mine, in which he went with great care into all the questions I had raised. It ended with these words: "My best wishes for any further discoveries you may make."

This is the first characteristic one encountered in Jung: his respect for the other person, whoever he or she might be, and his concern for the individual value in anyone. When I first went to visit him at Küsnacht, I was full of appre-

[1] "A Psychological Approach to the Dogma of the Trinity," CW II, originally was a lecture at the Eranos Conference in 1940. The "new version" was prepared for *Symbolik des Geistes* (1948).

hension as to how I should fare in meeting the great man—
but the moment I entered his intimate little study I felt
completely at ease.

. . .

Once he wanted me to understand that one should not feel
guilty about events which happen on their own account.
"They are just like acts of God," he said. "Think of it as if
a building had been hit by lightning; that, also, is an act of
God. There was a church in a Swiss village which had been
damaged by lightning, and the pastor went round the village to collect money for the repairs, and one shrewd old
peasant said to him: 'What—you are not going to make
me give you anything, if he destroys his own house!' That
man had got it right," Jung said and laughed.

On another occasion Jung explained to me what happens
when one mistrusts one's feelings and refuses to act on
them. "You can see from the window my boathouse down
by the lake," he said. "Some time ago I went for a swim
and then lay on the balcony of the boathouse to sun myself.
The level of the lake was so high that the boathouse was
surrounded by water. There came my dog in search of me.
He could not see me, and was not sure whether I was there.
Being of a somewhat cowardly disposition and not very
fond of the wet, the dog first put one paw into the water,
then withdrew it, and then another paw and withdrew it,
too. And this went on for some time. Eventually I made
the faintest little noise, and the dog shot through the water
and up the steps of the boathouse in one jump. The dog
is conditioned by instinct and has no will-power of his own,
except when a little noise from his master releases it." Jung,
of course, wanted to convey to me, although he left it to me
to draw the conclusion, that a person who mistrusts his own
feelings or thoughts and does not utilize his will to put them
to the test is hardly distinguishable from an animal; as a
conscious human being he hardly exists.

Another time Jung reverted to the problem of self-doubt, using a further example by way of illustration. "Our needs and desires are always active," he said. "Trouble occurs only if they are active in the unconscious, if we do not take them consciously in hand so as to give them a definite form and direction. If we refuse to do this we are dragged along by them and become their victim. Then they are like a sledge rushing downhill in the snow, with no one at the steering-ropes. You must place yourself firmly at the steering-ropes, not hang on at the back or, worse, be unwilling to take the ride at all—that only lands you in panic. Our unconscious energies give momentum to our journey through life and, if we direct their course, our actions will have strength; we may even sense that God is behind us."

.   .   .

He told me that he once met a distinguished man, a Quaker, who could not imagine that he had ever done anything wrong in his life. "And do you know what happened to his children?" Jung asked. "The son became a thief, and the daughter a prostitute. Because the father would not take on his shadow, his share in the imperfection of human nature, his children were compelled to live out the dark side which he had ignored."

.   .   .

I remember Jung stating on one occasion: "Every human being is inherently a unique and individual form of life. He is made like that. But there is something which man can do over and above the given material of his nature, and that is he can become *conscious* of what makes him the person he is, and he can work *consciously* towards relating what is himself to the world around him. And," Jung added reflectively, "this is perhaps all we *can* do."

Another time he said to me, as if he were speaking to himself: "This is how you must live—without reservation, whether in giving or withholding, according to what the circumstances require. Then you will get through. After all, if you should still get stuck, there is always the en- antiodromia from the unconscious, which opens new ave- nues when conscious will and vision are failing."

KENNETH LAMBERT (LONDON)

. . .

One way to express a personal debt to Jung is to recall cer- tain personal experiences of him in action as a person at certain points of time, communicating his experience to another person—as compared with him as a theoretician. I have two such memories. The first was of him in London in 1939, when he answered questions put to him by a group of doctors, psychotherapists, and clergymen, including a bishop. The result was a series of communications on "The Symbolic Life,"[2] and the poverty and neurotic potential of individuals and groups for whom such an experience was meaningless. At that time Jung's personal exuberance and physical size were noticeable, and we last saw him marching out, with a certain playful humor, arm-in-arm with the gaitered bishop—arm-in-arm, although communication on the subject of the symbol had not greatly advanced between them.

Eleven years later Jung gave me half a morning for a personal interview. He spoke with a spontaneous frankness and an unashamed sense of paradox. He remembered the group and the bishop, and asserted that the theologian is now passé, owing among other things to his inability to understand projection. But, he added, "Always I have a feeling of compassion for the clergyman. He has a devil of a problem." He had, of course, participated in this, for he

[2] A seminar talk given on April 5, 1939, to the Guild of Pastoral Psychology, published 1954 as Guild Lecture No. 80, and included in CW 18. Richard Parsons, Bishop of Southwark, was a participant.

spoke with feeling for his father "with all his intelligence, who had to be helpless over all this—so restricted and out of touch with nature and the dreams." Indeed, the intensely personal and historical basis of Jung's scientific motivation revealed itself as he showed me photographs of his grandfather the doctor and of his father the pastor—high-foreheaded and sensitive in facial expression. "I had the whole problem of the father to solve," he said, "I am always unpopular—with the theologians and with the doctors. I am always *mettant mes pieds sur le plat*. The medical chaps have no intelligence," he added. "They work too much from the outside, whereas everybody's psychology is making careful plans to get them into a state in which they have to face themselves, and the shadow. It's their chance to realize the self. If you can get them out of their hole by giving them a kick in the pants you've cheated them of their birthright." The same feet were put on the priest's plate. For he emphasized how Christianity forces people to meet the shadow, and he outlined an argument he had worked at to show that St. Thomas Aquinas really believed that the world was created by the Diabolus. Jung's own sense of the difficulty made him tell a rabbinical story of how God wanted to make a world with his mercy and his justice. The trouble was that if he used his mercy there would be too many sins, and if he used his justice you couldn't live. So he mixed both of them up and said: "Oh, how I wish there would be a world." Jung roared with laughter, and went on to mention the symbolism attached to Christ, indicating opposites in his nature, as, for instance, the Leviathan, the Lion, the Serpent, the Black Raven, and his crucifixion between two thieves. Then the symbolism became astrological. Jung stated that, at the birth of Christ, Saturn the maleficent god and Jupiter the beneficent god were so near to each other that they were almost one star, that is, the star of Bethlehem, when the new self, Christ, good and evil, was born. Jung then associated to this by telling two stories about people. A man told Jung about a Quaker who seemed a perfectly good man. So where was his shadow? Jung asked about his wife. Apparently she was perfect, too. His children? "Oh," said the inquirer, "one of them is a thief." In Jung's words, "He went out wagging his tail." The second story concerned a theologian without a shadow, but it turned out that his son was "getting into the way of forging checks." Jung's comment was, "The son assumes the father's shadow. His father was stealing, you see, from God his sins. The son was punished for the father's sins not rendered to God."

. . .

RENÉE BRAND (SAN FRANCISCO)

. . .

The year was 1955, in the fall. We were stepping from the living-room where tea had been served into the garden of 228 Seestrasse in Küsnacht. Ten students from the Institute had been delegated to celebrate with Jung the planting of a *Ginkgo biloba* tree given to him for his eightieth birthday. We stood in a semicircle by the place chosen for the tree while two gardeners started digging the hole. Between them they fell into an alternating rhythm, accentuated by the spades breaking up the earth and the thud of throwing it out. Jung was giving directions about the width and breadth of the hole, concerned that the roots should get enough space. As I looked at him in the outdoor light of the afternoon, he suddenly seemed less sturdy, his frame less powerful—different than in his study at my recent visit, or even a few minutes ago at tea. He looked all of his eighty years and very frail, with the frailty of old age. With the shock of this realization, a sinister crescendo seemed to get into the rhythm of spades going in and earth thumping down. Irrationally, it seemed that this hole was not for planting a tree, that these were not gardeners, they were grave-diggers. The feeling about death was so strong that the scene became unbearable, and I stood in utter helplessness, wishing and praying for it all to stop. Suddenly I heard Jung saying: "This has nothing to do with death. They are planting new life." He was looking straight in front of him, addressing no one. Having my unspoken thought picked out of my head and answered was so startling that the irrational panic turned into a numinous experience.

ELIZABETH OSTERMAN (SAN FRANCISCO)

The heavy wooden door on which I had just knocked was set in a thick stone wall which seemed solidly part of the earth. This was the entryway to the medieval-looking, secluded country place which Jung had built by hand through the years at Bollingen on the shore of Lake Zurich. On my way to the Aegean Islands on this first trip away from the western United States, I had stopped in Switzerland for this visit. Leaving the highway some distance from the town of Rapperswil, I had traversed a footpath which skirted a dense wood at the rear of a complex of walls and stone towers. A few feet away to my left the lake water lapped among the reeds. The July sun warmed the rain-dampened earth, and a soft haze covered the distant mountains.

As I stood waiting before the door I was somewhat nervous, but was reassured by sounds of wood-chopping coming from behind the wall. . . . Now the door opened, and I was invited into the inner garden by his household companion. There, beyond a second doorway, was the strong-bodied, white-haired, eighty-three-year-old man in his green workman's apron, seated before the chopping block. Behind him was a large square stone carved by him in earlier years when he was attempting to give form to his emerging realizations. I felt as though I had stepped out of time and had entered into an inner world where everything was relevant, unhurried, natural.

At the water's edge we settled into comfortable chairs, and through that afternoon the conversation wandered back into the prehistory of the earth, into the depths of the psyche, into the wonders of nature around us. Once I looked at my watch and he said, "Never mind a watch; I'll tell you." He returned frequently to the theme of what man is doing to himself by living in a fast and meaningless way, how he has become estranged from himself. With immediacy and great simplicity he said: "We must give time to nature so that she may be a mother to us. I have found the way to live here as part of nature, to live in my own time. People in the modern world are always living so that something better is to happen tomorrow, always in the future, so they don't think to live their lives. They are up in the head. When a man begins to know himself, to discover the roots of his past in himself, it is a new way of life."

The force that emanated from this man sitting beside me was amazing. He seemed at once powerful and simple; real, the way the sky and rocks and trees and water around him were real. He seemed to be all there in his own nature, but what made it so exciting was his *awareness* of it.

A knock on the door broke into the conversation; the taxi man had arrived. Jung remarked, "That says it." It was time to leave.

ON CREATIVE ACHIEVEMENT

••••••••••••••••••••••••••

Emil A. Fischer undertook to interview twenty Swiss men and women prominent in cultural life, and he published the resulting articles in a small book entitled *Schöpferische Leistung* (Thalwil, 1946)—"Creative Achievement." Fischer began his conversation by asking Jung about "the strange aphorism that is carved into stone above the entrance door of the house: *Vocatus atque non vocatus deus aderit.*" This was an opening that interviewers often hit upon. Jung had the inscription carved over the door when he built the house, in 1909. It came from an old copy of Erasmus that he had bought while a university student.[1]

Is there any special relationship between this saying and your Weltanschauung or your life's work?

"Called or uncalled, God is present!" It is a Delphic oracle. The translation is by Erasmus. You ask whether the oracle is my motto. In a way, you see, it contains the entire reality of the psyche. "Oh God!" is what we say, irrespective of whether we say it by way of a curse or by way of love.

Isn't the psyche of the artist and the intellectual particularly complex and worthy of closer consideration?

So far, too much one-sided attention has been focused on the morbid aspect of the matter. I wonder why there is so much nonsensical theorizing about the pathology of outstanding people. Most psychopaths are not geniuses; and on the other hand there are many geniuses who do not show the slightest traces of pathology.

What is much more significant in this context is the

---

[1] See *The Freud/Jung Letters*, p. xviii, n. 18.

theory of the shadow: the brighter the light, the darker the shadow!

It is important to see also the negative sides of great men. On Palm Sunday, Christ temporarily played the role of a political Messiah. His negative side and his power are symbolically displayed in the temptation by the Devil.

Biographies should show people in their undershirts. Goethe had his weaknesses, and Calvin was often cruel. Considerations of this kind reveal the true greatness of a man. This way of looking at things is better than false hero worship!

Where do you get the incentive for your creative work, Professor?

One is always in the dark about one's own personality. One needs others to get to know oneself.

Having said this—I actually started out by simply doing routine scientific work. I always followed the motto that it is worth doing something only if you do it right!

The incentives for my creative work are rooted in my temperament. Diligence and a strong desire for knowledge accompanied me throughout life. I do not derive any satisfaction from knowing things superficially: I want to know them thoroughly. When I came to the conclusion that I had only hazy notions of the primitives, and that it was not possible to acquire full knowledge about them through books, I started traveling in Africa, New Mexico, and India. For the same reason I also started learning Swahili.

What were the circumstances that induced you to work in the field of psychological research?

Even as a small boy I noticed that people always did the contrary of what was said of them. I found some of the people who were praised quite unbearable, whereas I thought others who were criticized quite pleasant.

I noticed the inconsistencies in the behavior of adults quite early on, because I spent my formative years in Basel, in a rather odd environment, which was frequented by people with a complicated psychic structure.

When I was barely four years old, someone said to me in an exaggeratedly childish tone: "Where do you think you are going with your rocking horse?" I reacted quite the enfant terrible: "Mama, why does this man say such nonsense?" Even as a child I clearly felt that people did not say what was really in their minds.

Isn't it possible for people to come to psychology in exactly the opposite way? Don't some people feel attracted to psychology because they want to find an explanation for the chaos within themselves?

Certainly! If you take a critical look at people, you will find that some of them are involved in psychology only in order to demonstrate that "the other person" is even more neurotic. However, in the kingdom of the blind the one-eyed man is king.

Isn't nature particularly important for you to sustain and enhance your personal productivity?

Nature can help you only if you manage to get time for yourself. You need to be able to relax in the garden, completely at peace, or to walk. From time to time I need to stop, to just stand there. If someone were to ask me: What are you thinking of just now?—I wouldn't know. I think unconsciously.

How important is the time factor in your scientific activity? Isn't it a great strain for you to work both as an analyst and as a research scientist?

My time has always been divided. Either I dealt with patients, or I did research work. For a time, I used to see patients only in the afternoons. The mornings were devoted to scientific work.

In earlier years I worked a lot at night, especially during the first World War. Until the middle of my life I worked chiefly in the morning, and after I was 36, chiefly in the afternoon. In the last ten years I've turned again to working in the morning.

How do you react to disturbances? Some occultist authors recommend that their adepts go into retreat to enhance their energies. Do you think that creative energy grows as a result of isolation?

The energy is there, but I must have the possibility of "casting my net." Once I have all the material, nothing and nobody must get near. I am not as sensitive to noise as Carlyle, who installed triple glass windows and saw to it that all the fowl and dogs near his property were bought up. But when I am in the active creative process, any disturbance is downright physically painful. I have a little house at Bollingen, to which I retreat and where I can work undisturbed when my notes and preparatory studies have reached the stage where I can start writing.

Do some Yoga systems offer the possibility of developing one's creative energies?

Yoga can liberate certain psychic contents and natural dispositions but it cannot produce them. You can't make something out of nothing, not even with will-power. And what is will-power? To have will-power means that you have a lot of drive. Creativeness is drive! A creative calling is like a *daimonion*, which, in some instances, can ruin a person's entire life.

[*Translated by Ruth Horine*]

A VISIT FROM A
YOUNG QUAKER

++++++++++++++++++++++++++

George H. Hogle, from Utah, went to see Jung at his Bollingen retreat during the summer of 1947. He wrote up his recollection of the meeting for a memorial booklet prepared by the Analytical Psychology Club of San Francisco in 1961, and he later added more details of the conversation in a letter.

Following Jung's advice, Hogle became an analysand of the psychotherapist Frances G. Wickes, in New York. Previously, he had worked in Wall Street, and subsequently he earned an M.D. degree at Columbia-Presbyterian and underwent psychiatric and analytical training in London. He is now clinical assistant professor of psychiatry at Stanford University, in Palo Alto, California, and a Jungian analyst.

While training for foreign relief work with the American Friends Service Committee in Philadelphia during 1946, I met several Quakers who were also interested in Jungian psychology. I had recently discovered medicine and now was searching for some connection between psychology and religion. The experience of trying to help heal the wounds of war in Germany a year later sharpened my search. During the summer of 1947, while on holiday in Zurich, I telephoned Dr. Jung's office on an impulse—here was the man who could give me the answers, I thought, not realizing it might take me several years. His secretary informed me that he did not see people while on holiday at a hideout (Bollingen) at the other end of the lake, but since she was in touch with him she would ask him anyway. To my delight and her surprise, the next day I was given an appointment.

After I had walked through the woods to what looked like a little fairy-tale castle by the side of the lake, the great wooden door was opened to my knock by the huge old hired man, smoking a pipe and with an ax in his hand. In lame German I asked for Herr Doctor, and in idiomatic English he introduced himself—not the dignified professor I had expected. As we stood on the beautiful shore, he put me somewhat at ease, chatting about building his hideaway. My hesitance and inhibitions were replaced soon after by the conviction that here was a very fallible, rigid old man, as we got into an enormously heated argument about the international situation.

I had told him that I was working with the Quakers in Germany to rebuild the bridges of friendship between enemies and that the next big job, I felt, was already looming on the horizon; namely, to reach out across the Iron Curtain and make some kind of friendship with the Russians. I felt that the Friends' approach would lessen tensions and be an example of mutual brotherhood.

He snickered, or something like that, and said he would not advise it; it would be quite impossible to work with the Russians or reach them, you could not trust them, they had broken their agreements many times. I replied, so had we, which was, of course, not mentioned in the Western press, and that somehow we needed to get beyond that. But he simply was adamant. Finally, he patted me on the shoulder and, with a big smile, said, "Well, we don't have to agree about everything."

Having helped me realize he was quite human and that it was safe to show some feeling, he escorted me up to an elegant Swiss tea, which we shared with Emma Jung. They inquired at length about the situation in Germany, no doubt the reason he was willing to see a non-German coming recently out of that country. I knew nothing of the controversy regarding his questionable sympathies for the Germans, but certainly at that time I got no impression that he had ever been warm in any way toward Nazism, rather that he only tried to understand what it all meant at a deeper level.

After tea, we were alone for about an hour, during which he dealt graciously and helpfully with my impossible inquiry as to what I should do with my life, knowing nothing about me and yet no doubt knowing much just by observing. Instead of answering my questions he gave me other better questions to ask myself over the succeeding months. I told him something of my belief that God is good and love, at which he inquired, "But do you think that God may also include hate and evil?" This rather shook me, but I explained his question to myself that he must be a Pantheist and that God includes all just as the individual self both the divine center and the shadow, that Satan must be another aspect of God. He encouraged me to go into psychology and gave me names of analysts, especially recommending Frances Wickes.

DOCTORS ON HOLIDAY
ON THE RIGI

✦✦✦✦✦✦✦✦✦✦✦✦✦✦✦✦✦✦✦✦✦✦✦✦✦✦

The founding of the C. G. Jung Institute in April 1948 brought many of Jung's friends and pupils to Zurich. (For Jung's address on the occasion, see CW 18, pars. 1129ff.) In June, for the first time since before the War, Esther Harding (see above, p. 25) and her friend and colleague Eleanor Bertine, M.D., traveled from New York. Dr. Bertine (1887–1968), American by origin and training, shared with Dr. Harding the leadership of the Jungian movement in the eastern United States. After returning from abroad, her *Report from Zurich* was brought out as a pamphlet by the Analytical Psychology Club of New York, 1948. It dealt chiefly with the organization of the Institute, but a more personal excerpt under the above title was included in *Memories and Perspectives Marking the Centennial of C. G. Jung's Birth* (published privately by the Club, 1975), and this version is printed here. Dr. Harding's journal entries for her visit at the same time are given afterward.

We arrived in Switzerland at the very height of rose-time. I think I never saw so many roses in my life, garden roses and climbing roses, wild roses and tame. One thing that strikes an American abroad, as a lot of you know, is that literally every inch of land is used, either fertilized for grazing or agriculture, or allocated to timber production, or else made into the ubiquitous gardens by which every peasant's cottage, as well as every mansion, is surrounded. All the villages looked like blooming rose-gardens. We well remembered, on this return, the majesty of the mountains, but we had almost forgotten the quaint loveliness of every little hamlet. For us, of course, the country round about Küsnacht was filled with memories of steps and stages on the inner way which had been accomplished there. It was under a particular tree that heavy thoughts had clustered like ripe fruit, yon forest had been a place of darkness of spirit, but clarification had come while swinging down the steep hill above the village just as twilight was falling. All the sounds, too, brought repercussions from the past, the thrice-repeated ding-dong, ding-dong, ding-dong announcing train time at the station, the splash of the little lake boats pulling up to a stop just under our window, the chimes of half a dozen churches ringing the quarter hour from near at hand and from across the lake. All were so utterly familiar, so unchanged by all the violence of the intervening years.

But the goal for which we had made the pilgrimage was, of course, to see Dr. Jung. So we were delighted to get a call bright and early the morning after our arrival giving us an appointment for the following morning. He had explained previously that he could no longer carry the burden of people's personal problems, but that he would be glad to talk with us about anything else we wished. We found him looking older, of course, for the twelve years since we had been there; his hair was snow white, but he appeared well and more full of ideas and of mental vitality than ever. He had so much to give that he seemed actually to need to give it. Physically, we were told, he readily gets over-tired and then he goes rapidly downhill. His illness has left him with only a small reserve, and he has to live within rather rigid limits. But within those limits, he is magnificent. Talking did not seem to tire him, and he poured out treasures lavishly, from what seemed to be an inexhaustible fund of wisdom. He said that he had thought old age would be a rather dull time of decrease and inaction, but actually it was most exciting. "You just sit quietly in one place and absolutely everything comes right to your doorstep!" The hard digging and delving that he has done all his life in pioneering this new way into the psyche seems now to be bearing fruit in the form of a great wealth of spontaneous ideas. Indeed all during his illness, he told us, ideas were flooding up, even in his delirium, which he is still trying to evaluate and record. His literary output is enormous. At present he is engaged in redoing *Psychology of the Unconscious*, writing another book on alchemy and one on the Self.[1] And of course he gives a lot of time to the Institute and to the working out of all the myriad details connected with getting it well started. And finally, he is continually visited by scholars interested in psychology and all the numerous fields which touch upon it, men and women who bring their special points of view to him and seek something of his integrating wisdom. So, in spite of physical limitations, he is an immensely hard worker. He said that, a while ago when he had gone off to the mountains for a much-needed rest and vacation, he had made up his mind that he had done his bit and had about come to the end of his assignment. So he wasn't going to have any more ideas, please. But that very night the conception of the central theme of the book on the Self forced itself upon him, and there was nothing for it but to set to work on another big undertaking.

Dr. Jung was, as he put it, "not quite pessimistic" about the inevitability of the destruction of our civilization. He found some indications—quite slight clues, to be sure—in the dreams of all sorts of people and in the particular way that certain things have happened, which suggest that this moment, with its upheaval and disorder, may be truly the transition to a new order, as we have all been hoping for so

---

[1] Jung greatly revised *Wandlungen und Symbole der Libido* (1912; tr. 1916, *Psychology of the Unconscious*) under the new title *Symbole der Wandlung* (1952; tr. 1956, *Symbols of Transformation*, CW 5). "Another book on alchemy" may have been *Mysterium Coniunctionis* (1955; CW 14), and the one on the Self was *Aion* (1951; CW 9 i).

long. He said that the uprush of brutality, which he had observed so generally in dreams of Germans before the War, was giving way to constructive symbols of a new phase. One rather interesting astrological fact, he noted, is that the line of the ecliptic, at present traversing the second fish of the sign of Pisces, the fish of the Anti-Christ, does not pass through its head but below. This would mean that, according to the stars, the sinister forces do not reach their maximum, do not quite "come to a head." Of course he made no claim to be a prophet, but merely an observer of whatever indications there might be.

At the end of the morning, Dr. Jung proposed that we join him for a long week-end trip, Thursday to Monday, on the Rigi. We had heard that he was planning a holiday and would be out of town for about a week, which we naturally took as our bad luck, never dreaming of such a windfall as this. He knew of a charming little inn recently built on a saddle just below the summit of the mountain, and said he would ask Miss Schmid to engage the rooms for us all. Mrs. Jung had hoped to go but couldn't manage it just then. Miss Wolff would try to get up by Saturday night.

So Thursday morning we met Dr. Jung at the railroad station. He was carrying a fat and heavy briefcase which held the manuscript of the book he had brought along to work on. That did not look much like a holiday to us, but fortunately it was never opened all the time we were there. The mountain and talk claimed every minute. Each morning, right after breakfast, we all fared forth for a tramp. The Rigi is a fairly domesticated mountain, at least a cogwheel railroad runs up to the top from each side, and there are many trails crisscrossing the slopes, where they are not too steep. Dr. Jung, needlessly apologetic, set the pace slow enough for us to keep up without having had a chance to get into training beforehand. For actually he was able to do as much as we cared to. There were benches placed here and there at particularly beautiful spots where we could sit down and divide our attention about evenly between the view and the talk. As you may remember, the Rigi rears steeply above Lucerne across from the sharp peaks of Pilatus, with the gem-like chain of lakes of the Vierwaldstättersee strung out at its feet. In the distance, across lower snow ranges, tower the giants of the Bernese Oberland. Wherever you look, your eye is caught and held by something you want to be able always to remember. Dr. Jung pointed to the sheer face of a cliff, asking, "Do you see that door?" We looked hard and could see nothing but unbroken rock. Then he pointed out the line of a ledge and above it the faintest bit of roughness. It was the door of a cave in the cliff, one of many made by the Swiss army as a means of defending the mountains when they momently expected invasion. The plan was to abandon the northern plain, where Zurich is located, and to retire into the mountains and fight there to the last ditch. The Swiss meant it, too, and that spirit was probably what saved them.

After lunch, and there is no problem in getting all you want to eat and drink in Switzerland if you can pay for it, there was time for a little rest, then we came together again for tea and another walk, then dinner and more talk until far into the night. And such talk! Dr. Jung was in top form, and the conversation ranged over everything conceivable, from the sublime to the ridiculous, from samples of his inimitable Rabelaisian wit to the meaning of faith. He told us about his experiences under threat of invasion during the war, about the visit of Churchill to Switzerland, which was like a triumphal procession, and the talks he had had with —or perhaps I should rather say had heard from—him. Dr. Jung spoke of the United States and its overwhelming job of world leadership. I said that this had not been sought or wanted by our country, and I questioned whether we were ready to carry such a responsibility. His answer was that the United States must not stay immature now, or it will be at the peril of the whole world. "Only you have the power, you must take the responsibility that goes with it." He thought it most necessary that we be firm with Russia or Russia will certainly control Europe. Like all the other Europeans I talked with, including some who had previously been far from pro-American, he was immensely appreciative of the Marshall Plan, and hoped that we would be firm and definite about laying down conditions for its operation. I asked whether that would not bring everybody down on us, with the accusation that we were using dollars to dominate the world. He agreed that it would, but said that such was the inevitable price of power. "You cannot at once hold power and avoid criticism, for what you don't do, if not for what you do." He thought we would have to accept that fact and go ahead, for the European countries could not agree among themselves. There was too much long and bitter history dividing them.

In these long hours in the mountains, Dr. Jung reminisced about his own past experiences, his trips to Africa and to India, the long anxiety during the period of Hitler's domination. And then, one morning, sitting in an outdoor terrace cafe looking over the deep valley with its emerald green lake and on to the snow peaks beyond, he took us to the mountains of the mind, as he told us of his latest idea of the psyche. This is the basis of his new book on the Self and will be the culmination of his life's work, the final great step in integration of a career outstandingly devoted to the integrative processes, both in knowledge and in life. He has found a symbol of the psychic structure which joins into an organic unity everything from the mineral world through the animal, the unconscious and ordinary consciousness up to the Anthropos, which is quality-less and so, like the old Uroboros, touches the primordial condition of Chaos with its forces constituting matter, from which the whole cycle springs again. It all was most suggestive and exciting, but too much to take in at one telling. Though he drew diagrams to elucidate his thought, I admit to a feeling

rather like my reaction many years ago when I first con-
tacted his work through *Psychology of the Unconscious*. It
was: "There speaks the master. I do not understand, but,
please God, I shall before I die." The elaboration of these
new ideas will, I think, bring some light to the dim inter-
region between psyche and body, as well as that between
psychology and physics. Anyway we felt that the companion with whom we sat waiting for the drinks to be
brought on that mountain terrace had himself given us a
drink from the cup of pure genius.

Of course the days on the Rigi were the high point of the
trip. It is impossible to be with Dr. Jung without a constant
sense that the inner world of the unconscious is a vital fact,
ever-present in the room. The habitual directness of his
connection with the actual libido of the moment is more
like that of the animal than of the usual man of today. One
feels that he has fully completed the cycle from the experience of blind instinct through ego-consciousness and
back to a broad conscious relation to the powerful but mysterious tides of the unconscious. His talk moves back and
forth from the obvious facts and events of the outer world
to the subtle and irrational manifestations of another to
which he grants an exactly equal validity and weight. That
this is no mere lip service, no mere intellectual point of view,
is shown in the freeing effect he produces upon practically
everybody, not too congealed by the fear that this man may
somehow be going to crack up his well-tailored persona and
reveal matters too disturbing to be welcome. But, though
Dr. Jung's talk is rich in references to experiences which
are ordinarily explained by *a priori* interpretations from the
realms of mysticism or superstition, he is utterly sure-footed
in keeping to the line that differentiates the facts which you
experience—the observed data—from what you think about
them and the names you call them by. He himself is frequently thinking about them, rescuing them from the scrap-
heap of mere fantasy and superstition and seeking an ex-

planation for them consonant with the findings of modern psychology. Certainly he does not hesitate to incur the criticism, once seriously levelled against him by a psychologist at the New School, to the effect that "Jung is more concerned with religious phenomena than is compatible with scientific respectability!" He even strayed so far into "scientific disrespectability" as to tell us about a magician whom he knows personally and who has talked freely to him. The man is a Swiss peasant who lives up in the hills above Bollingen, conscientiously practicing his profession. He trusted Dr. Jung, and told him willingly many stories of his successes with magic, producing in evidence a drawer full of testimonials and letters of appreciation from "grateful patients." He even brought out his greatest treasure, a book of spells for making magic in the name of Baldur, or of Venus, or of other thoroughly pagan gods. This little volume, believe it or not, he claimed had been presented to him by a monk! Apparently these invocations of highly questionable powers had not disturbed the peace of mind of the good friar in the least. Indeed magic flourishes, very much as of yore in out-of-the-way places in Switzerland. And not only there, one might add.

I have been repeatedly asked since our return, How does Dr. Jung really feel about the campaign against him as a Nazi sympathizer? That question cannot be answered quite simply, even if I could be sure of interpreting his reaction correctly, for the reply would have to depend upon the level of consciousness with which the interrogation was concerned. On the surface level it is deeply painful to him to have his name associated with the unspeakable horrors perpetrated with deliberate intent by the German government. Such vilification as he has received, and even the simple lack of understanding it implies, of all he has stood for in his entire life and work, cannot fail to hurt a man of his sensibility. But on another plane, it just does not touch him. While there are undoubtedly some venomous motives at work, the whole attack can also be regarded as one more manifestation of the fact that he stirs the unconscious to such an extent that he is inevitably mythologized as god or devil. He has had that experience before many times, and takes it in his stride as a part of life, a phenomenon to be accepted, rather than an offense to be personally resented. Indeed, Dr. Jung has a deep realization that, to be complete, the very godhead must include the devil, and human beings must accordingly find an adjustment to that fact and not just childishly reiterate that it oughtn't to be. So, with respect to the attacks against himself, he pulls up his collar and goes about his business, without getting unduly involved.

But to get on with my story. Saturday Miss Wolff arrived with her little dog. Though badly hampered by rheumatism, from which she has been a great sufferer, she gamely came along Sunday morning when we climbed to the pinnacle of the Rigi. Mrs. Jung, who had expected to get up that evening, was delayed by the death and funeral of a long-standing member of the Zurich Club, whom some of you will undoubtedly remember, Herr Dr. Schlegel.[2] Dr. Jung asked us to stay over until Tuesday in order to see her, but we had a dinner engagement with friends who had come to Zurich from southern Switzerland for a visit with us, so we had to leave before she arrived, greatly to our regret.

[2] The lawyer Eugen Schlegel, an old friend of the Jungs, died on June 10, 1948.

FROM ESTHER HARDING'S
NOTEBOOKS: 1948

•••••••••••••••••••••••••••

Küsnacht, 8 June

C. G. came in, the old C. G., smiling, welcoming, with both arms outstretched. He looked at us and said to Eleanor, "You have not changed." And to me, "But you have changed." I said, "There has been a world cataclysm since I last saw you."

He himself is very little changed. Older, yes, face a little thinner, with harder lines and planes, throwing the width and height of the head into greater prominence. Hair a little thinner, softly wispy around his head. He spoke of it, calling it his "feathers."

"Yes, my head is growing feathers. But the barber won't cut it."

I said, "Is it the same barber whom Zosimos[1] tells of?"

But he evidently did not hear all I said, for he replied, "No, it is not the same one. We have one who lives just across the road."

We spoke of how glad we had been to get his letters from time to time, which had kept us in touch. He said it had been very strange during the war in Switzerland, that little island of peace, how, in spite of the constant threat of invasion, he had not been really uneasy (putting his hand on his abdomen), that he had always had a sense they would be left uninterfered with.

He told of their great anxiety in 1939 over the Hitler-Stalin pact, which made it look as if they would be swal-

[1] A symbolic barber appears in the visions of Zosimos, a Greek alchemist of the 3rd cent. A.D., which Jung treated in an Eranos lecture, 1937. See "The Visions of Zosimos," CW 13, p. 60.

lowed up without doubt. He said he had had a dream at that time:

He found himself in a castle, all the walls and buildings of which were made of trinitrotoluene (dynamite). Hitler came in and was treated as divine. Hitler stood on a mound as for a review. C. G. was placed on a corresponding mound. Then the parade ground began to fill with buffalo or yak steers, which crowded into the enclosed space from one end. The herd was filled with nervous tension and moved about restlessly. Then he saw that one cow was alone, apparently sick. Hitler was concerned about this cow and asked C. G. what he thought of it. C. G. said, "It is obviously very sick." At this point, Cossacks rode in at the back and began to drive the herd off. He awoke and felt, "It is all right."

He emphasized that Hitler was treated as *divine*. Consequently, he felt, we had to view him like that, that Hitler is not to be taken primarily as a human man, but as an instrument of "divine" forces, as Judas, or, still better, as the Antichrist must be. That the castle was built of trinitrotoluene meant that it would blow up and be destroyed because of its own explosive quality. The herds of cattle are the instincts, the primitive, pre-human forces let loose in the German unconscious. They are not even domestic cattle, but buffalo or yaks, very primitive indeed. They are all male, as is the Nazi ideology: all the values of relationship, of the person or individual, are completely repressed; the feminine element is sick unto death, and so we get the sick cow. Hitler turns to C. G. for advice, but he limits his comment to the diagnosis, "The cow is very sick." At this, as though the recognition of the ailment released something, the Cossacks burst in. Even before that, the herd had been disturbed and nervous, as indeed the male animal is if separated too long or too completely from its complement, the female. The Cossacks are, of course, Russians. From that, C. G. said, he deduced that Russia—more barbaric than Germany, but also more directly primitive, and therefore of sounder instinct—would break in and cause the overthrow of Germany.

June

On more than one occasion Dr. Jung talked about parapsychological phenomena. He said he felt that the observed phenomena could only be explained with the hypothesis that time is a psychic phenomenon, i.e., a conditioning of our psyches, or of our consciousness. If one can once get outside this ego conditioning, time becomes entirely relative, and the present moment is as if eternal. This observation, however, does not tell us anything about immortality, or life after death. It refers only to the quality of our experience.

He gave as evidence the variable length of experience of a measured period of time. There is also the experience of long-continued happenings in dreams. And the story Zimmer[2] told of the saint who wanted to know the karma of Vishnu and was sent to get water, then met a maiden and lived a whole lifetime, and, when he returned, found the god just finishing his cigarette!—or something of the sort.

C. G. said it was to explain such things that he formulated his theory of synchronicity,[3] viz., that everything that occurs in any one moment is, in some way, an expression of that particular, unique moment in time, which never was before and will never recur. He explained the falling of the yarrow sticks for the *I Ching* in this way. Then he recounted several happenings that had an aptness of coincidence which caused the greatest surprise and wonder. For instance: the woman whose dreams had held much sexual material, which she kept trying to explain symbolically, till

[2] Heinrich Zimmer (1890–1943), German Indologist, close to Jung. For the parable, see his *Myths and Symbols in Indian Art and Civilization* (1946), pp. 32–34.

[3] Jung's first extensive treatment of his synchronicity theory was an Eranos lecture of 1951. For that, and the lengthy monograph "Synchronicity: An Acausal Connecting Principle" (1952), see CW 8.

C. G. felt he really must enlighten her; and at the next appointment two sparrows fluttered to the ground at her feet and "performed the act." Or the patient who dreamed of a scarab, and one flew at the window. . . .

Then he spoke of ESP experiences, dreams of events still unknown to the dreamer, which subsequently do occur. These dreams usually only come when the news is close at hand, rather than at the moment of occurrence. . . .

He related several experiences having to do with psychic phenomena connected with death of persons at a distance. There sometimes were what he called "spooks" about, cracklings and snappings in furniture. Occasionally, he had warning dreams about a person who was about to die, or he felt an unseen presence at the time of their departure. He twice dreamed of Baynes[4] after his death, each time in connection with Churchill, and each time when Churchill was actually in Switzerland, though C. G. did not know this at the time. For instance, he dreamed that he was sitting at a dinner table with Churchill or Roosevelt when a group of English officers, among whom was Baynes, in civilian clothes, came in. At this time Churchill had landed near Zurich for his plane to refuel on his way to Africa. A second dream was similar to the first, except that Roosevelt was not there. This time, Churchill was spending one night in Geneva on his way to Yalta.

He told us a lot about this visit and his contact with Churchill.[5]

He told us that in 1934 he had gone to Bollingen to work and had put up his yellow flag to warn Professor Fierz[6] that he was not "at home." He was unable to work, however. He felt terribly depressed. A heavy cloud seemed to oppress him. But he kept his flag up and struggled with the oppression

[4] For H. G. Baynes, see above, p. 33, n. 1.
[5] For Jung's meeting with Winston Churchill in Zurich in 1946, see *Letters*, vol. 1, index, under "Churchill."
[6] Professor H. E. Fierz.

all day Sunday and into Monday. At last, he pulled down the flag, feeling it was no use trying to work any longer. Immediately, Professor Fierz came over and told him of the Nazi purge, which had taken place on Sunday morning.

He spoke of exteriorized libido: how, when there was an important idea that was not yet quite conscious, the furniture and woodwork all over the house creaked and snapped, and that Mrs. Jung was aware of it as well as he. One time there came a sharp snap at the door just as he was falling asleep. This was repeated, and it woke him quite up. Then, as he began to fall asleep again, he had a vision of a fish, and, just as he lost consciousness, his wardrobe gave a great crack. He opened his eyes to see a large fish emerging from the top corner.

He told us of his hallucinations of the Ravenna mosaics.[7] When they went into the piscina, he and Miss Wolff, there was a misty blue light, and through it they saw the mosaics. They stood and discussed them for about half an hour and were amazed to find the Peter symbol, Peter walking on the water and being rescued by Christ, combined with the others (Moses bringing water from the rock; Jonah and the whale; the miraculous draft of fishes). He came back and narrated this in the seminar (of 1929?). When Dr. Meier[8] was going to Ravenna, a year or two later, C. G. told him he must not fail to see the mosaics and to get him pictures of them, for he and Miss Wolff had failed to find any in the town. (I was present at that seminar.) When Dr. Meier returned, he told C. G. that no such mosaics existed. He could not believe it. It was only some years that he ran across the story of the countess who had vowed to make such a gift of mosaics if she were delivered from shipwreck. The mosaics were made, but were destroyed by fire while in nearby St.

[7] Published in *Memories, Dreams, Reflections* (1963), Chapter 9, sec. v.
[8] C. A. Meier, then Jung's assistant, later director of the C. G. Jung Institute.

Giovanni's Church. Jung learned that a sketch does exist, but he has not seen it. . . .

Another time, he talked about "haunted houses." In Africa once he heard music and the sound of people talking, though he could not distinguish the words. The natives told him, "Those are the people who talk." This occurred more than once to him. And other travellers also have reported such experiences. Always at these places there are evidences that there has at some past time been a settlement—for example, there are plants there only grown under cultivation.

. . .

A VISIT FROM MORAVIA

The Italian novelist Alberto Moravia, whose writings had been censored by the Fascists, was working during the postwar period as a correspondent for *L'Europeo* (Milan). In the issue of December 5, 1948, he published a brief article on a visit to Zurich; the title translates as "The Psychoanalyst Jung Teaches How to Tame the Devil," though only the latter half is devoted to an interview with Jung, extracted here. The first part is about Swiss banking and Italo Svevo, his fellow novelist. In 1952, incidentally, the Roman Catholic Church put all of Moravia's books on the Index.

. . .

I am on my way to visit C. G. Jung in one of Zurich's suburbs. Here are the luxurious villas of the banking and commercial bourgeoisie, surrounded by vast gardens. They have their offices in modern, austere, and bare buildings in the center of town. Looking for Jung's villa along the main thoroughfare, in pouring rain, I am reminded of the American novelist Scott Fitzgerald, writer of another post-war generation. In one of his beautiful novels[1] he describes to

---

[1] *Tender Is the Night* (1934), in which—whether or not Moravia had it in mind—Fitzgerald mentions Jung several times, most notably in a passage in which the American psychiatrist Diver, practicing in Zurich, reflects on the personalities he might encounter at a psychiatric congress: "Articulate among them would be the great Jung, bland, super-vigorous, on his rounds between the forests of anthropology and the neuroses of school-boys" (Book Two, sec. XVI, in the original version). When his wife Zelda had a psychotic episode in late 1930, she was a patient of Dr. Oscar Forel at the sanitarium of Prangins, on Lake Geneva. A consultation was necessary, and Eugen Bleuler, of the Burghölzli in Zurich, "had been chosen after careful consideration. Dr. Jung was Fitzgerald's alternative choice, but Jung handled cases of neurosis primarily" (Nancy Milford, *Zelda: A Biography*, 1970, p. 179).

perfection the psychoanalytic milieu of Zurich: An American millionaire, much disturbed by his daughter's state of mind, brings her to Zurich to one of the most famous and expensive psychiatric clinics. There it is simply discovered that the daughter, at the age of fifteen, had been seduced by just that loving father. She falls in love with her physician, who cures her, marries him, and goes to live with him on the Riviera. . . . But here, at last, is No. 228 Seestrasse, the street of the lake. The rain is pelting down on the yellow leaves of the tree-lined avenue, at the end of which one can see the entrance to a villa. I ring the bell and Jung's secretary opens the door. In a few minutes Jung himself ushers me through the waiting room into his study.

Jung is an elderly man (he is 74), of stocky build, with a strong face reddened by the continuous flames of a cheerful fireplace. He has a white mustache, penetrating eyes, and white, dishevelled hair. A man of middle-class appearance, dressed in rough woolen sporty clothes, breathing a bit laboriously, stout, and with a pipe in hand. He asks me to sit down in an armchair, in front of a bright lamp which nearly blinds me. He, instead, possibly because it is the habit of a psychoanalyst, sits down facing me, his face in shadow as if he wants to study me without being himself scrutinized. Thus, with my face illuminated and his in darkness, we begin our conversation.

We talk in French, which Jung speaks fluently despite a somewhat harsh German accent. The first questions and answers are awkward. Then, no doubt because his examination of my face has given him a favorable impression, Jung warms up and begins to talk with greater ease.

Naturally the discussion revolves around his theories and books, all of which I know only superficially, and in particular the theory expounded in his last book, *Symbolik des Geistes*.[2] Digressing at times, Jung explains to me some of

[2] Published 1948, containing the final German version of "A Psychological Approach to the Dogma of the Trinity," CW 11.

the ideas of this latest work and its connection with the theory which gave him fame.

In the new book, the most important part apparently concentrates on an "attempt at a psychological explanation of the dogma of the Trinity." This book has caused much talk in Switzerland, precisely because of his interpretation of the Christian Trinity. In short, according to Jung, the Christian dogma represents a symbol for the collective psyche; the Father symbolizes a primitive phase; the Son an intermediate and reflective phase; and the Spirit a third phase in which one returns to the original phase, though enriching it through the intermediate reflections. Jung would like to add to that Trinity a fourth figure so as to transform the whole into, so to speak, a Quaternity. This fourth figure is the direct antithesis to the clear and conscious function of the first three: it would possess an obscure, subconscious function, and would represent—according to Jung—the devil.

In order to make this idea of a Quaternity comprehensible, Jung connects it with his well known theory of the psychology of the unconscious. He roughly reasons as follows: In ancient times the devil, i.e., the unconscious, existed in direct relationship to the spirit, or the conscious. This relationship was highly beneficial; the conscious nourished with its light the shadows of the unconscious; with its positivity the negativity of the unconscious; with its rationality the instinctuality of the unconscious. The ancient religions were aware of the relationships between conscious and unconscious; and what is more, they encouraged them. Yahweh, for instance, was not only God but also Devil. However, beginning with Christianity and particularly the Reformation, the unconscious, that is to say the devil, has become increasingly thwarted, suppressed, forgotten, obliterated. With Luciferian pride the Nordic Protestant believes he can do without the devil. And so, acquiring strength in direct proportion to that excess of repression, the unconscious suddenly explodes catastrophically in various diabolic and destructive ways. Jung explains that thus one can understand the clearly demonic and suicidal tendency of European civilization on the threshold of the first World War. At that time the devil, i.e., the unconscious, for too long repressed and even forgotten, took his revenge by driving men to regard with sensual joy destruction and death. At this point Jung graphically conjures up the picture of trains full of exuberant soldiers, the locomotives bedecked with flowers, leaving Berlin for the front in 1914, and he explains this joy at the imminent massacre with the joy of a finally achieved union with blood and death, i.e., the unconscious. Jung proposes the same explanation for the monstrous and automatic cruelty of the Nazis during the second World War. He says that this time once again the absence of a healthy relationship with the devil gave origin to an explosion of unprecedented and destructive fury. He concludes that it is necessary to restore as quickly as possible these relationships: and if necessary, to create precisely that Quaternity.

On this strange prediction, much in tune with the Faustian atmosphere, I leave Jung. Outside it continues to rain. Through the rain I make my way back to Zurich.

[*Translated by Beata Sauerlander*]

FROM CHARLES BAUDOUIN'S
JOURNAL: 1949

++++++++++++++++++++++++++

In January 1935, Jung had led in organizing the Swiss Society for Practical Psychology, which was the Swiss branch of the International General Medical Society for Psychotherapy. The Society brought together medical psychotherapists and lay psychologists of various schools, and it continued its activity after the International Society was dissolved.

Sarconnex d'Arve, July 4, 1949[1]

On Saturday I went to Hurden for the meeting of the Jung Society. This time I crossed a summer Switzerland in beautiful weather. The birch trees, trembling in the breeze, glittered with a rain of light; the foliage, after days of dryness, was touched here and there with gold as if on the verge of autumn. The lakes succeeded one another with felicitous diversity: the one of Geneva with blues and marine violets, that of Neuchâtel an emerald green, and the gray shades of the lake of Zurich were shot with lead. I made the acquaintance of the small town of Rapperswil and found it charming. . . .

Hurden is reached by a causeway that bestrides the lake for a kilometer. There on a peninsula—that could be called an island—one finds oneself in lake country, bounded on all sides by the profiles of peaks of unequal height; one is surrounded by red-plumed reeds and the lightning flights of water birds.

Here in a room of the Adler Hotel open to the gardens, Jung gave his lecture on mandalas.[2] He arrived, his step a

[1] From *L'Oeuvre de Jung* (1963); see above, p. 76.
[2] Apparently an early version of "Concerning Mandala Sym-

190

little slow, leaning on the gold-headed cane that his close friends say he has been using lately, and wearing a straw boater (boaters which have been so unfashionable are coming back this year), with his rather long white hair falling down on his neck behind. Yet his bearing was vigorous enough, with his good humor and his ready bursts of laughter. This time he spoke sitting, which is certainly permissible at seventy-four, rising from time to time to point with his stick to the designs pinned on the wall; it was hot, and he had been so bold as to take off his vest.

We dined on the terrace at the edge of the water. . . . During the lecture I was struck by Jung's profile, which when he removed his glasses to bend over his notes appeared to me to be incised with a rare energy, a mordancy and keenness seemingly belying the sanguine good nature and mischievousness of the person seen face to face.

[*Translated by Jane A. Pratt*]

---

bolism," CW 9 i, which originally appeared in *Gestaltungen des Unbewussten* (1950).

ON THE ATTACK IN THE
"SATURDAY REVIEW
OF LITERATURE"

....

In 1948 the Bollingen Foundation, which had been formed three years earlier, donated funds at the request of the Library of Congress to establish an annual prize in poetry. The Library named it the Bollingen Prize in Poetry and designated the Fellows in American Letters of the Library as its jury of award. In February 1949 the Library announced that the first annual award had been made, on the recommendation of the Fellows, to Ezra Pound. Pound at that time was under indictment for treason, being charged with propagandistic activities in support of the enemy during the War; and, having been judged insane by a medical board, he had been confined in a government mental hospital. At first, the reactions to the award were relatively mild, but in June, a poet and critic, Robert Hillyer, published two articles in the *Saturday Review of Literature* that arbitrarily dragged Jung into the controversy, through the Foundation's interest in his work, and presented him as a Nazi and anti-Semite and part of a conspiracy to prepare for "a new authoritarianism." The affair has been well documented in a booklet, *The Case Against "The Saturday Review of Literature,"* published by the magazine *Poetry* (Chicago), in October 1949.

Carol Baumann, an American pupil of Jung's residing in Switzerland, felt that it was "high time that Jung's own voice be heard, and I therefore asked for an interview." It was published in the *Bulletin of the Analytical Psychology Club of New York* (a mimeographed private publication), December 1949.

(Dr. Jung received me in his garden at Küsnacht, and we sat at a round stone table in the shade of a circle of great trees.

I had already sent Dr. Jung a list of the quotations which had been cited against him, and he glanced through these again.)

When people have jumped to false conclusions they often prefer to cling to their prejudices. There is little use in answering people who wish to misunderstand, for they are not interested in ascertaining the objective truth.

Yes, but many readers are mystified by the general uproar. Will you not answer a few questions about the most important accusations against you, to make your viewpoint clear to those who are really interested in learning the truth?

It must be clear to anyone who has read any of my books that I never have been a Nazi sympathizer and I never have been anti-Semitic, and no amount of misquotation, mistranslation, or rearrangement of what I have written can alter the record of my true point of view. Nearly every one of these passages has been tampered with, either by malice or by ignorance. Furthermore, my friendly relations with a large group of Jewish colleagues and patients over a period of many years in itself disproves the charge of anti-Semitism. Let us take the most important misquotation (*SRL*, June 11): "The Jew is a relative nomad, never has had and never will have his own culture. . . . The Aryan unconscious is a higher unconscious than the Jewish." It is significant that when the full context is read, these phrases acquire exactly the opposite meaning from that attributed to them by the "researchers." These mistranslated phrases have been taken from a paper entitled "On the Present Situation of Psychotherapy," which appeared in the *Zentralblatt für Psychotherapie* (Vol. 7, Nos. 1 and 2).[1] An extensive presentation of the main points in this paper has been printed in a thirty-two page article by Dr. Ernest Harms: "Carl Gustav Jung— Defender of Freud and the Jews" (*Psychiatric Quarterly*, April, 1946).[2] In order to evaluate the meaning of these

---

[1] "The State of Psychotherapy Today," CW 10.
[2] See above, p. 59, n. 1.

questionable phrases, I will give you the whole paragraph in which they appear:

"In consequence of their more than twice as ancient culture, they (the Jews) are vastly more conscious of human weaknesses and inferiorities and therefore much less vulnerable in this respect than we are ourselves. They also owe to the experience of ancient culture the ability to live consciously in benevolent, friendly and tolerant neighborhood with their own defects, while we are still too young to have no illusions about ourselves. . . . The Jew, as a member of a race whose culture is about 3,000 years old, like the educated Chinese, is psychologically conscious in wider areas than we are. . . . *The Jew, as relatively a nomad, never has produced, and presumably never will produce a culture of his own, since all his instincts and gifts require a more or less civilized host-people for their development.* Therefore, the Jewish race as a whole has, according to my experience, an unconscious which can only conditionally be compared to the Aryan. Aside from certain creative individuals, the average Jew is already much too conscious and differentiated to be pregnant with the tensions of the unborn future. *The Aryan unconscious has a higher potential than the Jewish; that is the advantage and the disadvantage of a youthfulness not yet fully estranged from barbarism.*"[3]

Since this article was to be printed in Germany (in 1934) I had to write in a somewhat veiled manner, but to anyone in his senses the meaning should be clear. I had to help these people. It had to be made clear that I, an Aryan outside Germany, stood for a scientific approach to psychotherapy. That was the point! I can not see anything in the least anti-Semitic in this statement. It is simply an appraisal of certain psychological differences in background, and in point of fact it is complimentary to the Jews to point out that they are in general more conscious and differentiated than the average

---

[3] Cf. CW 10, par. 353. The translation here is the interviewer's and likewise the italics.

Aryan, who has remained close to barbarism! And it is an historical fact that the Jews have shown a remarkable ability to become carriers of the cultures in all lands where they have spread. This shows a high degree of civilization, and such adaptability is a matter for admiration. Some people show a funny kind of resentment when one speaks of differences in psychology—but one must admit that different nationalities and different races have different outlooks and different psychologies. Take the difference between the French and the English, or for that matter, between the English and the Americans! There is a marked difference in psychology everywhere. Only an idiot can not see it. It is too ridiculous to be so hypersensitive about such things. They are facts of experience not to be ignored.

What can you say about the quotation: "The American presents to us a strange picture: a European with Negro mannerisms and an Indian soul"?[4]

This must be taken from a popular interview back in 1930 or thereabouts. The psychology of the unconscious does not lend itself to popular treatment. It is too easily misunderstood—all the more so when journalists try to make a sensational splash. Such an isolated bald statement naturally reads like blatant nonsense to anyone familiar with the workings of the unconscious mind. Before one can make any sense out of such a statement one needs to know how we can be influenced through the unconscious. I can just as well speak of the primitive contents of the European unconscious. There is no critical slur in these things. Indeed, for a wide-awake person, the primitive contents may often prove to be a source of renewal. The American unconscious is highly interesting, because it contains more varied elements and has a higher tension, owing to the melting-pot and the transplantation to a primitive soil, which caused a break in the traditional background of the Europeans who became Amer-

---

[4] "Mind and Earth" (orig. 1927), CW 10, par. 103.

icans. On the other hand, Americans are in a way more highly civilized than Europeans, and on the other hand their wellspring of life energy reaches greater depths. The American unconscious contains an immense number of possibilities. I cannot pretend to have attained a comprehensive view of it, and even that view which I have can not be compressed into a few sentences for an interview.

Mr. Hillyer claims that in 1936 you said that "Hitler's new order in Germany seemed to offer the only hope of Europe." [5]

Many Americans asked me what I thought about Hitler and his ideas, in the autumn of 1936, and I always expressed concern for the *future of Europe*. It is not true that I ever admired Hitler. However, in the early years, before the power devil finally took the upper hand with Hitler, he brought about many reforms and to a certain extent served the German people constructively. I may have said something of this kind as well as talking of the dangers ahead, which I had already written about. If I state an historical fact people immediately jump to the conclusion that that implies admiration! The mockery of it! My whole life work is based on the psychology of the individual, and his responsibility both to himself and his milieu. Mass movements swallow individuals wholesale, and an individual who thus loses his identity has lost his soul. Such a widespread phenomenon has well-nigh destroyed our civilization, and the danger is by no means over yet!

Hitler became the mouthpiece of all the undercurrents seething in the German people. This fact was aptly expressed by the oft-repeated phrase that Hitler followed his intuition with the false "assurance and accuracy of a sleepwalker"—until he came to the edge of the precipice from which there was no escape. In my paper on "Wotan" [6] I de-

---

[5] This quotation could not be documented.
[6] Orig. in *Neue Schweizer Rundschau* (Zurich), March 1936. A

scribed how the wind god of old provided a very apt picture of the force which seized on the German people, stirring up the long-buried barbaric past. I wrote this article in 1936 as a warning for those who could understand its implications. When the unconscious of a whole people is stirred to such an extent, and there is no *conscious and responsible leader* to canalize the released forces, then the devil takes hold and the destructive forces rush headlong to their final destruction, but only after half destroying the world around them. That is the tragedy.

Anyone who takes the trouble to read what I wrote both before and during the war will find my real views concerning mass psychology and its dangers, but my warning voice was not heard.

Can you say anything about the work of your Jewish followers?

There is plenty of evidence of their friendly collaboration with me. Dr. Gerhard Adler, in London, has continually defended me against the accusation of anti-Semitism. Dr. Ernest Harms, in America, as I already mentioned, painstakingly wrote up the true history of my connection with the *Zentralblatt.* He, incidentally, studied with both Freud and myself, but does not count himself as belonging to either school. Dr. Erich Neumann, of Tel Aviv, has written several books based on his study of my psychological views. There are many others I might mention, and, as you know, there is a large group of Jewish pupils here in Zurich.

The fact that you accepted the editorship of the Zentralblatt für Psychotherapie *and the honorary chairmanship of the International Society for Psychotherapy, in 1933, has greatly influenced Americans against you. Could you say something about this?*

---

shortened version appeared in *Saturday Review of Literature*, Oct. 16, 1937. Now in CW 10.

197

An objective review of the facts concerning this critical period in the history of European psychotherapy, and the motives which led me to try to save an international scientific organization of physicians, has been written by Dr. Harms, as I just said. I can add little to what he has written. However, I may sum up that when I, as a Swiss, accepted this position it was my aim to preserve a spirit of scientific cooperation among all European doctors in face of the Nazi anti-Semitism then first raising its head. It was impossible to fight the Nazi intolerance openly without endangering the position of all German doctors, and of German Jewish doctors in particular. But I did what I could as quietly as possible, and succeeded in getting a special paragraph adopted by the international society, whereby German Jewish physicians (who were barred from membership in the German branch society) could individually become members of the international organization. Thus they were able to become full members with equal rights. Later, when through the influence of the Nazis, Dr. M. H. Göring (a cousin of Hermann Göring) became co-editor of the *Zentralblatt*, and other Nazi doctors were foisted upon us (in 1936 and '37) my position gradually became untenable. During this fateful time the Nazis played double with my name. On the one hand, my name was placed on their black list on account of various things I had written which they could not swallow, as, for instance, my lecture on the "Theory of Complexes,"[7] held in Bad Nauheim in May 1934, in which I paid tribute to Freud. Still later, my Swiss publisher received news that my books were banned and destroyed. On the other hand, the Nazis were only too pleased to publicize my name, as a Swiss feather in their caps, in an effort to prop their waning reputation in the eyes of the world. Many false and conflicting rumors were circulated about me: that I was anti-Semitic, that I was a Jew, that I was Hitler's

[7] "A Review of the Complex Theory," CW 8, pars. 212ff.

doctor, etc., etc. The fact that my name became associated with Göring's on the *Zentralblatt* editorial board naturally put me in an increasingly false position, especially when he printed his famous pronouncement about *Mein Kampf*. This was inserted in the *Zentralblatt* without my consent, and I had not laid eyes on the manuscript before it appeared in print. Of course this statement represented the point of view of the German society only, never of the international society as a whole. Since the *Zentralblatt* was published inside of Germany, the Nazis enforced their influence whenever they could.

The task which I had accepted, namely the preservation of a non-political international society, finally became too heavy a burden and in fact an impossible undertaking. In the meantime, I attempted to do my duty in this respect as any other decent man would have done in my place. Several times I wanted to withdraw and I attempted to resign, but at the urgent request of the English and Dutch representatives, who begged me "for the sake of the whole organization to stay on," I stayed on. You can not quit people when they are in a hole. It has helped many people that I stuck to my post. One can say it was a foolish idealism which caused me to stand by, but it seemed to me unfair to all the people clinging to me to leave them in the lurch. My standpoint was: I'm not a rat which runs from a sinking ship; and so I did not actually resign until the end of 1939, when the war began and I could be of no further use. Then all international communications were disrupted.

I have never desired to get involved in political events, but as a troubled Swiss onlooker and a conscientious psychological observer, I have naturally had certain reactions to the disturbing events of the time we live in. I might add that in 1941 I delivered a lecture before a meeting of Swiss psychotherapists entitled "Psychotherapy Today"[8] in which I con-

[8] The opening address to the Kommission für Psychotherapie,

demned the totalitarian state at a time when the victorious panzer divisions were barely sixty-five miles away, and I knew the Nazis planned to make short work of me when and if they crossed the Swiss border.

Schweizerische Gesellschaft für Psychiatrie, Zurich, July 19, 1941. First published 1945, except for the private publication of a translation in *Spring*, 1942. Now in CW 16.

MAN AND HIS ENVIRONMENT

++++++++++++++++++++++++++++

The eminent Swiss geographer Hans Carol (1915–1971), a member of the Institute of Geography at Zurich University, was developing guidelines for regional planning in the Canton of Zurich when, in 1950, he sought the views of various people important in Swiss intellectual life. One of these was Jung, who gave him a half hour's appointment on February 8, 1950. The subject so engrossed Jung that he kept Carol nearly an hour longer. In 1958 Carol came to America, and from 1962 until his death he was professor of geography at York University, Toronto, where his chief interest was the geography of Africa. He came across the notes of his conversation with Jung much later and wrote them up for the *Neue Zürcher Zeitung*'s literary supplement, June 2, 1963; this version is translated here, with Carol's introduction reduced to the question. The account was published in slightly different form (translated) in *Landscape* (Santa Fe), spring 1965, and the paragraph beginning with an asterisk, on page 203, is from that version.

I would be grateful if you, as a leading psychologist, would comment on the subject of man and his environment. Although we planners try not to look at the human being as a mere product of his physical environment, we believe nonetheless that the environment is a crucial factor in human existence. Just as men are influenced by education, they are surely also influenced by the environment society designs for them.

I am very pleased that you are devoting your attention to this question. The abstract nature of work in a technological age leaves the worker dissatisfied. Dissatisfaction induces people to look for compensation elsewhere, Suggestibility increases geometrically according to the number of persons involved. Mass mental disorder may reach epidemic proportions. Decentralization, on the other hand, allows for small social units. Every man should have his own plot of land so that the instincts can come to life again. To own land is important psychologically, and there is no substitute for it. We keep forgetting that we are primates and that we have to make allowances for these primitive layers in our psyche. The farmer is still closer to these layers. In tilling the earth he moves around within a very narrow radius, but he moves on his own land. The industrial worker is a pathetic, rootless being, and his remuneration in money is not tangible but abstract. In earlier times, when the crafts flourished, he derived satisfaction from seeing the fruit of his labor. He found adequate self-expression in such work. But this is no longer the case. First of all, he is responsible for only a small part of the finished product. Secondly, the product is sold, it disappears, and he has no further stake in it. Because the psychological reward is inadequate, the worker rebels against his employer and against "capitalism" as a whole. We all need nourishment for our psyche. It is impossible to find such nourishment in urban tenements without a patch of green or a blossoming tree. We need a relationship with nature. I am just a culture-coolie myself, but I derive a great deal of pleasure from growing my own potatoes. People tend to look for the Kingdom of God in the outer world rather than in their own souls. This is particularly true of socialism. Individuation is not only an upward but also a downward process. Without any body, there is no mind and therefore no individuation. Our civilizing potential has led us down the wrong path. All too often an American worker who owns only one car considers himself a poor devil, because his boss has two or three cars. This is symptomatic of pointless striving for material possessions.

Yet, we need to project ourselves into the things around us. My self is not confined to my body. It extends into all the things I have made and all the things around me. With-

out these things, I would not be myself; I would not be a
human being, I would merely be a human ape, a primate.
Everything surrounding me is part of me, and that is precisely why a rented apartment is disastrous. It offers so few
possibilities for self-expression. In a standardized apartment,
in a standardized milieu, it is easy to lose the sense of one's
own personality, of one's individuality.

A community is based on personal relationships. No
community can evolve where people can easily move house-
holds from one place to another. The one-family house, the
house owned by its inhabitants, is much better because it
necessarily engenders a sense of permanence.

If man has a hand in shaping his environment, it will
reflect his personality. A Soviet collective farm lacks soul,
and the people who live on it are a dull, unhappy lot because they have been deprived of any opportunity for personal expression.

* When capitalism takes everything out of the hands of the
worker, he feels he has been robbed. Therefore our economic system must put something else within his grasp. In
particular, the worker must be enabled to have a personal
leisure-time occupation, and this again is best suited to the
private dwelling, the family, the garden. The economic
drawbacks of fixed permanent residence are less important.

Life in a small city is better than life in a large one,
politically, socially, and in terms of community relations.
Big cities are responsible for our uprootedness.

The Swiss are mentally more balanced and not so neurotic as many peoples. We are fortunate to live in a great
number of small cities. If I do not have what my psyche
needs, I become dangerous.

Because in our country the government is reluctant to aid
community projects, the projects that do materialize are all
the more genuine and valuable.

A captive animal cannot return to freedom. But our
workers can return. We see them doing it in the allotment

gardens[1] in and around our cities; these gardens are an expression of love for nature and for one's own plot of land. As our working hours become shorter, the question of leisure time becomes increasingly essential to us, time in which we are free of commands and restraints and in which we can achieve self-realization. I am fully committed to the idea that human existence should be rooted in the earth.

[*Translated by Robert and Rita Kimber and Ruth Horine*]

---

[1] On the continent and in England, small garden plots usually on the outskirts of a city.

COMMENTS ON A DOCTORAL
THESIS

+++++++++++++++++++++++++

Toward a Ph.D. degree at the New School for Social Research, New York, in early 1952, Ira Progoff submitted as his thesis a presentation of Jung's psychological theories and an interpretation of their significance for the social sciences. This was, most probably, the first serious notice of Jung's work by a social scientist. Progoff sent his manuscript to the Bollingen Foundation, which was about to begin the publication of the Collected Works of Jung, and it came to the attention of one of the Foundation's advisers, Cary F. Baynes, an old friend of Jung's. Recognizing the significance of Progoff's monograph, she sent the thesis to Jung to read and asked her daughter, Ximena de Angulo, who lived in Switzerland and had known Jung since her childhood, to facilitate matters by taking down Jung's comments. Miss de Angulo sent Progoff her report of the interview—as the discussion turned out to be—and he took account of Jung's remarks in revising his thesis for eventual publication as a book: *Jung's Psychology and Its Social Meaning* (1953).

Progoff, who had been a welfare worker while studying at the New School, was enabled through a Bollingen Fellowship to go to Switzerland in 1953. He met Jung for discussions and attended the Eranos Conference in August, where he came under the influence of the Zen scholar, D. T. Suzuki. Out of his experiences he wrote *The Death and Rebirth of Psychology* (1956). In 1966, Progoff founded Dialogue House, of which he is director, and which fosters a program for personal development through the "intensive journal" process.

A copy of Ximena de Angulo's interview was placed in the archives of Bollingen Foundation, where it was found nearly twenty years later and made available for publication in the present collection, with the permission of Miss de Angulo and Dr. Progoff. It is published in full, except for the deletion of

205

page numbers in the thesis, as these have no systematic relationship to the revised book.

The interview took place in the summerhouse at the bottom of the garden. We each had a copy of the thesis, and I had brought along pad and pencil so as to be able to take notes.

As a starting question I asked Jung if he thought the thesis merited expansion into a book, and he said without a moment's hesitation: "Oh, yes, most definitely." He went on to say that as it stood, its most obvious shortcoming was a certain onesidedness, that it told "only half the story." "You see, I am not a philosopher. I am not a sociologist—I am a medical man. I deal with facts. This cannot be emphasized too much." This, in a way, turned out to be the *leitmotiv* of the interview; he recurred to it again and again. I received the impression that what bothered him about the work was that it was phrased as though he had had social theories in mind from the beginning. I pointed out that in a thesis designed to prove the relevance of his ideas to the social sciences that had perhaps been unavoidable. He said yes, yes, that was probably so; but it was clear that he attaches the greatest possible importance to accentuating his standpoint as a medical man, as an empiricist who discovers certain facts and erects hypotheses to explain them, but who is not responsible for the implications, philosophical or otherwise, that may be drawn from his statements. He said that he was all the time being accused of making philosophical statements, because he made use of *philosophical concepts*, and because he didn't shy away from making his assumptions clear, but that his statements were not intended as philosophy, they were intended as descriptions of fact. "I am not particularly well read in philosophy. I simply have had to make use of philosophical concepts to formulate my findings."

He went on to say that he thought the *derivation* of these philosophical concepts should be clarified. "My conceptions are much more like Carus than like Freud." Kant, Schopenhauer, C. G. Carus, and Eduard von Hartmann "had provided him with the tools of thought." He had read their works when young, perhaps as early as his sixteenth year, at any rate well before the beginning of his medical studies, and they had influenced his thinking decisively. "To Schopenhauer I owe the dynamic view of the psyche; the 'Will' is the libido that is back of everything." It is a force outside consciousness, something that is *not* the ego. Kant had shown that the world is tied to the "I," to the thinking subject, but here was this non-ego, this "Will" that was outside the Kantian critique. When Jung came to study the dissociation of consciousness observable in schizophrenia, where people talk under the influence of something other than the ego, this non-ego struck him as the same thing as Schopenhauer's "Will." "The great question was, is there a non-ego, is there something that can pull me out of the isolation-in-the-ego of the Kantian world picture?"

It is correct that Burckhardt and Nietzsche influenced him; however, they were indirect, "side influences," Jung said. They were part of the atmosphere of Basel at the time he was growing up, though Nietzsche had already left the city then; "Burckhardt was our daily bread. I used to see him every day, going to his work." Everybody read him.

Nietzsche was a great psychological critic. "We were living at a time when there had been no wars within men's memory, but here was a man who saw war coming, who wrote that the next century would be the most warlike of all. I felt that he was right." But it was as a phenomenon that Nietzsche made the deepest impression on Jung. He saw the non-ego at work in him; Nietzsche was in a fever, in a passion, a passion that "gripped" Jung. He told how Nietzsche's insights and visions had tremendous fascination to a person living at that time who thought about the contemporary situation. "In his thirty-seventh year, Zarathustra happened to Nietzsche . . . 'da ward die eins zu zwei, Zarathustra ging an mir vorbei.' In 1888 he went mad. That was a tremendous event; it made a deep impression on me."

Bachofen also influenced him. "He influenced my understanding of the nature of symbols."

Jung thought that if the thesis were expanded, it might be a good idea to take his later writings more into consideration, especially *Aion* and *Die Psychologie der Übertragung*.[1] These, he said, were the generalities. Then he drew out a list, and we began going through the thesis point by point:

"(it is not) that the unconscious is held in common. . . ." Jung: "That is leaning over backwards. It *is* collective, *is* held in common. 'Collective' may be objectionable in some ways, but it does convey the fact that we share unconscious contents, that there is *participation mystique*."

". . . Jung's use of the term (unconscious) may partly be accounted for by the fact that he developed his thought while working under the influence of Sigmund Freud, and that he naturally adapted for his own system the terms with which he had been accustomed to working." This is not true, Jung said. "I had these thoughts long before I came to Freud. *Unconscious* is an *epistemological* term deriving from von Hartmann. Freud was not much of a philosopher, he was strictly a medical man. I had read these philosophers long before I ever saw Freud. I came to Freud for *facts*. I read *The Interpretation of Dreams*, and I thought Oh, here is a man who is not just theorizing away, here is a man who has got *facts*. This was not Freud's first publication, but it was the first one I read, then I read the others. We met in 1906."[2]

---

[1] *Aion* (orig. 1951) is CW 9 ii; "The Psychology of the Transference" (orig. 1946) is in CW 16.

[2] Freud and Jung actually met first, in Vienna, on March 3, 1907,

From the beginning, Jung said, he had occupied himself very much with zoology, with comparative zoology. Here he looked at me keenly to see if I took in the import of this statement. When I responded, he went on with a gleam in his eye: "I was especially interested in palaeontology; you see, my life work in historical comparative psychology is like palaeontology. That is the study of the archetypes of the animals, and this is the study of the archetypes in the soul. The *Eohippus* is the archetype of the modern horse, the archetypes are like the fossil animals."

This led me to ask him what had first taken him into psychiatry. "Oh," he said, "that was not until the very end of my medical studies. I had been acting as assistant to von Müller[3], the internist, who had received a call to Germany, and he wanted to take me along. In my last semester, I was preparing for my final exams, and I also had to know something about psychiatry, so I took up Krafft-Ebing's textbook on psychiatry. I read first the Introduction . . . and then it happened. Then it happened. I thought, this is it, this is the confluence of medicine and philosophy! This is what I have been looking for! They all thought I was crazy, they couldn't understand me at all, they thought I was giving up the chance of a fine career to enter a blind alley of medicine! You see, my professors all knew that in internal medicine they had facts to work with, something to build on, and they saw a great future for it, but psychiatry, that was sort of a strange no man's land tacked onto medicine, no one really knew anything. It was all up in the air, and it led nowhere."

I said that looking back now, his professors' reaction was really not surprising because, before his and Freud's work, psychiatry really didn't have any solid foundation and no

---

but their correspondence began in 1906. See *The Freud/Jung Letters*.

[3] Friedrich von Müller, at Basel University, later Munich. See *Memories, Dreams, Reflections*, p. 107/110.

place much to go. "Well, yes, that is so," he assented. "But I knew absolutely that this was the thing for me; it came over me with the most tremendous rush. You know, my heart beat so"—he spoke with great emphasis and looked at me intently—"I could hardly stand it; I was in a regular state!" And even at this distance in time he managed, by his voice and the forceful way he gestured, to convey something to me of the intensity of this experience! To me this was the high point of the interview—well, no, perhaps there was another one, which I'm coming to later—but at any rate it made the greatest possible impression on me to see how vividly he was able to reproduce this event before the mind's eye; one could feel the sense of destiny, the nervous excitement that must have gripped him.

". . . term 'persona' . . . derived from Etruscan, meaning mask." Jung said the Latin word *persona* came from *per sonare*, to sound through, because masks had a sort of tube inside, from the actor's mouth into the mouth of the mask, a built-in megaphone to amplify the sound so it would carry. The mask came to be called *persona* after this megaphone. Not Etruscan.

". . . the therapy of individuation . . ." Jung: "Why therapy? It is not a therapy. Is it therapy when a cat becomes a cat? It is a natural process. Individuation is a natural process. It is what makes a tree turn into a tree; if it is interfered with, then it becomes sick and cannot function as a tree, but left to itself it develops into a tree. That is individuation." I said I had always understood that individuation involved con- sciousness. "Oh," he said, "that is an overvaluation of consciousness. Consciousness is a part of it, perhaps, yes, but that depends on how much consciousness there is naturally there. Consciousness can also block individuation by not allowing what is in the unconscious to develop." He said it was therapy to restore the free flow from the unconscious, but the process itself is natural, and it will force itself through whether therapy is applied or not. If a person is meant to be an artist, but does something else, then pretty soon this development which is blocked will produce all kinds of symptoms, and in the end he will find himself painting whether he wants to or not, or else he will be very sick.

I asked him if it was what made a tree grow into a tree, if it was not the same thing as the Aristotelian entelechy, the inherent potentialities within the acorn which develop it into the oak. He hesitated, and I had to say it again another way, but then he said it was the same thing. (I think his prejudice against Aristotle is so great that it made him unwilling to commit himself; probably because "Aristotelian" thinking within the Church produces such intellectual aridity and doctrinaire rigidity.)

I was still not quite sure I had understood aright, and I said it had always bothered me whether, say, a Hindu yogin or a primitive medicine man, a truly wise one, of course, could be considered to be individuated, since they were not "conscious" in our sense of what went on inside them. "Well, I don't know about that," he said. "They may not be conscious but they hear the inner voice, they *act* on it, they do not go against it—that is what counts. The primitive may not *formulate* it in the way you mean, but he has a pretty clear idea what goes on; I understand his language. When I go to him, we speak the same language."

"You know, it is possible to have 'consciousness' *in globo*, so to speak, without its being differentiated." It is on this that the Church bases the development of its dogma; otherwise we today would be in the position of knowing more than the apostles, since the dogma has been set down in the intervening centuries. What has been defined and differentiated into dogma was present *in globo* in the inspiration of the apostles.

He repeated that individuation was a natural process; that "it can happen without consciousness."

These statements, and especially the decisiveness and assurance with which he made them, made a deep impression on me. The part about how he came to specialize in psychiatry was the most exciting of the interview, because it is a moving thing to hear how a person received the "call," and because it opened up new perspectives for my own private research into his philosophical antecedents, the subject I had originally meant to write my thesis on. But this part held the most *meaning* for me. The thought of this *principium individuationis* at work through all nature and through all mankind, East and West, has something awe-inspiring and majestic about it. I can't explain exactly why it came as a revelation to me. I had previously had a slightly different perspective on it, with more of an accent on effort and less on nature and process. That he knew so definitely what he was talking about gave me a direct intuition of the importance of "fact" and "experience" in psychology. I could see that it was a *fact* that he was talking about, though it might escape definition, just as a tree is a fact. A tree is not a bad analogy, because we do not understand how a tree functions either, how it raises up to its crown the huge volume of water that circulates in its system, for example, yet the tree is an indisputable fact, a natural process.

". . . meaning of terms 'introvert,' 'extravert' depends on context of Jung's theory of types, can only be grasped in terms of his total system . . ." Jung's comment here was that this was misleading; his terms are not *deduced*, they arise from the facts. He feels that whatever application is made of his ideas, in fairness to him it should always be phrased so that this fact of cardinal importance is clear. For the same reason he objects strenuously to the word "system"; he says he has no system, he deals with facts and attempts to construct hypotheses to cover them. "System" sounds closed, dogmatic, rigid. He wants the experimental, empirical, hypothetical nature of his work emphasized.

As to the spelling of extravert, he says extrovert is bad Latin and should not be used. He also prefers archetype.

Paragraph on incest. Jung suggests looking up *Die Psychologie der Übertragung* for a clearer view of the meaning of incest. Paragraph as it stands is insufficient.

(Immediately following the preceding sentence is a notation which is clear enough in itself, but which doesn't seem to me now to have much connection with the incest paragraph. However, I shall set it down here.) "The archetype is the *form* of instinct, it is how the instinct appears to us; cf. 'Der Geist der Psychologie,' *Eranos Jahrbuch* 1946."[4] Jung went on to say that an example of what he meant was the story of King Albrecht and Johannes, later known as Johannes Parricida.[5] The king and his suite were riding from Zurich to Basel. Johannes and some companions wished to murder the king, but they couldn't seem to make up their minds to do the deed. Johannes kept hesitating. When they came to the ford over the Limmat, at Baden, then he did it, he murdered the king. "That is the archetype; you see, the ford is the natural ambush, the place where the hero slays the dragon. Then suddenly Johannes found it in him to do the deed; the archetype was constellated."

". . . Jung considers the libido intensity of the anima to be so great that he refers to it as 'mana,' that is, as having a miraculous quality." (Ref. to *Two Essays*.)[6] Jung says he never could have said "miraculous" but *ausserordentlich*

---

[4] Augmented and revised as "On the Nature of the Psyche," CW 8.
[5] Cf. the version of this story in "The Houston Films," p. 293. The murder of the Habsburg king, Albert I, in 1308, actually occurred at Windisch, on the Reuss River.
[6] *Two Essays on Analytical Psychology*, CW 7.

wirksam, i.e., effective, or even numinous. But not miraculous.

". . . Jung's concept of individuation . . . opens the possibility of new conceptions of the nature of Man." Jung said to put "of the nature of the psyche."

". . . as Jung uses the term 'consciousness,' it signifies a part, a small part of consciousness in general." Jung said this is unclear, should be a "part of the cognitive" or something like that. Consciousness simply is consciousness, not part of it.

"The *représentation collective* refers to the condition in which there is a failure to distinguish between the individual and the group as a whole." According to Jung, the above is *participation mystique*. A *représentation collective* is a generally held idea, like "democracy is the best form of government," which everyone accepts without questioning; a kind of basic premise which is simply assumed to be true, which nobody dreams of investigating. All sorts of cultural and political slogans would come under this heading.

He went on to say that he had known Lévy-Bruhl personally, that he had been Jung's house guest in Küsnacht. Lévy-Bruhl had had many good ideas, but contemporary sociologists and anthropologists had completely failed to understand him, had misunderstood his idea that primitives think a-logically, and especially the conception of *participation mystique*. These attacks had rattled him so much that later he took a lot back, and in later editions dropped the "mystique" out of the term, but Jung has stuck to the formulation of the first edition because he thinks it accurately describes the facts.

In this connection, Jung told of having gone to hear a lecturer who attacked the concept of *participation mystique*, and who told an anecdote to illustrate the fact that natives distinguish perfectly between themselves and others, and between persona and objects. While the railroad from Mombasa to Nairobi was being built, a great deal of Native labor had to be employed, and the white engineers had the greatest trouble in getting them to work without constant supervision. As soon as the engineer's back was turned, they dropped their work. One man thought he would fix that. He had a glass eye, and when he had to leave, he called the Natives together and said: "I am going, but I am leaving my eye to watch you," and he took the eye out and placed it on the table. "You keep working, because this eye will see you if you stop." When he returned he found to his consternation that nobody had worked. "We put a hat over your eye so it couldn't see us loafing," the Natives told him.

Far from disproving Lévy-Bruhl's conception, as the lecturer thought, this anecdote backs it up: so little were the Natives able to separate the glass eye from its wearer that they went to the trouble to put a hat over it to prevent it from "seeing." When Jung afterward wrote a polite letter to the speaker pointing out this fact, he received an irate reply, and the lecturer became his life-long enemy!

". . . Jung's failure to be able to give an absolute definition of consciousness . . ." Jung commented: "How can consciousness explain itself?"

"The 'collective representations' by which society contains the individual, etc . . ." Again, it should be "participation mystique." Jung reworded the sentence to read as follows: "The *participation mystique* by which society contains the individual may be understood as a statement of the fact that individuals are still undifferentiated from each other, that is to say, they have not yet been self-consciously broken up into individual personalities."

"On this 'pre-conscious' level, the individual contains himself within his own archetype . . ." Jung corrected this to read: "On this 'pre-conscious' level the individual is un-conscious of himself." He said "within his own archetype" was misleadingly worded, that a clear distinction must be made between the archetype and archetypal *images*, which is how the archetype appears to us.

"The archetypes exist in the unconscious as undifferentiated symbols . . ." Jung suggests rereading "Der Geist der Psychologie" (*Eranos* 1946): the archetypes are *psychoeides*, are *noumena* (not numina!). Only the image is empirical, he said.

". . . the individual in society may be understood as a piece of the archetype, a piece that has been differentiated out of the collective representation." Jung: ". . . differentiated out of *participation mystique*, i.e., out of the collective uncon-scious." He said, "The archetype of the individual is the Self. The Self is all embracing. God is a circle whose center is everywhere and whose circumference is nowhere."[7]

". . . symbol . . . in other areas it appears with metaphysical or ontological overtones where it leads into the philosophical side of his system." Jung said if one studied the definitions of "symbol" in the *Types*[8] one saw that it was *not* meta-physical. (I think what he is getting at here and in other places is that he does not *aim* for a metaphysical overtone or for philosophical aspects. If we find such overtones it is be-cause general usage has given some of the concepts he makes use of such overtones. He could, of course, have chosen entirely new terms, but I think he did not do so because he wants to redefine the traditional terms, show where they arise out of experience, and thus keep the tradition alive, but with a different foundation.)

[7] "God is an intelligible sphere whose center is everywhere and whose circumference is nowhere."—St. Bonaventure, *Itinerarium mentis in Deum* (13th cent.), cited by Jung in *Mysterium Coniunctionis*, CW 14, par. 41, n. 42, and elsewhere.

[8] *Psychological Types*, CW 6.

"Only by the fact that (the libido analogue) comes from the collective suprapersonal layer of the unconscious is it able to function as a transformer of psychic energies . . ." Jung said this was well-expressed and showed the correct understanding of what he means by "collective" in collective unconscious.

". . . psychological problems of Western man . . ." Jung said Protestantism also belongs in the context, i.e., pre-Christian paganism, Greco-Hebrew religiosity, and Protestantism.

This brought to my mind the reference to his Swiss *Calvinist* background, and I asked if it was correct. He said no, no touch of Calvinism. The Reformation was introduced in Basel by Oecolampadius (in 1529), according to Jung the mildest of all the Reformers. Important factors in keeping the Reform within bounds were the fact that the city was a bishop's seat and that the university had been founded by Aeneas Silvius (Piccolomini) when he became Pope Pius II. Of all Swiss Protestant cities, Basel has always had the most tolerance and understanding of Catholic ways, viz., the celebrated Basler Fastnacht. Jung attributes his own attempts at a sympathetic understanding of Catholicism to this element in his background.

". . . when a culture becomes too highly rationalized . . . individuals are not able to experience the natural flow of unconscious materials." Jung commented that symbols can lose their efficiency; they age.

"The result is a vacuum in the psyche between the upper and lower layers." Jung: "What should that be?" He seemed to think the idea ought to be worded differently.

"The mechanisms of convention . . . keep people unconscious. . . . (They) follow their customary runways without the effect of conscious choice." Jung suggested saying "without bothering about conscious choice, without being confronted with the necessity of making up their minds."

"The lunatic is an individual completely overcome by the unconscious." Jung says it must read: "more or less overcome by the unconscious." I pointed out that it appeared to be a direct quotation from his writings, but that didn't bother him. He said in that case it must be incorrectly translated.

". . . (demons) involve the reactivation of archaic images stored in the unconscious from past historical eras . . ." Jung corrected this to read "they are the archetypal images which are always in the unconscious." He commented in general that it is important to differentiate the terminology correctly.

". . . Jung's statement that the entire tradition of psychoanalysis—*commencing with Freud* and extending through his own work—has been possible only because Western civilization has been passing through a crisis in its deepest beliefs." (My italics.) Jung says this must be taken much further back; the tradition begins with the German Romantics, comes down through Schopenhauer, Carus, etc., i.e., requires to be set in a larger historical perspective.

". . . Jung's conception of consciousness . . . two levels of meaning: *one as the totality of the psyche, that is to say, as cognition in general*; . . . the other as the small segment of awareness that centers around the ego." (My italics.) Jung said the first (italicized) part is wrong, only the second is correct.

". . . contemporary situation . . . searching for new religions, . . . etc." Jung asked to have the words "and moral" inserted into the latter part of the sentence, i.e., "the total questioning of intellectual and moral values and the search throughout Western civilization for the meaning of life."

THE HELL OF INITIATION

+++++++++++++++++++++++++++

J. P. Hodin, a British art critic and historian, of Czech origin, had studied Jung's statements about art and creativity, particularly in his essays on Joyce and on Picasso. Feeling dissatisfaction with Jung's explanation of his point of view, he requested an appointment to discuss psychology and modern art, and Jung received him at his house in Küsnacht on June 17, 1952. Hodin's account of the interview was published in his book *Modern Art and the Modern Mind* (Cleveland, 1972), in a chapter titled as above, part of which had been included in a lecture, "C. G. Jung and Modern Art," at the Institute of Contemporary Arts, London, in February 1954. The present version is recast in dialogue form.

(In a small study, its windows opening on the garden and the lake beyond it, Jung awaited me: a writing-desk in one corner, bookcases, a few insignificant pictures of small size in dark frames on the wall—landscapes, figures. Jung bade me welcome and asked me to be seated in a chair near the window. He was over medium height, had a strong frame which suggested peasant stock, and walked with a rather heavy gait. The soundness of his shape was matched by his strong gaze. His hair and moustache were white, but he seemed younger than his years although he was, he told me, just recovering from one of the illnesses which assail old age. That is why, when I mentioned in passing an incident from the life of the aged Swiss poet Hermann Hesse, Jung spoke of having many times lately thought of Freund Hein, *which is a German expression for death. But he must have embarked on one of his most ambitious works, the* Mysterium Coniunctionis,[1] *at about this same time.*

[1] Published 1955–57; CW 14.

He listened attentively to my objections. When I mentioned that in England his psychology had again and again been attacked as unscientific, he was at first indignant. Only later followed an even stream of evidence.)

In comparative anatomy, we speak of morphological phenomena in man, of organs which resemble the organs of animals. We know, for instance, that man has lived through early stages of development in the course of his evolution. We know the complete genealogy of the horse dating back millions of years, and on these facts the science of anatomy is founded. There is also a comparative morphology of psychic images. Folklore is another field of research into motivation. What I have practiced is simply a comparative phenomenology of the mind, nothing else. If someone has a dream and we find that dream in identical form in mythology, and if this constantly repeats itself, are we not justified in saying with certainty: We are still functioning in the same way as those who created that mythological image?

Take the Eucharist. A god is slain, pierced with a spear, is dismembered, eaten. To this day, the piercing of a loaf of bread with a silver spear is a ritual of the Greek Church. In the Aztec rites, Huitzilopochtli is slain, pierced with a lance. His body consists of a dough made from the seeds of plants just as the Host is made of white flour, and the pieces are distributed and eaten. The undivided and the divided God. Think of the use made of the cross in Yucatan. It is the same as our adoration of the Cross. Or the myth of Dionysos.[2] [Jung gave several other examples.]

The psychiatrists, in treating their cases, know that these things happen in the soul of the patients. There are countless ideas, images of the unconscious, which have been compared to mythological concepts, because they proved to be identical. There is only one method: the comparative method. Comparative anatomy, the science of comparative

[2] Cf. "Transformation Symbolism in the Mass," CW 11, pars. 340ff.

religion. Why not then comparative psychology? If we draw a circle and divide that circle into four equal parts and think of it as a philosophical idea, and the Chinese does the same thing, and the Indian too—do you think that it is something different when I do it? Unscientific! There are only a few heaven-inspired minds who understand me. In America it was William James. But most people are ignoramuses. They take no pains to find out the essential things about themselves. It requires too much Latin and Greek!

(I asked him if he had any inclination to interpret works of other modern artists—Paul Klee, for example. I had just come from Bern, where I had visited Klee's aged sister and his son Felix and had seen very early works of this artist.)

No. I cannot occupy myself with modern art any more. It is too awful. That is why I do not want to know more about it.[3] At one time I took a great interest in art. I painted myself, sculpted and did wood carving. I have a certain sense of color. When modern art came on the scene, it presented a great psychological problem for me. Then I wrote about Picasso and Joyce.[4] I recognized there something which is very unpopular, namely the very thing which con-

[3] Note by J.P.H.: I did not give up the idea that he might one day change his mind, and perhaps produce a piece of writing of a more positive character on modern art. But a letter which he wrote me on September 3, 1955, convinced me of the contrary: ". . . and I regret to tell you that I cannot fulfill your wish to write something on Kokoschka. I would first have to familiarize myself with the *oeuvre* of this artist and this would be too troublesome a task for me. My capacity, unfortunately, is very limited. Nor do I pretend to have very much to say about modern art. Most of it is alien to me from the human point of view and too disagreeably reminiscent of what I have seen in my medical practice. If I were to write something in the nature of what you have in mind, I would want to come to grips with the subject by way of a critical inquiry. Art is, after all, intimately connected with the spirit of the times, and there is a great deal in just this spirit of the times to which one could take exception. I cannot say that such a task would not attract me, but I am afraid it would go beyond my strength."

[4] These essays, orig. published in 1932, are in CW 15.

fronts me in my patients. These people are either schizo-phrenics or neurotics. Neurotics smart under the problems of our age. They smart under the conditions of its time. Art derives its life from and expresses the conditions of our time. In that sense art is prophetic. It speaks as the plant speaks of nature and of the earth, of ground and background. My patients make similar pictures. When they are in a chaotic state, all forms dissolve. Then panic grips them. Everything threatens to fall to pieces and we are in a state of panic—though it is an unadmitted panic. What does this art say? This art is a flight from the perceptible world, from the visible reality. What does it mean, to turn one's eye inward? The first thing people see there is the debris of destruction, and the infantilism of their own souls. That is why they imitate the tyro. People admire the art of the primitives. True, it is art, but it is primitive. Or one imitates the draw-ings of children. The schizophrenics do that too. To the extent that it is a manifestation of a yearning for the pri-mary it may have a positive value. But dissolution demands synthesis. And I am always concerned with the pile of wreckage, with the ruins of that which has been, with infantile attempts at something new. The fact is we have not yet reached the point when things can be put together. And we cannot reach it yet, because the world is cut in two. The iron curtain ...

A political factor. Has it anything to do with it?

I should think it has! It hangs over our lives like the sword of Damocles. Since 1933 we have witnessed uttermost destruction. First it was the Nazis. On two occasions they almost got here. If they had, I should have been put against the wall. Well, I had settled my accounts with the next world. If the Russians come we shall have the "pile of wreckage," for even if we are the victors, we know very well that we shall do the same thing as they do and with the same methods. In America, when they want to cope with the gangsters, they do it with the help of G-men. That means we become like them. I am pessimistic about the pile of wreckage. A new revelation from within, one that will enable us to see behind the shattered fragments of infantilism, one in which the true image appears, one that is constructive—that is what I am waiting for. We have to visualize this image empirically, as at once an idea and a living form, the ground for which has long been prepared historically. I have always pointed it out. The alchemist called it the Round. It is the idea of completeness. The Chinese call it Tao—the unity of opposites in the whole. Psychologically seen, the process takes place in the center of the personality which is not the "I," but another center, the greater man in us. For this, too, the ground has been prepared psychologically. I see it as form, or, if you like, as an idea. Except that an idea without living form is merely intellectual. My idea which is also form is like a man who has a body. If he has no body, we should not see him. It must be visible form and idea at the same time.

Do you consider science to have had a negative influence on modern man?

Science is only one source of evil. Besides science there are technology, religion, philosophy, art. Modern art preaches the same fatality. The destructive role of the intellect, of rationalism, not only of science, must share the guilt. Everything that should represent the irrational and fails to do so is responsible. "La Déesse raison a ses raisons" [the goddess of Reason has her own reasons]. This doctrine took the stage as a mass movement in the French Revolution, and it is the same revolution which we are still experiencing, because we have raised Reason to a seat above the gods. *(What Jung meant by this, I felt, was not God or gods as objective realities. As a psychologist all he says is that God is an archetype of what is to be found in the soul of man and which may be called the image of God. I misunderstood him intentionally in order to make him express himself more specifically, and suggested that modern man could not reconcile himself to dogmas, and that this was understandable if viewed historically.)*

Dogmas would be all right. They are symbols. One could not do it better. But the theologians rationalize them. We only interpret it psychologically, this drama of the Heavens. Theology is one of the causes of soullessness. Science, because it claims exclusiveness; the priest, when he subordinated himself to the intellect; art, which has all of a sudden lost its belief in beauty and looks only inwardly where there is nothing to be found but ruins, the mirror of our world: they all want to descend into the realm of the mothers without possessing Faust's key. In my own way I try to get hold of a key and to open closed doors with it.

ELIADE'S INTERVIEW
FOR "COMBAT"

✦✦✦✦✦✦✦✦✦✦✦✦✦✦✦✦✦✦✦✦✦✦✦✦✦

Mircea Eliade interviewed Jung at the 1952 Eranos Conference, near Ascona, in August. Jung had given his last Eranos lecture the previous year, after lecturing at nearly every conference beginning with the first, in 1933. Eliade's first Eranos lecture was given in 1950, and he continued as a frequent lecturer through the 1960's. Rumanian by birth, Eliade had studied in Calcutta and Bucharest, and at the beginning of the war he went to western Europe. Since 1958 he has been at the University of Chicago as Sewell L. Avery Distinguished Service Professor of the history of religions.

Eliade's article, "Rencontre avec Jung," was published in *Combat: de la Résistance à la Révolution* (Paris), Oct. 9, 1952. In the present version, Eliade's introductory remarks and interpolations have been much abridged, and some corrections and explanatory notes by Jung, which he sent to Eliade too late for inclusion in *Combat,* have been put in the text. Professor Eliade kindly supplied these additions.

(At seventy-seven years of age, Professor C. G. Jung has lost nothing of his extraordinary vitality, his astonishing youthfulness. He has just published, one after the other, three new books: on the symbolism of Aion [Time], on synchronicity, and "Answer to Job,"[1] which has already given rise to sensational reactions especially among theologians.)

This book has always been on my mind, but I waited forty years to write it. I was terribly shocked when, still a child, I read the Book of Job for the first time. I discovered

---

[1] *Antwort auf Hiob,* published earlier in 1952, provoked much discussion. English tr., 1954; in CW 11 (1958).

that Yahweh is unjust, that he is even an evildoer. For he allows himself to be persuaded by the devil, he agrees to torture Job on the suggestion of Satan. In the omnipotence of Yahweh there is no consideration for human suffering. There are plenty of examples of Yahweh's injustice in certain Jewish writings. But that is not the point; the point is the believer's *reaction* to the injustice. The question is: Is there in the midrashic literature any evidence for the existence of critical reflection or of a reconciliation of this conflict in the Deity? In one late text, Yahweh asks for the blessing of the high priest Ishmael, and Ishmael answers him: "May it be Thy will that Thy mercy may suppress Thy anger, and that Thy compassion may prevail over Thy other attributes. . . ."[2] The Almighty feels that a truly sanctified man is superior to himself.

It may be that all this is a question of language. It may be that what you call the "injustice" and the "cruelty" of Yahweh are only approximate and imperfect formulas for expressing God's total transcendence. Yahweh is "He that is," so he is beyond good and evil. He is impossible to apprehend, to understand, to formulate; consequently he is both merciful and unjust at once. This is a way of saying that no definition can circumscribe God, no attribute exhaust his potentialities.

I speak as a psychologist, and above all I am speaking of the anthropomorphism of Yahweh and not of his theological reality. As a psychologist, I say that Yahweh is contradictory and I also think this contradiction can be interpreted psychologically. In order to test Job's faithfulness, Yahweh allows Satan an almost boundless license. Now this fact is not without consequences for humanity. Very important events impend in the future because of the role that Yahweh felt obliged to assign Satan. Faced with Yahweh's cruelty, Job is silent. This silence is the most beautiful

---

[2] *Zera'im* I, Berakoth 7, in *The Babylonian Talmud* (tr. I. Epstein), p. 30. Cf. *Aion* (orig. 1951), CW 9 ii, par. 110.

and the most noble answer that man can give to an all-powerful God. Job's silence is already an annunciation of Christ. In fact, God made himself man, became Christ, in order to redeem his injustice to Job.

Yahweh did wrong but didn't recognize it. Perhaps Job knows this? At any rate, posterity has realized the agonizing conflict caused by Yahweh's immorality. There is a story of a pious sage who could not bear to read the Eighty-ninth Psalm.[3] Job is certainly conscious of divine injustice and thus is more consciouness than Yahweh. It is the subtle superiority of man's advance in moral consciouness *vis-à-vis* a less conscious God. That is the reason for the Incarnation.

The great problem in psychology is the integration of opposites. One finds this everywhere and at every level. In *Psychology and Alchemy* (CW 12) I had occasion to interest myself in the integration of Satan. For, as long as Satan is not integrated, the world is not healed and man is not saved. But Satan represents evil, and how can evil be integrated? There is only one possibility: to assimilate it, that is to say, raise it to the level of consciousness. This is done by means of a very complicated symbolic process which is more or less identical with the psychological process of individuation. In alchemy this is called the conjunction of the two principles. As a matter of fact, alchemy actually takes up and carries on the work of Christianity. In the alchemical view, Christianity has saved man but not nature. The alchemist's dream was to save the world in its totality: the philosophers' stone was conceived as the *filius macrocosmi*, which saves the world, whereas Christ was the *filius microcosmi*, the savior of man alone.[4] The ultimate aim of the alchemical opus is the *apokatastasis*, cosmic salvation.

For fifteen years I studied alchemy,[5] but I never spoke

[3] Cf. "Answer to Job," CW 11, par. 685.
[4] Cf. "Paracelsus as a Spiritual Phenomenon," CW 13, pars. 162f.
[5] Eliade had also been a student of alchemy prior to this interview. Cf. his *Alchemia asiatica* (Bucharest, 1935).

to anyone about it; I did not wish to influence my patients or my fellow workers by suggestion. But after fifteen years of research and observation, ineluctable conclusions were forced upon me. The alchemical operations were real, only this reality was not physical but psychological. Alchemy represents the projection of a drama both cosmic and spiritual in laboratory terms. The *opus magnum* had two aims: the rescue of the human soul and the salvation of the cosmos. What the alchemists called "matter" was in reality the [unconscious] self. The "soul of the world," the *anima mundi*, which was identified with the *spiritus mercurius*, was imprisoned in matter. It is for this reason that the alchemists believed in the *truth* of "matter," because "matter" was actually their own psychic life. But it was a question of freeing this "matter," of saving it—in a word, of finding the philosophers' stone, the *corpus glorificationis*.

This work is difficult and strewn with obstacles; the alchemical opus is dangerous. Right at the beginning you meet the "dragon," the chthonic spirit, the "devil" or, as the alchemists called it, the "blackness," the *nigredo*, and this encounter produces suffering. "Matter" suffers right up to the final disappearance of the blackness; in psychological terms, the soul finds itself in the throes of melancholy, locked in a struggle with the "shadow." The mystery of the *coniunctio*, the central mystery of alchemy, aims precisely at the synthesis of opposites, the assimilation of the blackness, the integration of the devil. For the "awakened" Christian this is a very serious psychic experience, for it is a confrontation with his own "shadow," with the blackness, the *nigredo*, which remains separate and can never be completely integrated into the human personality.

In interpreting the Christian's confrontation with his shadow in psychological terms, one discovers the hidden fear that the devil may be stronger, that Christ did not completely succeed in conquering him. Otherwise, why did one believe and still believes in the Antichrist? Why did one wait and continue to wait for the coming of Antichrist? Because only after the reign of Antichrist and after the second coming of Christ will evil finally be conquered in the world and in the human soul. On the psychological level, all these symbols and beliefs are interdependent: it is always a question of struggling with evil, with Satan, and conquering it, that is to say assimilating it, integrating it into consciousness. In the language of the alchemists, matter suffers until the *nigredo* disappears, when the "dawn" (*aurora*) will be announced by the "peacock's tail" (*cauda pavonis*) and a new day will break, the *leukosis* or *albedo*. But in this state of "whiteness" one does not *live* in the true sense of the word, it is a sort of abstract, ideal state. In order to make it come alive it must have "blood," it must have what the alchemists call the *rubedo*, the "redness" of life. Only the total experience of being can transform this ideal state of the *albedo* into a fully human mode of existence. Blood alone can reanimate a glorious state of consciousness in which the last trace of blackness is dissolved, in which the devil no longer has an autonomous existence but rejoins the profound unity of the psyche. Then the *opus magnum* is finished: the human soul is completed integrated.

I am and remain a psychologist. I am not interested in anything that transcends the psychological content of human experience. I do not even ask myself whether such transcendence is possible, because in any case the trans-psychological is no longer the concern of the psychologist. But on the psychological level I have to do with religious experiences which have a structure and a symbolism that can be interpreted. For me, religious experience is real, is true. I have found that through such religious experiences the soul may be "saved," its integration hastened, and spiritual equilibrium established. For me, as a psychologist, the state of grace exists: it is the perfect serenity of the soul, a creative equilibrium, the source of spiritual energy. Speaking always as a psychologist, I affirm that the presence of God is manifest, in the profound experience of the psyche, as a *coincidentia oppositorum*, and the whole history of religion, all the theologies, bear witness to the fact that the *coincidentia oppositorum* is one of the commonest and most archaic formulas for expressing the reality of God. Religious experience is *numinous*, as Rudolf Otto calls it, and for me, as a psychologist, this experience differs from all others in the way it transcends the ordinary categories of space, time, and causality. Recently I have put a great deal of study into synchronicity[6] (briefly, the "rupture of time"), and I have established that it closely resembles numinous experiences where space, time, and causality are abolished. I bring no value judgments to bear on religious experience. I affirm that an inner conflict is always the source of profound and dangerous psychological crises, so dangerous that they can destroy a man's integrity. This inner conflict manifests itself psychologically in the same images and the same symbolism testified to by every religion in the world and utilized also by the alchemists.

That is why I became interested in religion, in Yahweh, in Satan, in Christ, in the Virgin. I understand very well that a believer sees something quite different in these images from what I, a psychologist, have the right to see. The faith of a believer is a great spiritual force, it is the guarantee of his psychic integrity. But I am a doctor and am interested in healing my fellow creatures. Faith and faith alone has no longer the power—alas!—to cure certain people. The modern world is desacralized, that is why it is in a crisis. Modern man must rediscover a deeper source of his own spiritual life. To do this, he is obliged to struggle with evil, to confront his shadow, to integrate the devil. There is no other choice. That is why Yahweh, Job, Satan,

---

[6] "Synchronicity: An Acausal Connecting Principle" (orig. 1952); in CW 8.

represent psychologically exemplary situations: they are like paradigms of the eternal human drama.

(Jung discovered the collective unconscious—that is to say, everything that precedes the personal history of the human being—and he applied himself to deciphering its structures and its "dialectic" with a view to facilitating man's reconciliation with the unconscious part of his psychic life and to leading him towards the integration of his personality. Unlike Freud, Jung takes history into account: the archetypes, those structures of the collective unconscious, are loaded with history. It is no longer a question, as with Freud, of a "natural" spontaneity of each individual's unconscious, but of an immense reservoir of historical memories, a collective memory wherein is preserved, in essence, the history of all humanity. Jung believes that man should make greater use of this reservoir; his analytical method is concerned precisely with working out the means of using it.)

The collective unconscious is more dangerous than dynamite, but there are ways of handling it without too many risks. Then, when a psychological crisis launches itself, you are in a better position than any other to solve it. You have dreams and waking dreams: take the trouble to observe them. One could almost say that every dream, in its own manner, carries a message. It not only tells you that something is amiss in the depths of your being, it also brings you a solution for getting out of the crisis. For the collective unconscious which sends you these dreams already possesses the solution: nothing has been lost from the whole immemorial experience of humanity, every imaginable situation and every solution seem to have been foreseen by the collective unconscious. You have only to observe carefully the message sent by the unconscious and then decode it. Analysis helps you to read these messages correctly.

(It was by observing his own dreams—which he tried in vain to interpret in terms of Freudian psychoanalysis—that Jung was led to assume the existence of the collective unconscious. This happened in 1909. Two years later he began to be aware of the importance of his discovery.[7] Finally, in 1914, still on the track of a series of dreams and waking dreams, he came to understand that the manifestations of the collective unconscious are, in part, independent of the laws of time and causality. Since Professor Jung has kindly given me permission to speak of these dreams and waking dreams which have played a capital role in his scientific career, here is a summary[8] of them.)

In October 1913, while travelling by train from Zurich to Schaffhausen, a strange incident befell me. Passing through a tunnel, I lost consciousness of time and place and was awakened an hour later only when the conductor announced the arrival at Schaffhausen. During all this time I was the victim of an hallucination, a waking dream. I was looking at the map of Europe and saw how, country by country, beginning with France and Germany, all Europe became submerged under the sea. Shortly afterwards, the entire continent was under water with the exception of Switzerland: Switzerland was like a high mountain that the waves could not submerge. I saw myself seated on the mountain. But then, on looking more closely

[7] This series of dreams began with the dream of the multistoried house, in 1909, when Jung and Freud analyzed each other's dreams on their trip to America. It is not referred to in *The Freud/Jung Letters* but is recorded and commented on in *Memories, Dreams, Reflections,* pp. 158ff./154f., and is mentioned in "Mind and Earth" (orig. 1927), CW 10, par. 54. It was then followed by the archetypal dreams recorded in *Memories, Dreams, Reflections,* pp. 163ff./158f. and 171ff./166ff., which led up to the "world catastrophe" dreams of 1913 and 1914.

[8] In the French original, the dreams in the following two paragraphs were reported in the third person. They contain some significant details which are not found in the first-person report of the same dreams in *Memories, Dreams, Reflections,* pp. 175f./169f.

around me, I realized that the sea was of blood. Floating on the waves were corpses, roof tops, charred beams.

Three months later, in December 1913, and again in the train which was taking me to Schaffhausen, the same waking dream was repeated, again on entering the tunnel. (I realized later that this was like an immersion in the collective unconscious.) As a psychiatrist I became worried, wondering if I was not on the way to "doing a schizophrenia," as we said in the language of those days. Finally, some months later, I had the following dream: I found myself on the Southern seas near Sumatra, in summer, accompanied by a friend. But we learned from the newspapers that a terrible cold-wave had swept over Europe, such as had never been known to occur before. I decided to go to Batavia and board a ship in order to return to Europe. My friend told me he would take a sailing ship from Sumatra to Hadramaut and from there continue on his way through Arabia and Turkey. I arrived in Switzerland. All around me I saw nothing but snow. Somewhere an enormous vine was growing; it had many bunches of grapes. I approached and began to pick the grapes and distributed them among a throng of people who surrounded me but whom I could not see.

Three times was this dream repeated, and finally I became extremely uneasy. I was just at this time preparing a lecture on schizophrenia to be delivered at a congress in Aberdeen,[9] and I kept saying to myself: "I'll be speaking of myself! Very likely I'll go mad after reading out this paper." The congress was to take place in July 1914—exactly the period when I saw myself in my three dreams voyaging on the Southern seas. On July 31st, immediately after my lecture, I learned from the newspapers that war had broken out. Finally I understood. And when I disembarked in Holland the next day, nobody was happier than

---

[9] Not on schizophrenia, but "On the Importance of the Unconscious in Psychopathology," CW 3.

I. Now I was sure that no schizophrenia was threatening me. I understood that my dreams and my visions came to me from the subsoil of collective unconscious. What remained for me to do now was to deepen and validate this discovery. And this is what I have been trying to do for forty years.

(Jung was glad to receive a second explanation of this dream shortly afterwards. The newspapers were not long in telling of a German naval captain by the name of von Mücke who in a sail-boat had crossed the Southern seas from Sumatra to Hadramaut, taken refuge in Arabia, and proceeded from there to Turkey.[10])

[*Translated by Helen Temple and edited by R. F. C. Hull*]

[10] Notice of Lieut.-Cdr. Helmuth von Mücke's voyage appeared in the *Neue Zürcher Zeitung*, August 4, 1915, and the route corresponds to that given here. Later that year, von Mücke published an account of his adventures in a book entitled *Ayesha* (name of his schooner).

FROM CHARLES BAUDOUIN'S
JOURNAL: 1954

++++++++++++++++++++++

Zurich. Sunday, July 25, 1954[1]
There was a reception at Jung's house this afternoon to
celebrate his seventy-ninth birthday tomorrow. He had
invited about thirty people, who scattered around the
garden in small groups, with the lake shining in the
shadows below. Jung always goes about with a cane now,
but he holds himself very straight and gives an impression
of strength still intact. He sat apart to begin with at a little
table with Rochedieu[2] and me, and showed us how much
he appreciated having disciples in French-speaking lands.
He conversed in this way with the two of us for quite a
while, only rising from time to time to greet a new arrival
with a friendly smile or a familiar pat on the shoulder. His
wit is still lively, his memories rich and precise. When I told
him about my current work on the symbols in St. John of
the Cross he immediately sent his secretary to his library
to find two old books for me, the *Mundus Symbolicus* of
Picinello (Cologne, 1681), an enormous tome which I
discovered suddenly under my arm, and the *De Symbolica
Aegyptiorum sapienta* of Caussinus (Cologne, 1623), in
which the hieroglyphs are explained by a great quantity of
Greek texts. The talk turned upon a Carmelite friar who
had asked Jung if Elijah could be considered an archetype.[3]
This led Jung to go into the history of the Carmelites, and

---

[1] From *L'Oeuvre de Jung* (1963); see above, p. 76. This extract
also appeared, in French, in *Contact with Jung* (1966).

[2] E. Rochedieu, analytical psychologist of Geneva.

[3] Père Bruno de Jésus-Marie, O.C.D. Jung's long letter to him of
Nov. 5, 1943, in CW 18, pars. 1518ff., discusses Elijah as an archetypal figure.

he learned that this Order, which counts on Elijah for support, also claims the Holy Family among its members. Thus the Order had acquired a robe of the Virgin, and anyone who had worn it was delivered from purgatory (since the Virgin who visited purgatory every Saturday knew her own). This brought great riches to the Order but also the hostility of the Jesuits. A lively quarrel went on until it was silenced by one of the Popes. Today the Order is returning to the charge discreetly with the notion of an archetype!

Jung would not be Jung if he did not tell good stories. Here is another: one of his pupils, an extreme rationalist, was unable to conceive of the autonomy of the imagination and could not bring himself to use the method of "active imagination." Jung advised him to pay attention to his hypnagogic images. And he did so. Thus he saw a rock wall on which a goat appeared. Suddenly the animal turned its head, and the subject was seized with panic. Leaping from his bed, he took refuge with his wife, and never again would he listen to a word about active imagination. With one of those thick and pungent condensations for which Jung has a knack, he added, "That was the only pupil of mine who became a Nazi." He left us then to join a larger group at the big table.

.   .   .

[Translated by Jane A. Pratt]

HORNS BLOWING,
BELLS RINGING

++++++++++++++++++++++++++++

An American writer on psychology, Claire Myers Owens, visited Jung on July 24, 1954, and wrote up the experience for a contest feature, "Tourists Abroad," in the Paris edition of the *New York Herald Tribune*. Her article was the winning entry for Aug. 12, 1954.

Nervously, I pulled the bell at the home of the Grand Old Man of Switzerland. It was a large old-fashioned house directly on the beautiful Lake of Zurich, with the snow-topped Alps in the dim distance, and a vegetable garden in front.

As the maid admitted me, I feared that my awe of his world-wide fame would make me tongue-tied. My fears were groundless. A large, tall man with very pink cheeks and an appearance that belied his 80 years entered and greeted me. We sat in his library overlooking the flower garden and the blue lake with its many boats. He was friendly, jovial, startlingly frank.

For an hour and a half, we discussed his analytical psychology, Freud, his early struggles, religion and the role of evil, politics and the psychological origin of the "-isms," the maternal woman and the *grande amoureuse*, his collected works now being published in the United States in 18 volumes, "self-realization," the cause and cure of neuroses, and how to find the meaning of life.

I said I had a chapter on him in the book[1] I was writing—but how could I endure it if the book were not accepted?

---

[1] *Awakening to the Good: Psychological or Religious? An Autobiographical Inquiry* (Boston, 1958), pp. 207–220.

He said, write the truth, and expect to be misunderstood, and take the consequences. That was what he had been doing all his life. People feared truth.

Suddenly, we heard horns blowing, bells ringing. The maid rushed up in great excitement. He said: *"Nein! Nein!"* Then his daughter called up from the garden below. "They" wanted to see him. He murmured: "Nonsense!" She begged him to come out on the balcony.

He stepped out. So did I. A large lake steamer had stopped. Its two or three hundred passengers were waving wildly. Finally, he waved back—once.

It was the International Congress of Psychotherapists,[2] and their ship had stopped in order that they might have a glimpse of the greatest of all psychotherapists—Prof. Carl G. Jung.

[2] The International Congress for Psychotherapy assembled at Zurich from July 20 to 24, 1954, and on the last day, the feature was a cruise by chartered boat along the lake of Zurich. The excursion was the idea of the president of the Congress, Dr. Medard Boss, who also arranged for horns to be sounded at 3:30 p.m., when the boat paused in the lake off Jung's house, at Küsnacht. The Congress honored Jung and two others—the existential analyst Ludwig Binswanger and the psychoanalyst Oskar Pfister—with honorary membership.

THE WORLD OF JAMES JOYCE

The English writer Patricia Hutchins set out to explore James Joyce's background in Ireland and in the Continental cities where he lived. In Zurich, she interviewed Jung at his house in Küsnacht, on a date not readily evident, but probably in late 1954. Miss Hutchins described her encounter with Jung in her book *James Joyce's World* (London, 1957), pp. 181–84. The passage as given here is slightly abridged, to omit a digression on other literary matters.

We could only arrange a meeting in the evening. Thus I went out to the village of Küsnacht and made my way down a long, villa-edged road. Going through white gates, at the end of a short avenue of trees I could see a lit doorway in the dark tower-shape of a house. Soon a girl took me to a small ante-room on the first floor. Indian dolls and toys were in glass presses and among books and papers on the table was a recent issue of *Punch*. Downstairs someone whistled and a deep clock struck six across the atmosphere of quiet and good order there.

As I was ushered into a large library, over parquet and Indian carpets, there was only a standard lamp in a corner by the window so that furniture and pictures were indistinguishable. Dr. Jung rose and shook hands, a bulky figure with a pleasant voice, and I sat down on a comfortable seat opposite him. By some effect of the light behind his chair, or the angle of his glasses which enlarged the pupils, a curious distortion gave his look the full-powered concentration of a child or an animal. It was so distracting that I shifted my position and it became more usual again.

We talked first of all of my study of Joyce's background, and Dr. Jung's brief glimpse of Ireland from a liner stopping at Cobh on the way back from America. I mentioned Joyce's years in Zurich during the First World War and how Mrs. Rockefeller McCormick[1] had helped Joyce financially for a time and then abruptly ceased to do so.

"It has been suggested," I said, "that you were in some way involved, and that perhaps Joyce had offended the lady by refusing to be analyzed?"

"Well, now you tell me the story I may well have been, in an indirect way." Dr. Jung explained that Joyce's name was then unknown to him and he had not met the writer personally until much later, when Joyce, whose daughter was then in a sanatorium, asked for a consultation. Yet he recollected that before 1920 Mrs. McCormick mentioned she was supporting both an author and another artist at that time. She was much troubled by the fact that the latter did not work. Dr. Jung hesitated to tell her to cease these payments, but when the artist himself became his patient and told him of a recurrent dream in which he was bleeding to death, he advised Mrs. McCormick to end an intolerable situation, with most satisfactory results. Although Dr. Jung was not informed, she may well have decided to have done with Joyce and the manuscript of *Ulysses* as well.

"In the thirties I was asked to write an introduction to the German edition of *Ulysses*,"[2] he told me, "but as such it was not a success. Later I published it in one of my books. My interest was not literary but professional. . . . The book was a most valuable document from my point of view; I expressed this, as you know."

"You said that the experiences related were part of 'the

[1] Edith Rockefeller McCormick (1872–1932), daughter of John D. Rockefeller, was a patient of Jung, a Jungian analyst during her long residence in Zurich, and patron of musicians and writers. For a detailed account of her relationship with Joyce, see Richard Ellmann, *James Joyce* (1959), pp. 435, 480–83.

[2] Jung's essay, "'Ulysses': A Monologue" (orig. 1932), is in CW 15, with an appendix by the Editors giving three separate explanations of its genesis.

cold shadow-side of existence"[3]—I do not think that Joyce cared about that."

"The peculiar mixture and the nature of the material as presented is the same as in cases of schizophrenia, but dealt with by an artist. The same things that you find in the madhouse, oh yes, definitely, but with a *plan*. I wrote and apologized to the publisher for not being able to provide what he needed for the edition."

. . .

When Joyce approached the psychologist professionally in 1934,[4] Jung had put the article and his apology for it out of his mind, but Joyce would hardly have done so.

"Certainly he seemed very restrained," Dr. Jung said when I mentioned this. "Yes, now I remember it, during the hour or so while we talked of his daughter, it was impossible not to feel his resistances. The interview was correspondingly uneventful and futile. His daughter, on the contrary, was far more lively. She was very attractive, charming—a good mind. And her writing, what she did for me, had in it the same elements as her father's. She was the same spirit, oh they cared for each other very much. Yet unfortunately it was too late to help her."

The neurotic, like the child, is often very absorbent of the atmosphere created by those around him, especially when it in some way involves himself. A remark disparaging the Doctor—"How could *he* know what is going on in my pretty little head"—purported to have been made by Lucia, suggests that no real rapport was possible between them.

"*Finnegans Wake?*" Dr. Jung replied to my query. "I read parts of it in periodicals but it was like getting lost in a wood. Oh no, I could not manage it. *Ulysses* yes, but still

[3] Ibid., par. 172: "the cold shadow-side of life."
[4] See Ellmann, pp. 688–93, for an account of Jung's psychiatric treatment of Lucia Joyce, based chiefly on an interview he had with Jung in 1953.

I do not understand why so many people read it, so many editions have been published."[5]

"Well, surely they needed certain things to be said. In the twenties people wanted to read in print what they could not express themselves, about life, sex. . . . That generation was freeing itself from so much; we hardly understand its situation now. Then it seems to me that many problems inherent in Joyce's work are also those of the present-day world, in particular the adjustment of personal relations to science, the question of over-population. . . ."

"Yes, yes, that is the *great* problem, all over the world. I have been in India and seen the under-nourished people, the thousands, thousands born there. There is the important question of food, of food production. How are they all to be fed?"

Dr. Jung enlarged on this theme in a flow of sentences, one upon another, and with that quick, unsought illustration which characterizes his prose. As he stood up to go I was aware of his fresh, full face, and that there was a particular attractiveness about the man by his very largeness and health of mind.

"I am glad," he concluded, "that I do not have to face the difficulties of the future. I shall be eighty in July 1955, you know. They are so very great indeed."

"Well, I think you have done your share in helping other people—enough for one lifetime. We'll have to try and find a way out anyway."

"Yes, yes." As I got my coat from the ante-room I knew that by long habit he was watching, assessing me. With more care than usual, as if to make a good impression, I turned off the light and shut the door.

"Is this an old house?" I asked, to fill the gap before saying good-bye.

[5] For Jung's rather complimentary letter to Joyce about *Ulysses*, Sept. 27, 1932, see CW 15, p. 133, and *Letters*, vol. 1.

"No, but built after an ancient style." He smiled. "I am, you know, a conservative."[6]

[6] Patricia Hutchins sent Jung a draft of her account, which he returned, corrected, with a letter on June 29, 1955; see *Letters*, vol. 2. Jung said he could not recall writing to Joyce in 1932, and he added an interesting paragraph on the relationship of Joyce and his daughter as a classic example of the anima theory.

MEN, WOMEN, AND GOD

◆◆◆◆◆◆◆◆◆◆◆◆◆◆◆◆◆◆◆◆◆◆◆◆◆◆◆◆

The popular English journalist Frederick Sands, then foreign correspondent for the London *Daily Mail*, interviewed Jung at Küsnacht and published the results as five successive articles in the *Daily Mail*, April 25–29, 1955. Jung had read and approved the text of the interview. Sands's articles were headed with provocative sentences drawn from Jung's words—"To Call Women the Weaker Sex is Sheer Nonsense," "You Must Quarrel to Be Happy," etc. On September 10, 1961, three months after Jung's death, the material of the first two articles was rearranged and published under the title "The Trouble with Women" in the Sunday magazine sections of several American papers—the Washington *Post*, the New York *Journal*, the *American Weekly*, and others. Sands wrote: "It was the last interview the erect, agile six-footer would ever give—and in many respects his most remarkable. Shortly thereafter . . . he died at 85."

The 1955 text is given here, but the interviewer's remarks are omitted and Jung's are slightly abridged.

A man's foremost interest should be his work. But a woman —man *is* her work and her business. Yes, I know it sounds like a convenient philosophy of the selfish male when I say that. But marriage means a home. And home is like a nest— not enough room for both birds at once. One sits inside, the other perches on the edge and looks about and attends to all outside business.

The vanity of men is in most cases a result of their professional activities. The extent it reaches is sometimes almost grotesque. Most men are afraid of something and are full of prejudices—which are not there in the case of most women. Men are inclined to resent any interference with their way of thinking and their hidebound convictions.

This is especially the case with their manly prestige, which they feel they have to guard even when it is not threatened. They may be afraid that they are ill—or of being told that they are ill; they may have financial or some other suppressed worries. But more often than not they are suffering merely from—fear. Men almost invariably are not honest, either with themselves or with me.

So many women are just crying out for a better understanding with their husbands. Their men are incapable of grasping this—which is not strange since men do not understand women anyway. But women are unable to realize that in business their husbands are not the monarchs of all they survey. As often as not they are underdogs who have to put up with a great deal—a bullying boss, for instance. And the best remedy for that is a woman's understanding. After a day at business in such uncongenial circumstances—having to be pleasant to people he doesn't like—a man comes home in the evening wanting to bang someone over the head. Instead he is expected to continue the torture by being very nice to his wife.

A woman, of course, has also had her day's worries with the children and the household. She would like to talk about them. She is, in fact, just in the mood for a chat. But her husband is tired and taciturn. The average woman cannot visualize a man's problems. His secretary understands her boss better than his wife does.

I have never said so much to anyone in an interview before. Probably I shall find myself in trouble—especially with the women—for some of the things I have said.

Women are much tougher than men underneath. To call women the weaker sex is sheer nonsense. Beware those angel-faced types who always appear weak and helpless and talk in a high-pitched voice. They are the toughest of them all. Be cautious and prepared for anything with quiet women. The old proverb says "Still waters run deep"—and that's particularly so in the case of women. I know it sounds malicious, but quiet women usually have some surprises in store for us once we start delving beneath the surface.

Talkative women should not be taken at their face value. Often their talk is only a blind. Many people talk too much because they do not want to discuss essential things. Women who talk most think least.

Women will call me cynical and dislike me for being so frank. It is women's instinct to capture and hold one man. It is man's instinct to get as many women as possible. Man tries not to be caught, at least for as long as he can readily elude his pursuer. That is the instinct of the fast-running animal: escape by flight.

A woman's best prey is the man that no other woman has been able to catch. To catch a man that any woman could have caught—that makes the prize relatively valueless. But once she gets her man, woman holds him in a strong grip and makes sure that no other women are in the offing. That is natural and necessary, for it is man's nature to alight here and there and then take flight again—if he can.

I have terrible trouble making people see what I mean! Every psychological statement is also true when it is turned round to mean the opposite. That is complicated—but that is nature.

There are, for instance, any number of quite virile men who have a certain idea of the woman they want; they make a beeline for that woman and are never troubled by any other women. Such men generally get a wife they have to watch, for they are not the kind to stay inside the nest. And if they are not careful they may find the female, perched outside, flying off on occasional sorties of her own.

❖

A woman is at her best only when she loves a man. Personal relationship is her basic need, and when that falters she grows dissatisfied and argumentative in a way that often leads to divorce. But this certainly doesn't mean that men and women should remain placid. On the contrary, some tension must prevail in their daily lives, for otherwise there cannot be the ideal relationship in sex—and this is a "must" between husband and wife.

I once had an "ideal-looking couple" who came to consult me. Something had gone wrong. When I looked at them I wondered what could have brought them to me. They appeared perfectly suited to one another in every way and, as I soon discovered, they were blessed with all the material things life could offer. But eventually I found that the real trouble was that they were *too* well suited. This prevented any tension existing in their intimate relations. They coincided so much that nothing happened—a situation as awkward as the opposite extreme of total incompatibility.

Look at it in terms of everyday life. Is a conversation likely to be in any way interesting when you know beforehand that your partner will agree with everything you say? What is the use of discussing a conviction already shared and accepted as a matter of course? The incentive to discussion dies—there is no potential. When you know that your opinion agrees with your partner's, there is no point in mentioning it at all. So what does there remain to talk about?

It is far more interesting and productive to discuss something about which different views are held. I do not particularly enjoy a discussion in which everybody agrees with me—there is no obstacle to overcome, no tension, no productive flow. Difference of opinion can be fruitful; so can quarrels. They are obstacles in the way of getting together, and one has to make an effort to surmount them. Mentally, morally, physically—in all these ways Nature has created an extreme difference between man and woman, so that he finds his opposite in her and she in him. That creates tension.

If man and woman were the same, that would be stalemate. The earth would be sterile. Where the land is flat there is no flow of water; it has nowhere to go; it stagnates. In order to produce energy you must have opposites—an above and a below. There must be a difference in level, and the greater it is the swifter and more forcefully does the water flow.

To me a particularly beautiful woman is a source of terror. A beautiful woman is as a rule a terrible disappointment; you cannot have your cake and eat it.

In men, beauty and brain are seldom found together. The brain of a highly attractive man of handsome physique becomes merely the appendage of his wonderful torso.

At my country retreat I do as I please. I write, I paint— but I spend most of the time just drifting along with my thoughts.

It seems to me we have reached the limit of our evolution —the point from which we can advance no further. Man started from an unconscious state and has ever striven for greater consciousness. The development of consciousness is the burden, the suffering, and the blessing of mankind. Each new discovery leads to greater consciousness, and the path along which we are going is merely an extension of it. This inevitably calls for greater responsibility and enforces a great change in ourselves. We must draw conclusions from what we know and discover, and not take everything for granted.

Man has come to be man's worst enemy. It is a clash between man and God, in which man's Luciferan genius has produced in the H-bomb the power to destroy more effectively than any ancient god could. We must begin to learn about man until every Jekyll can see his Hyde.

The strains and stresses of twentieth-century living have so affected the modern mind that in many countries children are no longer able to concentrate. Here in Zurich the schoolteachers of the upper part of the lake asked me why it is that they are no longer able to carry out the full curriculum. The children, they said, seemed unable to concentrate. I told them that the fault lay with the cinema, the radio, television, the continual swish of motor-cars and the drone of planes overhead. For these are all distractions.

The same distractions affect adults as well. You cannot go into a hotel or a restaurant and carry on an intelligent conversation over a meal or a cup of tea because your words are drowned by music. Some time ago I was in a New York hotel and wanted to have a discussion with an American professor. It was impossible—we gave it up. I have nothing against music at the proper time and place, but these days one can't get away from it. I have just returned from the Ticino, in Italian Switzerland, where they love music. But when they turned on the radio in the restaurant I got so exasperated that I pulled out the plug.

Jazz and all that sort of stuff is silly and stultifying. But it is even worse when they play classics in such a place. Bach, for instance. Bach talks to God. I am gripped by Bach. But I could slay a man who plays Bach in banal surroundings.

Cocktails and all they stand for are just as bad. They simply kill all sensible conversation. Why, most of the people who go in for cocktail drinking are only able to keep up a decent conversation after the third. Worst of all is television.

✧

Without knowing it man is always concerned with God. What some people call instinct or intuition is nothing other than God. God is that voice inside us which tells us what to do and what not to do. In other words, our conscience.

In this dark atomic age of ours, with its lurking fear, man is seeking guidance. Consciously or unconsciously he is once more groping for God. I make my patients understand that all the things which happen to them against their will are a superior force. They can call it God or devil, and that doesn't matter to me, as long as they realize that it is a superior force. God is nothing more than that superior force in our life. You can experience God every day.

There are for instance, the "strange recurrences" that happen in the lives of certain individuals. Many patients come to see me about them. They want, quite naturally, to know why these things recur, whether the cause lies in themselves, and whether there is anything they can do to end it. These recurrences may be so conspicuous that—especially if they are unpleasant—the person concerned may begin to feel himself the victim of some sinister form of persecution. We must make a clear difference between this and the persecution mania of an unhinged mind. The recurrences are often quite genuine and not merely imagined.

Once I was walking in the garden of my house with a lady who had consulted me. She had told me, among other things, that whenever she was in the country she was attacked by birds—black birds. Hardly had we got away from the house than several crows approached and swooped down on us, fluttering about and cawing angrily. They left me alone, but kept on flying at my patient. One of them even nipped her on the back of the neck before I drove them off.

Another strange case: I treated three daughters and their mother. The three young women kept on having terrible dreams about the elder lady, who was a model mother. They dreamt of her as a wild animal. Years later she became prone to fits of melancholia in which she acted like a wild beast.[1]

The fact is that what happens to a person is characteristic

[1] Cf. *The Development of Personality*, CW 17, par. 107.

of him. He represents a pattern and all the pieces fit. One by one, as his life proceeds, they fall into place according to some predestined design.

All that I have learned has led me step by step to an unshakable conviction of the existence of God. I only believe in what I know. And that eliminates believing. Therefore I do not take His existence on belief—I *know* that He exists.

THE STEPHEN BLACK
INTERVIEWS

++++++++++++++++++++++++++++

Stephen Black interviewed Jung in July 1955, in order to record material for broadcast in connection with Jung's 80th birthday, 26 July. Besides a radio interview (no. 3, below), Black conducted an interview for the BBC television feature "Panorama," of which a segment of about six minutes (no. 2, below) was broadcast. The conversation took place on the terrace of Jung's house at Küsnacht; the sounds of a motorboat on the lake and music at the beach resort next door are sometimes audible. Emma Jung sat beside her husband—one sees her in the film—but did not take part in the interview.

Subsequently, Stephen Black left broadcasting, became a physician, and emigrated to New Zealand.

1

Professor Jung, could you tell me how it came about that psychological medicine came to be divided so sharply in the first half of this century into Freudian and Adlerian and Jungian philosophies?

Well, that is so. Always in the beginning of a new science, or when a new problem is tackled in science, there are necessarily many different aspects, particularly in a science like psychology, and particularly so when an absolutely new factor has been brought into the discussion.

Which was that?

In this case, it was the unconscious—the concept of the unconscious. It has been a philosophical concept before—in the philosophy of Carl Gustav Carus and then his follower

252

Eduard von Hartmann. But it was a mere speculative concept. The unconscious was a kind of philosophical concept at first, but through the discoveries by Freud it became a practical medical concept, because he discovered these mechanisms or connections. . . . He made of it a medical science. This is empirical.

An empirical medical science.

That was an entirely new proposition. And naturally quite a number of opinions are possible in the beginning, where one is insufficiently acquainted with the phenomena. It needed many experiments and experiences until one could establish a general terminology, for instance, or even a doctrine. Now, I never got as far as to produce a general doctrine, because I always felt we don't know enough. But Freud started the theory very early and so did Adler, because that can be explained by the human need for certainty. You feel completely lost in such an enormous field as psychology represents. And there you must have something to cling to, some guidance as it were, and that is probably the reason why this kind of psychology set out with almost ready-made theories. At least, the theories were conceived in a moment when one didn't know enough about the role of the psychology of the unconscious. That is my private view, and so I've refrained from forming theories.

When you first met Freud—when was that, 1906?

That was 1907.

Will you describe that meeting to me?

Oh, well, I just made a visit to him in Vienna and then we talked for thirteen hours without interruption.

Thirteen hours without interruption?

Thirteen hours without interruption! We didn't realize that we were almost dead at the end of it, but it was tremendously interesting.

Did you argue?

Yes, I did, to a certain extent. Of course, seeing him for the first time I had to get my bearings first. I had naturally also to listen to what he had to say. And I was then a very young man still, and he was the old man and had great experience and he was of course way ahead of me and so I settled down to learn something first.

And then in 1912 you published "The Psychology of the Unconscious."

Well, by 1912 I had acquired a lot of my own experience and I had learned a great deal from Freud and then I saw certain things in a different light.

So you dissociated yourself from Freud.

Yes, because I couldn't share his opinions of his convictions anymore with reference to certain things. I mean in certain points I have no argument against him, but in other respects I disagree with him.

What was it you disagreed most over at that time?

Well, that was chiefly the interpretation of psychological facts. You know, he was on the standpoint of scientific materialism, which I consider as a prejudice, a sort of metaphysical presupposition, which I exclude.

What in your view will be the final outcome of this kind of scientific quarrel between the various schools of medical psychology?

For the time being it is certainly a sort of quarrel, but in the course of time it will be as it always has been in the history of science. You will see that certain points will be taken from Freud's ideas, others from Adler's ideas, and something of my ideas. There is no question of victory of one idea, of one way of looking at things. Such victories are only obtained where it is a matter of pretension, of convictions, for instance, philosophical or religious convictions. In science there is nothing of the kind, there is merely the truth as one can see it.

Thank you. Professor Jung, there's a body of opinion in the world today that all is not well with the technique of psychoanalysis, that it takes too long, it uses up too many medical man-hours, it costs too much money. Have you felt that about your technique of analytical psychology?

That is perfectly true. It takes time, it costs money, it takes the right people and there are too few. But that is foreseen. That is in the nature of the thing. Man's soul is a complicated thing and it takes sometimes half a lifetime to get somewhere in one's psychological development. You know it is by no means always a matter of psychotherapy or treatment of neuroses. Psychology has also the aspect of a pedagogical method in the widest sense of the word. It is something—

A system of education.

It is an education. It is something like antique philosophy. And not what we understand by a technique. It is something that touches upon the whole of man and which challenges also the whole of man—in the patient or whatever the receiving party is as well as in the doctor.

2

But it's a therapeutic process also.

Yes, you know, this procedure has many stages or levels. If you take an ordinary case of neurosis, it may only go as far as healing the symptoms or giving the patient such an attitude that he can deal with his neurosis. Sometimes it takes him a week, sometimes a few days, sometimes it is just one consultation in which I clean up a case. It is of course a question of knowing where, or what—it needs a good deal of experience. But other cases take very long, and you couldn't send them away because they wouldn't go.

They want to know more, to make the whole process of development, which goes from stage to stage, a widening out of the mental horizon. You cannot imagine how one-sided people are nowadays. And so it needs no end of work to get people rounded out, or mentally more developed, more conscious. And they are so keen on it that for nothing in the world would they quit. And they are not shy of spending money on it.

Professor Jung, how does this compare with religion, with religious practice?

I rather would prefer to say, how does it compare with antique philosophy. You see, our religions are known as confessions. One confesses a certain creed. Now, of course, this has nothing to do with a creed. It has only to do with the natural individuation process, namely, the process that sets in with birth, as it were. As each plant, each tree grows from a seed and becomes in the end, say, an oak tree, so man becomes what he is meant to be. At least, he ought to get there. But most get stuck by unfavorable external conditions, by all sorts of hindrances or pathological distortions, wrong education—no end of reasons why one shouldn't get there where one belongs.

Do more people get stuck today than fifty years ago when you started?

There are no statistics, and I wouldn't have an opinion about it. But I only know that there is an uncanny amount of people that get stuck unnecessarily. They could get much further if they had heard the proper things or if they had spent the necessary time on themselves. But this is not popular, you know, to spend time on oneself, because our point of view is entirely extraverted.

One last question. You have defined these personality types of extravert and introvert. Which are you?

Oh well. [Laughs.] Everybody would call me an introvert.

You're an introvert. And what was Freud?

Now, that is a very difficult question. You know, Freud is—and he doesn't conceal it—he's a neurotic type. And there it is very difficult to make out what the real type is. For a long time you have to observe which mental contents are conscious and which are unconscious. And then only you can say this must be the original type. I will say Freud's point of view is an extraverted point of view. But as to his personal type I wouldn't speculate.

And Adler?

He is equally introverted.

He extended your definition of the complex to the inferiority complex. What are your views on this all important inferiority complex?

Well, that is a thing that surely plays a very great role, almost just as great as the sex complex. You see, the sex complex belongs to a hedonistic type of man who thinks in terms of his pleasure and displeasure, while there is another class of man, chiefly the man who has not arrived, who thinks in terms of power and defeat, and to him it is far more important to win out somewhere than his whole sex problem.

What should we think in terms of, in your view?

Obviously, life has the two aspects, namely, self preservation and the preservation of species. There you have the two things. Nobody in his senses dismisses the one or the other thing. We always have both aspects, because we are meant to be balanced.

3

During his visit to Küsnacht, Stephen Black also conducted an interview for BBC radio. According to the BBC transcript, it was recorded on July 29, 1955, and broadcast as part of a series, "Personal Call," on October 3. The text was printed as an appendix to E. A. Bennet's book *C. G. Jung* (London, 1961), and Dr. Bennet dated it July 24. He had been given the copyright in the transcript by the BBC and kindly permitted its publication here.

"Vocatus atque non vocatus deus aderit" is a Latin translation of the Greek oracle, and, translated into English, it might read, "Invoked or not invoked the god will be present," and in many ways this expresses the philosophy of Carl Jung. I am sitting now in a room in his house at Küsnacht, near Zurich, in Switzerland. And as I came in through the front door, I read this Latin translation of the Greek, carved in stone over the door. For this house was built by Professor Jung. How many years ago, Professor Jung?

Oh, almost fifty years ago.

Why did you choose to put this over your front door?

Because I wanted to express the fact that I always feel unsafe, as if I'm in the presence of superior possibilities.

Professor Jung is sitting opposite to me now. He is a large man, a tall man, and this summer reached his eightieth birthday. He has white hair, a very powerful face, with a small white mustache and deep brown eyes. He reminds me, with all respect, Professor Jung, of a typical peasant of Switzerland. What do you feel about that, Professor Jung?

Well, I think you are not just beside the mark. That is what I often have been called.

And yet Professor Jung is a man whose reputation far transcends the frontiers of this little country. It's a reputation which isn't only European; it is world-wide and has made itself felt considerably in the Far East. Professor Jung, how did you, as a doctor, become interested in psychological medicine?

Well, when I was a student of medicine I already then became interested in the psychological aspect—chiefly of mental diseases. I studied, besides my medical work, also philosophy—chiefly Kant, Schopenhauer and others. I found it very difficult in those days of scientific materialism to find a middle line between natural science or medicine and my philosophical interests. And in the last of my medical studies, just before my final exam, I discovered the short introduction that Krafft-Ebing had written to his textbook of psychiatry, and suddenly I understood the connection between psychology or philosophy and medical science.

This was due to Krafft-Ebing's introduction to his textbook?

Yes; and it caused me tremendous emotion then. I was quite overwhelmed by a sudden sort of intuitive understanding. I wouldn't have been able to formulate it clearly then, but I felt I had touched a focus. And then on the spot I made up my mind to become a psychiatrist, because there was a chance to unite my philosophical interests with natural science and medical science; that was my chief interest from then on.

Would you say that your sudden intuitive interest in something like that, your intuitive understanding, had to some extent been explained by your work during all the years since?

Oh, yes; absolutely. But, as you know, such an intuitive moment contains the whole thing *in nucleo*. It is not clearly formulated; it's an indescribable totality; but this moment had been the real origin of my career as a medical psychological scientist.

So it was in fact Krafft-Ebing and not Freud that started you off.

Oh, yes, I became acquainted with Freud much later on.

And when did you meet Freud?

That was only in 1907. I had some correspondence with

him before that date, but I met him only in 1907 after I had written my book on *The Psychology of Dementia Praecox*.[1]

That was your first book?

That wasn't really my first book. The book on dementia praecox came after my doctor's thesis in 1904.[2] And then my subsequent studies on the association experiment[3] paved the way to Freud, because I saw that the behavior of the complex provided the experimental basis for Freud's ideas on repression. And that was the reason and the possibility of our relationship.

Would you like to describe to me that meeting?

Well, I went to Vienna and paid a visit to him, and our first meeting lasted thirteen hours.

Thirteen hours?

For thirteen uninterrupted hours we talked and talked and talked. It was a *tour d'horizon*, in which I tried to make out Freud's peculiar mentality. He was a pretty strange phenomenon to me then, as he was to everybody in those days, and then I saw very clearly what his point of view was, and I also caught some glimpses already where I wouldn't join in.

In what way was Freud a peculiar personality?

Well, that's difficult to say, you know. He was a very impressive man and obviously a genius. Yet you must know the peculiar atmosphere of Vienna in those days: it was the last days of the old Empire, and Vienna was always spiritually and in every way a place of a very specific character. And particularly the Jewish intelligentsia was an impressive and peculiar phenomenon—particularly to us Swiss, you

[1] In CW 3.
[2] "On the Psychology and Pathology of So-called Occult Phenomena," CW 1.
[3] In CW 2.

know. We were, of course, very different and it took me quite a while until I got it.

Would you say, then, that the ideas and the philosophy which you have expressed have in their root something peculiarly Swiss?

Presumably. You know, our political neutrality has much to do with it. We were always surrounded by the great powers—those four powers, Germany, Austria, Italy, and France—and we had to defend our independence, so the Swiss is characterized by that peculiar spirit of independence, and he always reserves his judgment. He doesn't easily imitate, and so he doesn't take things for granted.

You are a man, Professor Jung, who reserves his judgment?

Always.

In 1912 you wrote a book called Psychology of the Unconscious,[4] *and it was at that time that you, as it were, dissociated yourself from Freud?*

Well, that came about quite automatically because I developed certain ideas in that book which I knew Freud couldn't approve. Knowing his scientific materialism I knew that this was the sort of philosophy I couldn't subscribe to.

Yours was the introvert, to use your own terminology?

No. Mine was merely the empirical point of view. I didn't pretend to know anything, I wanted just to make the experience of the world to see what things are.

Would you accuse Freud of having become involved in the mysticism of terms?

No; I wouldn't accuse him; it was just a style of the time. Thought, in a way, about psychological things was just, as it seems to me, impossible—too simple. In those days one

---

[4] The translation of *Wandlungen und Symbole der Libido* (1912); revised 1952 as *Symbole der Wandlungen = Symbols of Transformation*, CW 5.

talked of psychiatric illness as a sort of by-product of the brain. Joking with my pupils, I told them of an old text-book for the Medical Corps in the Swiss Army which gave a description of the brain, saying it looked like a dish of macaroni, and the steam from the macaroni was the psyche. That is the old view, and it is far too simple. So I said: "Psychology is the science of psychic phenomena." We can observe whether these phenomena are produced by the brain, or whether they are there in their own right—they are just what they are. I have no theory about the origin of the psyche. I take phenomena as they are and I try to describe them and to classify them, and my terminology is an empirical terminology, like the terminology in botany or zoology.

You've travelled a great deal?

Yes; a lot. I have been with Navaho Indians in North America, and in North Africa, in East and Central Africa, the Sudan and Egypt, and in India.

Do you feel that the thought of the East is in any way more advanced than the thought in the West?

Well, you see, the thought of the East cannot be compared with the thought in the West; it is incommensurable. It is something else.

In what way does it differ, then?

Well, they are far more influenced by the basic facts about psychology than we are.

That sounds more like your philosophy.

Oh, yes; quite. That is my particular understanding of the East, and the East can appreciate my ideas better, because they are better prepared to see the truth of the psyche. Some think there is nothing in the mind when the child is born, but I say everything is in the mind when the child is born, only it isn't conscious yet. It is there as a potentiality. Now, the East is chiefly based upon that potentiality.

Does this contribute to the happiness of people one way or the other? Are people happier in themselves in the East?

I don't think that they are happier than we are. You see, they have no end of problems, of diseases and conflicts; that is the human lot.

Is their unhappiness based upon their psychological difficulties, like ours, or it is more based upon their physical environment, their economics?

Well, you see, there is no difference between, say, unfavorable social conditions and unfavorable psychological conditions. We may be, in the West, in very favorable social conditions, and we are as miserable as possible—inside. We have the trouble from the inside. They have it perhaps more from the outside.

And have you any views on the reason for this misery we suffer here?

Oh, yes; there are plenty of reasons. Wrong values—we believe in things which are not really worthwhile. For instance, when a man has only one automobile and his neighbor has two, then that is a very sad fact and he is apt to get neurotic about it.

In what other ways are our values at fault?

Well, all ambitions and all sorts of things—illusions, you know, of any description. It is impossible to name all those things.

What is your view, Professor Jung, on the place of women in society in the Western world?

In what way? The question is a bit vague.

You said just now, Professor Jung, that some of our difficulties arose out of wrong values, and I'm trying to find out whether you feel those wrong values arise in men as a result of the demands of women.

Sometimes, of course, they do, but very often it is the

female in a man that is misleading him. The anima in man, his feminine side, of which he is truly unaware, is causing his moods, his resentments, his prejudices.

So that the woman who wants two cars because a neighbor has two cars, is only stimulating . . . ?

No, perhaps she simply voices what he has felt for a long time. He wouldn't dare to express it, but she voices it—she is, perhaps, naïve enough to say so.

And what does the man express of the woman's animus?

Well, he is definitely against it, because the animus always gets his goat, it calls forth his anima affects and anima moods; they get on each other's nerves. Listen to a conversation between a man and wife when there is a certain amount of emotion about them. You hear all the wonderful arguments of an anima in the man; he talks then like a woman, and she talks like a man, with very definite opinions and knows all about it.

Do you feel that there's any hope of adjusting this between a man and a woman, if they understand it in your terms?

Well, you see, that is one of the main reasons why I have developed a certain psychology of relationship—for instance, the relationship in marriage, and how a man and his wife should understand each other or how they misunderstand each other practically. That's a whole chapter of psychology and not an unimportant one.

Which is the basic behavior? The Eastern?

Neither. The East is just as one-sided in its way as the West is in its way. I wouldn't say that the position of the woman in the East is more natural or better than with us. Civilizations have developed styles. For instance, a Frenchman or an Italian or an Englishman show very different and very characteristic ways in dealing with their respective wives. I suppose you have seen English marriages, and you know how an English gentleman would deal with his wife in the event of trouble, for instance; and if you compare this with an Italian, you will see all the difference in the world. You know, Italy cultivates its emotions. Italians like emotions and they dramatize their emotions. Not so the English.

And in India or Malaya?

In India, presumably the same; I had no chance to assist in a domestic problem in India, happily enough. It was a holiday from Europe, where I had had almost too much to do with domestic problems of my patients—that sort of thing was my daily bread.

Would you say, then, as a scientific observation that there is, in fact, less domestic trouble in the East than in the West?

I couldn't say that. There is another kind of domestic problem, you know. They live in crowds together in one house, twenty-five people in one little house, and the grandmother on top of the show, which is a terrific problem. Happily enough, we have no such things over here.

At the end of his life, Freud, one feels, had some dissatisfaction with the nature of psychoanalysis, the length of time involved in the treatment of mental illness and so on. Have you, now you're eighty years old, felt any dissatisfaction with your work?

No; I couldn't say so. I know I'm not dissatisfied at all, but I have no illusions about the difficulty of human nature. You see, Freud was always a bit impatient; he always hoped to find some short-cut. And I knew that is just the thing we would not find, because anything that is good is expensive. It takes time, it requires your patience and no end of it. I can't say I am dissatisfied. And so I always thought anything, if it is something good, will take time, will demand all your patience, it will be expensive. You can't get around it.

How did you meet your wife? Is she connected with your work?

Well, I met her when she was quite a young girl, about fifteen or sixteen, and I just happened to see her, and I said to a friend of mine—I was twenty-one then—I said, "That girl is my wife."

Before you'd spoken to her?

Yes. "That's my wife." I knew it. I saw her on top of a staircase, and I knew: "That is my wife."

How many children have you got?

Five children, nineteen grandchildren, and two great-grandchildren.

Has any of this large family followed in your footsteps?

Well, my son is an architect and an uncle of mine was an architect. None has studied medicine—all my daughters married—but they are very interested and they "got it" at home, you see, through the atmosphere. One nephew is a doctor.

Were you interested in architecture at all?

Oh, yes; very much so. I have built with my own hands; I learned the work of a mason. I went to a quarry to learn how to split stones—big rocks.

And actually laying bricks, laying the stones?

Oh, well, in Europe we work with stone. I did actually lay stones and built part of my house up in Bollingen.

Why did you do that?

I wanted to handle and get the feeling of the stone and to touch the earth—I worked a lot in the garden, I have chopped wood, felled trees, and all that. I liked sailing and rowing and mountain climbing when I was young.

Could you explain what you think are the origins of this desire to touch the earth? We in England have it very much; every Englishman has his little garden. We all love the earth.

Of course. Well, you know, that is—how can we explain it?—you love the earth and the earth loves you. And therefore the earth brings forth. That is so even with the peasant who wants to make his field fertile, and in the night of the full moon he sleeps with his wife in the furrow.

Professor Jung, what do you think will be the effect upon the world of living, as we have been living, and may still have to live, under the threat of the hydrogen bomb?

Well, that's a very great problem. I think the West is more affected by it than the East, because the East has a very different attitude to death and destruction. Think, for instance, of the fact that practically the whole of India believes in reincarnation, so when you lose this life you have plenty of others. It doesn't matter so much. Moreover, this world is illusion anyhow, and if you can get rid of it, it isn't so bad. And if you hope for a further life, well, you have untold possibilities ahead of you. Since in the West there is one life only, therefore I can imagine that the West is more disturbed by the possibility of utter destruction than the East. We have only one life to lose and we are by no means assured of a number of other lives to follow. The greater part of the European population doesn't even believe in immortality anymore and so, once destroyed, forever destroyed. That explains a great deal of the reaction in the West. We are more vulnerable because of our lack of knowledge and contact with the deepest strata of the psyche. But the East is better defended in that way, because it is based upon the fundamental facts of the human soul and believes more in it and in its possibilities than the West. And that is a point of uncertainty in the West. It is a very critical point.

AN EIGHTIETH BIRTHDAY
INTERVIEW

++++++++++++++++++++++++++++

Michael Schabad interviewed Jung at his house in Küsnacht on a rainy Friday, July 22, 1955. His article was published on July 26 in the *National-Zeitung* (Basel). This translation is somewhat condensed. (Who was Herr Schabad? The editors of *National-Zeitung* cannot recall.)

Jung welcomes me with perfect courtesy and great charm. His tall, erect figure is by no means that of a patriarch. His face is ruddy, the white hair is clipped short and displays a broad forehead, brown eyes, and a Dinaric nose. The voice is resonant, his manner of speech lively, and the gestures expressive. He bubbles with ideas, memories, and quotations, and gives a much younger impression than his photographs.

I began with his relationship with Sigmund Freud during the last years in the life of the brilliant father of psycho-analysis. My question was a very concrete one: "Professor, did you congratulate Freud on the occasion of his eightieth birthday?"

The answer was no, and Jung explained it at length. Some time around 1933, he had sent a patient to Freud in Vienna with a detailed medical report and a friendly letter.[1] Freud did not respond. Since then they had never had any contact.

"I always recognized Freud's greatness and genius, but he was extremely headstrong. He came out of nowhere and

---

[1] Actually 1923. See *The Freud/Jung Letters,* final letter.

the world was hostile toward him. He *had* to be obstinate to gain acceptance. Had he not been obstinate, his theory would have remained unknown. He had to tell himself: 'Je m'établirai comme un rocher de bronze.' Once he said to me: we have to turn the theory of the unconscious into a dogma, to make it immovable. Why a dogma, I replied, since sooner or later truth will have to win out? Freud explained: We need a dam against the black tide of mud of occultism."[2]

C. G. Jung laughed and his eyes sparkled. He quickly went on: "Even at the beginning of my work on the association test, i.e., after 1904, I realized that complexes are not always the result of repressions. Complexes are autonomous and follow laws of their own. There are complexes which have never been conscious and therefore cannot have been repressed. For Freud the unconscious was mainly repressed material, a garbage dump for disagreeable experiences. But the unconscious is more than that."

I referred to another Freudian concept of the unconscious and quoted Freud from memory: "Everything in the psyche was unconscious to begin with: the quality of consciousness may or may not develop subsequently." Jung admitted this, but insisted that when Freud developed his theory he focused mainly on repression. I suggested that this had probably been necessary for practical reasons since, according to Freud, it was repression that was pathogenic.

I turned our discussion to Alfred Adler. To underscore Freud's great superiority to Adler, Jung made a sweeping gesture: "Adler had only *one* idea. It was a good idea, but he did not get beyond schoolmaster psychology."

(Adler's one correct idea was, of course, the one concerned with inferiority feelings and their compensation.)

I turned to certain modern schools of psychotherapy that

[2] See *Memories, Dreams, Reflections,* p. 150/147f.

question the existence of the Jungian archetypes, and mentioned the names of a number of living authors. Jung described these criticisms as pure verbalism. "It is as if I had a collection of minerals, with different rocks in many drawers. For the purpose of orientation I label the drawers with descriptions of the rocks. These critics are not in the least concerned with the rocks but only the labels. Talk of existence is not the same as existence proper. Words and names are not objects. I am an empiricist and I am concerned with facts. The thinking of these critics is two-dimensional, and they have no respect for psychological facts."

With the catch-phrase "psychological facts" Jung gets into his element. He relates at great length and vividly what he observed on his visits to the Pueblo Indians in New Mexico, the Africans in Kenya; he speaks of emotional knowledge, the reality of the image, of certain Buddhist forms of perception that are not rational or tied to language. Undoubtedly Jung himself is deeply convinced of the reality of the psyche, i.e., that it works. "You see," he said, "I have my life story, and you have yours. I know that I am sitting here and that I am talking to you, and you know the same thing as far as you are concerned. We are exchanging words. But aside from words, which address themselves to the intellect, there is so much more in the air between us: feelings, images, part-souls, or segments of the psyche. The people who rely on natural science and the so-called realistic view of the world, based on it, are unaware of the abstracting and isolating nature of science. True reality can only be approached and surmised spiritually."

"You must be thinking of Goethe's *Farbenlehre* and his *Urpflanze*,"[3] I interject.

"You are quite right, And I try to confirm Goethe's intuitions on the basis of experience."

[3] Works on the theory of colors (1810) and the metamorphosis of plants (1790).

I venture to question him about the parentage of his grandfather, Carl Gustav Jung, after whom he was named.

"There is circumstantial evidence that my grandfather was one of Goethe's sons," says Jung. "However, my grandsons don't know about it. I haven't made it a family tradition. My grandfather's mother played an important role in the theater world of Mannheim."[4]

Three times I make a move to get up and leave, as I do not wish to tire Jung, but he is in excellent spirits and does not want to let me go. "I have time for you, go on, just ask questions!"

I voice my amazement about his universal erudition. "Your productivity is unbelievable," I observe. Jung smiles. "Some people believe that others write my books for me. But as regards universality, it isn't as bad as all that: for example, I had to give up studying ancient Egyptian hieroglyphs and Arabic."

The subject of conversation turns to the English edition of his Collected Works and his correspondence with Freud, which has not yet been published, Jung says: "The Anglo-Saxons understand me better than the French. The French are either Cartesians, or Catholics." At the same time, however, he has much praise for the psychological wisdom of the Catholic Church and makes a number of interesting comments on the recently proclaimed dogma of the Assumption. "It is because the Jews and the Protestants—those mitigated Jews—have no pictures of God, because they are not allowed to represent the archetypes, that they top the statistics for neurosis."

Taking up a reference I made to the affinity between his theories and those of William James, Jung confirms my remark, saying that he had known James personally. "But do you know who anticipated my entire psychology in the

---

[4] For the legend of Jung's descent from Goethe, see *Memories, Dreams, Reflections*, ch. II, n. 1.

eighteenth century? The Hasidic Rabbi Baer from Meseritz, whom they called the Great Maggid.[5] He was a most impressive man."

In conclusion I ask for another interview in ten years time. Jung laughs: "In ten years you can shake hands with my shadow in Hades."

[*Translated by Ruth Horine*]

[5] Rabbi Dow Baer, or Beer, successor to the Baal Shem, lived from 1710 to 1772—M. S. (Cf. G. Scholem, *Major Trends in Jewish Mysticism*, 3rd edn., 1954, pp. 334ff.)

THE THERAPY OF MUSIC

++++++++++++++++++++++++++++

Margaret Tilly, a concert pianist of San Francisco, English by origin, became interested in experimentation with the therapeutic value of music when used specifically in certain cases. This interest grew out of her own experience with Jungian analysis, and Miss Tilly was urged by analysts to acquaint Jung with her work. In 1956, while in Geneva to give a concert on radio, she decided to send Jung some papers that she had written. A reply came by return mail, from Jung's secretary, asking her to come to Küsnacht two days later.

Miss Tilly (1900–1969), later the chief music therapist at the Langley-Porter Clinic in San Francisco, wrote up her encounter with Jung for a memorial booklet prepared by the Analytical Psychology Club of San Francisco in 1961. It is slightly abridged for the present version.

References to music are relatively few in Jung's writings—fewer than twenty citations in the general index to the Collected Works. One of Jung's rare comments is found in a letter to Serge Moreux, Jan. 20, 1950, in *Letters*, vol. 1.

When I walked into his hall, Dr. Jung came with hands outstretched to welcome me, and I felt that here was one of the warmest and friendliest persons I had ever been with —so easy to talk to that one did not feel overawed.

We sat at a round table in the window of his study. My papers were lying in front of him and he seemed to be literally bursting with interest and curiosity. He said, "I have read and heard a great deal about music therapy, and it always seemed to me so sentimental and superficial that I was not interested. But these papers of yours are entirely different, and I simply cannot wait to hear what you do. I can't imagine what it is. You must please use your language, not mine." I didn't immediately understand what he meant by the last sentence, but said, "Before I talk, Dr. Jung, may I ask what your own relationship to music has been?" And his reply was a surprise. "My mother was a fine singer, so was her sister, and my daughter is a fine pianist. I know the whole literature—I have heard everything and all the great performers, but I never listen to music any more. It exhausts and irritates me." When I asked why, he replied, "Because music is dealing with such deep archetypal material, and those who play don't realize this." And then I understood at last why the idea has grown up that Jung is not particularly sympathetic to music. He cares too much, not too little.

At this point he said, "With your permission I have asked Miss Bailey and my daughter to join us this afternoon, as they will be so interested in what you are going to tell us. Now let us have a cup of tea together." And we proceeded into his large, dark, cozy living room, where he introduced me to his daughter and Miss Bailey,[1] who were sitting in front of a fire. On the far side of the room was a Bechstein grand with its top raised. We had a gay and delightful time around the fire, Dr. Jung full of fun and charm, and as I swallowed my last drop of tea, he said, "I can't wait another minute—let's begin, but you use your language." I said, "Do you mean you want me to play?" and he said, "Yes. I want you to treat me exactly as though I were one of your patients. Now—what do you think I need?" We both roared with laughter and I said, "You really *are* standing me up, aren't you?" He said, "Yes, I am. Now, let's go to the piano. I am very slightly deaf, so may I sit close?" And with that he sat down just behind me, so that I had to turn round a little to see him.

I began to play. When I turned round, he was obviously

---

[1] Jung's third daughter, Marianne Niehus-Jung (1910–1965), and Ruth Bailey, who kept house and cared for Jung after the death of his wife in 1955. Cf. below, p. 365.

very moved, and said, "Go on—go on." And I played again. This second time he was far more deeply moved, saying, "I don't know *what* is happening to me—what are you doing?" And we started to talk. He fired question after question at me. "In such and such a case what would you try to accomplish—where would you expect to get—what would you do? Don't just tell me, *show* me—*show* me"; and gradually as we worked he said, "I begin to see what you are doing—show me more." I told him many case histories, and we worked on for over two hours. He was very excited and as easy and naïve as a child to work with. Finally he burst out with "This opens up whole new avenues of research I'd never even dreamed of. Because of what you've shown me this afternoon—not just what you've said, but what I have actually felt and experienced—I feel that from now on music should be an essential part of every analysis. This reaches the deep archetypal material that we can only sometimes reach in our analytical work with patients. This is most remarkable."

At this point some evil genie made me look at my watch, and I said, "Dr. Jung, I have to go, or I miss my train back to Paris." "Oh, you mustn't go," he said. "Can't you stay a few days and be with us? Can't you come back?" I most reluctantly took my leave. His daughter drove me to the train and I sat in a daze all the way to Paris.[2]

[2] Alan Watts, in his autobiography *In My Own Way* (New York, 1972), p. 394, refers briefly to Margaret Tilly's meeting with Jung and adds: "Shortly afterwards, Jung's daughter said to Margaret, 'Perhaps you don't realize that you did something very important for me and my father. I have always loved music, but he has never understood it, and this was a barrier between us. Your coming has changed all that, and I don't know how to thank you.' "

THE HOUSTON FILMS

Richard I. Evans, professor of psychology at the University of Houston (Texas), conducted four interviews with Jung at the Eidgenössische Technische Hochschule (Federal Institute of Technology), in Zurich, on August 5–8, 1957. They were filmed by John Meaney, director of the Radio-TV-Film Center at the same university, as part of an educational project designed for students of the psychology department. The films, four hours in duration, have been shown at Houston and other American colleges and to other audiences. Later, the analytical psychologist Joseph Henderson, M.D., at Jung's express request and under the sponsorship of the Bollingen Foundation, edited a somewhat abridged version, of about two and one-half hours, which is shown more often by Jungian organizations. This was the first of a series of filmed interviews by Evans with notable contributors to psychology, including B. F. Skinner, Erik Erikson, Gordon Allport, Jean Piaget, and R. D. Laing.

A film transcript, made in Houston, was edited by Evans and published as a paperback, *Conversations with Carl Jung and Reactions from Ernest Jones* (Insight Books, Princeton and London, 1964), in which the text of the Jung interviews was rearranged under various subject-headings; the Jones interview had no relation to Jung. Twelve years later, Evans republished his version of the interview with corrections and with a verbatim transcript.[1]

[1] Dr. Richard I. Evans's interview with C. G. Jung is reprinted by permission of Dr. Evans and the University of Houston. It is a transcript of the four one-hour interviews which Dr. Evans conducted with Jung at the latter's home in Küsnacht, Switzerland, in August 1957, and contains editorial changes and corrections by R. F. C. Hull, Aniela Jaffé, William McGuire, and others. Permission to use the original transcript was granted by Dr. Evans and subsequently agreed to by E. P. Dutton & Co. The transcript also appears as an appendix in the book *Jung on Elementary Psychology: A Discussion between Carl Jung and Richard Evans* (New York: E. P. Dutton & Co., Inc.), 1976.

For the present publication, the Houston transcript was compared with the tape of the film soundtrack, through numerous auditions by the editors and Mrs. Jaffé, as well as Marie-Louise von Franz and Barbara Hannah, and all possible errors of transcription were corrected. Then the text was edited in the customary way. Questions have in some cases been abbreviated. Deletion of some impenetrably obscure passages in the soundtrack is indicated by ellipses, and editorial interpretations are in square brackets. There are some editorial differences between the two published versions of the verbatim transcript. The editors have annotated the present version.

FIRST INTERVIEW

Dr. Jung, many of us are aware of the fact that in your early work you were to some degree at least in association with Dr. Sigmund Freud, and I know it would be of very great interest to many of us to hear how you happened to become involved in his work and ideas.

Well, as a matter of fact it was in the year 1900, in December, soon after Freud's book about dream interpretation had come out, that I was asked by my chief, Professor Bleuler, to give a report on the book.[2] I studied the book very attentively and I didn't understand many things in it, they were not at all clear to me. But from other parts I got the impression that this man really knew what he was talking about, and I thought that this is certainly a masterpiece—full of future. I had no ideas then of my own; I was just beginning my career as assistant in the psychiatric clinic. I began with experimental psychology, or psychopathology; I applied the experimental association methods of Wundt, the same that had been applied at [Kraepelin's] psychiatric clinic in Munich, and I had studied the results and I had the idea that one should go over them again. So

[2] See Jung's 1901 report on Freud's *On Dreams*, CW 18, pars. 841 ff. No report on *The Interpretation of Dreams* has come to light.

I made these association tests[3] and I found out that the important thing in them had been missed, because it is not interesting to see that there is a reaction—a certain reaction —to a stimulus word. That is more or less uninteresting. The interesting thing is why people could *not* react to certain stimulus words, or in an entirely inadequate way.

And then I began to study these places in the experiment where the attention or the capability of the test person began to waver or to disappear, and I soon found out that it was intimate personal affairs people were thinking of, or which were in them even if they momentarily did not think of them, when they were unconscious in other words; but that nevertheless an inhibition came from the unconscious and hindered the expression in speech. Then, in examining all these cases as carefully as possible, I saw that it was a matter of what Freud called repressions. I also saw what he meant by symbolization.

In other words, from your word association studies, some of the things in The Interpretation of Dreams *began to fall into place?*

Yes. And then I wrote a book about the psychology of dementia praecox,[4] as it was then called—now it is schizophrenia—and I sent the book to Freud and wrote to him about my association experiments and how they confirmed his theory thus far. That is how my friendship with Freud began.

There are other individuals who also became interested in Freud's work, and one of them was Dr. Alfred Adler. As you remember Dr. Adler, what was it in your estimation that led him to become interested in Freud's work?

Well, he belonged; he was one of the young doctors that belonged to the Freud circle there. There were about

[3] The "Studies in Word Association" (originally 1905–1907), now in CW 2.
[4] In *The Psychogenesis of Mental Disease*, CW 3.

twenty young doctors who followed Freud, who had a sort of little society, and Adler was one who happened to be there, and he studied Freud's psychology in that circle.

Another individual who joined this group was Otto Rank, and of course he, unlike yourself, Dr. Adler and Dr. Freud, was not a physician—did not have a medical degree. Was this regarded by your group as something unusual?

Oh no. I met many people from different faculties who were interested in psychology. All people who have to do with human beings were naturally interested—theologians, lawyers, teachers. They all have to do with the human mind and these people were naturally interested. I'm naturally prejudiced, you know!

Then your group, including Freud, did not feel that this was exclusively an area of interest for the physician? This was something that might appeal to many?

Oh my, yes! Mind you, every patient you have gets interested in psychology. Inevitably. Nearly everyone thinks he is meant to be an analyst.

One of the very fundamental ideas of the original psychoanalytic theory was Freud's conception of the libido as a sort of broad, psychic sexual energy. Of course we all know that you began to feel that Freud might have laid, perhaps, a little bit too much stress on sexuality in his theories. When did you first begin feeling this?

Well you see, in the beginning I naturally had certain prejudices against his conceptions, but after a while I overcame them. I could do that owing to my biological training. I could not deny the importance of the sexual instinct, you know. But later on I saw that it was really one-sided, because you see man is not governed only by the sex instinct —there are other instincts as well. For instance, in biology you see that the nutritional instinct is just as important as the sex instinct, so in primitive societies sexuality plays a role much smaller than food. Food is the all-important interest and desire. Sex, that is something they can have everywhere, they are not shy. But food is difficult to obtain, you see, and so it is the main interest. Then in other societies—I mean in civilized societies—the power drive plays a much greater role than sex. For instance, there are many big business men who are impotent, even, because their whole energy is going into moneymaking or dictating the laws to everybody else. That is much more interesting than affairs with women.

So as you began to look over Freud's emphasis on the sexual drive, you began to think in terms of other cultures, and it seemed to you that this emphasis wasn't sufficiently universal to be of primary importance?

Well you know, I couldn't help seeing it because I had studied Nietzsche. I knew the works of Nietzsche very well. He had been a professor at Basel University, and the air was full of talk about Nietzsche. So naturally I had studied his works, and there I saw an entirely different psychology, a perfectly competent psychology, but all built upon the power drive.

Do you think it possible that Freud hadn't wanted to be influenced by Nietzsche?

You mean his personal motivation?

Yes.

Well of course it was a personal prejudice. It happened to be his main point, you know, that certain people are chiefly looking for this side and other people for another side. So you see, the inferior Dr. Adler, the younger, the weaker, naturally had a power complex. He wanted to be the successful man. Freud *was* a successful man, he was on top, so he was interested only in pleasure, in the pleasure principle, while Adler was interested in the power drive.

You feel that it was a sort of function of his own personality?

Yes, it is quite natural, it is one of two ways of dealing with reality. Either you make reality an object of pleasure if you are powerful enough already, or you make it an object of your desire to grab it, or to possess it.

Some observers have thought that perhaps the patients Freud saw in Vienna of this period were often repressed sexually, and this may have been one thing that reinforced Freud's ideas. In other words, the Viennese society was a rather—quotes—"repressed" society.

Well, it is certainly true that at the end of the Victorian age there was a reaction going on all over the world against the sex taboos, so-called. One didn't understand properly any more why or why not, and Freud belonged to that time. It was a sort of liberation of the mind from such taboos.

There was a reaction, then, against the tight, inhibited culture he was living in.

Oh yes. Freud in that way really belonged to the category of a Nietzschean mind. Nietzsche had liberated Europe from a great deal of such prejudices, but only concerning the power drive and our illusions as to the motivations of our morality. It was a time critical of morality.

So Freud, in a sense, was taking another direction?

Yes. And moreover, sex being the main instinct, the predominating instinct, then, in a society where the social conditions are more or less safe, sexuality is apt to predominate because people are taken care of. They have their positions, they have enough food—no question of hunting and seeking food or anything like that—and then it is quite probable that the patients you meet practically all have a certain sexual complex.

So this is the drive in that particular society most likely to be inhibited?

Yes. It is a sort of finesse, almost, when you find out that somebody has a power drive and his sex only serves the purpose of power. For instance, a charming man whom all women think is the real hero of all hearts, he is a power-devil, like a Don Juan, you know. The woman is not his problem, his problem is how to dominate. So in the second place after sex comes the power drive, and even that is not the end.

Now going still further into the development of Freud's theory, which of course was a significant factor as you say in the development of many of your own early ideas—Freud talked a great deal about the unconscious.

As soon as research comes to the question of the unconscious, things necessarily become blurred, because the unconscious is something which is *really* unconscious, and so you have no object, you see nothing! You can only make inferences, you know, and so we have to create a model of this possible structure of the unconscious because we can't see it. Now Freud came to the concept of the unconscious chiefly on the basis of the same experience I had in the association experiment. People reacted, they said things, they did things, without knowing that they had done or said them. This is something you can observe in the association experiment, where people cannot remember afterwards what they did or what they said when a stimulus word hits the complex. In the so-called reproduction experiment you go through the whole list of words, and you see that the memory fails where there was a complex reaction. That is the simple fact Freud had based his idea of the unconscious on. Because that is what we can see, time and again, when people make a mistake in speech or say something they didn't mean to say; they just make ridiculous mistakes. There is no end of stories, you know, about how people can betray themselves by saying something they didn't mean to say at all, yet the unconscious *meant* them to say just that thing. For instance, when you want to express your sympathy at a funeral, you go to someone and you say "I congratulate you." That's pretty painful, you know, but it happens, and it is true.

Now this is something that goes parallel with the whole school of the Salpetrière, in Paris. There was Pierre Janet, who had worked out that side of the unconscious reactions quite particularly. Freud refers very little to Pierre Janet, but I studied with Pierre Janet in Paris and he formed my ideas very much. He was a first-class observer, though he had no dynamic psychological theory. It was a sort of physiological theory of unconscious phenomena, the so-called *abaissement du niveau mental*, that is, a certain depotentiation of the tension of consciousness. A content sinks below the level of consciousness and thus becomes unconscious. That is Freud's view too, only he says it sinks down because it is helped, it is repressed from above. That was my first point of difference with Freud. I said there were cases in my observation where there was no repression from above, but the thing itself is true. Those contents that became unconscious had withdrawn all by themselves, they were not repressed. On the contrary, they have a certain autonomy. I discovered the concept of autonomy because these contents that disappear have the power to move independently of my will. Either they appear when I want to say something definite, they interfere and speak themselves instead of what I wanted to say, or they make me do something I didn't want to do at all, or they withdraw at the very moment I want to use them. They certainly disappear!

And this is independent of any of the pressures on consciousness Freud suggested?

Yes. There can be such cases, sure enough. But besides them there are also the cases that show that the unconscious contents acquire a certain independence. All mental contents that have a feeling-tone that is emotional, that have the value of an affect, have the tendency to become autonomous. So you see, anybody in an emotion will say and do things which he cannot vouch for. He must excuse himself for being in a state, he was *non compos mentis*.

Freud recognized that in a sense the individual is born entirely a victim of what he later called the Id, which is unconscious and undeveloped, a collection of animal drives. It is not easy to see where all these drives, these instincts, come from.

Nobody knows where instincts come from. They are there, you find them. It is a story that was played out millions of years ago. There sexuality was invented, and I wasn't there so I don't know how this happened. Feeding was invented very much longer ago even than sex, and why and how it was invented I don't know, I wasn't there. So we don't know where instinct comes from. It is quite ridiculous to speculate about such an impossibility. The question is only: Where do those cases come from where instinct does not function? That is something within our reach, because we can study the cases where instinct does not function.

Could you give us some rather specific examples of what you mean by cases where the instinct does not function?

Well, instead of instinct, which is a habitual form of activity, take any other form of habitual activity. Once, suddenly, that thing doesn't function. Take a singer who is in absolute control of his voice, suddenly he can't sing. Or take a man who writes fluently, suddenly he makes a ridiculous mistake, his habit doesn't function. You see, when you ask me something, I'm supposed to be able to react to you. Suddenly I am *bouche béante* [open-mouthed] —for instance if you succeed in touching one of my complexes, you can see that I am absolutely perplexed. I am *dépossédé*, and words fail me! [Laughter.]

We haven't seen you very perplexed yet, Dr. Jung.

Or look for instance at exam psychology, a fellow who knows his stuff quite well. The professor asks him something and he cannot say a word.

A block, yes. Another part of Freud's theory was the idea that out of this sort of unconscious instinctual structure— and of course the word "structure" has to be put in quotation marks as you point out it is only a model—which Freud called the Id, an ego emerges as a result of the organism's contact with reality, in a sense perhaps also a product of frustration as reality is imposed on the developing individual. Now do you accept this conception of the ego?

Whether the individual has an ego at all, that is your question? Ah, that is again such a case—I wasn't there when it was invented! However, you can observe it to a certain extent with a child, because a child definitely begins in a state where there is no ego. And then about the fourth year or before, but about that time, the child develops a sense of ego, "I," "myself," and that is in the first place an identity with the body. For instance, when you ask primitives they always emphasize the body. You ask, "Who has brought this thing here?" And the Negro will say, "Uh [a grunt] brought it"—no accent on the "I," simply "brought it." You say, "But have *you* brought it?" and then he says, "In here, me, me, yes, I, myself, this given object, this thing here." So the identity with the body is one of the first things which makes an ego; it is the spatial separateness that induces, apparently, the concept of an ego. Then, of course, there are lots of other things. Later on it is mental differences, personal differences of all sorts, etc. You see, the ego is continuously building up; it is not a finished product, never, it builds up. No year passes when you do not discover a new little aspect in which you are more ego than you thought.

There has been much discussion about how certain experiences in the early years influence the formation of the ego. One of the most extreme views was advanced by Otto Rank. He spoke of the birth trauma and said that the actual trauma of being born would have a very powerful impact on the ego and show itself throughout life.

I should say it is very important for an ego that it is born. It is highly traumatic, you know, when you fall out of heaven! [Laughter.]

But do you take literally Otto Rank's position that the birth trauma has a profound psychological effect?

Of course. For instance, if you are a believer in Schopenhauer's philosophy you say it is a hellish trauma to be born. There is a Greek saying, "It is beautiful to die in youth, but the most beautiful of all things is not to be born." Philosophy, you see.

But you don't take this as a literal psychic event?

Don't you see, this is an event which happens to everybody that exists—that he once has been born! Everybody who is born has undergone that trauma, so the word trauma has lost its meaning. It is a general fact, and you cannot say it is a "trauma." It is just a fact. Because you cannot observe a psychology that hasn't been born; only then could you say what the birth trauma is. Until then you cannot even speak of such a thing. It is just a lack of epistemology.

Yes, I see. Going a little further, in the more or less orthodox psychoanalytic view, as you well know, there is a great deal of attention paid to what Freud called psychosexual development. Step by step the individual encounters a series of problems which he must resolve in order to mature. One of the earliest problems seems to center round, you might say, primitive oral satisfactions, or oral zone experiences—

In other words, the nutritional instinct was more important than sex. That's not very interesting.

Do you interpret this, then, as a sort of nutritional hunger drive? You do not see it as an early representation of the sexual drive?

I think, you see, that when you say one of the first and foremost interests is to feed, it doesn't need a peculiar kind of terminology like "oral zone." *Of course* they put it into the mouth.

So you look at it in a much simpler sense?
Science consists to a great extent of mere talk.

Another rather fundamental point in the development of the ego in the more or less orthodox psychoanalytic view is that the oral zone is followed by another critical level, an anal level of development. At this level another crucial, early frustration arises, centering on toilet training. Would you regard this so-called anal level as having broad sexual implications and being significant from the standpoint of ego-development and character formation?
Well, one *can* use such a terminology because it is a fact that children are exceedingly interested in all the orifices of the body and in doing all sorts of disgusting things, you know, and sometimes such a peculiarity keeps on into later life. It is quite astonishing what you can hear in that respect. Now it is equally true that people who have such preferences also develop a peculiar character. In early childhood a character is already there. You see, a child is not born a *tabula rasa*, as one assumes. The child is born as a highly complex organism, with existing determinants that never waver throughout life and that give the child his character. Already in earliest childhood a mother recognizes the individuality of her child, and if you observe carefully you can see tremendous differences even in very small children. These peculiarities express themselves in every way, first in all childish activities, in the way they play, in the things they are interested in. There are children who are tremendously interested in all moving things, in movement chiefly—all the things that affect the body. They are interested in what the eyes do, what the ears do, how far you can bore into your nose with your finger, you know.

They will do the same with the anus, they will do whatever they please with their genitals. When I was a boy at school we once stole the class-book where all the punishments were noted, and there our professor had noted, So-and-so punished with two hours for toying with his genitals during the religious hour.

These interests express themselves in a typically childish way in children. And later on they express themselves in other peculiarities which are still the same, but this doesn't come from the fact that once they had done such and such a thing in childhood. It is the character that is doing it. There is a definite inherited complexity, and if you want to know something about the possible reasons you must go to the parents. So in any case of a child's neurosis I go back to the parents and see what is going on there, because children have no psychology of their own, in the literal sense. They are so much in the mental atmosphere of the parents, so much *en participation mystique* with them, they are imbued with the paternal or maternal atmosphere, and they express these influences in their childish way. Take an illegitimate child. He is particularly exposed to environmental difficulties, such as the misfortune of the mother, etc., etc., and all the other complications. Such a child will miss, say, a father. Now in order to compensate for this it is just as if he were choosing or nominating a part of his body for a father, instead of the father, and he develops, for instance, masturbation. That is very often so with illegitimate children. They become terribly autoerotic, even criminal.

With reference to the role of the parents, one of the central parts of the so-called psychosexual development in the more or less orthodox psychoanalytic theory is the so-called Oedipus complex—

That is just what I call an archetype. It was the first archetype Freud discovered, the first and only one. He thought this *was* the archetype. Of course there are many such archetypes. You look at Greek mythology and you find them, any amount of them. Or look at dreams and you find any amount of them. But incest was so impressive to him that he even chose the term "Oedipus complex" because that was one of the outstanding examples of an incest complex. And it is only the masculine form, mind you, because women have an incest complex too. But there it is not an Oedipus, so it is something else. It is only the term for an archetypal way of behavior, in the case of a man's relation, say, to his mother; but this also means to his daughter, because whatever he was to the mother he will be it to the daughter too. It can be this way or that way. It depends.

Then you will accept the Oedipus complex but not as being the only important such influence. You see it as just one of many.

One of the many, many ways of behavior. The Oedipus gives you an excellent example of the behavior of an archetype. It is always a whole situation. There is a mother, there is a father, there is a son, there is a whole story of how such a situation develops and to what end it finally leads. And that is an archetype. An archetype is always a sort of abbreviated drama. It begins in such and such a way, it extends to such and such a complication, and it finds its solution in such and such a way. That is the usual form. Take for instance the instinct of building a nest with birds. In the way they build the nest there is the beginning, the middle, and the end. It is built just to suffice for a certain number of young. So you see the end is already anticipated. That is the reason why, in the archetype itself, there is no time. It is a timeless condition where beginning, middle, and end are just the same, they are all given in one. This is only a hint of what the archetype can do, you know. But that's a complicated question.

To discuss more specifically Freud's concept of the Oedipus complex, it is commonly held, again in fairly orthodox psychoanalytic circles, that the child's early family patterns of behavior with the mother, the father, etc., are relived over and over again. For example, when the young man gets married, he may react to his wife as he did to his mother, or he may be searching for someone like his mother, or the daughter will be searching for a father. Does this recapitulation of the very early Oedipus situation fit in with your conceptions?

Oh no. No, no. You see, Freud speaks of the incest complex just in the way you describe, but he omits completely the fact that with this Oedipus complex there is already given the contrary, namely the resistance against it. If the Oedipus complex were really predominant, we would have been suffocated in incest half a million years ago at least. But there is a compensation. In all early levels of civilization you find the marriage laws, exogamous laws. The first form, the most elementary form, is that a man can only marry his cousin on the maternal side. The next form is that he can only marry his cousin in the second degree, from the grandmother. There are four-class systems, eight- and twelve-class systems, and in China there are still some traces of a twelve-class and a six-class system. Those are developments beyond the incest complex and against the incest complex. Now if sexuality is predominant, particularly incestuous sexuality, how can it develop? These things developed in a time long before there was any idea of the child, say, of my sister. That's all wrong. On the contrary it [sister-incest] was a royal prerogative as late as the Achaemenid kings of Persia, and among the Egyptian Pharaohs. If the Pharaoh had a daughter by his sister, he married that daughter and again had a child with her and then married his grand-daughter, because that was the royal prerogative. And so you see, the preservation of the royal blood is always a sort of attempt at the highly appreciated incestuous restriction of the number of ancestors, because this is a loss of ancestors. Now you see that must be explained too. It is not only the one thing, there is also its compensation. You know this plays a very great role in the history of human civilization.[5] Freud is always inclined to explain these things by external influences; for instance, you would not feel hampered in any way *if* there were not a law against it, no one is hampered by himself. And that is what he never would admit to me.[6]

Apropos that point, Freud in his later writings introduced a sort of part ego which he called the super-ego—

Yes, the super-ego, the codex of what you can and what you cannot do.

[5] Jung's statements are very condensed here and several steps in the argument are missing. The incest complex is discussed in detail in "The Psychology of the Transference," CW 16, pars. 410ff. Briefly, the incestuous or endogamous tendency is kept in check ("compensated") by the exogamous tendency, resulting in the sociological compromise of the primitive "sister-exchange" or "cross-cousin marriage" and the development of marriage classes (pars. 431ff.). The cross-cousin marriage rests upon the foundation of the "archetypal marriage quaternio which is not a human invention at all but a fact that existed long before consciousness" (par. 437). The endogamous tendency was permitted expression in the form of sister-incest until quite late times only as a royal prerogative, the kings being the representatives of the gods, who on a primitive level were believed to propagate their kind incestuously (par. 419). By reducing the number of merely human ancestors, incest preserved the divinity of the royal blood. "The idea of the incestuous hierosgamos does in fact appear in civilized religions and blossoms forth in the supreme spirituality of Christian imagery (Christ and the Church, *sponsus* and *sponsa,* the mysticism of the Song of Songs, etc.)" (par. 438). Thus the endogamous tendency must also be considered "as a genuine instinct which, if denied realization in the flesh, must realize itself in the spirit" ("compensation") (par. 438).

[6] That is, would not admit that man does check himself and that his resistance to incest, for example, is partly "built-in" and not determined solely by sexual taboos. The super-ego is "a natural and inherited part of the psyche's structure." Cf. "A Psychological View of Conscience," CW 10, pars. 830f.

Built-in prohibitions—

Yes, but Freud doesn't see that it is in himself, he has it in himself. Otherwise there could be no balance in the individual. And who in hell would have invented the decalogue? That was not invented by Moses. But there is an eternal truth in man himself, because he checks himself.

You mentioned earlier that Freud's Oedipus situation was an example of the archetype. Could you please elaborate on this concept?

Well, you know what a behavior pattern is.[7] The way in which, say a weaver bird builds his nest. That is an inherited form in him which he will apply. Or certain sorts of symbiotic phenomena between insects and plants. They are inherited patterns of behavior. And man, of course, has an inherited scheme of functioning too. His liver, his heart, all his organs, and his brain will always function in a certain way, each following its pattern. You would have great difficulty in seeing it because we cannot compare it with anything. There are no other beings like man that are articulate and could give an account of their functioning. If that were the case we would know—I don't know what— but because we have no means of comparison we are necessarily unconscious about our own conditions. Yet it is quite certain that man is born with a certain way of functioning, a certain pattern of behavior, and that is expressed in the form of archetypal images.

For instance, the way in which a man should behave is given by an archetype. That is why primitives tell the stories they do. A great deal of education goes through storytelling. They call a palaver of the young men and two older men *perform* before the eyes of the younger all the things they should not do. Then they say, "Now that's exactly the thing you shall not do." Another way is to *tell* them of all the things they should not do, like the decalogue—"Thou

[7] Cf. "On the Nature of the Psyche," CW 8, pp. 200ff.

shalt not." And that is always supported by mythological tales. Our ancestors have done so and so, and so shall you. Or such and such a hero has done so and so, and this is your model. Again, in the teachings of the Catholic Church there are several thousand saints. They show us what to do, they serve as models. They have their legends and that is Christian mythology. In Greece there was Theseus, there was Heracles, models of fine men, of gentlemen, you know, and they teach us how to behave. They are archetypes of behavior.

Or take a more concise archetype like the archetype of the ford, the ford through a river. That again is a whole situation. You have to cross the ford, you are in the water, there is an ambush, or there is a water animal, say a crocodile or something like that. There is a danger and something is going to happen, and the question is how you escape. Now this is a whole situation that makes an archetype. And that archetype now has a suggestive effect upon you. For instance, you get into a situation, you don't know what the situation is. Suddenly you are seized by an emotion or by a spell, and you behave in a certain way you have not foreseen at all. You do something quite strange to yourself.

You'd call it spontaneous?

Quite spontaneous, and that is done through the archetype that is constellated. We have a famous case in our Swiss history of King Albrecht,[8] who was murdered at the ford of the Reuss not very far from Zurich. His murderers were riding behind him for the whole stretch from Zurich to the Reuss, and they deliberated and couldn't agree whether they wanted to kill the king or not. And the moment the king rode into the ford Johannes Parricida, the father murderer, shouted, "Why do we let that"—and used a swearword—"live on!" And they killed him. Because this

[8] Albert, d. 1308, killed by his nephew, John the Parricide.

was the moment when they were seized, this was the right moment.

So you see, when you have lived in primitive conditions, in the primeval forest among primitive people, you know that phenomenon. You are seized by a spell, and then you do something that is unexpected. Several times when I was in Africa I got into such situations and afterwards I was amazed. One day I was in the Sudan, and it was really a very dangerous situation which I didn't recognize at the moment at all. But I was seized by a spell, and I did something I wouldn't have expected, I couldn't have invented it. The archetype is a force. It has an autonomy and it can suddenly seize you. It is like a seizure. Falling in love at first sight is something like that. You see, you have a certain image in yourself, without knowing it, of woman, of *the* woman. Then you see that girl, or at least a good imitation of your type, and instantly you get a seizure and you are gone. And afterwards you may discover that it was a hell of a mistake. A man is quite able, he is intelligent enough, to see that the woman of his "choice," as one says, was no choice, he has been caught! He sees that she is no good at all, that she is a hell of a business, and he tells me so. He says, "For God's sake, doctor, help me to get rid of that woman!" He can't, though, he is like clay in her fingers. That is the archetype, the archetype of the anima.[9] And he thinks it is all his soul, you know! It's the same with the girls. When a man sings very high, a girl thinks he must have a very wonderful spiritual character because he can sing the high C, and she is badly disappointed when she marries that particular number. Well, that's the archetype of the animus.

Dr. Jung, to be even a little bit more specific, you have suggested that in all societies there are symbols that in a sense

[9] For the anima see *Two Essays on Analytical Psychology*, CW 7, pars. 296ff.; "Concerning the Archetypes, with Special Reference to the Anima Concept," CW 9 i; *Aion*, CW 9 ii, ch. III.

direct or determine what a man does. You also suggest that somehow these symbols become inborn and—quotes—"inbred."

They don't *become.* They *are.* They are there to begin with. You see, we are born into a pattern, we *are* a pattern. We are a structure that is pre-established through the genes.

Would you say, then, that the archetype is just a higher order of an instinctual pattern, such as your earlier example of a bird building a nest?

It is a biological order of our mental functioning, just as our biological or physiological functioning follows a pattern. The behavior of any bird or insect follows a pattern, and it is the same with us. Man has a certain pattern that makes him specifically human, and no man is born without it. We are deeply unconscious of this fact only because we all live by our senses and outside of ourselves. If a man could look into himself he could discover it. When a man discovers it in our days he thinks he is crazy—and he may be crazy.

Would you say the number of such archetypes are limited, prefixed, or can the number increase?

Well, I don't know what I do know about it, it is so blurred. You see, we have no means of comparison. We know there is a behavior, say, like incest, or there is a behavior of violence, a behavior of panic, a behavior of power, and so on. Those are areas, as it were, in which there are many variations. It can be expressed in this way or that way, you know. And they overlap, often you cannot say where one form begins or ends. It is nothing concise, because the archetype in itself is completely unconscious and you can only see the effects of it. When you know a person is possessed by an archetype, you can divine and even prognosticate possible developments. For instance, when you see that a man is caught by a certain type of woman in a very specific way, you know he is caught by the anima. Then the whole thing will have such and such complications, such and such developments, because it is typical. And the way the anima is described is exceedingly typical. I don't know if you know Rider Haggard's *She*, or *L'Atlantide* by Benôit. Those are anima types, and they are quite unmistakable. *C'est la femme fatale.*

You have used the concepts anima and animus and I wonder if you could perhaps elaborate more specifically on those terms?

Well, this is a bit complicated, you know. The anima is an archetypal form, expressing the fact that a man has a minority of female genes, and that is something that does not disappear in him. It is constantly present, and it works as a female in a man. Therefore already in the sixteenth century the humanists discovered that man has an anima; each man carries his female within himself, they said.[10] So that is not a modern invention. It is the same with the animus. It is a masculine image in a woman's mind which is sometimes quite conscious, sometimes not conscious, and it is called into life the moment that woman meets a man who says the right things. Then because he says it, it is all true, and he is the fellow, no matter what he is. Those are particularly well-founded archetypes, those two. They are extremely well defined. And there you can lay hands on the basis, as it were, of the archetype.

SECOND INTERVIEW

Dr. Jung, we have been discussing some of the factors in the development of the personality, and you have very kindly elaborated for us some of your fundamental conceptions such as the archetype, and the anima and animus. Now another concept which seems to be a very interesting one in

[10] *Hermetis Trismegisti Tractatus vere Aureus . . . cum scholiis Dominici Gnosii* (Leipzig, 1610). Cf. "Psychology and Religion," CW 11, p. 30, n. 32.

your work is the persona. I wonder if you would mind telling us something about this?

Well, this is a practical concept we need in elucidating people's relations.[11] I noticed with my patients, particularly with people in public life, that they have a certain way of presenting themselves. For instance, take the doctor. He has good bedside manners, and he behaves as one expects a doctor to behave. He may even identify himself with his role and believe that he is what he appears to be. He must appear in a certain form, or people won't believe he is a doctor. The same with a professor, he is supposed to behave in a certain way so that it is plausible that he is a professor. So the persona is a complicated system of behavior which is dictated by the demands of society and partly by one's fiction of oneself.

Now this is not the real personality. In spite of the fact that people will assure you it is all quite real and honest, it is not. The performance of the persona is quite all right as long as you know that you are not identical with the way you appear. But if you are not conscious of this fact you sometimes get into very disagreeable conflicts. People can't help noticing that at home you are quite different from what you appear to be in public. And individuals who are not aware of this stumble over it in the end. They deny they are like that, but they *are* like that. Then you don't know which is the real man. Is he the man he is at home in his intimate relations, or is he the man that appears in public? It is often a question of Jekyll and Hyde. Occasionally there is such a difference that you could almost speak of a double personality. And the more pronounced it is, the more people get neurotic. They got neurotic because they have two different ways, they contradict themselves all the time, and being unconscious of themselves they don't know it. They think they are all one, but everybody sees that they

---

[11] For the persona see *Two Essays*, pars. 243ff.

are two. Some know them only from one side, others only from the other side. And then there are situations that clash, because the way you are creates situations in your relationships with people, and these two situations don't chime, in fact they are just dishonest. And the more this is so, the more people are neurotic.

Would you say that the individual may even have more than two personas?

Oh, rarely. We can't afford very well to play more than two roles. But there are cases of people who have up to five different personalities. In cases of dissociation of personality, for instance, where the one person—call him person A—doesn't know of the existence of person B, but B knows of A. There may be a third personality, C, that doesn't know of the two others. There are such cases in the literature, but they are rare.

Very rare.

In ordinary cases, it's just an ordinary dissociation of personality. One calls that a systematic dissociation, in contradistinction to the chaotic or unsystematic dissociation you find in schizophrenia.

Do you distinguish between the term "persona" and the term "ego"? Are they two different things?

Well you see, the ego is supposed to be the representative of the real person. For instance, when B knows of A but A doesn't know of B, one would say that the ego is more on the side of B, because the ego has a more complete knowledge, and A is a split-off personality.

You also use the term "self." Does it have a different meaning from "ego" and "persona"?

Yes, oh quite. When I say "self"[12] you mustn't think of "I myself," because that is only your empirical self which

[12] For the self see *Aion*, chs. I and IV.

is covered by the term "ego." But when it is a matter of the "self" it means a personality that is more complete than the ego, because the ego consists only of what you are conscious of, what you know to be yourself. In our example of B who knows A though A doesn't know B, B is relatively in the position of the self. The self is, on one side, the ego, on the other side it is the unconscious personality which is in the possession of everybody. Very often it is just the other way round: the unconscious is in possession of consciousness. But that is a different case.

You see, while I am talking I am conscious of what I say; I am conscious of myself, yet only to a certain extent. Quite a lot of things happen. For instance, I make gestures but am not conscious of them. They happen unconsciously, you can see them. I may use words and can't remember at all having used those words, or even at the moment I may not be conscious of them. So any amount of unconscious things occur in my conscious condition. I'm never wholly conscious of myself. While I am trying to elaborate an argument, at the same time there are unconscious processes that continue perhaps a dream I had last night, or a part of myself thinks of God knows what, of a trip I'm going to take, or of such and such people I have seen. Or when I am writing a paper, I continue writing that paper in my mind without knowing it. You can discover these things, say, in dreams, or if you are clever, by direct observation of the individual. Then you see in the gestures, or in the expression of the face, that there is an *arrière pensée*, something behind consciousness. So that you finally have the feeling, Well, that man has something up his sleeve, and you can even ask him, "What are you really thinking of? You are thinking all the time of something else." Yet he is not conscious of it. Or again, he may be. There are individuals who have an amazing knowledge of themselves, of the things that go on in themselves. But even those people wouldn't be capable of knowing what is going on in their unconscious.

For instance, they are not conscious of the fact that while they live a conscious life, all the time a myth is being played out in the unconscious, a myth that extends over centuries, a stream of archetypal ideas that goes on through the centuries through an individual. Really it is like a continuous stream, and it comes to light in the great movements, say in political or spiritual movements. For instance, in the time before the Reformation, people dreamt of the great change. That is the reason why such great transformations could be predicted. If somebody were clever enough to see what is going on in the unconscious mind, he would be able to predict it. I predicted the Nazi rising in Germany through the observation of my German patients. They had dreams in which the whole thing was anticipated, and in considerable detail. And I was absolutely certain, in the years before Hitler—I could even say the year, in the year 1918—I was sure that something was threatening, something very big, and very catastrophic.[13] I knew it only through the observation of the unconscious.

There is something very particular in the different nations. It is a peculiar fact that the archetype of the anima plays a very great role in Western literature, French and Anglo-Saxon. Not in Germany. There are exceedingly few examples in German literature where the anima plays a role.[14] That is simply due to the fact that not one woman is buried unless she is buried as "alt Kaminfegersgattin"[15] at least. She must have a title, otherwise she hasn't existed. And so it is just as if—now mind you, this is a bit drastic, but it illustrates my point—as if in Germany there really are no women. There is Frau Doktor, Frau Professor, Frau Kommerzienrat,[16] the grandmother, the mother-in-law, the

[13] "The Role of the Unconscious," CW 10, par. 17.
[14] Cf. "Flying Saucers: A Modern Myth," CW 10, par. 775.
[15] "Old chimney sweep's wife."
[16] "Councillor of Commerce," a quite meaningless title which sounds impressive to successful tradesmen, etc.

grandfather, the father, the son, the daughter, the sister. No woman—*la femme ça n'existe pas*. That is the idea, you see. Now that is an enormously important fact which shows that in the German mind there is going on a particular myth, something very peculiar, and psychologists really should look out for these things. But they prefer to think that I am a prophet. Ha!

This is of course a very interesting and remarkable set of statements. How do you look at Hitler in this light? Would you see him as a personification, a symbol of the father?

No, no, no, not at all. I couldn't possibly explain the very complicated fact that Hitler represents. It is too complicated. You know, he is a hero figure, and a hero figure is far more important than any fathers that have ever existed.

Much broader—

He was no father at all, he was a hero in the German myth. And mind you, a religious hero. He was a savior, he was meant to be a savior. That is why they put his photo upon the altars, even. Or someone declared on his tombstone that he is happy that his eyes had beheld Hitler, and now he can lie in peace. He is just a hero myth, you see.

Now getting back to the idea of the self, the self incorporates those unconscious factors—

The self is merely a term that designates the whole personality. The whole personality of man is indescribable. His consciousness *can* be described, his unconscious *cannot* be described because the unconscious—and here I must repeat myself—is always unconscious. It is really unconscious, we really don't know it, so we don't know our unconscious personality. We have hints, we have certain ideas, but we don't know it really. Nobody can say where man ends. That is the beauty of it, you know; it's very interesting. The unconscious of man can reach God knows where. There we are going to make discoveries.

Now another set of ideas, which of course are very, very well known to the world but which you have originated, centers round the terms "introversion" and "extraversion."[17]

Like the word "complex"—I invented it too, you know, from the association experiment. Well you see, this is simply practical, because there are certain people who definitely are more influenced by their surroundings than by their own intentions, while other people are more influenced by the subjective factor. Now the subjective factor, and this is very characteristic, was understood by Freud as a sort of pathological autoeroticism. This is a mistake. The psyche has two important conditions. One is the environmental influence, and the other is the given fact of the psyche as it is born. As I told you yesterday, the psyche is by no means a *tabula rasa*. We are a definite mixture and combination of genes, and they are there from the very first moment of our life, and they give a definite character even to the little child. That is the subjective factor, looked at from the outside.

Now if you look at it from the inside, it is just as if you were observing the world. When you observe the world you see people, you see houses, you see the sky, you see tangible objects. But when you observe yourself within, you see moving images, a world of images, generally known as fantasies. Yet these fantasies are facts. You see, it is a fact that a man has such and such a fantasy, such a tangible fact that when a man has a certain fantasy another man may lose his life. Or a bridge may be built—these houses were all fantasies. Everything you do here, all of the houses, everything was fantasy to begin with, and fantasy has a proper reality. This should not be forgotten, fantasy is not nothing. It is of course not a tangible object, but it is a fact nevertheless. It is like a form of energy, despite the fact that we can't measure it. It is a manifestation of something, and that is a reality just as much as the peace treaty of Versailles, or

[17] Cf. *Two Essays*, pars. 56ff., and *Psychological Types*, CW 6, ch. X.

something like that. It no longer exists, you can't show it, but it has been a fact.

So psychic events are facts, are realities, and when you observe the stream of images within, you observe an aspect of the world, of the world within. Because the psyche, if you understand it as a phenomenon occurring in living bodies, is a quality of matter, just as our body consists of matter. We discover that this matter has another aspect, namely a psychic aspect. It is simply the world seen from within. It is just as though you were seeing into another aspect of matter. This is an idea that is not my invention. Old Democritus talked of the *spiritus insertus atomis*, the spirit inserted in atoms. That means the psyche is a quality which appears in matter. It doesn't matter whether we understand it or not, but that is the conclusion we come to if we draw conclusions without prejudices.

And so, you see, the man who goes by the influence of the external world—say society or sense perceptions—thinks he is more valid because this is valid, this is real, and the man who goes by the subjective factor is not valid because the subjective factor is nothing. No, that man is just as well based, because he bases himself on the world from within. So he is quite all right even if he says, "Oh, it is nothing but my fantasy." Of course that is the introvert, and as the introvert is always afraid of the external world, he will be apologetic about it when you ask him. He will say, "Yes, of course, I know those are my fantasies," and he has always a resentment. And as the world in general, particularly America, is extraverted as hell, the introvert has no place, because he doesn't know that he beholds the world from within. And that gives him dignity, that gives him certainty, because, nowadays particularly, *the world hangs by a thin thread, and that thread is the psyche of man.* Suppose certain fellows in Moscow lose their nerve or their common sense for a bit, then the whole world is in fire and flames. Nowadays we are not threatened by elemental catastrophes.

There is no such thing in nature as an H-bomb—that is all man's doing. *We* are the great danger. The psyche is the great danger. What if something goes wrong with the psyche? And so it is demonstrated in our day what the power of the psyche is, how important it is to know something about it. But we know nothing about it. Nobody would give credit to the idea that the psychic processes of the ordinary man have any importance whatever. One thinks, "Oh, he is just what he has in his head. He is all from his surroundings." He is taught such and such a thing, believes such and such a thing, and particularly if he is well housed and well fed, then he has no ideas at all. And that's the great mistake, because he is just what he is born as, and he is not born as a *tabula rasa* but as a reality.

One of the very common, I think, misconceptions of your work among some writers in America is that they have characterized your discussion of introversion and extraversion as suggesting that the world is made up of only two kinds of people, introverts and extraverts. Would you like to comment on that?

Well, Bismarck once said, "God preserve me from my friends, with my enemies I can deal alone!" You know what people are. They catch a word and then everything is schematized to fit that word. There is no such thing as a pure extravert or a pure introvert. Such a man would be in the lunatic asylum. They are only terms to designate a certain penchant, a certain tendency. For instance, the tendency to be more influenced by environmental factors, or more influenced by the subjective factor, that's all. There are people who are fairly well balanced and are just as much influenced from within as from without, or just as little. And so with all the finer classifications, they are only *points de repère*, points for orientation.

There is no such thing as a schematic classification. Often you have great trouble even to make out to what type a man belongs, either because he is very well balanced or because he is very neurotic. When you are neurotic you always have a certain dissociation of personality. And then the people themselves don't know when they react consciously or when they react unconsciously. You can talk to somebody and you think he is conscious and knows what he says, and to your amazement you discover after a while that he is quite unconscious of it, doesn't know it. It is a long and painstaking procedure to find out what a man is conscious of and what he is not conscious of, because the unconscious plays in him all the time. Certain things are conscious, certain things are unconscious, but you couldn't tell.

Then this whole matter of extremes, introvert and extravert, is a sort of scheme to hang an idea on?

My scheme of typology is only a scheme of orientation. There is such a factor as introversion, there is such a factor as extraversion. The classification of individuals means nothing, nothing at all. It is only the instrumentarium for the practical psychologist to explain, for instance, the husband to a wife or vice versa. It is very often the case—I might say it is almost a rule, but I don't want to make too many rules in order not to be schematic—that an introvert marries an extravert for compensation, or another type marries the countertype to complement himself. For instance, a man who has made a certain amount of money is a good business man, but he has no education. His dream is, of course, a grand piano at home, artists, painters, singers or God knows what, and intellectual people, and accordingly he marries a wife of that type in order to have that too. Of course he has nothing of it. She has it, and she marries him because he has a lot of money.

These compensations go on all the time. When you study marriages, you can see it easily. We alienists have to deal with a lot of marriages, particularly those that go wrong, because the types are too different sometimes and they don't understand each other at all. You see, the main values of the extravert are anathema to the introvert, so he says, "To hell with the world, I *think*!" His wife interprets this as his megalomania. But it is just as if an extravert said to an introvert, "Now look here, fellow, these are the facts, this is reality!" And he's right. And the other type says, "But *I* think!" and that sounds like nonsense to the extravert because he doesn't realize that the other, without knowing it, is seeing an inner world, an inner reality. And he may be right, as he may be wrong, even if he based himself on God knows what solid facts. Take the interpretation of statistics, you can prove anything with statistics. What is more a fact than a statistic?

Of course, tied in with your typology of—quotes—"intro-version" and "extraversion" we know of your concepts of thinking, feeling, sensation, intuition, and it would be very interesting to have some expansion of these particular terms as related to the introvert-extravert dichotomy.

Well, there is quite a simple explanation of those terms, and it shows at the same time how I arrived at such a typology. Sensation tells you that there *is* something. Thinking, roughly speaking, tells you *what* it is. Feeling tells you whether it is agreeable or not, to be accepted or rejected. And intuition—now there is a difficulty. You don't know, ordinarily, how intuition works. When a man has a hunch, you can't tell exactly how he got at that hunch, or where that hunch comes from. There is something funny about intuition.

I will tell you a little story. I had two patients, the man was a sensation type, the woman was an intuitive type. Of course they felt attracted. So they took a little boat and went out on the lake of Zurich. And there were those birds that dive after fish, then after a while they come up again, and you can't tell where they will come up. And so they began to bet who would be the first to see the bird. Now you would think that the one who observes reality very care-fully—the sensation type—would of course win out. Not at all. The woman won the bet completely. She was beating him on all points, because by intuition she knew it before-hand. How is that feasible? Sometimes, you know, you can really see how it works by finding out the intermediate links. Intuition is a perception by intermediate links, and you only get the result of that whole chain of associations. Sometimes you succeed in finding out, but more often you don't.

So my definition is that intuition is a perception via the unconscious. That is as near as I can get. It is a very im-portant function, because when you live under primitive conditions a lot of unpredictable things are likely to happen. Then you need your intuition because you cannot possibly tell by your sense perceptions what is going to happen. For instance, you are traveling in a primeval forest. You can only see a few steps ahead. You go by the compass, perhaps, but you don't know what there is ahead. It is uncharted country. If you use your intuition you have hunches, and when you live under primitive conditions you are instantly aware of hunches. There are places that are favorable, there are places that are not favorable. You can't tell for your life what it is, but you'd better follow those hunches because anything can happen, quite unforeseen things. For instance, at the end of a long day you approach a river. You don't know that there is a river, and when you come to that river it is quite unexpected. For miles there is no human habita-tion. You cannot swim across, it is all full of crocodiles. So what? Such an obstacle hadn't been foreseen, but it may be you have had a hunch that you should remain in the least likely spot and wait for the following day when you can build a raft or something, or look for possibilities.

You can also have intuitions—and this constantly hap-pens—in our jungle called a city. You can have a hunch that something is going wrong, particularly when you are driving an automobile. For instance, it is the day when nurses appear in the street. And they always try to get something interesting, like a suicide, you know—to be run over, that's more marvellous apparently. And then you get a peculiar feeling, and really, at the next corner there is a second nurse that runs in front of the automobile. Duplication of cases, that is a rule, you know; such chance happenings come in groups.

So you see, we constantly have warnings, hints, that consist perhaps in a slight feeling of uneasiness, uncertainty, fear. Under primitive conditions you would pay attention to these things, they mean something. With us in our man-made, absolutely—apparently—safe conditions, we don't need that function so very much, yet we still use it. You will find the intuitive types among bankers, Wall Street men; they follow their hunches, and so do gamblers of all descriptions. You find the type very frequently among doctors, because it helps them in their prognoses. Sometimes a case can look quite normal, as it were, and you don't foresee any complications, yet an inner voice tells you, Now watch out, here is something not quite right. You can't tell why or how, but we have a lot of subliminal sense perceptions, and from them we probably draw a good deal of our intuitions. That is perception by way of the unconscious, and you can observe it with intuitive types.

Intuitive types very often do not perceive by their eyes or by their ears, they perceive by intuition. For instance, it once happened that I had a woman patient in the morning at nine o'clock. I often smoke my pipe and have a certain smell of tobacco in the room, or a cigar. And she came and said, "But you begin earlier than nine o'clock"—earlier, I said, you call that early?—"you must have seen somebody at eight o'clock." I said, "How do you know?" There *had* been a man there that had come at eight o'clock already. And she said, "Oh, I just had a hunch that there must have been a gentleman with you this morning." I said, "Hum, but how do you know it was a gentleman?" And she said, "Oh well, I just had the impression, the atmosphere was just like a gentleman here." And all the time, you know, the ash tray was under her nose, and there was a half-smoked cigar! But she wouldn't notice it. The intuitive is a type that doesn't see, doesn't see the stumbling block before his feet, but he smells a rat for ten miles.

More specifically, what would be an example of the differ-
ence between an intuitive extravert and an intuitive in-
trovert?

Well, you know, you have chosen a somewhat difficult ease, because one of the most difficult types is the intuitive introvert. The intuitive extravert you find among hunters, bankers, gamblers; that is quite understandable. But the introvert variety is more difficult because he has intuitions about the subjective factor, the inner world. That is very difficult to understand because what he sees are most uncommon things, and he doesn't like to talk about them if he is not a fool. He would spoil his own game by telling what he sees, because people won't understand it.

Once I had a patient, a young woman about 27 or 28. Her first words were when I had seated her, "You know, doctor, I come to you because I have a snake in my abdomen." "*What?!*" "Yes, a snake, a black snake coiled up right in the bottom of my abdomen." I must have made a rather bewildered face at her, for she said, "You know, I don't mean it literally, but I should say it was a snake, a snake." In our further conversation a little later—that was about the middle of her treatment which lasted only for ten consultations—she said she had foretold me, "I'll come ten times, and then it will be all right." "But how do you know?" I asked. "Oh, I've got a hunch." And really, about the fifth or sixth consultation she said, "Oh, doctor, I must tell you, the snake has risen, it is now about here." Hunch! Then on the tenth day I said, "Now this is our last consultation. Do you feel cured?" And she said, beaming, "You know, this morning it came up, it came out of my mouth, and the head was golden." Those were her last words.

Now that same girl—when it comes to reality—came to me because she couldn't hear the step of her feet any more, because she walked on air, literally. She couldn't hear it, and that frightened her. When she came to see me I asked for her address, and she said, "Oh, pension so and so. Well, it is not called a pension exactly but it is a sort of pension." I had never heard of it. "Now that is curious," I said, "I have never heard of that place." "Well, it's a very nice place. Curiously enough, there are only young girls there, very nice and very lively young girls, and they have a merry time. I often wish they would invite me to their merry evenings." I said, "And do they amuse themselves all alone?" "Oh, no, they have plenty of young gentlemen coming in, and they have a beautiful time, but they never invite me." It turned out that it was a private brothel. She was a perfectly decent girl, you know, of a very good family, not from here. She had found that place, I don't know how, and she was utterly unaware that they were all prostitutes. And I said, "For heaven's sake, you fell into a very dark place! You hurry up and get out of it."

That was her sensation, she didn't see reality, but she had hunches like anything, and they came off. Such a person cannot possibly speak of her experiences because everybody would think she's absolutely crazy. I myself was quite shocked, and I thought, For heaven's sake, is that a case of schizophrenia? You don't hear that kind of talk, but she assumed that the old man, of course, knows everything, and even understands that kind of language. So you see, if the introverted intuitive were to speak of what he really perceives, practically no one would understand him. They learn to keep things to themselves, and you hardly ever hear them talking of these things. That is a great disadvantage, but it is an enormous advantage in another way, not to speak of the experiences they have in that respect and also in their human relations. For instance, they come into the presence of somebody they don't know, and suddenly they have inner images, and these images give them more or less complete information about the psychology of the partner. It can also happen that they come into the presence of somebody they don't know at all, not from Adam, and they know an important piece out of the biography of that person, and are not aware of it, and they tell the story, and then the fat is in the fire.[18] So the introverted intuitive has in a way a very difficult life, although one of the most interesting lives, but it is often difficult to get into their confidence.

Yes, because you say they are afraid people will think they are sick.

The things that are interesting to them, or are vital to them, are utterly strange to the ordinary individual, and a psychologist should know of such things. When people make a psychology, as a psychologist ought to do, his very first question is, Is he extraverted or is he introverted? They will look at entirely different things. Is he a sensation type, is he an intuitive type, is he a thinking or a feeling type? These things are complicated. They are still more complicated because the introverted thinker, for instance, is compensated by inferior, archaic, extraverted feeling. So an introverted thinker may be very crude in his feeling: the introverted philosopher who is always carefully avoiding women will be married by his cook in the end! [Laughter.]

So we can take your introvert-extravert category and describe the introverted sensation type, the extraverted sensa-

[18] For an example from Jung's own biography see *Memories, Dreams, Reflections,* p. 51/61.

tion type, the introverted thinking type, and so on. In each case it does not stand for a real category but is simply a model that helps us to understand the individual.

It is just a sort of skeleton to which you have to add the flesh. Or you could say it is like a country mapped out by triangulation points. That doesn't mean the country consists of triangulation points, it is only in order to have an idea of the distances. It is a means to an end. It only makes sense, such a scheme, when you deal with practical cases. If you have to explain an introverted intuitive husband to an extravert wife it is a most painstaking affair, because, you see, an extraverted sensation type is the furthest away from inner experiences and the rational functions. She adapts and behaves according to the facts as they are, and she is always caught by those facts. She, herself, is those facts. But if the introvert is intuitive, to him that is hell, because as soon as he is in a definite situation he tries to find a hole where he can get out. Every given situation is just the worst that can happen to him. He is pinched and he feels caught, suffocated, chained. He must break those fetters because he is the man who will discover a new field. He will plant that field, and as soon as the young plants are coming up, he's finished, he's done, he's no more interested. He is all right, and others will reap what he has sown. When those two marry each other there is trouble, I assure you.

Yes indeed. Now speaking of the intuitive type, you are of course familiar with the work of J. B. Rhine at Duke University. Some of his work in extrasensory perception, clairvoyance, and telepathy sounds quite a bit like your research into the intuitive function. Would you say that a person who has clairvoyance would be an intuitive type?

That's quit probable. Or it can be a sensation type, say an extraverted sensation type who is very much influenced by the unconscious. He has introverted intuition in his unconscious, you see. There are two groups, the rational and the irrational. The rational group is thinking and feeling. The ideal thinking is a rational result, and so is feeling, it is a rational value. That is differentiated feeling. But sensation is necessarily irrational because it may *not* prejudice facts. The ideal perception of reality is that you have an accurate perception of things as they are, without additions or corrections. Intuition doesn't look at things as they are; that is prison, that is anathema to the intuitive. He looks, oh, ever so shortly at things as they are and makes off into an unconscious process, at the end of which he has seen something nobody else would have seen. The people who yield the best results [in Rhine's experiments] are always those who are introverted, or where introverted intuition comes in. But that is a side aspect of it, it is not interesting. There is another question which is far more interesting, and that is the terms they use. Rhine himself uses them—precognition, telepathy, etc. They mean nothing at all. They are words, but he thinks he has said something when he says "telepathy."

The word itself is not a description of the process.
Not a description. It means nothing, nothing at all.

Now of course, a lot of the things you are describing I think scientists will say are due to chance. Chance occurrences, chance factors. Rhine uses statistical methods, and he reports these occurrences more often than would be expected by chance.
Well, you see, he proves that it is more than chance, it is statistically graspable. That is the important point and it hasn't been contradicted. There was some such proof to the contrary in England, and they said, Oh, Rhine, that's nothing but guesswork. Exactly! That's it, it is guessing, what you call guessing. A hunch is guessing; a definite guess, you know, is a hunch—just that. But it means nothing. The point is that [with Rhine the result] is more than

merely probable, it is beyond chance. That is the great problem. But people hate problems they can't deal with, and they can't deal with this one. Even Rhine very often does not understand our argument in this respect, because it is a relativation—now I am going to say something which in these sacred rooms is anathema—a relativation of time and space through the psyche. That's the fact, and that is what Rhine has made evident. Now swallow that! Well, that's difficult.

May I go a little further into some of your recent work, which is indeed very profound, and is not too well known to many of our students—

Of course not! Nobody reads these things, only the general public. Because my books are at least sold. [Laughter.]

I'm referring to the concept of synchronicity—[19]
Uh-huh!

which would have some relevance at this point in our discussion. Would you care to comment a little bit?

That is awfully complicated, one wouldn't know where to begin. Of course this kind of thinking started long ago, and when Rhine brought out his results I thought now we have at least a more or less dependable basis to argue on. But the argument was not understood at all because it is really very difficult. When you observe the unconscious you come across plenty of instances of a very peculiar kind of parallel events. For example, I have a certain thought, or a certain subject is occupying my attention and my interest. At the same time something else happens, quite independently, that portrays just that thought. Now this is utter nonsense, you know, looked at from the causal point of view. That it is not nonsense is made evident by the results of Rhine's experiments. There is a probability, it is something more than chance that such an event occurs.

[19] Cf. "Synchronicity: An Acausal Connecting Principle," CW 8.

I have never made statistical experiments except one in the way Rhine did. I made it for another purpose.[20] But I have come across quite a number of cases where it was most astonishing to find that two causal chains happened at the same time, but independently of each other, so that you could say they had nothing to do with each other. Of course that's quite clear. For instance, I speak of a red car and at that moment a red car comes along. I hadn't seen it, it was impossible because it was behind the building until just this moment when the red car appears. Now this seems mere chance. Yet the Rhine experiment proves that these cases are not mere chance. Of course many of these things are occurrences to which we cannot apply such an argument, otherwise we would be superstitious. We can't say, "This car has appeared because some remarks had been made about a red car. It is a miracle that the red car appears." It is not, it is chance, just chance. But these "chances" happen more often than chance allows, and that shows there is something behind it. Rhine has a whole institute with many co-workers and has the means. We have no means here, you know, to make such experiments, otherwise I would probably have done them. But it is just physically impossible. So I had to content myself with the observation of facts.

Third Interview

Dr. Jung, one question which is quite important as we attempt to understand the psychology of the individual centers around the problem of motivation, why the person does what he does. To some degree you have already talked about that when you discussed the archetypes. However, to go further into this problem, earlier when we spoke of the libido you felt it was more than just sexual energy. You thought it could be something much broader. Now you

[20] "An Astrological Experiment," ibid., pp. 459ff.

have certain principles concerning psychic energy which are very provocative, and one of these principles, I believe, you refer to as the principle of entropy.

Well I only allude to it,[21] you know. The main thing is the standpoint of energetics as applied to psychic phenomena. There you have no possibility of exact measurement, so it always remains a sort of analogy. Freud uses the term "libido" in the sense of sexual energy, and that is not quite correct. If it is sexual, then it is a power like electricity or any other manifestation of energy. Now energy is a concept by which you try to express by analogy all the manifestations of power. They have a certain quantity, a certain intensity, there is a flow in one direction tending towards the ultimate suspension of opposites, for instance "high" and "low." A lake on a mountain flows downwards until all the water is down, then it is finished.

Something similar is the case in psychology. We get tired from intellectual work, or from consciously living, and then we must sleep to restore our powers. It is just as if in the night the water were pumped from a lower level to a higher level so that we can work again the next day. Of course that simile is lame too, so it is only in an analogous way that we use the term "energy." I used it because I wanted to express the fact that the power manifestation of sexuality is not the only power drive, say the drive to conquer or the drive to aggression. There are many forms, you see. Take the animals, the way they build their nests, or the urge of traveling birds that migrate. They are all driven by a sort of energy manifestation, and the meaning of the word "sexuality" would be entirely lost if everything were that. Freud himself saw that it was not applicable everywhere, and later on he corrected himself by assuming that there are also ego drives. That is something else, that's another manifestation. Now in order not to presume or to prejudice things I speak

[21] "On Psychic Energy," ibid., pp. 25ff.

simply of energy, a quantity of energy that can manifest itself via sexuality or any other instinct. That is the main feature, not the existence of one single power, because that is not warrantable.

Another thing about motivation is that there seem to be two views in much of our American psychology today. One might be called an historical view, where we try to look at the history and development of the individual for answers as to why he is doing a certain thing at a certain moment. Then there is another view postulated by Kurt Lewin, which is a sort of field theory. He thinks that history, the past, is not as important in motivation as all the conditions which affect the individual at the moment. We can predict behavior by knowing these conditions and don't have to go back into the past to understand why a person does what he does. Do you think Lewin's "present field" theory has any merit?

Well, obviously. I always insist that even a chronic neurosis has its true cause in the present moment—now.[22] You see, neurosis is made every day by the wrong attitude the individual has, but that wrong attitude is a historical fact and needs to be explained historically by things that have happened in the past. Yet that is one-sided too, because all psychological facts are oriented not only to a cause but also to a goal. They are, in a sense, teleological because they serve a certain purpose. The wrong attitude can have originated, in a certain way, long ago, but it wouldn't exist today any more if there were not immediate causes and immediate purposes that keep it alive. And so a neurosis can be finished suddenly on a certain day in spite of all causes. Further, at the beginning of the war one observed that cases of compulsion neurosis which had lasted for many years suddenly were cured because they got into an entirely

---

[22] Cf. "The Theory of Psychoanalysis," CW 4, pp. 157ff.

new condition. It is like a shock, you see that with shock. Even schizophrenics can be vastly improved by a shock, because that's a new condition; it is a very shocking thing that shocks them out of their habitual attitude. They are no longer in it, and then the whole thing collapses, the whole system that has been built up for years.

So in working with a patient, you would not say it is absolutely imperative to have to reformulate all of his past life in order to help him with his present neurosis?

There is no system about it in therapy. In therapy you treat the patient as he is in the present moment, irrespective of causes and such things. That is all more or less theoretical. There are cases who know just as much about their own neurosis as I do, in a way. In such cases I can start right away with posing the problem. For instance, there is a case, a professor of philosophy, and he imagines that he has cancer.[23] He shows me several dozen X-ray plates that prove there is no cancer. He says, "Of course I have no cancer, but nevertheless I am afraid I could have one. I've consulted ever so many surgeons and they all assure me there is none, and I know there is none, but I *might* have one, you see, and that's enough." Such a case can stop from one moment to the next, he simply stops thinking such a foolish thing. But that is exactly what he cannot do.

In such a case I say, "Well, it's perfectly plain to you that it's nonsense what you believe. Now why are you forced to believe such nonsense? What is the power that makes you think such a thing against your free will? You know it is nonsense, so why should you think it?" It's like a possession, you know. Exactly like a demon in him that makes him think like that, in spite of the fact that he doesn't want to. That is the problem for an intellectual man. Then I say, "Now you don't know, you have no answer. I have no answer. So what are we going to do?" I say, "Now we

23 Cf. "Psychology and Religion," pp. 10ff.

will see what you dream, because a dream is the manifestation of the unconscious side." He has never heard of the
unconscious side, so I must explain to him that he has an
unconscious and that the dream is a manifestation of it,
and if we succeed in analyzing the dream we might get an
idea about that power that makes him think like that. In
such a case one can begin right away with the analysis of
dreams, and in all cases that are a bit serious. Mind you,
this is not a simple case, it is a very serious and difficult case
in spite of the simplicity of the phenomenology and the
symptomatology.

In all cases after the preliminaries, such as the history of
the family, the whole medical anamnesis, etc., we come to
that question, What is it in your unconscious that makes
you wrong, that hinders you from thinking normally?
Then we reach a point where we can begin with the observation of the unconscious, and day by day we proceed
by the data the unconscious produces. We discuss the dream
and that gives a new surface to the whole problem. Then
he will have another dream, and the next dream again
gives an answer, because the unconscious is in a compensatory relation to consciousness, and after a while we get the
full picture. And if he has the full picture and has the
necessary moral stamina, well then he can be cured. But in
the end it is a moral question whether a man applies what
he has learned or not.

*Then in this situation the unconscious plays a very impor-
tant part. But as you see it, what you have found in the
dream is not necessarily an image or symbol of what has
happened in the past?*

Oh no, not at all! It is just the symbol. The symbol, you
see, is a special term. The symbolic expression in a dream
is a manifestation of the situation of the unconscious,
looked at from the unconscious. Suppose I tell you something which is my personal subjective view, and if I ask

myself, "Now are you really quite convinced of it?" I must admit I have certain doubts—not in the moment when I tell you, but these doubts are in the unconscious. And when I have a dream about it, these doubts come to the forefront in my dreams. That is the way the unconscious looks at the thing, it is just as though it says, It is all very well what you are saying, but you omit entirely such and such a point.

Now if the unconscious acts on the present situation, looking at this in broad motivational terms, this effect of the unconscious is not the result of repression in the way the orthodox psychoanalyst looks at it?

No, it may be that what the unconscious has to say is so disagreeable that one prefers not to listen. And in most cases people would probably be less neurotic if they could admit these things. But these things are always a bit difficult, or disagreeable, or inconvenient, or something of the sort. So there is always a certain amount of repression, but that is not the main thing. The main thing is that they are really unconscious. If you are unconscious about certain things that ought to be conscious, you are dissociated. Then you are a man whose left hand never knows what the right is doing and counteracts or interferes with the right hand. Such a man is hampered all over the place.

Would you say that the unconscious of a particular individual who was raised in an entirely different culture, say in India, would be in many respects similar to the unconscious of another individual who, we'll say, had lived in Switzerland all his life?

Well, that question is also complicated because when we speak of the unconscious we should almost say "which unconscious?" Is it the personal unconscious which is characteristic of a particular individual?

You have the personal unconscious as one kind of unconscious.

Yes. In the treatment of neurosis you have to do with that personal unconscious for quite a while, and only then do dreams come which show that the collective unconscious is being touched upon. As long as there is material of a personal nature you have to deal with the personal unconscious. But when you get to a problem which is no more merely personal but also collective, you get collective dreams.

The distinction between the personal unconscious and the collective unconscious, then, is that the personal would be more involved with the immediate life of the individual, and the collective would be universal, having the same elements in all men?

Yes. Every society has collective problems, collective convictions, and so on. We are very much influenced by them. For instance, you belong to a certain political party, or profess a certain creed, and that can be a serious determinant of your behavior. Now as long as a personal conflict doesn't touch upon it, the collective unconscious is no problem, it doesn't appear. But the moment you transcend your personal sphere and come to your impersonal determinants, say to a political question or any other social question which really matters to you, then you are confronted with a collective problem, and then you have collective dreams.

I wonder if it would be too presumptuous of me to ask if you could think of an actual case of a patient or a friend that would show us how the personal and the collective unconscious were acting in his neurosis or in a problem he may have had.

Well you see, there is an enormous amount of personal dreams and I couldn't possibly tell you just one from such an *embarras de richesse*. There are millions of personal dreams that simply deal with your relation to your father, or to your mother, or to your wife, and so on, with all sorts of individual variations. But suppose a patient comes to that deeper level, or that his conflict begins to get really serious so that his mind might suffer, then he can have a collective dream in which clearly mythological motifs appear. There are plenty of examples in the literature. I wrote a book, you know, called *Psychology of the Unconscious*,[24] about such dreams.

I remember the case of a very learned man, very rational.[25] He had of course a lot of personal problems, but they got so bad that he got into very disagreeable relations with his whole surroundings. He was a member of a society and he got into a brawl with the people of that society, it was really quite shocking. Now, he started with collective dreams. Suddenly he dreamt of things he had never in his life thought of before—mythological motifs, and he thought he was crazy, because he couldn't understand it at all, it was just as if the whole world were transformed. That is what you see in cases of schizophrenia, but this wasn't a case of schizophrenia. As examples you can take any of these collective dreams I have published, there are plenty. For the moment I cannot remember a suitable example. To make it clear I should have to tell a long story and then you would see what I mean, otherwise it makes no sense to give you something short.

I told you the case of that intuitive girl who suddenly came out with the statement that she had a black snake in her belly. Well now, that is a collective symbol. That is not an individual fantasy, it is a collective fantasy. It is well known in India. She had nothing to do with India, but though it is entirely unknown to us we have it too, for we are all similarly human. So I even thought in the first moment that perhaps she was crazy, but she was only highly intuitive. In India the serpent is at the basis of a whole philosophical system, of Tantrism; it is Kundalini, the Kundalini serpent. This is something known only to a few specialists, generally it is not known that we have a serpent in

---

[24] Revised as *Symbols of Transformation*, CW 5.
[25] This case forms Part II of *Psychology and Alchemy*, CW 12.

the abdomen. That is a collective dream or a collective fantasy.

In the day to day life of the individual, is it possible that things that trouble him and cause tension lead to repression, and these become part of the personal unconscious?

Yes, but he doesn't repress consciously always. These things disappear, simply, and Freud explains that by an act of repression. But you can prove that these things have never been conscious before. They simply don't appear, and you don't know why they don't appear. Of course, *après le coup*, you can say that is why they didn't appear, they were disagreeable or incompatible with one's conscious views, one's conscious attitude. But that is afterwards, you couldn't predict it.

So you see, these things that have an emotional tone, they are partially autonomous, they can appear or, on the contrary, not appear. They can disappear at will, not of the subject, but of their own, though you can also repress them. It is the same with projections. People say, One makes projections. It's nonsense, one doesn't make them, one finds them. They are already there, because *here* the unconscious is not conscious, but *there* it is conscious, in my brother. There I see the beam in my own eye as a mote in my brother's eye. It is right there because I am unconscious of the beam in my own eye. And so these disappearances, or so-called repressions, are just like projections. Instead of being projected into somebody or something outside, they are introjected. But you are not the one that is doing it, they are already unconscious. There are cases [of conscious repression], sure, but I should say the majority aren't repressions. That was my first point of difference with Freud. I saw in the association experiment that certain complexes are quite definitely not repressed. They simply won't appear. Because, you see, the unconscious is real, it is an entity, it works by itself, it is autonomous.

So looking at the so-called defense mechanisms, projection, rationalization, etc., you would differ from the orthodox psychoanalytic view in that you would not say they are developed by way of repression as a means of defending the ego?

Yes, take the example of that serpent. That never had been repressed, otherwise it would have been conscious to her. On the contrary it was unconscious to her and appeared only in her fantasy, quite spontaneously. She didn't know how she came to it. She said, Well, I just saw it.

Some orthodox psychoanalysts might have said it was a phallic symbol.

Yes, of course, but you can say anything, you know. You can say a church spire is a phallic symbol, but when you dream of a penis, what is that? You know what an analyst said, one of the orthodox, the old guard, he said, "In this case the censor has not functioned." Now, you call that a scientific explanation? [Laughter.]

Very interesting, Dr. Jung, very interesting indeed. Now another concept related to motivational development is the process of individuation, which you frequently refer to in your writings. Would you care to comment on this process of psychic development towards a whole, a totality?

Well, you know, that is something quite simple. Take an acorn, put it in the ground, it grows and becomes an oak. That is man. Man develops from an egg, and grows into the whole man, and that is the law that is in him.

So you think psychic development is in many ways like biological development?

It is a fact that people develop psychically on the same principle as they develop in the body. Why should we assume it is a different principle? It is really the same kind of evolutionary behavior as the body shows. Take those animals that have specially differentiated anatomical characteristics, those of the teeth, or something like that. Well, those characteristics are in accordance with their psychic behavior, or their psychic behavior is in accordance with those organs.

So as you see it there is no need to bring in other theories to explain psychic development?
The psyche is no different from the living being, it is the psychic aspect of the living being. It is even the psychic aspect of matter, a quality of matter [. . .] I couldn't discuss the [physical] implications.

Well, you yourself have a background in physics—
Nothing to speak of.

Reading your work one is aware that you know archaeology, anthropology—
Well, inasmuch as my work is concerned with it, but I have no mathematical gifts, you know. You cannot get a real knowledge or understanding of nuclear physics without a good deal of mathematics, higher mathematics. There I only have a certain relation with it on the epistemological questions. Modern physics is truly entering the sphere of the invisible and intangible.

It is in reality a field of probabilities, you know, that is exactly the same as the unconscious. I have often discussed this with Professor Pauli.[26] He is a nuclear physicist, and to my amazement I found that they have terms which are used in psychology too, and simply on account of the fact that we are entering a sphere—the one from without, and we from within—which is unknown. That's the reason for the parleys between psychology and higher mathematics. For instance, we use the term "transcendent function."[27] Now the

---

[26] Wolfgang Pauli, awarded the Nobel Prize, d. 1958. His paper "The Influence of Archetypal Ideas on the Scientific Theories of Kepler" appears in Jung and Pauli, *The Interpretation of Nature and the Psyche* (1955).
[27] Cf. "The Transcendent Function," CW 8.

transcendental function is a mathematical term for the function of irrational and imaginary numbers. That is higher mathematics with which I have nothing to do. But we come to the same terminology.

When you spoke of Dr. Einstein in your earlier discussion,[28] *you were saying that he more or less tried out some of his ideas on you. Did you ever suggest the possibility that relativity might apply to psychic functions?*

Well, you know how it is when a man is so concentrated on his own ideas. And when he is a mathematician on top of everything, you are not welcome.

What year was it that you were friends with Einstein?

I wouldn't call myself a friend, I was simply the host. I tried to listen and to understand, so there was little chance to insert any of my own ideas.

Was this after he had formulated his relativity theory?

It was just when he was working on it, right in the beginning. It was very interesting, very interesting.

In your dealings with Professor Toynbee, have you gotten rather interested in his ideas of history?

Ah yes, his ideas about the life of civilizations and the way they are ruled by archetypal forms. Toynbee has seen what I mean by the historical function of archetypal developments. That is a mighty important determinant of human behavior that lasts for centuries or for thousands of years. It expresses itself in symbols, sometimes symbols you would think nothing of at all. You know that Russia, the Soviet Republics, have that symbol of the red star. It is a five-rayed red star. America has the five-rayed white star.

---

[28] As the reader may have observed, there has been no previous reference to Einstein. Such a reference may be among the passages cut out of the tape, or it may have been made to Prof. Evans in private conversation. Cf. "The Tavistock Lectures," CW 18, par. 140.

They are enemies, they can't come together. Now you see in the Middle Ages, in alchemy, for at least two thousand years the red and the white were the royal pair, ultimately destined to marry each other.

I see. Very interesting. Very, very interesting.

America is a sort of matriarchy, most of the money is in the hands of women. And Russia is the land of the little father, it's a patriarchy. So the two are mother and father. In the Middle Ages they were called the white woman, the "femina candida," and the "servus rubeus," the red slave. The two lovers have quarrelled with each other![29] [Laughter.]

Now after this very pleasant little digression I would like to ask you about something that seems to be a very fundamental part of your writing, and that is the term "mandala." I would be most interested to have your observations on this.

The mandala is just one typical archetypal form.[30] It is what they called in alchemy the *quadratura circuli*, the square in the circle or the circle in the square. It is an age-old symbol that goes right back to the prehistory of man. It is found all over the earth and it expresses either the deity or the self. These two terms are psychologically very much related—which doesn't mean that I believe that God is the self or that the self is God. I simply state that there is a psychological relation between them. There is plenty of evidence for this.

The mandala is a very important archetype. It is the archetype of inner order, and it is always used in that sense, either to make an arrangement of the many, many aspects of the universe, a world scheme, or to make a scheme of our psyche. It expresses the fact that there is a center and a periphery, and it tries to embrace the whole. It is the

[29] Cf. "Flying Saucers," par. 790.
[30] Cf. "Concerning Mandala Symbolism," CW 9, Part I.

symbol of wholeness. So you see, when during the treatment there is a great disorder and chaos in a man's mind, this symbol can appear in the form of a mandala in a dream, or else he makes imaginary, fantastical drawings, or something of that sort. The mandala appears spontaneously as a compensatory archetype, bringing order, showing the possibility of order. It denotes a center which is not coincident with the ego but with the wholeness which I call the self—this is the term for wholeness. I am not whole in my ego, my ego is a fragment of my personality. The center of a mandala is not the ego, it is the whole personality, the center of the whole personality. The mandala plays a very great role in the East, but in our Middle Ages equally. Then it got lost, and was thought of merely as a sort of allegorical, decorative motif. But as a matter of fact it is a highly important and highly autonomous symbol that appears in dreams and so on, or in folklore. We could easily say that it is the main archetype.

Speaking of this totality which as you say is a sort of unified self, sometimes we try in psychology to start from whatever totality does exist in the individual and to look into the underlying motivation, and we have recently used a great deal of what we call "projective tests." We all know you played a major role in developing this point of view with your word association method. What are the ingredients of the word association test? What is involved in the use of it?

You mean the practical use of it?

Yes.

Oh well, you see, in the beginning when I was a young man I was of course completely disoriented with patients. I didn't know where to begin or what to say, and the association experiment gave me access to their unconscious. I learnt about the things they did not tell me, and I got a deep insight into the things they did not know, and I discovered many things.

In other words, from these responses you discovered complexes, or emotional blocks—of course, this word "complex" originated with you and it's very widely used now—

Yes, the *gefühlsbetonter Komplex*, that is one of my terms.

Did you hope from these complexes or emotional blocks to get at materials of the personal unconscious or the racial unconscious?

In the beginning there was no question of a collective unconscious or anything like that. It was chiefly the ordinary personal complexes.

I see. You weren't expecting to get into such depths.

Among hundreds of complex associations there might appear an archetypal element, but that wouldn't show particularly. That is not the point. You know it is like the Rorschach, a superficial orientation.

You knew Hermann Rorschach, I believe, did you not?

No, he circumvented me as much as possible.

But did you get to know him personally?

No, I never saw him.

In his terms "introtensive" and "extrotensive," of course, he is reflecting your conceptions of introversion and extraversion.

Yes, but I was anathema because I had said it first, and that is unforgiveable. I should never have done it.

So you really didn't have any personal contacts with Rorschach?

No personal relation at all.

Are you familiar with his test?

Yes, I know it. But I never applied it because later on I didn't apply the association test any more, because it wasn't necessary. I learned what I had to learn from the exact examination of psychic reactions. I think it is a very excellent means.

Would you recommend the practising psychiatrist, the clinical psychologist, to use projective tests like the Rorschach test?

For the practical training of psychologists who do actual work with people, I think it is one of the best means of making them see how the unconscious works. It is exceedingly didactic. You can demonstrate repression and the amnestic phenomena, the way people cover up their emotions, and so on. It is like an ordinary conversation, but seen and measured in its principles. That is what makes it so interesting. You observe all the things you observe in a conversation. You ask people something and discuss certain things, and you observe little hesitations, mistakes in speech, certain gestures. All that comes into the foreground, and it is measurable, you know, in the experiment. And so I think I don't overrate the didactic value of it, I think very highly of it. And we still use it in the training of young alienists. Or, if I have a case that doesn't want to talk, I can make such an experiment and find out a lot of things through the experiment. I have, for instance, discovered a murder.[31]

Is that right?
Yes.

Would you like to tell us how this is done?
You have that lie detector in the United States. Well, that is the association test I worked out with the psychogalvanic phenomenon.[32] And we did a lot of work also with

[31] This may be the case discussed in "The Tavistock Lectures," CW 18, par. 108. Cf. also *Memories, Dreams, Reflections*, pp. 115ff./ 117f.
[32] "Psychophysical Investigations wtih the Galvanometer and Pneumograph in Normal and Insane Individuals," CW 2.

the pneumograph, to show the decrease in the volume of breathing under the influence of a complex.[33] That is one of the causes of tuberculosis, it arises from such a condition. Some people have a very shallow breathing, don't ventilate the apices of their lungs any more, and get tuberculosis. Half of the tubercular cases are psychic.

This question of psychic tubercular cases, etc., gets us into a particularly interesting area of motivation that we're talking a lot about in the United States, and I'm sure is of interest to you, as this is the whole area of psychosomatic medicine.

I have seen a lot of astounding cures of tuberculosis, chronic tuberculosis, by analysis, where people learnt to breathe again. It would not help them if they had learned to breathe normally, but understanding what their complexes were, that helped them.

When did you first become interested in the psychic factors of tuberculosis? Was it many years ago?

I was an alienist to begin with, I was always interested, naturally. Presumably because I understood so little of it, or I noticed they understood so little.

Right now we are becoming more and more interested in the very thing you are saying, how the emotional, unconscious personality factors can actually have an effect on the body. The classic example in the United States is the peptic ulcer. We believe this is a case where emotional factors have actually created the pathology. These ideas have been extended into many other areas. It is felt that where there already is a pathology these emotional factors can intensify it. Many of our physicians say that sixty to seventy per cent of their patients do not have anything physically wrong with them, but instead have disorders of psychosomatic origin.

[33] "Further Investigations on the Galvanic Phenomenon and Respiration in Normal and Insane Individuals," CW 2.

Yes, that is well known for more than fifty years. But the question is how to cure them.

Do you have any ideas as to why the patient selects this type of symptom?

He doesn't select them, they happen to him. You could just as well ask when you are eaten by a crocodile, how you happened to select that crocodile. He has selected you. [Laughter.]

Of course it means that, in a sense, you selected unconsciously—

No, not even unconsciously.

You don't believe there is any way of tracing in the personality of the individual the reasons why—

That is an extraordinary exaggeration of the importance of the subject, as if he were choosing such things. They get him.

So even unconsciously there isn't this degree of freedom. But to get back to psychosomatic medicine, recently it has hinted that cancer may have psychosomatic involvements.

Yes, yes.

And this doesn't surprise you?

Not at all. We knew these things long ago, you know. Fifty years ago we already had these cases, ulcer of the stomach, tuberculosis, chronic arthritis, skin diseases. All are psychogenic under certain conditions.

Even cancer?

Well, you see, I couldn't swear, but I have seen cases where I wondered whether there was not a psychogenic reason for that particular ailment. It came too conveniently.

And some of these studies in the United States show that Jewish women practically never get cancer in the vaginal region, but more often say in the breast region.

332

Well, many things can be found out about cancer, I'm sure. You see, to us it was always a question of how to treat these things, and anything is possible. Every disease has a psychological accompaniment, and it all depends—perhaps life depends—on whether you treat such a patient psychologically in the proper way or not. That can help tremendously, even if you cannot prove in the least that the disease in itself is psychogenic. Or you can have an infectious disease in a certain moment when you are in a psychic predicament, because then you are particularly accessible to an infection. Tonsillitis is a typical psychological disease, yet it is not psychological in its physical causation. It's just an infection. But why did you get it then? Well, it was just the psychological moment. When it is established and there is high fever and an abscess, you cannot cure it by psychology. Yet it is quite possible to avoid it by a proper psychological attitude.

So all this interest in psychosomatic medicine is pretty old stuff to you?

These things were all known here long ago. For instance, there is the toxic aspect of schizophrenia. I published it fifty years ago, just fifty years ago,[34] and now everyone discovers it. You are far ahead in America with technological things, but in psychological matters and suchlike you are fifty years behind the times. You simply don't understand them, and that's a fact. I'm sorry, I don't want to offend you, that's a general collective statement, you are simply not yet aware of what there is. There are plenty more things than people have any idea of. I told you the case of that theologian who didn't even know what a hierosgamos was and thought it was an apparition.[35] Everyone who says I am a mystic is just an idiot. He doesn't understand the first word of psychology.

[34] Cf. "The Psychology of Dementia Praecox," CW 3, pp. 35f., 97f.
[35] No previous reference. Cf. n. 28, above.

There is certainly nothing mystical about the statements you have just been making, Dr. Jung. Now to pursue this a little further, another development that falls right into line with this whole discussion of psychosomatic medicine has been the use of drugs to deal with psychological problems. A particular development has been the so-called non-addictive drugs which began in France with chlorpromazine, reserpine, serpentina, and a great variety of milder tranquillizers known by such trade names as Miltown and Equinal. They are now being administered very freely to patients by general practitioners and internists, not only to schizophrenics and others who are not approachable, but are being dispensed almost as freely as aspirins to reduce everyday tensions.

It is very dangerous.

Why do you think it is dangerous? They say these drugs are non-addictive.

It's just like the compulsion that is caused by morphine or heroin. It becomes a habit. You don't know what you are doing, you see, when you use such drugs. It is like the abuse of narcotics.

But the argument is that these are not habit-forming; they are not addictive, not physiologically.

Oh yes, that is what one says.

But you feel that psychologically there is still addiction?

Yes. There are many drugs that are not habit-forming like morphine, yet it becomes a psychic habit, and that is just as bad as anything else.

Have you actually seen any patients or had any contact with individuals who have been taking these particular drugs, these tranquillizers?

I can't say. You see with us there are very few. In America, you know, there are all those little tablets and powders.

Happily enough we are not yet so far. You see, American life is, in a subtle way, so one-sided and so *déraciné*, uprooted, that you must have something to compensate the earth. You have to pacify your unconscious all along the line because it is in an absolute uproar, so at the slightest provocation you have a big moral rebellion. Look at the rebellion of modern youth in America, the sexual rebellion, and all that. The real natural man is just in open rebellion against the·utterly inhuman form of life. You are absolutely divorced, you know, from nature in a way, and that accounts for the drug abuse.

But what about the treatment of seriously ill mental patients? We have the problem of hospitalized patients, the schizophrenics, manic-depressives. Certain schizophrenics are so withdrawn that you can't deal with them. In many hospitals they have been using drugs like chlorpromazine and the patient comes back to reality for a short time. I don't think most of our practitioners believe the drugs cure the patients in themselves, but at least they make the patient more amenable to psychotherapy.

Yes, the only question is whether that amenability is a real thing or drug-induced. I am sure that any kind of suggestive treatment will have an effect, because the patients simply become more suggestible. You see, any drug or shock undermines the moral stamina, making these people accessible to suggestion. And then they can be led, they can be made into something, but it is not a very happy result.

Fourth Interview

Dr. Jung, I know our students would be very interested in your opinion concerning the kind of training and background a psychologist should have. For example, there is one view that says he should be trained only in statistics and the rigorous scientific method, and this is the greatest tool he can have. However, there may be more to this problem of studying the individual than this rather narrow type of training. Would you like to comment on the type of training and background you think should be required of an individual as he tries to understand the human organism?

I don't quite understand what you mean.

Just to be a little bit more specific, do you think the humanities are important for the study of the individual?

Well, of course, when you study human psychology you can't help noticing that man's psychology doesn't consist only of the ramifications of instinct in his behavior. These are not the only determinants, there are many others, and the study of man from his biological aspect only is quite insufficient. To understand human psychology it is absolutely necessary that you study man also in his social and general environment. You have to consider the fact that there are different kinds of societies, different kinds of nations, different traditions, and for that purpose it is absolutely necessary to treat the problem of the human psyche from many standpoints. Each is a very considerable task, naturally.

Thus, after my association experiments, when I realized that there is obviously an unconscious, the question arose, Now what is this unconscious? Does it consist merely of remnants of conscious activities, or are there things that are practically forever unconscious? In other words, is the unconscious a factor in itself? I soon came to the conclusion that the unconscious must be a factor in itself, because I observed, time and again, that people's dreams, or schizophrenic patients' delusions and fantasies, contain motifs which they couldn't possibly have acquired in our surroundings. This is due to the fact, as I said earlier, that the child is not born a *tabula rasa* but is a definite mixture or combination of genes, and although the genes seem to contain chiefly dynamic factors, *arrangeurs* of certain types of behavior, they also have a tremendous importance for the arrangement of the psyche, as soon as the psyche appears, naturally. Before its appearance you cannot study it, but once it appears it has certain qualities, it has a certain character, and that must necessarily depend on the elements born in the child. So, factors determining human behavior are born with the child and determine its further development.

Now that is one side of the picture. The other side of the picture is that the individual lives in connection with others in certain surroundings that will influence the given combination of qualities. And that too is a very complicated factor, because the environmental influences are not merely personal. There are any amount of objective factors. The general social conditions, laws, convictions, ways of looking at things, of dealing with things, these are not of an arbitrary character. They are historical. There are historical reasons why things are as they are. And as there are historical reasons for the qualities of the psyche that is formed, there is such a thing as the history of man's evolution in past aeons, and that shows that a real understanding of the psyche must consist in the elucidation of the history of the human race. The history of the mind, for instance, as of the biological data.

So, when I wrote my first book on the psychology of the unconscious, I had already formed a certain idea of the nature of the unconscious. To me it was then a living remnant of the original history of man living in his surroundings—a very complicated picture. My material then, my empirical material, was supplied chiefly by lunatics, by cases of schizophrenia, and I had observed that there are, chiefly at the beginning of the disease, invasions of fantasies into conscious life, fantasies of an entirely unexpected sort, most bewildering to the patient. He is quite confused by these ideas and gets into a sort of panic because he never before had thought of such things; they are quite strange to him, and equally strange to his physician. You see the

337

alienist is equally dumfounded by the peculiar character of those fantasies. Therefore he says, That man is crazy. He is crazy to think such things, nobody thinks such things, and the patient agrees with him, and all the more he gets into a panic. So as an alienist I thought it was really the task of psychiatry to elucidate these things that broke into consciousness. These voices, these delusions. In those days— that is, mind you, more than forty or fifty years ago—I had no hope of being able to treat these cases or help them, but I had a very great scientific curiosity, and I wanted to know what these things really were. I thought that these things had a system, that they were not merely chaotic, decayed material, because there was too much sense in those fantasies.

So what I did then was, I studied cases of psychogenic diseases, like hysteria, hysterical somnambulism, and such things, where the contents that came from the unconscious were in a readable condition and could be understood. And then I saw that, in contradistinction to the schizophrenics, the mental contents of hysterics were of a humanly understandable character, they were even elaborate, dramatic, suggestive, insinuating, so one could make out a second personality. Now this is not the case in schizophrenia. There the fantasies are, on the contrary, unsystematic, chaotic, and you cannot make out a proper second personality, apart from rare cases of a complicated nature.

Now I knew of psychopathic cases, on the borderline between schizophrenia and hysteria, where ideas came up, delusions that were not exactly hysterical, because they were singularly difficult to understand, sort of strange, strange eruptions, and I thought that these cases could give me a better understanding. So I took the opportunity when Professor Flournoy, the old professor of psychology and philosophy at the university of Geneva, published a case of an American girl who had bestowed on him a series of half poetic and romantic fantasies. He published that material without commenting on it. He gave it as an example of creative imagination.[36] Now, when I read those fantasies I saw this was exactly the material I needed. I was always a bit afraid to tell of my personal experiences with patients because I felt people might say it was merely suggestion, you know. I took that case because I surely had no hand in it. It was old Professor Flournoy, an authority, he was a friend of William James. I knew him personally very well, a fine old man, and he certainly wouldn't be accused of having influenced the patient. And that is the reason why I analyzed these fantasies.

That case then became the subject of a whole book called *Psychology of the Unconscious*. It is now called *Symbols of Transformation*, and I have revised it after forty years. It needed it, because it was a first attempt. There I tried to show that there is a sort of unconscious—at that time I simply called it "the unconscious"—that clearly produces things which are historical and not personal. It was mythological material, the nature of which was not understood either by Professor Flournoy or by the patient. And there I tried for the first time to produce a picture of the functioning of the unconscious, a functioning which allowed certain conclusions to be drawn as to the nature of the unconscious.

Writing that book cost me my friendship with Freud, because he couldn't accept it. To him the unconscious was a product of consciousness, and simply contained all the remnants; it was a sort of store-room where all the things consciousness had discarded were heaped up and left. To me the unconscious then was already a matrix, a basis of consciousness of a creative nature, capable of autonomous acts, autonomous intrusions into consciousness. In other words, I took the existence of the unconscious for a real fact, a real autonomous factor capable of independent action.

[36] "Quelques Faits d'imagination créatrice subconsciente," *Archives de psychologie* (Geneva), V (1906), pp. 36–51. Translated in *Symbols of Transformation*, CW 5, appendix.

Now that was a psychological problem of the very first order, and it made me think furiously, because the whole of philosophy even in our day has not yet recognized that we have a counter-actor in our unconscious, that in our psyche there are two factors: consciousness is one, and there is another, equally important, the unconscious, that can interfere with consciousness any time it pleases. Of course I said to myself, "Now this is very uncomfortable, because I think I am the only master in my house." But I must admit there is another somebody in that house that can play tricks, and I have to deal with the unfortunate victims of that interference every day in my patients.

So the next thing I wrote was in 1916, a disquisition on the relations between the ego and the unconscious. There I tried to formulate the experiences that are more or less regularly observable in cases where consciousness is exposed to unconscious data, to interferences or intrusions; where the unconscious is considered an autonomous factor that has to be taken seriously, and one doesn't undervalue it any more by assuming that it is nothing but a discarded remnant of consciousness. It is a factor in its own right, and a very important factor, because it can create the most horrible disturbances. That was the pamphlet I wrote;[37] it was published in French, and nobody understood it. I saw that the reason why nobody understood it was that nobody had had a similar experience, because the question hadn't been pursued that far. Nobody had taken the unconscious seriously and considered it as a real factor that can determine human behavior to a very considerable degree.

So then I began an examination of human attitudes, how our consciousness functions. I couldn't help seeing, for instance, the difference between Freud and Adler, a typical

[37] "La Structure de l'inconscient," *Archives de psychologie*, XVI (1916), pp. 152–79. See "The Structure of the Unconscious," Appendix II in *Two Essays*, the original version of "The Relations between the Ego and the Unconscious" (ibid).

difference.[38] The one assumes that things evolve along the line of the sex instinct, the other assumes that things evolve along the line of the power drive. And there I was, in between the two. I could see the justification for Freud's view, and could see the same for Adler, and I knew that there were plenty of other ways in which things could be envisaged. And so I considered it my scientific duty to examine first the condition of the human consciousness. That is the originator of ways of envisaging; it is the factor that produces attitudes, conscious attitudes towards certain phenomena. When you know, for instance, that there are people who see the difference between red and green, you take it for granted that everybody sees that difference. Not at all. There are cases of trichromatism, and so on. The one sees this, the other sees that, and I tried to find out what the principal differences were.

That is the book about types. I saw first the introverted and extraverted attitudes, then the functional aspects, then which of the four functions is predominant. Now mind you, these four functions were not a scheme I had invented and applied to psychology. On the contrary, it took me quite a long time to discover that there is another type than the thinking type, as I thought my type to be—of course, that is human. It is not. There are other people who decide the same problems I have to decide, but in an entirely different way. They look at things in an entirely different light, they have entirely different values. There are, for instance, feeling types. And after a while I discovered that there are intuitive types. They gave me much trouble. It took me over a year to become a bit clearer about the existence of intuitive types. And the last, and the most unexpected, was the sensation type. And only later I saw that these are naturally the four aspects of conscious orientation.

You see, you get your orientation, you get your bearings

[38] Cf. *Two Essays*, pars. 56ff.

in the chaotic abundance of impressions, by the four functions. If you can tell me of any other aspect by which you get your orientation I shall be very grateful. I haven't found more. I tried. But those are the four that covered the thing. The intuitive type, which is very little understood, has a very important function because he goes by hunches, he sees around corners, he smells a rat a mile away. He can give you perception and orientation in a situation where your senses, your intellect and your feeling are no good at all. When you are in an absolute fix, an intuition can show you the hole through which you can escape. That is a very important function under primitive conditions, or wherever you are confronted with vital issues you cannot master by rules or by logic.

So, through the study of all sorts of human types, I came to the conclusion that there must be as many different ways of viewing the world. The aspect of the world is not one, it is many—at least 16, and you can just as well say 360. You can increase the number of principles, but I found the most simple way is the way I told you, the division by four, the simple and natural division of a circle. I didn't know the symbolism then of this particular classification. Only when I studied the archetypes did I become aware that this is a very important archetypal pattern that plays an enormous role.

I also found that the study of types gives you a lead as to the personal nature of the unconscious, its personal quality in a given case. If you take an extravert you will find his unconscious has an introverted quality, because all the extraverted qualities are played out in his consciousness and the introverted are left in the unconscious; therefore it has introverted qualities, and with the functions it is the same. That gave me a lead of diagnostic value, it helped me to understand my patients. When I knew their conscious type I got an idea about their unconscious attitude. And since a neurotic is influenced as much by the unconscious as he is by the conscious, he is influenced by another type, as it were. It is as if he were another type, and in certain cases it is almost impossible to say whether the individual is to be judged by his conscious quality or by his unconscious quality, because you cannot tell at first sight which is which. This helped me to understand the Freudian and the Adlerian aspect. It gave me an important lead, also, as to the way an individual is going when he is under actual analytical treatment. Because there the point is that you try to integrate unconscious contents into consciousness, to confront the individual who has a definite conscious attitude with its unconscious content that acts against him in his neurosis. It is just as if another personality of the opposite type were influencing him or disturbing him. And so, in the course of the years, I got a great deal of empirical material about the peculiar way in which the conscious and unconscious contents interact.

So through your typology you gradually developed a sort of psychology of opposites, where the conscious would reveal one side of the type and the unconscious would be the other side. This would be a very important way, then, of helping you to analyze and understand the individual.

From a practical point of view, it is diagnostically quite important. The point I wanted to elucidate is that in analyzing a patient you make typical experiences. There is a typical way in which the integration of consciousness takes place. The ordinary way is that through the analysis of dreams you become acquainted with the contents of the unconscious. I already told you this. To begin with it is all personal material: subjective problems, the individual's difficulties in adapting to environmental conditions, and so on. Now, it is a regular observation that when you talk to an individual and he gives you insight into his inner preoccupations, interests, emotions—in other words, hands over his personal complexes—you gradually get into a position of authority whether you like it or not. You become a point of reference, you are in possession of all the important items in a person's development. I remember, for instance, I analyzed a very well-known American politician, and he told me, oh, any amount of the secrets of his trade, and suddenly he jumped up and cried, "My God, what have I done! You know you could get a million dollars for what I have told you!" I said, "Well, I'm not interested. You can sleep in peace, I shall not betray you. I'll forget it within a fortnight."

Now you see, that shows that the things people hand out are not merely indifferent things. When it comes to something important, emotionally important, they hand out themselves. They hand out a big emotional value, as if they were handing over a large sum, as if they were trusting you with the administration of their estate, and they are entirely in your hands. Often I hear things that could ruin those people, utterly and permanently ruin them, things which would give me, if I should have any blackmailing tendencies, unlimited power over them.

Now that, you see, creates an emotional relationship to the analyst, and that is what Freud called the transference, which is a central problem in analytical psychology.[39] It is just as if these people had handed over their whole existence, and that can have very peculiar effects upon the individual. Either they hate you for it, or they love you for it, but you are never indifferent to them. When they hand out such material its context is associated with all the most important persons in the life of a patient. The most important persons are usually father and mother—that comes up from childhood. The first troubles are with the parents as a rule. So in handing over your infantile memories about the father or about the mother, you also hand over the image of father and mother. Then it is just as if the analyst had

[39] Cf. "The Psychology of the Transference," CW 16.

taken the place of the father, or even of the mother. I have had quite a number of male patients who called me "Mother Jung," because they handed over the mother to me, curiously enough. But that's quite irrespective of the personality of the analyst. It is simply disregarded. He functions as if he were the mother, or as if he were the father, the central authority. That is what one calls transference, a typical instance of projection. Freud doesn't exactly call it projection, he calls it transference. That is an allusion to the old and superstitious idea of handing over a disease, transferring the disease to an animal or laying the sin upon a scapegoat, and the scapegoat takes it out into the desert and makes it disappear. So the patients hand themselves over in the hope that I can swallow that stuff and digest it for them. I am *in loco parentis* and have a high authority. Naturally I am also persecuted by the corresponding resistances, by all the manifold emotional reactions they have had against their parents.

Now that is the structure you have to work through first in analyzing the situation, because the patient in such a condition is not free, he is a slave. He is utterly dependent on the analyst, like a patient with an open abdomen on the operating table. He is in the hands of the surgeon, for better or worse, and so the thing *must* be finished. This means we have to work through that condition in the hope of reaching a situation where the patient is able to see that I am not the father, not the mother, that I am an ordinary human being. Everybody would naturally suppose such a thing to be possible, that the patient could arrive at such an insight if he or she is not a complete idiot, that they could see I am just a doctor and not that emotional figure of their fantasies. But that is very often not the case.

I once had a very intelligent young woman patient, a student of philosophy with a very good mind.[40] One might easily think she would see I was not the parental authority,

[40] This case is discussed in *Two Essays*, pars. 206ff.

but she was utterly unable to get out of this delusion. In such a case one always has recourse to the dreams. It is just as if one were asking the unconscious, Now what do *you* say about such a condition? She says through the conscious, "Of course I know you are not my father, but I just feel like that, it *is* like that, I depend upon you." Then I say, "Now we will see what the unconscious says."

The unconscious now produces dreams in which I really assume a very curious role. In her dreams she was a little infant, sitting on my knees, and I held her in my arms. I was a very tender father to the little girl, you know, and more and more her dreams became emphatic in that respect. I was a sort of giant and she was a very little, frail human thing, quite a little girl in the hands of an enormous being. And the last dream of that series (I cannot tell you all the dreams) was that I was out in the midst of nature, standing in a field of wheat, an enormous field of wheat that was ripe for harvesting. I was a giant and I held her in my arms like a baby, and the wind was blowing over that field of wheat. Now you know, when the wind is blowing it makes waves in the wheatfield, and with these waves I swayed— like that—as if I were putting her to sleep. And she felt as if she were in the arms of a god, of the Godhead, and I thought, "Now the harvest is ripe, and I must tell her." And I told her, "You see, what you want and what you are projecting into me, because you are not conscious of it, is the idea of a deity you don't possess. Therefore you see it in me."

That clicked. Because, you know, she had a rather intense religious education—of course it all vanished later on and something disappeared from her world. The world became merely personal, and that religious conception of the world no longer existed, apparently. But the idea of a deity is not an intellectual idea, it is an archetypal idea. Therefore you find it practically everywhere under one name or another. You know even if it has the name "mana" it is an all-powerful, extraordinary effect or quality, even if it is not personal at all. So she suddenly became aware of an entirely pagan image that comes fresh from the archetype. She didn't have the idea of a Christian God, or of an Old Testament Yahweh. It was a pagan god, a god of nature, of vegetation. He was the wheat himself, he was the spirit of the wheat, the spirit of the wind, and she was in the arms of that numen.

Now that is the living experience of an archetype. It made a tremendous impression on that girl, and instantly it clicked. She saw what she really was missing, that missing value which she projected into me, making me indispensable to her. And then she saw that I was not indispensable, because, as the dream says, she is in the arms of that archetypal idea. That is a numinous experience, and that is the thing people are looking for, an archetypal experience that gives them an incorruptible value.

You see, they depend upon outer conditions, they depend upon their desires, their ambitions. They depend upon other people because they have no value in themselves. They have nothing in themselves. They are only rational, and they are not in possession of a treasure that would make them independent. But when that girl can hold that experience, then she doesn't depend any more. She *cannot* depend any more, because that value is in herself. And that is a sort of liberation, and it makes her complete. If she can realize such a numinous experience she is able to continue on her path, her way, her individuation. Nature will take her course. The acorn can become an oak, and not a donkey. She will become that which she is from the beginning.

I have seen quite a number of such cases, and that gave me a motive to study the archetypes, because I began to see that the structure of what I then called the "collective unconscious" is really a sort of agglomeration of such typical images, each of which has a numinous quality. The archetypes are, at the same time, dynamic; they are instinctual images that are not intellectually invented. They are always there and they produce certain processes in the unconscious one could best compare with myths. That's the origin of mythology. Mythology is a dramatization of a series of images that formulate the life of the archetypes. The statements of every religion, of many poets, and so on, are statements about the inner mythological process, which is a necessity because man is not complete if he is not conscious of that aspect of things.

And so, you see, a man is not complete when he lives in a world of statistical truth. He must live in the world of his mythological truth, and that is not merely statistics. It is the expression of what he really is, and what he feels himself to be. A man without mythology is merely a product of statistics, as it were, an average phenomenon. Our natural science makes everything into an average, reduces everything to an average, while the truth is that the carriers of life are individuals, not average numbers. And of course, all the individual qualities are wiped out, and that is most unbecoming. It is unhygienic. It deprives people of their specific values, of the most important experiences of their life, where they experience their own value, the creative background of their personality.

The trouble is that nobody understands these things, apparently. It is quite strange that one doesn't see what an education without the humanities is doing to man. He loses connection with his family, as it were, with the whole stem, the tribe—the connection with the past that he lives in, in which man has always lived. Man has always lived in the myth, and we think we are able to be born today and to live in no myth, without history. That is a disease, absolutely abnormal, because man is not born every day. He is born once in a specific historical setting, with specific historical qualities, and therefore he is only complete when he has a relation to these things. If you grow up with no connection with the past, it is just as if you were born without eyes and ears. From the standpoint of natural science you need no connection with the past, you can wipe it out, but that is a mutilation of the human being. I have seen from practical experience that this realization has a most extraordinary therapeutic effect, and I can tell you such a case.

There was a young Jewish girl.[41] Her father was a banker, and she had received an entirely worldly education. She had no idea of tradition, but then I went further into her history and found out that her grandfather had been a saddik in Galicia, and when I knew that I knew the whole story. That girl suffered from a phobia, a terrific phobia, and had already been under psychoanalytic treatment to no effect. She was really badly plagued by that phobia, anxiety states of all sorts. And then I saw that the girl had lost the connection with her past, had lost the fact that her grandfather had been a saddik, that he lived in the myth. And her father had fallen out of it too. So I simply told her, "You will stand up to your fear. You know what you have lost?" She didn't, of course not. I said, "Your fear is the fear of Yahweh." You know, the effect was that within a week she was cured after all those years of bad anxiety states, because that went through her like lightning. But I could say that only because I knew she was absolutely lost. She thought she was in the middle of things, but she was lost, gone.

Her life made no sense, for what is our existence when we are just "average numbers"? The more you make people into average numbers the more you destroy our society. If you want the "ideal state," the "slave state," go to Russia. There it is wonderful, there you can be an "average number." But you pay very dearly, your whole life goes to blazes.

I have seen plenty of cases of a similar kind, and that, naturally, led me on to a profound study of the archetypes. I got more and more respectful of archetypes, and now,

---

[41] Cf. *Memories, Dreams, Reflections*, pp. 138ff./137f. Also "The Symbolic Life," CW 18, par. 635.

by Jove, that thing should be taken into account. That is an enormous factor, very important for our further development and for our well-being. It was, of course, difficult to know where to begin, because it is such an enormously extended field. So the next question I asked myself was, "Now where in the world has anybody been busy with that problem?" And I found nobody had, except a peculiar spiritual movement that went together with the beginnings of Christianity, namely Gnosticism.[42] That was the first thing, actually, that I saw, that the Gnostics were concerned with the problem of archetypes. They made a peculiar philosophy of it, as everybody makes a peculiar philosophy of it when he comes across it naïvely and doesn't know that the archetypes are structural elements of the unconscious psyche.

The Gnostics lived in the first, second, and third centuries. And what was in between? Nothing. And now, today, we suddenly fall into that hole and are confronted with the problems of the collective unconscious which were the same then two thousand years ago—and we are not prepared to meet that problem. I was always looking for something in between, you know, something that linked that remote past with the present moment. And I found to my amazement it was alchemy,[43] which is understood to be a history of chemistry. It is, one might almost say, anything *but* that. It is a peculiar spiritual or philosophical movement. The alchemists called themselves philosophers, like the Gnostics. And then I read the whole accessible literature, Latin and Greek. I studied it because it was enormously interesting. It is the mental work of seventeen hundred years, in which is stored up all they could make out about the nature of the archetypes, in a peculiar way, that's true—it is not simple. Most of the texts haven't been published since the Middle Ages; the last editions date from the

[42] *Memories, Dreams, Reflections*, ch. VII.
[43] Ibid.

middle or end of the seventeenth century, practically all in Latin. Some texts are in Greek, not a few very important ones. That gave me no end of work, but the result was most satisfactory, because it showed me the development of our unconscious relations to the collective unconscious and the variations our consciousness has undergone, and why the unconscious is concerned with these mythological images.

Take a phenomenon like Hitler. That is a psychic phenomenon, and we've got to understand these things. It is just as if a terrific epidemic of typhoid fever were breaking out, and you said, "Now this is typhoid fever, isn't that a marvellous disease?" It can take on enormous proportions and nobody knows anything about it. Nobody takes care of the water supply, nobody thinks of examining the meat or anything like that, but simply states that this is a phenomenon. Yes, but one doesn't understand it. To me, of course, it was an enormous problem because it is a factor that has determined the fate of millions of European people and of Americans. Nobody can deny that he has been influenced by the war. That is all Hitler's doing, and that's all psychology, our foolish psychology. But you only come to an understanding of these phenomena when you understand the background from which they spring.

Of course I cannot tell you in detail about alchemy. It is the basis of our modern way of conceiving things, and therefore it is as if it were right under the threshold of consciousness. It gives you a wonderful picture of how the development of archetypes, the movement of archetypes, looks when you see them as if from above. From today you look back into the past, and you see how the present moment has evolved out of the past. Alchemical philosophy —it sounds very curious. We should give it an entirely different name. It does have a different name, it is called Hermetic philosophy, though of course that conveys just as little as the term alchemy. It is the parallel development, as Gnosticism was, to the conscious development of Christianity, of our Christian philosophy, of the whole psychology of the Middle Ages.

And so, you see, in our days we have such and such a view of the world, such and such a philosophy, but in the unconscious we have a different one. We can see that from the example of alchemical philosophy, which stands in exactly the same relation to the medieval consciousness as the unconscious stands in relation to ourselves. And we can reconstruct, or even predict, the unconscious of our day when we know what it has been yesterday. Now that, in a few words, is the development of my ideas, without going into details.

You've gone into great detail elsewhere in much of your writing, of course.

Well, yes. People have to read the books, by golly, in spite of the fact that they are thick! I'm sorry.

We are hoping this will stimulate many of them to read the books.

Well, now you could stop, I think.

Well done! Well done, Dr. Jung.

JUNG AND THE CHRISTMAS TREE

Georg Gerster (b. 1928), having earned a Ph.D. in German literature at Zurich University in 1956, embarked on a remarkable career as a freelance writer and photographer specializing in science—he has worked on every continent including Antarctica. Shortly before Christmas 1957 he interviewed Jung for *Die Weltwoche* (Zurich), and his article was published on Christmas Day. It is slightly condensed here. Jung is speaking:

An Indian swami knocked on the door of a villa on the Zürichberg. "Forgive me for disturbing you," he said to the householder. "I come from Madras, and am making a study of local religious customs in Europe. Perhaps you could . . .?" The householder backed away. "I'm afraid you have come to the wrong house. We are enlightened people here. Of course we go to church, at least now and then, but as you probably know we Protestants are not on the best of terms with the world of religious symbols. If you were thinking of finding any religious customs here like the ones in your own country, I'm afraid you will go home disappointed." The swami retired crestfallen. But let us suppose he comes back again, say in December, and catches the householder in the act of decorating the Christmas tree. "But you told me you had no religious customs," he says reproachfully. "And yet you cut down a fir tree just to let it dry up in the drawing-room, and cover it with little candles which are no use at all for heating purposes. Tell me, is this prescribed by your religion or its holy writings?" The householder shakes his head in astonishment. "Not that I know of. It's something that's always been done. . . ."

On one of my expeditions to Africa, I lived for a while with a tribe on the slopes of Mount Elgon, in Kenya. Every

353

morning, at sunrise, they stepped out of their huts, spat into their hands, and held them palm outwards to the sun. Asked why they did this, they were at a loss for an answer. They could only say: "It's something that's always been done. . . ."[1] Such ignorance has earned them the name of primitives in the judgment of the whites. Now if our Indian friend were to publish in Madras his researches among the inhabitants on the slopes of the Zürichberg, he would have some remarkable things to report. "Although they deny it, they worship rabbit idols which lay colored eggs, and on the day they call Easter they look for these eggs in the garden, with much shouting. They also worship, on another day they call Christmas, an illuminated tree which they hang all over with spangles, shiny balls, and sweetmeats. Yet they do not know why they do this. They are very small-minded and primitive people."

The very existence of such things as the May-pole, the May-tree, and the greasy pole tell us a great deal about the Christian claim to the Christmas tree. At best it was a matter of reinterpreting old customs, in much the same way as the feast of Christ's nativity was grafted on to the already existing mid-winter vegetation festivals. The tree-symbol has a very venerable history; the Finnish scholar Uno Holmberg, who investigated the symbolism of the tree of life, called it "mankind's most magnificent legend."[2] The countless changes of meaning the tree-symbol has undergone in the course of its history are proof of its richness and vitality. The tree has a cosmic significance—it is the world-tree, the world-pillar, the world-axis. Only think of Yggdrasill, the world-ash of Nordic mythology, a majestic, evergreen tree growing at the center of the world. The tree, particularly its crown, is the abode of the gods. Hence the village tree in India and the German village linden tree

[1] Cf. "Archaic Man" (orig 1931), CW 10, pars. 143f.
[2] *Der Baum des Lebens* (Helsinki, 1922–23), p. 9.

round which the villagers gather in the evenings: they are sitting in the shadow of the gods. The tree also has a maternal aspect. In Germanic mythology the first human beings, Ask and Embla, come from the ash and the alder, as their names show. Among the Yakuts of Siberia, a tree with eight branches was the birthplace of the first man. He was suckled by a woman the upper part of whose body grew from its trunk. These and many similar ideas are not invented, they simply came into men's heads in bygone times. It is a sort of natural revelation.

To give an example. One evening an English District Commissioner in Nigeria heard a tremendous racket going on in the barracks of the native troops. Six soldiers had to put a raving comrade in chains. When the D.C. arrived, the black man lay quiet and was released at his order. In explanation of his strange behavior, he said that he had wanted to go home because his tree was calling him, but now it was too late. The D.C. learnt further that when he was a little child the man's mother had once put him to rest under a tree while she went to work. The tree then talked to him and made him promise that he would hasten to it without delay whenever he heard it calling and would bring it food. Several times the tree had called him, said the soldier, and each time he had brought it the best he had in his miserable hut. On this evening, far from his village, he had heard the tree calling for food, yet could not obey the voice because of his military duties. Often, as here, the tree symbolizes the numen, the psychic fate of the person, his inner personality.[3] In the dream of Nebuchadnezzar the king himself is symbolized by the tree. There is also an old Rabbinic idea that the ageing Adam was granted one look into paradise. In the branches of the withered tree there lay a child. We might further mention the old patristic ideas of Christ as the tree of life.

[3] Cf. "The Spirit Mercurius," CW 13, par. 247.

Doesn't the custom, still practiced today in many places, of planting a tree at the birth of a child also belong in this context?

Certainly. The reason for this unthinking ritual act is the *participation mystique* between man and the tree: both share the same fate.

To come back to the Christmas tree. Haven't several quite different sets of symbols fused into one? The tree, the lights, the evergreen branches, the decorations, the distribution of Christmas presents—all these have their own symbolic value, and in numerous folk customs some of the components are differently combined.

Agreed. But let us not forget that the total combination, the lighted and decorated tree, is also found outside Christ's nativity and in non-Christian contexts. For instance in alchemy, that well-known reservoir for the symbols of antiquity.

(Here Jung produced an alchemical picture of the tree with the sun, the moon, and the seven planets in its branches, surrounded by allegories of the alchemical process of transformation.)

Now you know what the shining globes on the Christmas tree mean: they are nothing less than the heavenly bodies, the sun, moon, and stars. The Christmas tree is the world-tree. But, as the alchemical symbolism clearly shows, it is also a transformation symbol, a symbol of the process of self-realization. According to certain alchemical sources, the adept climbs the tree—a very ancient shamanistic motif. The shaman, in an ecstasy, climbs the magical tree in order to reach the upper world where he will find his true self. By climbing the magical tree, which is at the same time a tree of knowledge, he gains possession of his spiritual personality. To the eye of the psychologist, the shamanistic and alchemical symbolism is a projected representation of the process of individuation. That it rests on an archetypal foundation is evidenced by the fact that patients who have not the slightest knowledge of mythology and folklore spontaneously produce the most amazing parallels to the historical tree-symbolism.[4] Experience has taught me that the authors of these pictures were trying to express a process of inner development independent of their conscious volition.

Your conception of the Christmas tree is in no way disturbed by the fact that the custom dates only from the seventeenth century?

Why should that be any objection to my view that the Christmas tree, which in the longest and darkest night of the year symbolizes the return of the light, is archetypal? On the contrary! The way the Christmas tree has caught on in various countries and rapidly took root, so that most people actually believe it is an age-old custom, is only further proof that its appeal is grounded in the depths of the psyche, in the collective unconscious, and far exceeds that of the crib, the ox, and the ass.

In one of your books you remark that people decorate the Christmas tree without knowing what is at the back of this custom.[5]

It is an old pagan one. It is not I who use this expression but the Church. "Omnis haec observatio est paganorum," it says in an old papal declaration with reference to decorating the houses with green branches. This and similar customs are pagan. And J. C. Dannhauer, an Evangelical theologian in Strasbourg, preached in the middle of the seventeenth century against the fir trees people set up in their houses at Christmas and bedecked with dolls and candles. These old divines were not so wrong according to their lights.

[4] Cf. "The Philosophical Tree," Part I, CW 13.
[5] "Archaic Man," CW 10, par. 145.

Now that you have elucidated its background as an empirical investigator, the increasing popularity of the Christmas tree must rejoice your heart as a psychotherapist. I conjecture you would agree that Christmas trees are healthy —as a measure of psychic hygiene?

Your conjecture is correct. The archetypes are, so to speak, like many little appetites in us, and if, with the passing of time, they get nothing to eat, they start rumbling and upset everything. The Catholic Church takes this very seriously. Just now it is setting about reviving the old Easter customs. The abstract greeting "Christ is risen!" no longer satisfies the craving of the archetypes for images. So in order to set it at rest, they have had recourse to the hare-goddess, a fertility symbol. And lately the Church has reintroduced an ancient fire ceremony: the Easter fire, the primordial fire, is lit not with matches but with flint and steel! A tremendously nourishing procedure for man's feelings. The inner man has to be fed—a fact that moderns, with their frivolous trust in reason, often overlook to their own harm. The Christmas tree is one of those customs which are food for the soul, nourishment for the inner man. And the more primordial the material they use, the more promising these customs are for the future.

A TALK WITH STUDENTS
AT THE INSTITUTE

◆◆◆◆◆◆◆◆◆◆◆◆◆◆◆◆◆◆◆◆◆◆◆◆◆◆

During May 1958, Jung came and talked with students at the C. G. Jung Institute of Zurich. Notes were taken by one of them, Marian Bayes, and published only twelve years later, in *Spring*, 1970. Mrs. Bayes's transcript has been edited to eliminate brackets around some phrases, supplied by the transcriber for tentative readings.

What is man to do with his passionate, primitive, chthonic nature?

We tend to identify our chthonic nature with evil and our spiritual nature with good. We must accept the dark forces and stop projecting them. What is acceptance? Some things *cannot* be accepted. If the analysis is honest it will come to an impossible problem—a problem that has no issue. A lot of instinctive nature is repressed, and it wells up. And now what? Nobody can deal with it; nobody knows what to do.

Go to bed. Think of your problem. See what you dream. Perhaps the Great Man, the 2,000,000-year-old man, will speak. In a cul-de-sac, then only do you hear his voice. The urge to become what one is is invincibly strong, and you can always count on it, but that does not mean that things will necessarily turn out positively. If you are not interested in your own fate, the unconscious is.

There is a mountain of symbolism. It is not designed to prove a theory, as people think. I have amassed symbols in order to give the analyst a chance to know about symbolism so that he can interpret dreams. As if *we* know nature! Or about the psyche! The 2,000,000-year-old man may know something.

I have no trouble talking to primitives. When I talk of the Great Man, or the equivalent, they understand. The Great Man is *something that reacts*.

The analyst needs knowledge in order to interpret what the unconscious says, and he must give credit to his own interpretation. He must have courage, he must help; it is as if a man is bleeding to death, and you *ponder!* You can only say, "My God, I don't *know*, but if it is an error, the unconscious will correct it. It seems to me it is like this."—And stand for it! It must be the best you can do. No cheating, no flippancy or routine; then the devil is after you. You must be honest about whether it is really the best you can do. If it is the best before God that you can do, then you can count on things going the right way. But it may be the wrong way. We go through difficult things; that is fate. Man goes through analysis so that he can die. I have analyzed to the end with the end in sight—to accompany the individual in order that he may die. The analyst must help life as long as he can.

There is a prejudice that analysis is the art of letting out the unconscious, like opening the cages in a zoo. That is part of analysis, but it must not be done in an irresponsible and foolish way. This is only the preparatory part. The main analysis is what to do with the things that have emerged from the unconscious. One must see what the underlying trend is—what the will of God is. You are damned if you don't follow it. It will ruin your life, your health. You have sold part of your soul, or have lost it.

To the primitives it is death to lose the soul.

Analysis is a long discussion with the Great Man—an unintelligent attempt to understand him. Nevertheless, it is an attempt, as both patient and analyst understand it. (The Naskapi[1] would have a great advantage, because he would

[1] On the Naskapi Indians of the Labrador Peninsula and their concept of the Great Man, see M.-L. von Franz, "The Process of Individuation," in *Man and His Symbols* (1964), pp. 161–62; also Frank G. Speck, *Naskapi* (Norman, Okla., 1935), pp. 41ff.

realize that it is a discussion with the Great Man.) Work until the patient can see this. It, the Great Man, can at one stroke put an entirely different face on the thing—or *anything* can happen. In that way you learn about the peculiar intelligence of the background; you learn the nature of the Great Man. You learn about yourself against the Great Man—against his postulates. This is the way through things, things that look desperate and unanswerable. The point is, *how are you yourself going to answer this?* There one is alone, as one should be, with the highest ethical distinctions. Ethics is not convention; ethics is between myself and the Great Man. During this process, you learn about ethics versus morality.[2] The unconscious gives you that peculiar twist that makes the way possible.

The way is ineffable. One cannot, one *must* not, betray it. It is like the way of Zen—like a sharp knife, and also twisting like a serpent. One needs faith, courage, and no end of honesty and patience.

Does the cycle of this dialogue continue permanently, or has man a special role in it?

That is what you learn: what your role is, where you are in the divine economy, in the order of things. You see yourself in a new light because you have added the information of the unconscious. You have added things you didn't dream of—a new aspect of yourself and of the world. This you cannot regulate, or it would be misused.

To clarify your mind you draw a mandala, and it is legitimate. Another says, "Oh, *that's* how to do it!" and draws a mandala. And *that* is a mistake; that is cheating, because he is copying.

Never say no or yes on principle. Say it only when you *feel* it is really *yes*. If it is really *no*, it is no. If you say yes for any outer reason, you are sunk.

[2] Cf. "A Psychological View of Conscience" (1958), CW 10.

What is the result of an attitude of free decision?

The result is that you are always in the game; you are included, you are taken for real. If you are dishonest, you are excluded from the individuation process. If you are dishonest, you are *nothing* for your unconscious. The Great Man will spit on you, and you will be left far behind in your muddle—stuck, stupid, and idiotic.

If you follow the unconscious closely, your intelligence will not sink below a certain level, and you will add a good deal of intelligence to what you already possess. If you take the unconscious intellectually, you are lost. It is not a conviction, not an assumption. It is a *Presence*. It is a *fact*. It is *there*. It *happens*.

How can we know it? By a certain amount of self-criticism. When you have an idea, *you* have not thought about that thing. It came to you. When you realize this, then you are honest. A certain amount of modesty is absolutely necessary. You have got to accept what the unconscious produces, and you have to understand its language. It is *Nature*, and it has to be translated into human forms. That is the reason for the dignity of man, that he has the ability to do this. There is no *reflection* in creation. To reflect is man's task, and he can do it when he is not sterilized. When he puts himself above it, he is sterile. The attitude is incommensurable with science. What scientist will observe and say that what he observes *does not exist?* When you observe, then you are scientific. People don't know whether a thought is theirs or whether they unhooked it in another house. The naïveté of the white man—that he identifies the ego with the Great Man!

Is not the human bond a central vital link in analysis?

The thing you are is so much stronger than your feeble words. The patient is permeated by what you are—by your real being—and pays little attention to what you say. The analyst has unsolved problems because he is alive—life is a problem daily. Otherwise he is dead. In the shortest time each puts his foot into it. If you take your mistake the right way, it is the way of analysis. The analyst must know about his complexes, because they will be touched during the work with the patient. When I dream of a patient, it is usually a sign that one of my complexes has been touched.

Each step ahead that the patient makes can be a step for the analyst. You cannot be with someone without being permeated by that personality, but the chances are you do not notice it; a certain feeling-atmosphere will take hold of you. If you are not a feeling type you may have to ask a feeling type about your own "weather" because you are unconscious of your own feelings.

Doesn't stress on the transference obviate . . . ?

One of the greatest hindrances to understanding is the projection of the shaman—the savior. As soon as you are elevated to such a rank, you are powerless, lost in a sea of mist. When signs of this inflation appear, this is a serious warning, and the inflation must be discouraged as soon as possible. You are just as unable to perform miracles as a shaman as a rule is. The father complex is at the bottom of it, and when this is analyzed, it is reduced to human size. But there is still the human being. The father transference, the Christ transference, etc., each is a mistake, a deviation, produced by the patient's perplexity. If the patient were a Naskapi, he would say that the transference is his Great Man. The analytic conversation is between two Great Men. (The Naskapi would have a great advantage because he would understand this.) Work until the patient can see that. That is the point of the transference. It is vital to the patient to find out about this, and the analyst must be able to answer these questions. He can only say, "I am this," when he knows what *this* is. The patient may come to the end of his perplexity and still have a transference. Awkward. Then it is something else—the archetypes are in play;

that is the Great Man, or whatever he calls it. At bottom, the transference is by no means a *personal* fantasy. You lose an enormous value when you reduce it to the personal, and you must teach the patient about this double possibility: that there is the personal and there is something more in the personality, namely the Great Man.

FROM CHARLES BAUDOUIN'S
JOURNAL: 1958

++++++++++++++++++++++++++++

The first International Congress for Analytical Psychology was held in Zurich in August 1958. The pleasant feature of a boat ride on the lake was included in the program, with a pause off-shore at Jung's house. After Emma Jung's death, in 1955, Ruth Bailey, a close family friend whom Jung had met during his trip to East Africa in 1925–26, had at Mrs. Jung's wish become his housekeeper and companion.

Sunday, August 10

Today a boat trip on the lake of Zurich in the late after-noon. The big moment came when the boat stopped off Küsnacht to salute Jung with a trumpet blast and hundreds of waving arms. The old master, dressed in summer white, had come down to the bank below his villa; standing with his lady companion beside him, he gestured with his hand for a long time as he watched the big boat loaded with his disciples disappearing—toward what destinies?—into the fair-weather haze. The young and affable Dr. Baumann,[1] who speaks excellent French—which does no harm—told me that he was Jung's grandson, and he explained that the lady companion who has been helping Jung "since my grandmother died" was an old friend met in the 1920's at the time of the trip to black Africa; then, as we passed it, he showed us the birthplace of Paracelsus.[2] But the vision— insistent and moving—that continued to dominate the re-

[1] Dieter Baumann, M.D., son of Jung's second daughter, Gret, and Dr. Fritz Baumann. He is an analytical psychologist.
[2] Paracelsus (see above, p. 39, n. 5) was born in 1493 at Einsiedeln, several miles south of the lake.

marks we exchanged and the water, land, and clouds passing by was the vision of Jung all in white, larger than life-size, one would have said—probably because of the white clothing—standing on his bank and repeating, as though to infinity, his gestures of farewell.

(It was a real farewell: I was not to see him again.)

[Translated by Jane A. Pratt]

FROM ESTHER HARDING'S
NOTEBOOKS: 1958

++++++++++++++++++++++++++++

Küsnacht, 23 August

We found him looking remarkably well, and he greeted us with great cordiality. . . .

We spoke of the Congress . . . and he talked of how, when the idea is not sufficiently real, it is couched in "fat words," "words of power," that seek to convince but are really a compensation for a weakness in the idea or in the understanding of the idea. . . .

[About the Assumption of the Virgin Mary] Jung said that she has already entered into the nuptial chamber and that thus, naturally, after a time there will be a child. The churchmen do not realize this, nor do they consider what it will mean. They stop at the idea that there may be some sort of feminine godhead, but do not speculate on what sort of child will be born, like the child of the Sun-Woman in the Revelation.[1] . . .

Over and over again, he came back to the need for humanness. The wise man needs to give a place to foolishness, to childishness. Otherwise he gets above his humanity and stumbles over a stone; then he goes back and kicks the stone "that ought to have known enough to get out of the way of Mr. So-and-So, while all the time he stumbled because he was not paying enough attention to his humble reality."

On Palm Sunday, the Master could not walk, but must ride, he said, speaking of the New Testament; so he stole the ass. He had said his kingdom was not of this world, yet

---

[1] Cf. "Answer to Job" (orig. 1952), CW 11, par. 710, referring to Revelation 12:1.

in this act he contradicted his own mission. So just afterwards he cursed the barren fig tree, for "it ought to have had food for the Master's lunch—just like the man who kicks the stone he stumbles over. But the theologians never see this. Satan, the power devil, whom he had cast behind his back, returned on Palm Sunday. In this way, he brought on himself the mocking as a Caesar, etc. He forsook his mission, and so, on the cross, he felt that God had forsaken him."

He said the gospels were full of all sorts of contradictory things. The mention of the fig tree episode led him to speak of the Lord's Prayer and its petition, "Give us this day our daily bread." He said the Greek word translated as *daily* occurred in this place only, never in classical Greek, so a guess had been made as to its meaning. St. Jerome translated it as suprasubstantial bread. Recently it had been found in the gnostic writings of some newly-discovered fragments. There, it seemed to have the meaning of daily portion, or ration. Here again, C. G. said, we have a contradiction, for the Lord's Prayer taught us to be concerned about our daily ration, while another time he taught, "Take no thought for the morrow, what ye shall eat or what ye shall drink or wherewithal ye shall be clothed, for your heavenly Father knoweth that ye have need of these things."[2]

He said he was sorry that St. Jerome's translation was not the correct one, for it was very meaningful.

Speaking of the foolishness of the wise, he said one must always recognize that one does not know what a dream means, especially one's own dream, for the unconscious always finds the chink in the wall of one's own theory or built-up system. The unconscious wants to come through into consciousness, and when we build up a systematic body of knowledge we necessarily keep the unconscious out. Nature is just what we do *not* know. So, he said, in

[2] Cf. Matthew 6:25 and Luke 12:22.

speaking of such things it is much better to use a symbolic way of speech, for that says much more—even what you do not know yourself. If you limit yourself to known facts, what you say may be true of the thousand other cases, but just *not* of this one. The truth escapes people who are always trying to systematize, and they have to use power to try to convince.

One must allow one's own foolishness, for Nature is naïve; there is always the joke, the *just-so*.

The user of fat words cannot put it into simple language. He is impressed with the powerful idea and tries to impress others with it. If he were *really* impressed with its reality, he would stammer and get great feelings of inferiority before it. Every true experience of the *numinosum* has this effect. But such a man is afraid to show his littleness in face of the great idea. He gets inflated and struts. He would be shown to be really wise if he could admit that he could say nothing in the face of the great experience. (A man who is truly in love can only stammer, "I love you.")

And yet, he said one must make a theory or system, especially for teaching purposes, only one must not take it as representing the facts. As an illustration of the use and limitations of a formulated system, he said, it is as though you find an uninhabited island. You must begin at once to orient yourself. There is a mountain over there, a group of trees here, and the coastline along there. The mountain is perhaps ten miles away, but it may be fifteen, then your calculations will be put out. Also you do not know how high it is, so you cannot triangulate from it. Or there may be a river between you and it that you cannot cross. Yet you must say, "Here is a map of the island I discovered, but, for goodness sake, don't believe it!" And you must say the same to students when you teach them the theory of analysis.

AT THE BASEL PSYCHOLOGY CLUB

++++++++++++++++++++++++++++

On November 1, 1958, Jung visited a small study group of the Psychologische Gesellschaft in Basel and answered a series of written questions, besides other questions spoken from the audience. The event was tape-recorded and transcribed, and it is first published here, in translation. Square brackets indicate lacunae in the text or conjectural readings.

I would like to thank you for crediting me with the ability to say something sensible in spite of my advanced years. This cannot be taken entirely for granted since I tend for the most part to be very absent-minded. Concentrating on your difficult questions might thus end in the fiasco of my getting lost in some train of thought. So I beg you to call me to order if it seems to you that I am wandering off somewhere into the blue.

QUESTION 1: *What is the criterion that indicates whether an archetypal dream or a vision should make an obligatory demand on an individual, or be evaluated only as an expression of a general contemporary event which the dreamer has picked up and which does not address him as an individual human being?*

The desired criterion here is whether the dreamer feels numinously addressed by the dream. If not, then it doesn't concern him—and it doesn't concern me either. At most it could initiate a theoretical bandying about of words, which of course is futile.

QUESTION 2: *Can myth be equated with a collective dream? If so, are we to assume that a historical event either precedes or follows it?*

Here you must define more precisely what you mean by myth. Strictly speaking, a myth is a historical document. It is told, it is recorded, but it is not in itself a dream. It is the product of an unconscious process in a particular social group, at a particular time, at a particular place. This unconscious process can naturally be equated with a dream. Hence anyone who "mythologizes," that is, tells myths, is speaking out of this dream, and what is then retold or actually recorded is the myth. But you cannot, strictly speaking, properly take the myth as a unique historical event like a dream, an individual dream which has its place in a time sequence; you can do that only *grosso modo*. You can say that at a particular place, at a particular time, a particular social group was caught up in such a process, and perhaps you can so to speak condense this process, covering it may be several thousand years, and say this epoch historically precedes such and such, and historically follows such and such.

This is a very troublesome undertaking. What precedes the myth of Osiris, for example? The Osiris myth goes back to approximately 4000 B.C. What preceded it? Total darkness. We just don't know. And what followed it? The answer to this is of course much easier: the Osiris myth was followed by the Christ myth. That is perfectly clear, even though theologians assure us that remarkably enough the mental outlook of the New Testament has nothing to do with Egyptology, or precious little; but it is simply that people know too little, that's all. I will give you only one example. As you know, Christ's genealogical table in the New Testament consists of 3 x 14 names.[1] The number 14 is significant, because at the great Heb-Sed festival of the ancient Egyptians, celebrated every thirty years to reaffirm Pharaoh as God's son, statues of 14 of his ancestors were carried before him at the procession, and if 14 ancestors

[1] Matthew 1:1–17.

couldn't be found, some invented ones were added—there had to be 14 of them.[2] Well, in the case of God's son Christ, who was of course infinitely more exalted than Pharaoh, there had to be 3 x 14 generations, and that is a Trishagion, the well-known triple formula for "Holy, holy, holy is the Lord God of Sabaoth." This triple repetition is simply an expression of the numinosity of the "Thrice Holy."

Here, then, we have one such trace [of Egyptian influence]. If you carefully study the statements about Christ that have been handed down historically, you will find they are mythological statements intimately connected with the myth of Osiris. That is why Christianity spread into Egypt without meeting the slightest resistance. The country was christianized in no time because all the necessary precedents already existed. Take for example the fish, the fish attribute of Christ: it was swallowed by the Egyptians without question because they already had a day on which a certain fish might be eaten and on other days not. All this quite apart from the spiritual content of the Osiris myth.

Now it is the case with most myths, when you examine them more closely, that the historical event can be established *post festum* but not *ante festum*, because the more numinous these mythological statements are, the further they recede into the dim bygone of human history. We at any rate are in the fortunate position of late epigoni, who, looking back on three Platonic months, three aeons of conscious history, can demonstrate that these myths form a continuity. Thus the Osiris myth was clearly superseded by the Christ myth. This is one of the finest examples of mythological continuity. It is as though in the course of the millennia slow upheavals took place in the unconscious, each new aeon being as it were ushered in by a new myth.

[2] Cf. *Mysterium Coniunctionis*, CW 14, par. 331, n. 9. For the Heb-Sed festival, cf. pars. 356ff.; also Erich Neumann, *The Origins and History of Consciousness* (1954), pp. 243ff.

The myth is not new, it is age-old, but a new version, a new edition of it, a new interpretation characterizes the new epoch. That is why, for the ancients, the transition from one age to another was an important event. For instance Hammurabi, the famous Babylonian lawgiver, felt he was the Lord of a new aeon; he lived around 2000 B.C. That is roughly the time when the Jewish tradition began. Think, also, of the Augustan Age another two thousand years later, which began with Divus Augustus, whose birth was regarded as the birth of a savior. And if you recall Virgil's 4th Eclogue,[3] you will see that the child who ushers in the coming age is a bringer of peace, a savior, who was naturally interpreted by the Christians as Christ. The date of Virgil's poem is prechristian. For him it was certainly the birth of Augustus that was meant. At that time there was a tremendous longing for redemption in Italy, because two thirds—please note—two thirds of the population consisted of slaves whose fate was hopelessly sealed. That gave rise to a general mood of depression, and in the melancholy of the Augustan Age this longing for redemption came to expression. Therefore a man who knew how to "mythologize," like Virgil, expressed this situation in the 4th Eclogue. Thanks to this prophetic gift he is also the psychopomp in Dante, the guide of souls in purgatory and in hell. Afterwards, of course, in the Christian paradise, he had to surrender this role to the feminine principle [Beatrice], and this is naturally highly significant in view of the future recognition of the feminine figure in Christianity. But all that was in Dante's time. Then, as you know, it was six hundred years until the dogma of the Immaculate Conception was promulgated by Pius IX,[4] and another hundred years until the promulgation of the Assumption.[5]

---

[3] For text, see *Symbols of Transformation*, CW 5, par. 121.
[4] In the Bull *Ineffabilis Deus,* December 8, 1854.
[5] By Pius XII in the Bull *Munificentissimus Deus*, November 1, 1950.

QUESTION 3: *Do you believe we are heading for complete barbarism in the new aeon, or is there still some likelihood that cultural disaster can be avoided?*

I must confess that in this matter I believe nothing, for I just don't know. I can't believe anything I don't know, and once I know it I don't need to believe it any more. I don't know whether we are heading for complete disaster, I only know that things look very black—but you know that too. I don't want to play the prophet, but you see, *the* great problem before us is over-population, not the atom bomb. The atom bomb, teleologically considered, makes provision for the disposal of the surplus. There are population statistics which already predict even more serious food shortages in 1965; India, the entire subcontinent of India is already in the grip of this crisis. The slightest disturbance in the seasonal fertility leads to frightful famines, and the same is true of China. Now they have stamped out malaria in India and that alone causes an immense population increase, quite apart from all the epidemics of cholera and plague that have been averted. However, it is likely that in time they will have to be allowed to spread again; it is the only possible way of skimming off the surplus population. This is not my idea; I have talked with the Chief of Public Hygiene who has a big laboratory on the Gulf of Kutch, the main import center for such articles as smallpox, cholera, and plague. He told me that they can imagine no other solution of the overpopulation problem in India except a colossal epidemic. In 1920, for instance, following the influenza epidemic, they had a loss of 675,000 lives. But that is exactly the surplus birthrate for one year and it goes on piling up like an avalanche.

QUESTION FROM THE AUDIENCE: *Can't something be done with birth control?*

Well, they have granted half a million pounds for that, and you should just ask the Indians what good it has done and how it went down with the masses—you can imagine. It amounts to nothing at all, a drop of water on a hot stove. The decrease of population doesn't begin with the educated classes who understand birth control; it must begin with the lower classes, and in India until recently only 20 per cent of them were not illiterate. Today about half the population is still illiterate. You can imagine what birth control means under these conditions: nothing. They are little better than cave-dwellers, and many of them are still completely wild tribesmen. Reasonable measures like these are quite hopeless. The birth rate can only be controlled by catastrophes, short of a miracle. The question naturally arises: What will happen if the world population goes on increasing and people are huddled together still more as a result? It will produce a frightful tension which can discharge itself in one way or another, and on the rational side we have no answer and on the irrational side we can expect heaven knows what, at any rate nothing particularly hopeful. You can put this down to the pessimism of old age. At all events, it is highly probable that we are heading for an extremely critical time, which all of us may perhaps not experience—the peak of it, that is—because we are the end of the Pisces aeon and can certainly expect that with the transition to the new aeon of Aquarius, approximately 150–200 years from now, our distant descendants will experience all sorts of things. This atom bomb business, for instance, is terribly characteristic of Aquarius, whose ruler is Uranos, the Lord of unpredictable events. But this is speculation. Have you any questions? I wouldn't want my esteemed audience to be left out of it!

QUESTION 4: *Since our consciousness is one of the contents of the self, can we assume that individual consciousness continues after death? Do you know any modern dream material which would corroborate such an assumption? Does the concept of eternal life mean the preservation of individual consciousness, or that the human soul enters into other forms and configurations, thereby losing its individuality?*

You realize that this is very difficult to answer. To put it briefly, it's a question of conscious immortality. This is a question our Lord Buddha was asked twice. For his disciples it was naturally a matter of great concern whether the *karma* that passes from one generation to another by metempsychosis is personal, and represents a personal continuity, or whether it is impersonal. In the latter case it's as though there were an unconscious *karma* suspended somewhere, which is seized upon in the act of birth and is reincarnated with no awareness of any personal continuity. That is one aspect. The other aspect is that this *karma* is by nature conscious, having a subjective consciousness, and when this is reincarnated it becomes potentially possible to remember one's previous births because of this *karma*'s transcendent self-awareness. Both times Buddha evaded the question, he didn't go into it, although he himself asserted that he was aware of his previous births, about 560 incarnations in all conceivable forms, plant, animal, and human.

So you see that in those times, when people were not exactly sparing with metaphysical assertions, there being as yet no theory of knowledge, Buddha rejected this question as useless. He thought it much more useful to meditate on the *nidana* chain, the chain of cause and effect, consisting of old age, sickness, and death, than to speculate about immortality. And in a sense such speculation is sterile, because we are never in a position to adduce any valid proofs in this respect. If we could eventually adduce any proof it would be of a man, say, appearing as a ghost one year or two years or ten years or maybe even twenty years after his death. But we still cannot prove that this ghost is identical with this dead man. There is thus no possibility whatever of furnishing proofs, because even if the ghost of a dead man were to reveal something that only he had known in his lifetime and no one else—and there are such cases, well authenticated cases—the question would still remain as to how that was related to the absolute knowledge of the unconscious. The unconscious has a kind of absolute knowledge, but we cannot prove it is an absolute knowledge, because the Absolute, the Eternal, is transcendental. It is something we cannot grasp at all, for we are not yet eternal and consequently can say nothing whatever about eternity, our consciousness being what it is. These are transcendental speculations, which may be so or may not be so. Hence for epistemological reasons it is absolutely impossible to make out anything with certainty in this matter.

On the other hand, the question of immortality is so urgent, of such immediacy, that one ought nevertheless to give some kind of answer. So I say to myself, Well then, if I am up against a question I cannot answer and yet ought to answer for the peace of my soul, for my own well-being, I can be so disquieted by this question that an answer is absolutely imperative. At any rate I ought to try to form an opinion about it with the help of the unconscious, and the unconscious then obliges and produces dreams which point to a continuation of life after death. There is no doubt of that, I have seen many examples of this kind. Now of course you can say these are only fantasies, compensating fantasies which we cannot hinder, which are rooted in our nature—all life desires eternity—but they are far from being a proof. On the other hand, we must tell ourselves that though this argument is all right as far as it goes, we have irrefutable evidence that at least parts of our psyche are not subject to the laws of space and time, otherwise perceptions outside space and time would be altogether impossible—yet they exist, they happen. All cases of telepathic clairvoyance, predictions of the future—they exist. I have been able to verify this from countless experiences, not to mention Rhine's experiments, which can't be refuted unless you stand the whole theory of probability on its head. This has actually been proposed, a whole new probability theory should be invented, though how this could be done without violations of logic is completely beyond me. At any rate we have at present no means of contesting Rhine's results, quite apart from the numerous instances of prediction, non-spatial perception, and the like.

This offers the clearest and most incontrovertible proof that our conceptions of space and time, as seen from the causal, rationalistic standpoint, are incomplete. To get a complete picture of the world we would have to add another dimension, or we could never explain the totality of the phenomena in a unified way. That is why rationalists maintain through thick and thin that no such experiences as clairvoyance and the like exist, because the rationalistic view of the world stands or falls with the reality of these phenomena. But if they do exist, our rationalistic view of the world is untenable. You know that in modern physics the possibility that the universe has several dimensions is no longer denied. We must reckon with the fact that this empirical world is in a sense appearance, that is to say it is related to another order of things below it or behind it, where "here" and "there" do not exist; where there is no extension in space, which means that space doesn't exist, and no extension in time, which means that time doesn't exist. There are experiences where space is reduced by 20 per cent, or time by 90 per cent, so that the time concept is only 10 per cent valid. If that is so—and I see no possibility of disputing it—we must face the fact that something of our psychic existence is outside space and time, that is, beyond changeability, or one could also say, changeable only in infinite spaces of time.

These are ideas which for us are logical deductions, but are commonly held views in India. For instance, if you read the Buddha stories in the [Pali Canon], you will find many examples. Here is one: When the Buddha was dwelling in the grove he suddenly heard that one of the highest Brahma gods had a wrong thought. He at once betook himself to the highest Brahma world and found the Brahma god in a fort—actually the palace of the Rajah or the Maharajah—and in the spacious paradisal gardens of this fort, set on a high peak of the Himalayas, the Brahma god was enjoying himself with his court ladies. They had climbed up a tree and were throwing flowers and fruit down and he found it delightful and said to the Buddha, This spectacle you see, this joy and this pleasure, will endure forever because I am immortal. Then said the Buddha, There you make your mistake. Your life will endure for *kalpas*, for cosmic ages, but sometime it will come to an end. The Brahma god wouldn't believe it. At this moment there was suddenly absolute silence. No flowers and no fruit fell down any more, the laughter of the court ladies froze, and the Brahma god was very astonished and said, What's up? Then said the Buddha, At this very moment the *karma* of your court ladies is extinguished and they are no more—and so it will fare with you. Then the Brahma god was converted to the Lord Buddha and vowed him true discipleship.

That is the story. Life may endure for an infinity of *kalpas* but it is not eternal. Of course that doesn't bother us much. But it does show that in India there was a realization of the relativity of time. It is an intuition, naturally evolved and become second nature, of what is probably the actual state of our world. We see a world of consciousness from which we can't really draw any conclusions, but then we know from experience that there is a background which is absolutely necessary, otherwise we couldn't explain the phenomena of this world. In consequence, we are unable to explain a prediction of the future or a spatial extrasensory perception in terms of special radar facilities, for even the finest radar cannot predict an event taking place a fortnight hence. We always use this radar comparison to explain seeing at a distance in space, but you get nowhere with it in explaining seeing at a distance in time.

QUESTION FROM THE AUDIENCE: *Some years ago you once talked about the physicist's concept of the time quantum, according to which there is not time in between two time quanta, so that what appears between them is a kind of timelessness. Would you elaborate on this?*

That is really beside the point, it is only an analogy for making comprehensible how timelessness must be implicit in the time concept, as is necessary for logical reasons. When you say "high" you also mean "low" without saying so. When we speak of time we must also have the concept of nontime. Just as we have the quantum concept in energy, so also, since time is a phenomenon of energy, we can speak [without any] difference of a succession of such [time quanta], that is, of these gaps then produced. The quantum theory is a theory of the discontinuity of events, and that is why Einstein tried to bridge over the gaps. It was a thorn in his eye that discontinuities exist; the perfect world-creator cannot afford discontinuities, everything should be rational, but it just isn't.

We are not in a position to prove that anything of us is necessarily preserved for eternity. But we can assume with great probability that something of our psyche goes on existing. Whether this part is in itself conscious, we don't know either. There is also the consideration, based on experience, that any split-off part of the psyche, if it can manifest itself at all, always does so in the form of a personality, as though it possessed a consciousness of itself. That is why the voices heard by the insane are personal. All split-off complexes speak in personal form whenever they express themselves. You can, if you like, or if you feel the need, take this as an argument in favor of a continuity of consciousness. In general one could say that since consciousness is an important psychic phenomenon, why shouldn't it be just that part of the psyche which is not affected by space and time? In other words, it goes on existing relatively outside space and time, which would by no means be a proof of immortality but rather of an existence for an indefinite time after or beyond death.

In support of this psychological hypothesis you can also adduce the experiential fact that in conditions which by all medical standards are profoundly unconscious, resulting from cerebral anemia or shock, the most complicated dreams can occur, presupposing a high degree of conscious activity as well as the presence of an individual consciousness, despite the fact that for sound commonsense any psychic activity is no longer possible. So if I fall into an absolute coma and am totally unconscious of my coma, it is possible for a big dream to take place in this coma. Well, who is doing that, and where? It is explained that because of the lack of blood the brain is incapable of sustaining consciousness. But how then does it sustain a dream in which an individual consciousness is present? Two German physiologists have published a very interesting work on subjective levitation phenomena following brain injuries.[6] Such cases have been observed fairly often, though these things are rather rare. For instance, a soldier is shot in the head in combat and lies there as if dead. But, in his subjective consciousness, he rises up in the air in the position in which he is lying. The noise of battle is completely extinguished, he sees the whole terrain, he sees the other people, but it is all utterly soundless and still; then he hears his name, a comrade is calling to him and he comes to himself and is now really a wounded man. But up to that point he is in a state of levitation, he is as though lifted out of this world, yet though it continues to exist and he has some perception of it, it no longer affects him. By any human standard such a person is profoundly unconscious. But in his unconsciousness he undergoes a subjective experience which is simply

---

[6] Hubert Jantz and Kurt Beringer, "Das Syndrom des Schwebeerlebnisses unmittelbar nach Kopfverletzungen," *Der Nervenarzt* (Berlin), XVII (1944), pp. 197–206. Cf. "Synchronicity: An Acausal Connecting Principle," CW 8, pars. 949ff.

psychic, and which can be placed on entirely the same foot-ing as consciousness. It is observations like these that have to be considered here.

The concept of immortality tells us nothing about the related idea of rebirth or metempsychosis. Here again we have to depend on dreams that give us a few hints. But it is worth bearing in mind that a highly civilized continent like India—that is, highly civilized in its spiritual culture—is absolutely convinced of the transmigration of souls, and that reincarnation is regarded as self-evident. This is as much taken for granted as our assumption that God created the world or that some kind of *spiritus rector* exists—that would be a fitting comparison. Educated Indians know that we don't think as they do, but that doesn't bother them in the least; they simply find it stupid that we don't think that way. When I was in India, a doctor gave me a whole dossier about a child of four, a little girl who remembered her previous life. She had been reborn a few years after her death and knew what her name was previously, her hus-band's name, what children she had and where she lived. So when she was four years old—in India children are very precocious—her father went with her to that distant city and let himself be shown round by the child. She led him to her house, where she had been the mother, where her children still were, where her husband was, and she recog-nized everybody, even the grandmother—an Indian house-hold always has a grandmother on top—she knew them all and was then accepted as the previous wife. I have never heard of such a thing in Europe. Certainly there are many people among us today who believe in reincarnation. Maybe it is simply a sign of our [. . .] and barbarism that we don't think like that and are only just beginning to take such thoughts seriously. But in India, whose civilization is so much older than ours and where there is also a much greater inner culture, these ideas were arrived at very early and the Indians have never got out of them. They took them over from the age of primitives, for practically all primitives believe that there is a continuity within the tribe. Hence the amusing [custom] of certain Eskimos who put one of the grandfather's lice on the head of the grandchild, so that the soul substance of the grandfather shall be passed on to him.

So you see, the matter is a bit complicated, but I hope you have understood what I mean. [Two members of the audience then relate examples of the transmigration of souls.] Individual instances like this certainly do exist but they are very uncommon. There is also an interesting story that allegedly happened in England. A house began to be haunted and the whole household was terribly frightened of the ghost. Now there was a society lady who had no connection with this house but had longed for years to own a certain house which she claimed was hers. She searched everywhere to find something answering to this description, saying she would buy it. Then she suddenly hit on this house, which was up for sale because it was haunted. And when she came the housekeeper opened the door and ran off with a shriek, and it turned out that she herself was the ghost who had been haunting the house for a long time because she had seen it in her imagination. So she got her house, or so the story goes. But—*si non e vero!*

QUESTION 5: *Can I help the spirit of my dead father by trying to live in accordance with the demands of the unconscious?*

Yes, provided—one must always add—that the spirit of the dead father [remains a living idea]. I call this idea hygienic, because when I think that way everything is right in my psychic life and when I don't think that way everything goes wrong, then somewhere things don't click, at least in the biological sense. It's as if I ate something that rationally considered is harmless but it doesn't agree with me—I get the stomach ache. But if I eat something that rationally considered is not good, it does agree with me so why shouldn't I eat it? It is even advisable to do so. For instance, for many people there is no harm in drinking a glass of red wine, while for others it is sheer poison and can have very bad consequences, but that doesn't mean that because it has bad consequences sometimes, one shouldn't drink wine. Rationally one can argue that the enjoyment of alcohol is harmful, but it is not true in general, only in certain cases. So it is much better that we do what agrees with us than what does not agree with us. It agrees with human beings to have ideas about things they cannot know. And if they have these ideas that suit them, they are better off psychologically. They feel better, they sleep better, have a better appetite, and that's the only criterion we have. It means a tremendous lot to people if they can assume their lives have an indefinite continuity; they live more sensibly, they don't need to hurry any more. They have centuries to waste, so why this senseless rush? But of course one always wants to know whether it is really so—as if anyone knew whether it is really so! We know nothing at all. Think of the physicists, they are the closest to reality, and yet they speak of models, of fields of probability. That's it, we just don't know.

QUESTION FROM THE AUDIENCE: *But the fact that such a need exists—*

We have many needs!

Yes, but just this one seems to indicate that something in the psyche proves that this idea—

Yes, but now go and ask a rationalist, he will say, Quite, quite! And if you feel the need for a large income, what then?—This need exists too, or to own a fine car, but that doesn't prove he'll get it. We have many needs, you see. The existence of a need proves only that it should be satisfied, and from that we deduce that we ought to have just those ideas which correspond to this need.

But for this need to arise, there must be something in it, like the psyche's striving towards a goal.

Yes, but that still doesn't prove anything. It's like when you have a patient who says, I simply must have a fine car, or else. So you tell him, Then get one, go to it, work! That is his reality, but it proves nothing. Similarly, when someone says, I want to be immortal, that doesn't make him immortal. He has that need, but you can find many people who don't admit to any such need. And when you come to think of it, how frightful it would be to have to sit on a cloud for ten thousand years playing a harp!

Now the idea of the spirit of the dead father is a transcendent idea, but it serves a purpose and I would call it "reasonable." It is reasonable to think that way. So supposing this spirit has a subjective existence, a consciousness of its own, then there also exists an ethical relation to what it is or what it wants or what it needs. And if I live in such a way that it helps this spirit, it is a moral achievement from which I can expect satisfaction. But the question we are being asked is: if I live in accordance with the demands of the unconscious. That is too general. In such a case I would say: What corresponds to the urgent need of the father should be compensated, not simply the unconscious—that's going too far. For instance, something the father has left unfinished.[7] Or the father appears to his daughter and tells her in a dream or in reality that he has buried a treasure somewhere which didn't belong to him, but was stolen property and she should give it back. These are situations that occur in reality. Or he tells her that he had a philosophy which actually made him unhappy and so the daughter must think differently. Only these specific relationships are really satisfactory. They must fit the real character of the father, then the corresponding reaction can be expected, in so far as these transcendent ideas are any use at all. This may be a quite ruthless question, but the real criterion is:

[7] Cf. *Memories, Dreams, Reflections,* p. 214/204.

Do they serve a purpose? Are they an advantage? For if they accomplish nothing, why should I have these ideas? But if I feel they are a positive advantage, then why shouldn't I have them? They cannot decide the issue one way or another, any more than we are in a position to understand actual reality and establish what it is: there are only fields of probability. There are average predictable phenomena and there are just as many that are unpredictable—were it otherwise there would be no statistics!

QUESTION 6: *May we assume that there is a connection between dual predestination and synchronicity, and that experientially they are the same thing? The same as being in Tao—the simultaneous reality of spirit and matter, simultaneously experienced with equal intensity, but always vibrating like a compass needle?*

What do you mean by dual predestination?

ANSWER FROM THE AUDIENCE: *Karl Barth has rethought Calvin's predestination theory along new lines and says it is not, as Calvin said, that people are either rejected or accepted from the very beginning, but that each person is both accepted at one moment and rejected at another.*

The theory of predestination has of course nothing to do with synchronicity. Synchronicity is a scientific concept and the predestination theory is a dogma. Synchronicity is a description of facts, whereas the predestination theory is riddled with contradictions. If predestination is true, then everything goes on as it *must*: there are some who are chosen to go to heaven, others are predestined to roast in hell and go down to the kitchen. If you fit the bill, you're chosen—or else the good Lord invalidates his own decree by suddenly sweeping up to heaven someone predestined for hell, or snatches someone down from heaven and sticks him in the pit. If you examine these things logically it is simply a juggling with words that has nothing to do with actuality. Dual predestination, indeed! So I am predestined for hell *and* predestined for heaven, and then suddenly, by a sleight of hand, I am either here or there. That is not a workable argument, it is a conjuring trick: you think the top hat is empty, and behold there is a white rabbit sitting in it!

MEMBER OF THE AUDIENCE: *I had hoped this was a point where depth psychology and theology could finally meet.*

Oh no, here we are not in agreement at all. Synchronicity states that à certain psychic event is paralleled by some external, non-psychic event and that there is no causal connection between them. It is a parallelism of *meaning*. That has nothing to do with the acrobatics of predestination. Theologians do perform the merriest pranks. One professor of theology reproached me for asserting, in contradiction to God's word, that a man must grow up and put aside childish things. Man, he said, must remain a child. Now it is precisely the teaching of the New Testament that one should not *remain a* child but *become* as a child. My view, he declared, was "en flagrant contradiction avec la parole du Maître." So I sent him a postcard citing the Biblical passages that say exactly the opposite.[8] The same is true of Catholics. A Jesuit father came to me, a very intelligent type, and said, I really can't understand you, you must explain to me how you can assert that Christ and Mary were not human beings. I replied, But it is very simple. According to the teaching of the Church you were born in sin, so was I, and all men, and that is how death came into the world. We are corruptible and have corruptible bodies, but Christ and Mary have incorruptible bodies. Therefore they were taken up to heaven in the body as was Elijah of old, and therefore they were not human beings. All men are mortal, all men are corruptible because of original sin. He had never thought of that! He was so dumfounded that he

---

[8] For example: Matthew 18:3–5, Mark 10:15, Luke 18:17; also I Cor. 13:11.

couldn't utter a word! There's the theologian for you—the general run of theological thinking is often simply incomprehensible. Now can a theologian not notice that Christ and Mary according to dogma have an incorruptible body? That is a divine attribute, only gods have it, or demons, but not men.

QUESTION 7: *What is the psychological difference between belief in a personal God and the concept of a divine impersonal principle?*

Men naturally have ideas about God, and as my dead friend Albert Oeri[9] quite rightly said, some imagine a good God, the conservatives imagine him as an elderly railway official with a beard, and the others as a little more gaseous. So it goes—we have all sorts of ideas of a personal fathergod with a beard, and a universal "principle" which is really more than "gaseous"—much more abstract. It is simply the difference between an infantile idea and a philosophical one. Or, it is the difference between being personally addressed, the personal encounter, and a general philosophical hypothesis.

If one has an idea, that is to say a rationalized idea which has been discussed and reflected upon, it is always a paradox. As Kant has already pointed out, only antinomial statements can be made about transcendental positions. He exemplifies this by: God is, God is not. Thus every statement about God is also represented by its opposite. Hence God is personal, he is my Father, he is a universal principle. An infinity of statements is possible, all of them valid in so far as they also state the opposite. The antinomy of the statements is a proof of their honesty. But naturally one cannot form any such ideas of which it could seriously be said that they must be so, because their object is one which we cannot know unless we were God himself, and in so far as we are "God" we are speaking of our unconscious, being

[9] See above, p. 3.

ourselves unconscious to the extent we are "God." Thus it is that all the statements we make about God are statements about the unconscious. It is local, it is universal, it is the One, it is the Many or the All, it is personal and impersonal because the unconscious appears to us in all these forms. One feels personally addressed by the unconscious—or one doesn't.

QUESTION 8: *Have you ever met any people who have seen Ufos, and were they prepared to interpret this experience purely psychologically and not insist on the physical reality of the Ufos?*

I actually do know of four cases of people who have seen Ufos or said they did. They are not in the least prepared to interpret the Ufos psychologically. They are more inclined to ask me, Do you think this is psychological? because for them it was felt as thoroughly real.

There was, for instance, the case of a doctor in an American city who together with many other people observed a Ufo for three-quarters of an hour in the form of a small silvery sphere or disc which then suddenly vanished. Knowing this man to be a regular camera fiend, I assumed he had taken a marvellous photo of this phenomenon. But astonishingly enough he hadn't, although he carried his camera with him, as always.[10]

Another man was driving with his wife over the Golden Gate bridge in San Francisco, when she saw in the west about twenty Ufos flying in the Pacific. She drew her husband's attention to them and he saw them too. The spheres or discs gleamed like silver in the sun. Both sent me eye-witness reports and some time later I saw the man personally, whereupon he expressed his astonishment at my interest in such things. But this, you see, is also a contribution to psychology. It is said that people who make the least fuss about these things are the most likely to see a Ufo.

[10] Cf. "Flying Saucers: A Modern Myth," CW 10, par. 613.

A former patient, now an analyst living in the southwest of America, also observed a silvery object in the sky for about four minutes, after which it vanished at great speed. She described it as "web-like" and as though sprayed with aluminum, so that one could make out its web-like structure. She evidently wanted to convey that the object was lighter than metal. Not for a moment did she doubt that it was real—it was like seeing a bus passing—with no connection whatever with any kind of psychology, so that one is absolutely flummoxed and thinks these people must have seen something real. I have not concerned myself at all with the question of whether these things can be real and if so how. Ufos in dreams should be treated like any other dream image, they play exactly the same role.

QUESTION 10: *Can our preoccupation with psychology and with Ufos be traced back to a decline of the belief in God, as though this left a void which the unconscious had to fill?*

Yes, we feel uneasy and dissatisfied and insecure and now under modern political conditions we are naturally afraid also. And naturally we ask, What is the matter with man's psychology? We cannot make anyone else responsible for what is happening in the world except man. There lies the great danger: why is man as he is? In our world miracles do not happen any more, and we feel that something simply must happen which will provide an answer or show a way out. So now these Ufos are appearing in the skies. Although they have always been observed[11] they didn't signify anything. Now, suddenly, they seem to portend something because that something has been projected on them—a hope, an expectation. What sort of expectation you can see from the literature: it is of course the expectation of a savior. But that is only one aspect. There is another aspect, a mythological one. The Ufo can be a ship of death, which means that ships of death are coming to fetch the

[11] Ibid., pars. 757ff.

living or to bring souls. Either these souls will fall into birth, or many people are going to die and will be fetched by fleets of these ships of death.[12] These are important archetypal ideas, because they can also be predictions. If an atomic war were to break out, an infinite multitude of souls would be carried away from the earth. How one is to explain the Ufos in individual cases, I cannot say. It depends on the circumstances, on a dream, or on the person concerned. There is indeed a void in individuals now that we are beginning to discover that our belief in metaphysical explanations has grown enfeebled. In the Middle Ages the Ufos would have been taken for divine manifestations, but we must say with Goethe: "For all our wisdom, Tegel still is haunted."[13]

[12] Ibid., pars. 697–99, 702–3.
[13] Cf. "The Meaning of Psychology for Modern Man," CW 10, par. 309. *Faust, Part One* (trans. P. Wayne, Penguin Books), p. 178.

TALKS WITH MIGUEL SERRANO:
1959

◆◆◆◆◆◆◆◆◆◆◆◆◆◆◆◆◆◆◆◆◆◆◆◆◆◆◆◆

In 1947, the Chilean diplomat and writer Miguel Serrano first read a book of Jung's, which he had taken along on a trip to the Antarctic, and during the next ten years, while living in India, he simultaneously studied Jung and yoga. In 1957 he first wrote to Jung (meanwhile, he had become Chile's ambassador to India), and finally, on February 28, 1959, Jung invited Serrano to visit him at the Hotel Esplanade, in Locarno, where he liked to go for rest and a change of scene. Serrano and Jung talked (in English) in a quiet corner of the hotel lobby.

Serrano's account of his meetings with Jung is in his book *C. G. Jung and Hermann Hesse: A Record of Two Friendships*, translated from the Spanish by Frank MacShane (London and New York, 1966). Here the conversation has been recast in dialogue form and slightly abridged.

I understand you have just come from India. I was there some time ago, trying to convince the Hindus that it is impossible to get rid of the idea of the ego or of consciousness, even in the deepest state of *samadhi*. When I was at the University of Calcutta in Bengal, I discussed this matter with various Brahman doctors and professors, but they were unable to understand. I tried to explain to them that if Ramakrishna, for example, had been able to get rid of his consciousness completely in his moments of profound ecstasy, then those very moments would have been nonexistent. He would never have been able to remember them or to record them, or even to consider them as having any existence at all.[1]

[1] Cf. "The Holy Men of India," CW 11.

(As he talked, I realized that I would have to keep myself very conscious of the moments that were passing between us, and I tried to be as observant as possible. I noticed that in addition to the energy which radiated from him while he talked, there was also in him a certain kindness, although it was sometimes mixed with a sense of irony, or even of sarcasm. Yet above all, I was aware of a certain air of absence or mystery about him, for I knew that this kind man was quite capable of transforming himself into a cruel and destructive being if, by chance, certain of the extremes within him happened to fuse. His eyes were penetratingly observant; they seemed to see beyond his glasses, and perhaps beyond time. I had seen a number of photographs of Jung showing him during his youth and mature years, but nothing connected those photographs with the person with whom I was sitting. I was struck with this transformation, for Jung now looked like an ancient alchemist. His hands were knotty, and on the ring finger of his left hand there was a dark stone mounted in gold and inscribed with strange characters.)

Since the unconscious really means the not-conscious, nobody can gain that state while he is alive, and be able to remember it afterwards, as the Hindus claim. In order to remember, one must have a conscious spectator, who is the self or the conscious being. I discussed all this with the Maharaja of Mysore's guru.

I have always thought that the Hindu tries to get rid of the ego in order to escape from the wheel of samsara; eternity for him would be like a continuous state of insomnia, and he therefore wants to blend himself into the concept of the Whole. That is what the modern Hindu wants, but as you know the Siddhas tried something quite different. Now I understand that you wish to establish a dialogue between the ego and that which transcends it, and that you wish to project the light of consciousness more and more into the

*unconscious . . . and that as a consequence you talk about
the collective unconscious; and I understand that by the law
of polarity, a collective conscious may also exist or even a
superconscious. Do you think that this is perhaps the state
to which the Hindu refers and to which he aspires when he
undergoes* samadhi *or, even more forcefully,* kaivalya?
*Perhaps to gain that state, to reach the superconscious, one
has to get rid of everyday rational consciousness. Thus the
difficulty between yourself and the Hindus may merely be
one of misunderstanding, or a failure to realize what the
Hindu really means when he says that he wishes to overcome the ego.*

That may well be, for the Hindus are notoriously weak
in rational exposition. They think for the most part in
parables or images. They are not interested in appealing to
reason. That, of course, is a basic condition of the Orient as
a whole. . . . As for your hypothesis about the superconscious, that is a metaphysical concept and as a consequence
outside of my interests. I wish to proceed solely on facts and
experiences. So far, I have found no stable or definite center
in the unconscious and I don't believe such a center exists. I
believe that the thing which I call self is an ideal center,
equidistant between the ego and the unconscious, and it is
probably equivalent to the maximum natural expression of
individuality, in a state of fulfillment or totality. As nature
aspires to express itself, so does man, and the self is that
dream of totality. It is therefore an ideal center, something
created. The Hindus have written wisely on this point.
According to the Sankhya philosophers, the *purusha* is the
self, and the *atman* may be similar to it. But the definition
always takes the form of a parable. Do you know the story
of the disciple who went to visit his Master to ask him
what the *atman* was? The Master replied, "It is everything."
But the disciple persisted: "Is it the Maharaja's elephant?"
"Yes," answered the Master, "you are the *atman* and so is
the Maharaja's elephant." After that, the disciple departed

very satisfied. On his way back, he met the Maharaja's elephant, but he did not move out of the road because he thought that if he and the elephant were both *atman,* then the elephant would recognize him. Even when the elephant driver shouted at him to move, he refused to do so, and so the elephant picked him up with his trunk and threw him to the side. The next day, covered with bruises, the disciple once again called on his Master and said, "You told me that the elephant and I were both *atman,* and now look what it has done to me." The Master remained perfectly calm and asked the disciple what the elephant driver had told him. "To get out of the way," answered the disciple. "You should have done what he told you to do," said the Master, "because the elephant driver is also *atman.*" Thus the Hindus have an answer for everything. They know a great deal.

The Hindus live entirely in symbols. They are penetrated and interpenetrated by them, but they don't interpret them, nor do they like anyone else to interpret them, since that would be like destroying them. I think that is why your work is not much known or discussed in India, even though you have devoted so much time to its culture and to the Orient in general. You interpret symbols. On the other hand, you are very well known and widely read in my own country.

I know, I am always receiving letters from Chile and from other countries in South America, and that surprises me, since all of my work has been directed towards myself; all of the books that I have written are but by-products of an intimate process of individuation, even when they are connected by hermetic links to the past and, in all probability, to the future. But since they are not supposed to be popular, and are not directed towards the masses, I am somewhat frightened by the sudden success I have had here and there. I am afraid it is not good, because real work is completed in silence and strikes a chord in the minds of only a very few. There is an old Chinese saying which states that if a man sitting alone in his own room thinks the right thoughts, he will be heard thousands of miles away.

Yes, India is an extraordinarily interesting country, and you should live that experience *right*, and you should live it intensely until the hour comes. I also wanted to confront that universe and, as a product of the Christian West, to use it to test my own ways and to give life to those zones within me which correspond to those of the Hindus, but which in the West for the most part remain dormant. And that is why I went to India in 1938.[2] Let me tell you what I now think of that country, and you can correct me later.

So far as I can see, an Indian, so long as he remains an Indian, doesn't *think*—at least in the same way we do. Rather, he *perceives* a thought. In this way, the Indian approximates primitive ways of thinking. I don't say that the Indian is primitive, but merely that the processes of his thought remind me of primitive methods of producing thoughts. Primitive reasoning is in essence an unconscious function which only perceives immediate results. We can only hope to find that kind of reasoning in a civilization which has progressed virtually without interruption from primitive times. Our natural evolution in Western Europe was broken by the introduction of a psychology and spirituality that had developed from a civilization higher than our own. We were interrupted at the very beginning when our beliefs were still barbarously polytheistic, and these beliefs were forced underground and have remained there for the last two thousand years. That, I believe, explains the divisiveness that is found in the Western mind. Still in a primitive state, we were forced to adopt the comparatively sophisticated doctrines of Christian grace and love. A dissociation was thus produced in Western man between the

[2] The visit is described in *Memories, Dreams, Reflections*, ch. IX, iv.

conscious and the unconscious part of his mentality. The conscious mind was undoubtedly freed from irrationality and instinctive impulses, but total individuality was lost. Western man became someone divided between his conscious and unconscious personality. The conscious personality could always be domesticated because it was separated from the primitive; and as a consequence we in the West have come to be highly disciplined, organized, and rational. On the other hand, having allowed our unconscious personality to be suppressed, we are excluded from an understanding or appreciation of the primitive man's education and civilization. Nevertheless, our unconscious personality still exists and occasionally erupts in an uncontrolled fashion. Thus we are capable of relapsing into the most shocking barbarisms, and the more successful we become in science and technology the more diabolical are the uses to which we put our inventions and discoveries.

But to make man aware of his conscious side is not the only way to civilize him, and in any case, is not the ideal way. A far more satisfactory approach would be to consider man as a whole instead of considering his various parts. What is needed is to call a halt to the fatal dissociation that exists between man's higher and lower being; instead, we must unite conscious man with primitive man. In India we can find a civilization which has incorporated everything that is essential to primitivism, and as a consequence we find man considered as a whole. The civilization and psychology of India are well represented in their temples, because these temples represent the universe. I make this point in particular in order to explain what I mean by *not thinking*. What I mean is simply that, thank God, there is still a man who has not learned how to think, but who still perceives his thoughts as though they were visions or living beings, and who perceives his gods as though they were visible thoughts, based on instinctive reality. He has made peace with his gods, and they live with him. It is true that the life he leads is close to nature. It is full of hope, of brutality, misery, sickness, and death; nevertheless, it has a completeness, a satisfaction, and an emotional beauty which is unfathomable. Undoubtedly, the logic of this civilization is imperfect, and thus we see fragments of Western science side by side with what we call superstition. But if these contradictions are improbable to us, they are not to the Indians. If these contradictions exist, they are merely the peculiarities of autonomous thought and are responsible only to themselves. The Indian himself is not responsible for these contradictions, since his thought *comes to him*. This phenomenon is illustrated by the Indian's lack of interest in the details of the universe. He is only interested in having a vision of totality. But alas, he does not realize that the living world can be destroyed in a struggle between two concepts.

Yes, that is what India is like. It is a great natural civilization, or rather, a civilization of nature. Indeed, it could be said of all of the Orient that, at least until very recently, it has not tried to dominate *nature, but to respect its laws and to understand them—to give them a meaning. Nevertheless, it has no sense of* persona; *it only knows the archetype. I realize, of course, that the idea of personality is not necessarily good; perhaps it's quite the opposite.*

Yes, India is archetypal. And that is why I made no plans to visit swamis or gurus when I went to India; I didn't even go to see Ramana Maharshi,[3] who had so interested Somerset Maugham, because I felt that it was not

---

[3] Jung, however, edited *Der Weg zum Selbst* (1944), a collection of the Maharshi's writings translated from English by Heinrich Zimmer. It has an introduction by Jung, reprinted in CW 11 as "The Holy Men of India," in which he develops the ideas in the above paragraph.

W. Somerset Maugham (1874–1965), the English writer, was also in India in 1938. In *A Writer's Notebook* (1949), pp. 250–76, he relates his experiences while there, including (pp. 273f.) a brief account of meeting an unidentified holy man, evidently Ramana

necessary to do so. I knew what a swami was; I had an exact idea of his archetype; and that was enough to know them all, especially in a world where extreme personal differentiation doesn't exist as it does in the West. We have more variety, but it's only superficial.

You said, Dr. Jung, that you went to India in order to know yourself better. I went to do something like that myself, because I want to discover what we South Americans are. We are neither Asian nor are we Europeans. You have said that the Hindu doesn't think *his thoughts, and I take that to mean that he doesn't think with his mind, with his brain, but that his thoughts are produced in some other center of his being. Do you think that is possible? It has always seemed to me that we South Americans do not think* from *the rational center, but from some other one, and consequently, our first task is to discover what that other center is, so that we can begin to understand our own being. Where do you suppose this center is located? Do you think we should take seriously the hypothesis of the* chakras[4]*— the psychic centers of yoga?*

Your question is very interesting. I once remember having a conversation with the chief of the Pueblo Indians, whose name was Ochwiay Biano, which means Mountain Lake. He gave me his impressions of the white man, and he said that they were always upset, always looking for something, and that as a consequence their faces were lined with wrinkles, which he took to be a sign of eternal restless-

---

Maharshi, at Tiruvannamalai, near Madras. In *Points of View* (1958), Maugham devotes a lengthy essay, "The Saint," to the Maharshi, by name, with a fuller account of their meeting and many vivid biographical details.

[4] For a detailed study of the *chakra* system see Arthur Avalon, *The Serpent Power* (Madras and London), 1931. Also Jung, "The Realities of Practical Psychotherapy," CW 16, 2nd edn., appendix, pars. 560–62, and Joseph Campbell, *The Mythic Image* (1975), pp. 330–80.

ness. Ochwiay Biano also thought that the whites were crazy since they maintained that they thought with their heads, whereas it was well known that only crazy people did that. This assertion by the chief of the Pueblos so surprised me that I asked him how *he* thought. He answered that he naturally thought with his heart.[5] And that is how the ancient Greeks also thought.

That is extraordinary. The Japanese, you know, consider the center of the person to be in the solar plexus. But do you believe that white people think with their heads?

No. They think only with their tongues. They think only with words, with words which today have replaced the Logos.

But what about the chakras, *Doctor, what do you think about them? Some peope claim that they correspond to the plexes of Western science. At the very least, they seem to be located in the same places as the plexes are. Of course the Tantric yogis say that the* chakras *and the nadis are psychic centers, rather than physiological or physical, and that they are located along a "vertebral column" which is also psychic. Thus the* chakras *only exist potentially; they come into being only by an act of the will, usually through the practice of yoga. Perhaps they are something like the self, which you mentioned a few moments ago—something which must be created. In any event, many questions remain to be answered about that ancient Oriental science, and many of the techniques now seem to be lost, perhaps in some huge cataclysm which overtook their civilization.*

The *chakras* are centers of consciousness, and Kundalini, the Fiery Serpent, which is to be found at the base of the spine, is an emotional current that runs along the spine, uniting what is below with what is above, and vice versa. [Pause.] I am very old now, and am losing my memory. . . .

[5] Cf. *Memories, Dreams, Reflections*, ch. IX, ii.

Starting from the bottom, at the base of the vertebral column is the *muladhara chakra*;[6] then in the solar plexus comes the *manipura*; after that there is the *anahata*, which is in the heart, the *vishudda*, which is in the throat, the *ajna*, which is found at a point between the eyebrows, and finally there is the *Brahma-chakra*, which is the coronary *chakra*.[7] These locations are useful only to give you an idea of what I mean. The *chakras* are centers of consciousness. The lower ones represent animal consciousness, and there are even others below the *muladhara*.

I suppose that if we were able to activate all of these centers, we would then achieve totality. Still, that would probably bring about the end of history, which seems to be like a pendular movement from one chakra to another. That is to say, each civilization seems to express a particular chakra, and different types of consciousness exist in various parts of the world and at various times. Can you define your concept of the self and what you believe to be the real center of personality?

The self is a circle whose center is everywhere and whose circumference is nowhere.[8] And do you know what the self is for Western man? It is Christ, for Christ is the archetype of the hero, representing man's highest aspiration. All this is very mysterious and at times frightening.

Serrano traveled on from Locarno to Montagnola, near Lugano, where he visited Hermann Hesse. Subsequently, May 5, 1959, Serrano was in Zurich and telephoned Jung's secretary, Aniela Jaffé, to ask for an appointment. Jung invited him to come that afternoon at 4 o'clock.

[6] This *chakra* is followed by the *svadhisthana*, localized near the bladder.
[7] Otherwise called *sahasrara*, localized at the top of the skull.
[8] See above, p. 216, n. 7.

On his previous meeting, Serrano had given Jung a copy in typescript of an English translation of a story, "The Visit of the Queen of Sheba," later published in book form (see below, p. 462).

Your story about the Queen of Sheba is more like a poem than an ordinary tale. The affair of the King and the Queen of Sheba seems to contain everything; it has a truly noumenal quality. But if you should ever meet the Queen of Sheba in the flesh, beware of marrying her. The Queen of Sheba is only for a magic kind of love, never for matrimony. If you were to marry her, you would both be destroyed and your soul would disintegrate.

I know.

In my long psychiatric experience I never came across a marriage that was entirely self-sufficient. Once I thought I had, because a German professor assured me that his was. I believed him until once, when I was visiting in Berlin, I discovered that his wife kept a secret apartment. That seems to be the rule. Moreover, a marriage which is devoted entirely to mutual understanding is bad for the development of individual personality; it is a descent to the lowest common denominator, which is something like the collective stupidity of the masses. Inevitably, one or the other will begin to penetrate the mysteries. Look, it's like this.

(Jung then picked up a box of matches and opened it. He separated the two halves and placed them on a table so that at a distance they looked the same. He then brought them together until the drawer of the box entered the shell.)

That's how it is. The two halves appear equal, but in fact they are not. Nor should they be, since one should always be able to include the other or, if you like, remain outside of the other. Ideally, the man should contain the woman and remain outside of her. But it's a question of degree, and the homosexual is fifty-five per cent feminine. Basically speaking, however, man is polygamous. The people of the Mussulman Empire knew that very well. Nevertheless, marrying several women at the same time is a primitive solution, and would be rather expensive today.

I think the French have found the solution in the Number Three. Frequently this number occurs in magic marriages such as your encounter with the Queen of Sheba. It is something quite different from Freud's sexual interpretations or from D. H. Lawrence's ideas. Freud was wrong, for example, in his interpretation of incest, which, in Egypt, was primarily religious and had to do with the process of individuation. In reality, the King was the individual, and the people were merely an amorphous mass. Thus the King had to marry his mother or his sister in order to protect and preserve individuality in the country. Lawrence exaggerated the importance of sex because he was excessively influenced by his mother; he over-emphasized women because he was still a child and was unable to integrate himself in the world. People like him frequently suffer from respiratory illnesses which are primarily adolescent. Another curious case is that of Saint-Exupéry:[9] from his wife I learned many important details about him. Flight, you see, is really an act of evasion, an attempt to escape from the earth. But the earth must be accepted and admitted, perhaps even sublimated. That is frequently illustrated in myth and religion. The dogma of the Assumption of Mary is in fact an acceptance of matter; indeed it is a sanctification of matter.[10] If you were to analyze dreams, you would understand this better. But you can see it also in alchemy. It's a pity we have no alchemical texts written by women, for then we would

[9] Antoine de Saint-Exupéry (1900–1944), French aviator, author of *Night Flight*, *The Little Prince*, and *Wind, Sand, and Stars*.

[10] Cf. "A Psychological Approach to the Dogma of the Trinity," CW 11, pars. 251–52, and "Answer to Job," ibid., par. 743, n. 4, and pars. 748ff.

know something essential about the visions of women, which are undoubtedly different from those of men.

Do you think it wise to analyze one's own dreams and to pay attention to them? I have talked with Krishnamurti, in India, and he told me that dreams have no real importance, and that the only important thing is to look, *to be conscious and totally aware of the moment. He told me that he never dreams. He said that because he looks with both his conscious and unconscious mind, he has nothing left over for dreams, and that when he sleeps he gains complete rest.*

Yes, that is possible for a time. Some scientists have told me that when they were concentrating with all their attention on a particular problem, they no longer dreamed. And then, for some unexplained reason, they began to dream again. But to return to your question about the importance of analyzing your own dreams, it seems to me that the only important thing is to follow nature. A tiger should be a good tiger; a tree, a good tree. So man should be man. But to know what man is, one must follow nature and go on alone, admitting the importance of the unexpected. Still, nothing is possible without love, not even the processes of alchemy, for love puts one in a mood to risk everything and not to withhold important elements.

(Jung then rose and took a volume from the bookcase. It was his own Archetypes and the Collective Unconscious [CW 9 i], *and he opened it at an essay called "A Study in the Process of Individuation." He showed me the extraordinary plates that are reproduced there, some of Tibetan tankas.)*

These were made by a woman with whom we planned a process of individuation for almost ten years. She was an American and had a Scandinavian mother.

(He pointed to one picture [no. 14] done in bright colors. In the center was a flower, rather like a four-leaf clover,

and above it were drawn a king and queen who were taking
part in a mystic wedding, holding fire in their hands. There
were towers in the background.)

The process of the mystic wedding involves various
stages and is open to innumerable risks, like the *Opus
Alquimia*. For this union is in reality a process of mutual
individuation, which occurs, in cases like this, in both the
doctor and the patient.

(*As he spoke of this magic love and alchemical wedding, I
thought of Solomon and the Queen of Sheba, Christ and
his Church, and of Shiva and Parvati on the summit of
Mount Kailas—all symbols of man and his soul and of the
creation of the Androgynous. Jung went on as though he
were talking to himself.*)

Somewhere there was once a Flower, a Stone, a Crystal,
a Queen, a King, a Palace, a Lover, and his Beloved, and
this was long ago, on an Island somewhere in the ocean five
thousand years ago. . . . Such is Love, the Mystic Flower of
the Soul. This is the center, the self. . . .

(*Jung spoke as though he were in a trance.*)

Nobody understands what I mean. Only a poet could
begin to understand. . . .

You are a poet. And that woman, is she still alive?

She died eight years ago. . . . I am very old. . . .

(*I realized that the interview should end. I showed Jung
some drawings of Hesse and gave him greetings from Step-
penwolf.*)

I met Hesse through a mutual friend, who was interested
in myths and symbols. His friend worked with me for a
while, but he was unable to follow through to the end. The
path is very difficult. . . .[11]

[11] The "friend" is Hesse himself, whom Jung refrained from
identifying as a patient. For Hesse's analysis with Jung, see Jung,
*Letter*s, ed. G. Adler, vol. I, pp. 573–76.

A VISIT FROM LINDBERGH

◆◆◆◆◆◆◆◆◆◆◆◆◆◆◆◆◆◆◆◆◆◆◆◆◆◆

In the summer of 1959, Charles A. Lindbergh (1902–1974) and his wife Anne Morrow Lindbergh were spending their vacation in Switzerland. They went to see Mrs. Lindbergh's publishers, Kurt and Helen Wolff, who were residing at that time in Zurich. Kurt Wolff had persuaded Jung to work with Aniela Jaffé on the composition of his autobiography, and the Wolffs saw Jung from time to time in order to discuss the work in progress. On August 2, the Wolffs invited the Lindberghs to go along with them on a visit to Jung at his Bollingen retreat. In a letter of December 11, 1968, to Helen Wolff, Lindbergh set down his recollection of the visit.

Jung had become interested in the phenomenon of flying saucers, or unidentified flying objects, in the early 1950's, had replied to written questions by Georg Gerster on the subject in 1954,[1] and published his own book in 1958.[2] In a statement that Jung issued to United Press International in August 1958, after the report had been spread by the press that he believed the "Ufos" to be physically real, Jung stated: "This report is altogether false. . . . I cannot commit myself on the question of the physical reality or unreality of the Ufos since I do not possess sufficient evidence either for or against. I therefore concern myself solely with the psychological aspect of the phenomenon. . . ."[3]

. . . I looked forward, especially, to the possibility of listening to Jung talk about "flying saucers," for I knew he was deeply interested in them.

I recall Jung talking about the depths of the lake at our

[1] In *Weltwoche* (Zurich), July 9, 1954. See "On Flying Saucers," CW 18, pars. 1431–44.
[2] *Flying Saucers: A Modern Myth of Things Seen in the Skies* (orig., 1958; tr. R.F.C. Hull, 1959; CW 10).
[3] CW 18, par. 1445.

side, and relating these depths to the human subconscious. We were sitting together in a small room, you, Kurt, Jung, Anne, and I. Finally, the conversation shifted to "flying saucers." I had expected a fascinating discussion about psychological aspects of the numerous and recurring flying-saucer reports. To my astonishment, I found that Jung accepted flying saucers as factual. On the one hand, he didn't seem in the least interested in psychological aspects. On the other, he didn't seem at all interested in factual information relating to the investigation of flying-saucer reports.

When I told Jung that the U. S. Air Force had investigated hundreds of reported flying-saucer sightings without finding the slightest evidence of supernatural phenomena, it was obvious that he did not wish to pursue the subject farther. He asked me how I accounted for recent flying-saucer reports in Europe—especially a series of sightings along an apparently straight line of flying-saucer flight. He referred to Donald Keyhoe's book about flying saucers.[4] I told Jung that, while I had not seen Keyhoe in recent years, I had known him intimately many years ago. (Keyhoe accompanied me, in another plane, when I made a three-month tour of the United States in the "Spirit of St. Louis," in 1927, under the auspices of the Daniel Guggenheim Fund for the Promotion of Aeronautics. He and I usually occupied the same suite of rooms at the hotels where I stopped.)[5]

.   .   .

I told Jung that, to substantiate the claims he made about the reality of flying saucers, Keyhoe, in the early chapters of

[4] In a recent communication, Major Donald E. Keyhoe says that either *Flying Saucers from Outer Space* (New York, 1953; London, 1954) or *The Flying Saucer Conspiracy* (New York, 1955; London, 1957) is referred to here.

[5] Keyhoe wrote a book about this, too: *Flying with Lindbergh* (New York, 1928).

his book, cited alleged reports that the British De Havilland Comets which disintegrated in air had been reported hit by "unidentified flying objects."[6] I said that I had been in close contact with the De Havilland Company and its engineers at the time, because Pan American Airways had on order and option a number of Comets, and I was a consultant to Pan American in this field. I told him that the cause of disintegration was fuselage rupture resulting from fatigue and inadequate basic design, and that in my conferences with De Havilland personnel and other engineers concerned, no mention had ever been made of "unidentified flying objects."

I also mentioned to Jung the high-level Pentagon conference cited by Keyhoe, again in the early chapters of his book, to substantiate his claims about the reality of flying saucers. Keyhoe wrote that this conference had been called because of the alarm caused by flying saucers and their sightings, that it was highly secret, and that the officials attending the conference felt the situation was so alarming and serious that the information discussed should be withheld from public knowledge. I told Jung I had been working closely with the Air Force, as a consultant, at the time, and that Pentagon officials were not alarmed by reports on flying saucers, but astonished at the stories they read about flying saucers in the newspapers. The conference was called as a result of the plea, "For God's sake, somebody tell us what it's all about." It was not a secret conference.

So far as I could judge, Jung showed not the slightest interest in these facts.

I then described a discussion on flying-saucer reports I had carried on with General Spaatz (an old friend and Chief of the United States Air Force). I had, laughingly, asked Spaatz how I could persuade one of my sons that the

[6] Keyhoe says that in *Flying Saucers from Outer Space*, pp. 1–2, he gave the official report that only *one* Comet disintegrated after being hit by an "unidentified flying body."

flying-saucer reports he had read in a *Reader's Digest* article were not true. Spaatz, in his dryly humorous way, had replied: "Slim, don't you suppose that if there was anything true about this flying-saucer business, you and I would have heard about it by this time?"

To this, Jung replied: There are a great many things going on around this earth that you and General Spaatz don't know about.

Thereafter, I departed from the subject of flying saucers. I can't believe that Jung was as uninterested in either psychological aspects or facts relating to flying saucers as the Bollingen meeting made it appear to me. I wonder if there wasn't some reason that day for his not wanting to talk about the subject, even though I can't explain in my own mind what it would be. I was fascinated by Jung. One intuitively feels the elements of mysticism and greatness about him—even though they may have been mixed, at times, with elements of charlatanism. I liked Anne's not unadmiring description of Jung as "an old wizard." In the highest sense, he seemed like that to me in the wizard setting of lakeside Bollingen. And in this instance, the "Old Wizard" just didn't open his mind to me on the subject of flying saucers.

It was a great experience for us, that visit with you and Kurt to Bollingen, one Anne and I are deeply grateful for and will never forget. Jung was such an extraordinary man, surely one of our time's great geniuses. My admiration and respect for him remain, and I continue to find tremendous stimulation in his writings; but I approach his statements and conclusions with even greater caution than in the past.

I realize I have used the term "fact" loosely, as though the physical and psychological could be completely separated, as though the real and the intangible have no relationship in essence. In a sense, every concept forms its own reality, and with this sense in mind, I think a more interesting discussion might have taken place with Jung.

ON THE FRONTIERS OF
KNOWLEDGE

••••••••••••••••••••••••••

This interview conducted by the French-Swiss writer Georges Duplain was first published in the *Gazette de Lausanne*, September 4–8, 1959, as the conclusion of a series of articles by Duplain, "Aux frontières de la connaissance," discussing Jung's book *Flying Saucers: A Modern Myth of Things Seen in the Sky* (orig. 1958). The articles and interview were reissued that same year by the *Gazette* as a pamphlet with a preface by Jung, also given here. The interview, with interpolations by Duplain citing Jung's writings, was published in *Spring*, 1960, in a translation by Jane A. Pratt, which translation is by her courtesy reproduced here but without the interpolations. A few omitted passages have been restored.

Preface

I am particularly grateful to Georges Duplain for having published a series of articles in the *Gazette de Lausanne* which are truly remarkable for their penetration and lucidity. Ordinarily my books are treated rather superficially by the press, and little attempt is made to get at their deeper meaning. This is true not only of the daily papers but also of scientific journals. Georges Duplain goes way beyond this sort of reporting. He is interested in the very essence of the subject under discussion and its relevance to our times. I greatly appreciate this attitude as well as that of the *Gazette de Lausanne*, which has always seen to it that my writings were fairly appraised.

The principal theme examined in this series of articles is a very strange one. It concerns the bizarre and doubtful apparitions of objects which seem to move through our atmosphere. It is surmised that they may come from other planets. It is extremely difficult to obtain reliable proofs of their objective existence, but there are none the less more than ordinary reasons for examining them more closely.

For whether these apparitions have a physical reality or not, they are in any case psychic realities, if only because they have given rise to copious discussions and to a whole literature. Even if there is nothing physically tangible about these phenomena, the rumor of the existence of such objects is an incontestable fact. Whether the rumor corresponds to a physical reality or not makes little difference to a psychologist. For him the interesting thing is to know why the human mind creates such products, because that throws particular light on the activity of our unconscious. The rumor is itself an extremely valuable source of information, since we discover in it new aspects of unconscious psychic activity. Experiences of this kind are especially important because some people still deny the existence of the unconscious part of the psyche, and even those who do admit its existence find themselves in the greatest perplexity as to how it should be understood. The universal spread of this rumor thus gives us a most valuable opportunity to penetrate more deeply into the still very controversial nature of psychic phenomena.

In taking the trouble to write such a thoughtful report, Georges Duplain has done a service not only to the interested public but to our psychological knowledge in general.

C. G. JUNG

INTERVIEW

I am astonished that you should be willing to see a journalist when so many of your own medical followers cannot get near you!

I am astonished, too, to see you here; that a journalist should want to see me—ever since the business of the flying saucers arose, they have been trying to pass me off as senile! But I must say that the French Swiss behave relatively well. I have met with a surprising understanding on your part.

As far as the flying saucers go I haven't much to add. I have received quantities of new documents since my book appeared;[1] they don't make the matter any clearer but they show more and more how important it is. Oh, there's an immense amount to this phenomenon.

You speak of a change of era, of a new Platonic month, of the passage into another sign of the zodiac.[2] What do you mean by that, what reality do such constellations have?

People don't like you to talk about that, you will get yourself laughed at. Nobody has read Plato—you haven't either. Yet he is one of those who have come closest to the truth. The influence of the constellations, the zodiac, they exist; you cannot explain why, it's a "Just-So Story," that proves itself by a thousand signs. But men always go from one extreme to the other, either they don't believe, or they are credulous, any knowledge or faith can be ridiculed on the basis of what small minds do with it. That's stupid and, above all, it's dangerous. The great astrological periods do exist. Taurus and Gemini were prehistoric periods, we don't know much about them. But Aries the Ram is closer; Alexander the Great was one of its manifestations.[3] That was from 2000 B.C. to the beginning of the Christian era. With that era we came into the sign of the Fishes. It was not I who invented all the fish symbols there are in Christianity: the fisher of men, the *pisciculi christianorum*.[4] Christianity has marked us deeply because it incarnates the symbols of

[1] "Flying Saucers: A Modern Myth," CW 10.
[2] Ibid., par. 589.
[3] The Arabic name for Alexander was Dhulqarnein, "two-horned." Cf. *Symbols of Transformation*, CW 5, par. 283, n. 32, also Pl. XXa.
[4] Cf. *Aion*, CW 9 ii, par. 148.

the era so well. It goes wrong in so far as it believes itself to be the only truth; when what it is is one of the great expressions of truth in our time. To deny it would be to throw the baby out with the bathwater. What comes next? Aquarius, the Water-pourer, the falling of water from one place to another. And the little fish[5] receiving the water from the pitcher of the Water-pourer, and whose principal star is Fomalhaut, which means the "fish's mouth." In our era the fish is the content; with the Water-pourer, he becomes the container. It's a very strange symbol. I don't dare interpret it. So far as one can tell, it is the image of a great man approaching. One finds, besides, a lot of things about this in the Bible itself: there are more things in the Bible than the theologians can admit.

It's a matter of experience that the symbolism changes from one sign to another, and there is the risk that this passage will be all the more difficult for the men of today and tomorrow because they no longer believe in it, no longer want to be conscious of it. Why, when Pope Pius XII in one of his last discourses deplored that the world was no longer conscious enough of the presence of angels, he was saying to his faithful Catholics in Christian terms exactly what I am trying to say in terms of psychology to those who stand more chance of understanding this language than any other.

But what recommendations can you make for the passage that is about to take place, whose difficulties you fear?

A spirit of greater openness towards the unconscious, an increased attention to dreams, a sharper sense of the totality of the physical and the psychic, of their indissolubility; a livelier taste for self-knowledge. Better established mental hygiene, if you want to put it that way. The religions have

---

[5] Piscis Austrinus, the Southern Fish. Cf. ibid., par. 173, n. 30, and par. 174. Cf. also *Memories, Dreams, Reflections*, p. 339/313 and n.

tried to be this, but the result is not entirely satisfactory, don't you agree?

What is very important is to exist, and that's rarer than one realizes. To have a daily task and to accomplish it; and at the same time to attend to what is going on, inside oneself as well as outside, conscious of all life's forms, all its expressions. To follow the major rules, but also to give free rein to the least familiar aspects of oneself. Drawing, and the fantasies and visions that it brought about, was a valuable thing. Now we take photographs, and that doesn't fill the same need at all. In return, the painters recognize no limits to the most impassioned fantasy. They are becoming specialists in certain needs for expression; but all of us have these needs, we can't divide up the personality's inside work the way we think we can divide its outside activity. That breaks up something essential in it and causes an appalling psychic illness. In writing about flying saucers, I explained why men are so attentive to anything resembling a circle or a ball, the symbols of unity, of the totality of a person's being, of what I have called the self. There is a terrible spiritual famine in our world, but there are also people who don't want to be beak-fed or fed with infant's pap.

May I ask you to repeat the principal points of your system which may assist man to discover his totality and allay his spiritual famine, when he no longer adheres to the words of Christianity?

In the first place, I have no system, no doctrine, nothing of that kind. I am an empiricist, with no metaphysical views at all. I have only hypotheses. From them I have gained some basic principles. There is the self, which is the totality of one's being, known and unknown, conscious and unconscious, as opposed to the distinction between physical and psychic. Then there are the archetypes, those images of instinct. For instinct is not just an outward thrust, it also takes part in the representation of forms. The animal, for example, has a certain idea of the plant, since he recognizes it.[6] Our instincts do not express themselves only in our actions and reactions, but also in the way we formulate what we imagine. Instinct is not only biological, it is also, you might say, spiritual. And it always repeats certain forms which can be studied down the ages among all peoples. These are the archetypes.

The crossing of a river, now, that is an archetypal situation. It's an important moment, a risk. There is danger in the water, on the banks. Not for nothing did Christianity invent great St. Christopher, the giant who carried the infant Jesus through the water. Today men don't have that experience very often, or others of that sort either. I remember river crossings in Africa with crocodiles, and unknown tribes on the other side; one feels that one's destiny —human destiny, almost—is at stake. Every man has his own way of approaching the crossing, you see. And think of King Albrecht's death near Wettingen, too: the knights were hesitant, not very determined, one can't be at all sure that they would have attacked the king just anywhere. But they surprised him in the middle of the ford, in the place where fate strikes—and jumped at the chance.[7]

There is also the collective unconscious, that immense treasury, that great reservoir, whence mankind draws the images, the forces, which it translates into very different languages, but whose common source is being found out more clearly all the time. So many coincidences come from there.

Is your explanation of man and the world understandable to simple people or reserved for the intellectual élite?

There are two distinct things: the use of psychotherapy

[6] Cf. "On the Nature of the Psyche," CW 8, par. 398, and "Instinct and the Unconscious," ibid., pars. 268, 277.
[7] Cf. above, "The Houston Films," p. 293.

is reserved for medical specialists—not everyone can fool around with that—but what you call the "explanation" reaches a lot more people than I would have thought possible myself.

I always remember a letter I received one morning, a poor scrap of paper, really, from a woman who wanted to see me just once in her life. The letter made a very strong impression on me, I am not quite sure why. I invited her to come and she came. She was very poor—poor intellectually too. I don't believe she had ever finished primary school. She kept house for her brother; they ran a little newsstand. I asked her kindly if she really understood my books which she said she had read. And she replied in this extraordinary way, "Your books are not books, Herr Professor, they are bread."

And the little travelling salesman of women's things, who stopped me in the street and looked at me with immense eyes, saying, "Are you really the man who writes those books? Are you truly the one who writes about these things no one knows?"

Yes, in the long run I am very optimistic. The people do follow it. In the French part of Switzerland the first edition of my *L'Homme à la découverte de son âme*[8] was sold out in three months. Who reads it? Not the professors.

How did you arrive at your global concept of the human being, of the totality?

Empiricism, I tell you, observation. One must admit that the psychological fact is everything. Perception makes reality psychic, we live in the sort of a world-image that our senses and intelligence can perceive; we do not know true reality, in so far as all of it is not conceivable to us.

---

[8] Five essays by Jung, tr. Roland Cahen-Salabelle, together with extracts from a seminar delivered in Basel (1934) and from "The Tavistock Lectures" (CW 18); Geneva and Annemasse, 1944 and subsequent edns. Jung's epilogue is in CW 18. Cf. above, p. 76.

But we have quantities of signs of the reality beyond. We should try to understand what is beyond us.

That is accomplished by stages. A whole evolution was needed before the idea of the unconscious was accepted. Nietzsche, Schopenhauer, Pierre Janet, Charcot, Freud: they were so many steps. The conjunction of several lines of study in one man was also needed. I have had the good luck to be able to study all my life. My father was a theologian, specializing in oriental languages; he passed on a bit of his gift for language to me. I studied the literature, I studied medieval and ancient alchemy. Comparative religion, of course, and, to begin with, philosophy at the same time as medicine. All of that was necessary to work out the line of thought and the mental attitude that have led me to uncover certain laws. And don't forget my travels, particularly in India and Africa,[9] where one meets men of other epochs. By dint of observation, of discovery, one notes relationships, resemblances, coincidences, and one tries to get back to their common source, for there certainly must be one. It's the sum of experience, that's all.

Let me tell you a story which happened a long while ago, to show you how empiricism leads to certain discoveries. The doctor of a small town in Canton Solothurn had sent me a young patient who suffered from incurable insomnia. She was pining away from lack of sleep and narcotics. He could think of no way to help her except hypnotism or this new psychoanalysis that they were beginning to talk about.

But she came to me. She was a teacher, twenty-five years old, of a very simple family, who had successfully completed her studies, but who lived in constant fear of making a mistake, of not being worthy of her position. She had gotten into an unbearable state of spasmodic tension. Clearly, what she needed was psychic relaxation. But we did not

[9] Cf. *Memories, Dreams, Reflections*, ch. IX.

know much about all those ideas then. There was no one in the locality where she lived who could handle her case, and she could not come to Zurich for treatment. I had to do, as best I could, whatever was possible in an hour. I tried to explain to her that relaxation was necessary, that I, for example, found relaxation by sailing on the lake, by letting myself go with the wind; that this was good for one, necessary for everybody. But I could see by her eyes that she didn't understand. She got it intellectually, that's as far as it went, though. Reason had no effect.

Then, as I talked of sailing and of the wind, I heard the voice of my mother singing a lullaby to my little sister as she used to do when I was eight or nine, a story of a little girl in a little boat, on the Rhine, with little fishes. And I began, almost without doing it on purpose, to hum what I was telling her about the wind, the waves, the sailing, and relaxation, to the tune of the little lullaby. I hummed those sensations, and I could see that she was "enchanted."

But the hour came to an end, and I had to send her away brusquely. I knew nothing more about her. I had forgotten her name and that of her physician. But it was a story that haunted me.

Years later, at a congress, a stranger introduced himself to me as the doctor from Solothurn and reminded me of the story of the young girl. "Certainly I remember the case," I said. "I should have liked so much to know what became of her."

"But," he replied in surprise, "she came back cured, as you know, and I was the one who always wanted to know what you had done. Because all she could tell me was some story about sailing and wind, and I never could get her to tell me what you really did. I think she doesn't remember. Of course, I know it's impossible that you only hummed her a story about a boat."

How was I to explain to him that I had simply listened to something within myself? I had been quite at sea. How was I to tell him that I had sung her a lullaby with my mother's voice? Enchantment like that is the oldest form of medicine. But it all happened outside of my reason: it was not until later that I thought about it rationally and tried to arrive at the laws behind it. She was cured by the grace of God.

How can you speak of the grace of God?

And why not? A good dream, for example, that's grace. The dream is in essence a gift. The collective unconscious, it's not for you, or me, it's the invisible world, it's the great spirit. It makes little difference what I call it: God, Tao, the Great Voice, the Great Spirit. But for people of our time God is the most comprehensible name with which to designate the Power beyond us.

The images of God—it's an immense story. I remember an African tribe whose members greeted the first rays of the sun by spitting in their hands and turning them towards it. That's classic: since breath is the soul, the saliva which accompanies the breath is the substance of the soul. What that gesture means exactly is: "My God, I offer you my soul." I tried to find out if they knew the meaning of their gesture. No, the young did not know, nor the fathers. But the grandfathers knew, it is they who guard the secrets. And elsewhere you see this gesture in the carved dog-headed baboons of Abu Simbel.

I watched the tribesmen and when I thought I had understood them I asked, "Your god Mungu, he is the sun?" Homeric gales of laughter from the tribesmen. This poor imbecile of a white man, imagining that we worship that ball of light and heat! I looked closer. The same rite also greeted the new moon. So, in the end, I understood their god: it was the moment when darkness changes into light, not the sun itself, but its appearing.[10] There is Horus, too, among the Egyptians. There are so many things and they all hang together.

The French writer Colette once said to her husband about some bit of animal behavior, "Maurice, there's just one *animal, just* one *animal!"*

I wasn't familiar with that but it's exactly the same idea, the same sense of totality, expressed in the language of someone very close to the animal world. There are so many possible forms of the truth. We must find simple words for the great truths; we must try to approach the living truth behind things, it's mankind's oldest effort.

In our time, it's the intellect that is making darkness, because we've let it take too big a place. Consciousness discriminates, judges, analyzes, and emphasizes the contradictions. It's necessary work up to a point. But analysis kills and synthesis brings to life. We must find out how to get everything back into connection with everything else. We must resist the vice of intellectualism, and get it understood that we cannot only understand.

Two or three more centuries will go by before the new era I spoke of in connection with the flying saucers. A lot will still have to happen to mankind. Many things will have to change before the new style comes to birth, the new formula for the realization of humanity.

I remember a marvellous sight I beheld one evening in India at the Darjeeling observatory. Sikkim was already in shadow, the mountains blue to about four thousand meters, violet to about seven thousand. And there in the middle of that ring of mountains was Kanchenjunga in all its glory, resplendent as a ruby. It was the lotus with the jewel without price in its center. And all the savants and scientists, lost in wonder at this spectacle, said "OM" without realizing

[10] For a fuller account see ibid., pp. 266ff., and concerning the dog-headed baboons, pp. 269/274.

it. That's the primal word, the sound that passes from mother to child, and what some primitives say when they approach a stranger. And after the learned men had regained consciousness, they felt the need of a word and they asked me to recite part of *Faust*.

Faust—you know how Goethe spoke of that work, of the research into the essential that it meant? As "das Hauptgeschäft," the main thing, the essential.

Man has need of the word, but number is a much more important thing. In essence, number is sacred. Lots of important things might be said about it. The quaternity, above all, is an essential archetype. The square, the cross. The squaring of the circle by the alchemists. The cross in the circle, or, for Christians, Christ in "glory." It is not I who have made up all that. It exists, and it's important.

What can men do, and especially we Swiss, to prepare ourselves and help everyone prepare himself to face a future already disturbing in its immediacy?

There is no entirely simple, thoroughly rational recipe. Most of us are too academic-minded to come face to face with living reality in its wholeness, its totality. We prefer to deny it because that's easier, and because we can find such a lot of good, honest, reasonable arguments for doing so. What would you have me do? I say what I know, what I believe, how I see things. But I know very well that truth is ineffable and all our approaches to it, gross. Just the same, we're moving ahead. But it's such a long story.

In the case of Switzerland there are some profound symbols which are very strange: the union of white and red in our flag, for example, is a "sign" of the reconciliation of opposites. I pointed out in my book on "flying objects" that the white star on American airplanes and the red star on Soviet planes also show this opposition of masculine and feminine colors. In Switzerland this symbolism may be said to point to their reconciliation, since the two colors are conjoined. And besides there is also (on our flag) the cross, which is the sign of the quaternity already to be found in the center of Switzerland, where the rivers take their rise, as though the play of nature had marked out that quaternity. If we were more conscious in our country, we might think more of this; we might allow these great symbols to penetrate us.

But there is no entirely simple, thoroughly rational recipe: though the Swiss want that above all. The sort of things that we have been talking about are, without doubt, harder to explain to the Swiss than to other people. We are extremely materialistic in the broadest sense of the term. Feet on the ground, heads not too high in the sky! We believe in nothing but what we see, what we touch, what we know. The Swiss is much too literal-minded to come face to face with live reality in its wholeness, its totality. He prefers to deny it because that is easier, and because such a lot of good, honest, reasonable arguments can be found to support his denial. What would you have me do? I say what I know, what I believe, how I see things. But I know very well that the Truth is ineffable, and all our approaches to it are gross. Just the same we are moving ahead. But it is such a long story.

There is one thing that counts, though: we're beginning to look at history in the light of perspectives gained from the study of the psyche and of human behavior. And not only history but economics, too. Men like Professor Karl Schmid[11] at the Federal Institute of Technology, Zurich, or Professor Böhler[12] and his Institute for Economic Research, have a very extensive acquaintance with psychology; their better knowledge of man and what motivates him should

[11] Cf. *Hochmut und Angst* (Zurich and Stuttgart, 1958).
[12] Cf. Eugen Böhler, "Ethik und Wirtschaft" (Ethics and Economy), *Industrielle Organisation* (Zurich), IV (1957); "Ideologies and Ideals," *Spring*, 1960; and "Conscience in Economic Life," in *Conscience* (Studies in Jungian Thought; Evanston, 1970).

permit a better understanding of political and economic conditions. With time and accumulated experience, we shall not only understand the past better, but maybe we shall also learn how to avoid the most dangerous situations in the future, to forestall political crises just as we now begin to know how to forestall economic crises. That would be progress, if men were wise enough.

But remember what the Pope said: "The world should be more conscious of the presence of angels." There was a man who was conscious of what the unconscious brings us, who was in contact with the living truth.

[Translated by Jane A. Pratt]

THE "FACE TO FACE"
INTERVIEW

++++++++++++++++++++++++++++

John Freeman's interview with Jung on the BBC television program "Face to Face" has undoubtedly brought Jung to more people than any other piece of journalism and any of Jung's own writings. Freeman and a team led by the producer Hugh Burnett filmed the interview in Jung's house at Küsnacht in March 1959, and, edited to one-half hour, it was broadcast in Great Britain on October 22, 1959. Subsequently, it has often been rebroadcast, and a cinema film version is frequently shown by educational organizations, Jungian groups, and such. Part of the transcript was published in a different form in *Face to Face*, edited by Burnett (London, 1964), containing a number of interviews conducted by Freeman.

Freeman was deputy editor of the *New Statesman* at the time of the interview with Jung. They formed a friendship that continued until Jung's death. Later, Freeman was editor-in-chief of the *New Statesman*; 1965–68, British High Commissioner to India; and 1969–71, British Ambassador to Washington.

Because of the success of Jung's interview by Freeman, the next year the BBC requested another interview, this time with a psychiatrist about medical problems. Jung declined, because he felt unequal to the exertion and was discouraged by his previous experience of interviews by psychologists poorly informed of his work. See his letter to Burnett, June 30, 1960, in *Letters*, ed. Adler, vol. 2.

Professor Jung, how many years have you lived in this lovely house by the lake at Zurich?

It's just about fifty years.

Do you live here now just with your secretaries and your English housekeeper?

Yes.

No children or grandchildren with you?

Oh no, they don't live here, but I have plenty of them in the surroundings.

Do they come to see you often?

Oh yes!

How many grandchildren have you?

Oh, nineteen.

And great grandchildren?

I think eight, and I suppose one is on the way.

And do you enjoy having them?

Well, it's nice to feel such a living crowd are out of one-self.

Are they afraid of you, do you think?

I don't think so. If you would know my grandchildren you wouldn't think so! They steal my things. Even my hat that belongs to me they stole the other day.

Now, can I take you back to your own childhood? Do you remember the occasion when you first felt consciousness of your own individual self?

That was in my eleventh year. There I suddenly was on my way to school I stepped out of a mist. It was just as if I had been in a mist, walking in a mist, and I stepped out of it and I knew, "I am." "I am what I am." And then I thought, "But what have I been before?" And then I found that I had been in a mist, not knowing how to differentiate my self from things. I was just one thing among other things.[1]

---

[1] Cf. Jung, *Memories, Dreams, Reflections*, pp. 32f./44f.

Now was that associated with any particular episode in your life, or was it just a normal function of adolescence?

Well, that's difficult to say. As far as I can remember, nothing had happened before that would explain this sudden coming to consciousness.

You hadn't, for instance, been quarrelling with your parents, or anything?

No. No.

What memories have you of your parents? Were they strict and old-fashioned in the way they brought you up?

Oh well, you know, they belonged to the later part of the Middle Ages. My father was a parson in the country, and you can imagine what people were then, you know, in the seventies of the past century. They had the convictions in which people have lived since one thousand eight hundred years.

How did he try to impress these convictions on you? Did he punish you, for instance?

Oh no, not at all, no. He was very liberal, and he was most tolerant and most understanding.

Which did you get on with more intimately—your father or your mother?

That's difficult to say. Of course, one is always more intimate with the mother, but when it comes to the personal feeling I had a better relation to my father, who was predictable, than with my mother, who was to me a very problematical something.

So at any rate fear was not an element in your relation with your father?

Not at all.

Did you accept him as being infallible in his judgments?

Oh no, I knew he was very fallible.

How old were you when you knew that?

Now, let me see. [Long pause.] Perhaps eleven or twelve years old. It was hanging together with the fact that I *was*, that I knew I *was*, and from then on I saw that my father was different.

Yes. So the moment of self-revelation was closely connected with realizing the fallibility of your parents?

Yes, one could say so. But I realized that I had fear of my mother, but not during the day. Then she was quite known to me, and predictable, but in the night I had fear of my mother.

And can you remember why? Can you remember what that fear—

I have not the slightest idea why.

What about your schooldays now? Were you happy at school—as a schoolboy?

In the beginning I was very happy to have companions, you know, because before I had been very lonely. We lived in the country and I had no brother and no sister. My sister was born very much later, when I was nine years old, and so I was used to being alone, but I missed it—I missed company—and in school it was wonderful to have company. But soon—you know in a country school I was far ahead—and then I began to be bored.

What sort of religious upbringing did your father give you?

Oh, we were Swiss Reformed.

And did he make you attend church regularly?

Oh, well, that was quite natural. Everybody went to church on Sunday.

And did you believe in God?

Oh, yes.

Do you now believe in God?

Now? [Pause.] Difficult to answer. I *know*. I don't need to believe. I know.

Well now, turning to the next staging point in your life. What made you decide to become a doctor?

I really—originally—I wanted to be an archaeologist; Assyriology, Egyptology, or something of the sort. I hadn't the money; the study was too expensive. So my second love then belonged to nature, particularly zoology, and when I began my studies I inscribed in the so-called Philosophical Faculty Two—that means natural sciences. But then I soon saw that the career that was before me would make a schoolmaster of me, you see. But I didn't—I never thought I had any chance to get any further, because we had no money at all. And then I saw that that didn't suit my expectations, you know. I didn't want to become a schoolmaster. Teaching was not just what I was looking for. And so I remembered that my grandfather had been a doctor, and I knew that when I was studying medicine I had a chance to study natural science and to become a doctor. And a doctor can develop, you see, he can have a practice, he can choose his scientific interests more or less. At all events, I would have more chance than being a schoolmaster, also the idea of doing something useful with human beings appealed to me.

And did you, when you decided to become a doctor, have difficulty in getting the training at school and in passing the exams?

I particularly had a difficulty with certain teachers. They didn't believe that I could write a thesis. I remember one case where the teacher had the custom, the habit, of discussing the papers written by the pupils, and he took the best first. And he went through the whole number of the pupils and I didn't appear, and I was badly troubled over it, and I thought well, it is impossible that my thesis can be *that* bad, and when he had finished he said: "There is still one paper left over and that is the one by Jung. That would be by far the best paper if it hadn't been copied. He has just copied this somewhere—stolen. You are a thief, Jung! And if I knew where you had stolen it I would fling you out of school!" And I got mad and said this is the one thesis where I have worked the most, because the theme was interesting, in contradistinction, you know, to other themes which are not at all interesting to me. And then he said, "You are a liar, and if we can prove that you have stolen that thing somewhere, then you get out of school."[2]

Now that was a very serious thing for me, because what else then, you see? And I hated that fellow, and that was the only man I could have killed, you know, if I had met him once at a dark corner! I would have shown him something of what I could do.

Did you often have violent thoughts about people when you were young?

No, not exactly. Only when I got mad. Well, then I beat them up.

And did you often get mad?

Not so often, but then for good!

You were very strong and big, I imagine?

Yes, I was pretty strong, and you know, reared in the country with those peasant boys, it was a rough kind of life. I would have been capable of violence, I know. I was a bit afraid of it, so I rather tried to avoid critical situations because I didn't trust myself. Once I was attacked by about seven boys and I got mad, and I took one, and just swang him round by his legs, you know, and beat down four of them, and then they were satisfied.

And were there any consequences from that afterwards?

Oh, I should say, yes! From then on it was always sus-

[2] Ibid., pp. 64ff./72ff. Also "The Gifted Child," CW 17, par. 232.

pected that I was at the bottom of every trouble. I was not, but they were afraid and I was never attacked again.

Well now, when the time came that you qualified as a doctor, what made you decide to specialize in being an alienist?

Well, that is rather an interesting point. When I had finished my studies practically, and when I didn't know what I really wanted to do, I had a big chance to follow one of my professors. He was called to a new position in Munich, and he wanted me as his assistant. But then in that moment I studied for my final examination, I came across a textbook of psychiatry. Up to then I thought nothing about it, because our professor then wasn't particularly interested, and I only read the introduction to that book, where certain things were said about psychosis as a maladjustment of the personality. That hit the nail on the head. In that moment I saw I must become an alienist. My heart was thumping wildly in that moment, and when I told my professor I wouldn't follow him, I would study psychiatry, he couldn't understand it. Nor my friends, because in those days psychiatry was nothing, nothing at all. But I saw the one great chance to unite certain contrasting things in myself, namely, besides medicine—besides natural science I always had studied the history of philosophy and such subjects. It was just as if suddenly two streams were joining.[3]

And how long was it after you took that decision that you first came in contact with Freud?

Oh, you know, that was at the end of my studies, and then it took quite a while until I met Freud. You see, I'd finished my studies in 1900 and I met Freud altogether much later. In 1900 I already read his *Dream Interpretation* and the Breuer-Freud studies about hysteria, but that was merely literary, you know, and then in 1907 I became acquainted with him personally.

[3] *Memories, Dreams, Reflections*, pp. 108f./111.

Will you tell me how that happened? Did you go to Vienna to meet him?

Oh well, then I'd written a book about the psychology of dementia praecox,[4] as we called schizophrenia then. And I sent him that book, and thus became acquainted. I went to Vienna for a fortnight and then we had a very long and penetrating conversation, and that settled it.

And this long and penetrating conversation was followed by personal friendship?

Oh yes, it soon developed into a personal friendship.

And what sort of man was Freud?

Well, he was a complicated nature, you know. I liked him very much, but I soon discovered that when he had thought something then it was settled, while I was doubting all along the line, and it was impossible to discuss something really *à fond*. You know he had no philosophical education, particularly; you see I was studying Kant, and I was steeped in it, and that was far from Freud. So from the very beginning there was a discrepancy.[5]

Did you in fact grow apart later, partly because of a difference in temperamental approach to experiment and proof and so on?

Well, of course, there is always a temperamental difference, and his approach was naturally different from mine because his personality was different from mine. That led me into my later investigation of psychological types. There are definite attitudes. Some people are doing it in this way and other people are doing it in another *typical* way, and there were such differences between myself and Freud, too.

Do you consider that Freud's standard of proof and experimentation was less high than your own?

[4] "The Psychology of Dementia Praecox," CW 3.
[5] For the meeting with Freud, see *Memories, Dreams, Reflections*, ch. V, and *The Freud/Jung Letters*, p. 24.

Well, you see, that is an evaluation I'm not competent of; I am not my own history, or my historiographer. With reference to certain results, I think my method has its merits.

Tell me, did Freud himself ever analyze you?
Oh yes, I submitted quite a lot of my dreams to him, and so did he.

And he to you?
Yes, oh yes.

Do you remember now at this distance of time what were the significant features of Freud's dreams that you noted at the time?
Well, that is rather indiscreet to ask. You know I have— there is such a thing as a professional secret.

He's been dead these many years.
Yes, but these regards last longer than life. [Pause.] I prefer not to talk about it.

Well, may I ask you something else, then, which perhaps is also indiscreet. Is it true that you have a very large number of letters which you exchanged with Freud which are still unpublished?
Yes.

When are they going to be published?
Well, not during my lifetime.

You would have no objection to them being published after your lifetime?
Oh, no, none at all.

Because they are probably of great historical importance.
I don't think so.

Then why have you not published them so far?
Because they were not important enough to me. I see no particular importance in them.

They are concerned with personal matters?

Well, partially. But I wouldn't care to publish them.[6]

Well now, can we move on to the time when you did eventually part company with Freud. It was partly, I think, with the publication of your book Psychology of the Unconscious.[7] *Is that correct?*

That was the real cause. No, I mean the final cause, because it had a long preparation. You know, from the beginning I had a *reservatio mentalis*. I couldn't agree with quite a number of his ideas.

Which ones in particular?

Well, chiefly, his purely personal approach, and his disregard of the historical conditions of man. You see, we depend largely upon our history. We are shaped through education, through the influence of the parents, which is by no means always personal. They were prejudiced, or they were influenced by historical ideas or what are called dominants,[8] and that is a most decisive factor in psychology. We are not of today or of yesterday; we are of an immense age.

Was it not partly your observation, your clinical observation, of psychotic cases which led you to differ from Freud on this?

It was partially my experience with schizophrenic patients that led me to the idea of certain general historical conditions.

Is there any one case that you can now look back on and feel that perhaps it was the turning point of your thought?

---

[6] By agreement of the Freud and Jung families, the letters were published in 1974. For an account of the events leading up to publication, see *The Freud/Jung Letters*, introduction, especially pp. xix–xxxiv.

[7] *Wandlungen und Symbole der Libido* (1912). Revised 1952 as *Symbole der Wandlung = Symbols of Transformation*, CW 5.

[8] Another term for archetypes.

Oh yes, I had quite a number of experiences of that sort, and I went even to Washington to study Negroes at the psychiatric clinic there,[9] in order to find out whether they have the same type of dreams as we have, and these experiences and others led me then to the hypothesis that there is an impersonal stratum in our psyche, and I can tell you an example. We had a patient in the ward; he was quiet but completely dissociated, a schizophrenic, and he was in the clinic or the ward twenty years. He had come into the clinic as a matter of fact a young man, a little clerk and with no particular education, and once I came into the ward and he was obviously excited and called to me, took me by the lapel of my coat, and led me to the window, and said: "Doctor! Now! Now you will see. Now look at it. Look up at the sun and see how it moves. See, you must move your head, too, like this, and then you will see the phallus of the sun, and you know, that's origin of the wind. And you see how the sun moves as you move your head, from one side to the other!" Of course, I did not understand it at all. I thought oh, there you are, he's just crazy. But that case remained in my mind, and four years later I came across a paper written by the German historian, Dieterich, who had dealt with the so-called Mithras Liturgy, a part of the Great Parisian Magic Papyrus. And there he produced part of the so-called Mithras Liturgy, namely it had said there: "After the second prayer you will see how the disc of the sun unfolds, and you will see hanging down from it the tube, the origin of the wind, and when you move your face to the regions of the east it will move there, and if you move your face to the regions of the west it will follow you." And instantly I knew—now this is it! This is the vision of my patient![10]

[9] At St. Elizabeths Hospital, Washington, D.C., September 1912. See *The Freud/Jung Letters*, 323J, n. 2.
[10] CW 5, pars. 150ff. Cf. also CW 8, pars. 228 and 318, and CW 9 i, par. 105.

But how could you be sure that your patient wasn't unconsciously recalling something that somebody had told him?

Oh, no. Quite out of the question, because that thing was not known. It was in a magic papyrus in Paris, and it wasn't even published. It was only published four years later,[11] after I had observed it with my patient.

And this you felt proved that there was an unconscious which was something more than personal?

Oh well, that was not a proof to me, but it was a hint, and I took the hint.

Now tell me, how did you first decide to start your work on the psychological types? Was that also as a result of some particular clinical experience?

Less so. It was a very personal reason, namely to do justice to the psychology of Freud, also to that of Adler, and to find my own bearings. That helped me to understand why Freud developed such a theory. Or why Adler developed his theory with his power principle.

Have you concluded what psychological type you are yourself?

Naturally I have devoted a great deal of attention to that painful question, you know!

And reached a conclusion?

Well, you see, the type is nothing static. It changes in the course of life, but I most certainly was characterized by thinking. I always thought, from early childhood on, and I had a great deal of intuition too. And I had a definite difficulty with feeling, and my relation to reality was not particularly brilliant. I was often at variance with the

[11] Albrecht Dieterich's *Eine Mithrasliturgie* actually was published first in the year 1903, before the delusion was observed. See "The Concept of the Collective Unconscious," CW 9 i, par. 105, n. 5.

reality of things. Now that gives you all the necessary data for a diagnosis!

During the nineteen thirties, when you were working a lot with German patients, you did, I believe, forecast that a second world war was very likely. Well now, looking at the world today, do you feel that a third world war is likely?

I have no definite indications in that respect, but there are so many indications that one doesn't know what one sees. Is it trees, or is it the wood? It's very difficult to say, because people's dreams contain apprehensions, you know, but it is very difficult to say whether they point to a war, because that idea is uppermost in people's minds. Formerly, you know, it has been much simpler. People didn't think of a war, and therefore it was rather clear what the dreams meant. Nowadays no more so. We are so full of apprehensions, fears, that one doesn't know exactly to what it points. One thing is sure. A great change of our psychological attitude is imminent. That is certain.

And why?

Because we need more—we need more psychology. We need more understanding of human nature, because the only real danger that exists is man himself. He is the great danger, and we are pitifully unaware of it. We know nothing of man, far too little. His psyche should be studied, because we are the origin of all coming evil.

Does man, do you think, need to have the concept of sin and evil to live with? Is this part of our nature?

Well, obviously.

And of a redeemer?

That is an inevitable consequence.

This is not a concept which will disappear as we become more rational; it's something which—

Well, I don't believe that man ever will deviate from the original pattern of his being. There will always be such ideas. For instance, if you do not directly believe in a personal redeemer, as it was the case with Hitler, or the hero-worship in Russia, then it is an idea, it is a symbolic idea.

You have written, at one time and another, some sentences which have surprised me a little, about death. Now, in particular I remember you said that death is psychologically just as important as birth and like it it's an integral part of life. But surely it can't be like birth if it's an end, can it?

Yes, if it's an end, and there we are not quite certain about this end, because you know there are these peculiar faculties of the psyche, that it isn't entirely confined to space and time. You can have dreams or visions of the future, you can see around corners, and such things. Only ignorance denies these facts, you know; it's quite evident that they do exist, and have existed always. Now these facts show that the psyche, in part at least, is not dependent upon these confinements. And then what? When the psyche is not under that obligation to live in time and space alone, and obviously it doesn't, then to that extent the psyche is not subjected to those laws, and that means a practical continuation of life, of a sort of psychical existence beyond time and space.

Do you yourself believe that death is probably the end, or do you believe that—

Well, I can't say. You see, the word belief is a difficult thing for me. I don't believe. I must have a reason for a certain hypothesis. Either I know a thing, and then I know it—I don't need to believe it. I don't allow myself, for instance, to believe a thing just for the sake of believing it. I can't believe it. But when there are sufficient reasons for a certain hypothesis, I shall accept . . . naturally. I should say: "We had to reckon with the possibility of so and so"—you know.

Well now, you've told us that we should regard death as being a goal—
  Yes.

—and that to shrink away from it is to evade life and make life purposeless.
  Yes.

What advice would you give to people in their later life to enable them to do this, when most of them must in fact believe that death is the end of everything?
  Well, you see, I have treated many old people, and it's quite interesting to watch what the unconscious is doing with the fact that it is apparently threatened with a complete end. It disregards it. Life behaves as if it were going on, and so I think it is better for an old person to live on, to look forward to the next day, as if he had to spend centuries, and then he lives properly. But when he is afraid, when he doesn't look forward, he looks back, he petrifies, he gets stiff and he dies before his time. But when he's living and looking forward to the great adventure that is ahead, then he lives, and that is about what the unconscious is intending to do. Of course, it's quite obvious that we're all going to die, and this is the sad finale of everything; but nevertheless, there is something in us that doesn't believe it apparently. But this is merely a fact, a psychological fact—it doesn't mean to me that it proves something. It simply is so. For instance, I may not know why we need salt, but we prefer to eat salt, because we feel better. And so when you think in a certain way you may feel considerably better, and I think if you think along the lines of nature then you think properly.

And this leads me to the last question that I want to ask you. As the world becomes more technically efficient it seems increasingly necessary for people to behave communally and collectively. Now do you think it possible that the

highest development of man may be to submerge his own
individuality in a kind of collective consciousness?

That's hardly possible. I think there will be a reaction. A
reaction will set in against this communal dissociation. You
know, man doesn't stand for ever his nullification. Once
there will be a reaction, and I see it setting in. You know,
when I think of my patients, they all seek their own
existence and to assure their existence against that complete
atomization into nothingness, or into meaninglessness. Man
cannot stand a meaningless life.

....

Küsnacht, 13 May

I spoke of the clergy and how they are reaching out for his ideas. . . . He said, "Only the clergy and we are concerned with the education of the soul. People may have to go back to the Church when they reach a certain stage of analysis. Individuation is only for the few." . . .

Jung went on to say that X. [a mutual acquaintance, a cleric] had never really faced his problem, nor taken up his cross, that is, the opposition that forms the cross (crossing his fingers as he spoke). He need not have been afraid; the Church would not have rejected him. A Jesuit said to X. once, "You make a fist in your pocket and go on with the ritual!" But he could not face the fact of evil—just as he denied that Jesus had a shadow, though that is clearly portrayed, even in the records we have. Not only did he fail on Palm Sunday, allowing himself to be venerated as an imperial savior, and then cursed the fig tree because it did not fall into line, but also he was actually unable to carry his cross, someone else had to carry it for him, a most significant point. And so he had to be *fixed* on the cross. If we do not carry our own cross, we will surely be crucified. So X., who had not enough backbone to carry his cross, had an illness and must die of cancer. . . .

Another cleric who had come to see Jung had said, "They cannot face the implications of their own doctrine." Jung said, "You will have read my *Answer to Job*." And he replied, yes, but that there was one thing he could not agree with: C. G. said there that Jesus and Mary were not real human beings. Jung had replied, "You and I and all men are born in sin and have the stain of sin upon us, but Jesus and Mary, according to the dogma, are immaculate, born without stain of sin. Therefore they are not real human beings at all." He went on, "I put something into his head, but he could not accept it." I said, "He must have gone away with a bad headache." C. G. agreed, "He probably had a migraine."

Then he began to speak of how you can only talk to people where they are. If they have a European background, you must begin from the Christian standpoint; and people should go back to the Church when freed from personal problems, as they are not all able to make an individual formulation or experience for themselves, which takes enormous courage.

He compared this to Buddhist or Hindu ideas. He said, "The clergy only deal with their own people. When asked, What about Buddhists? the clergy say they are not our concern—except as missionaries, of course." . . .

He said he had met one philosopher, or yogi, in India,[1] who was of great understanding. He had asked him about *bodhi*, enlightenment, and was told it was achieved through separating oneself from the *kleshas*. "And then what is it like?" he had asked. "It is the nothingness." "Then who experiences the enlightenment?" Jung went on to say that obviously there is no one to experience it. It is a state of unconsciousness, in which anything may happen, or nothing. But as no one is there to experience it, there can be no enlightenment. "The Indians," he said, "are in the fourteenth century." . . .

Later, during the dinner for Dr. Jacobi's[2] seventieth birthday, I was seated next to Dr. Jung. He told me that he was

---

[1] Jung went to India in January 1938 as an honorary delegate to the Silver Jubilee of the Indian Science Congress, in Calcutta. He also visited Bombay, Khajuraho, Benares, Darjeeling, Allahabad, and Ceylon.

[2] See above, p. 38.

born in the Chinese year of the swine and said, "I think that we are again in that year." The Buddha too was born in the year of the swine, and there is a certain resemblance between himself and the Buddha. The Buddha was born the son of a king, yet had to go away alone until he found the Noble Eightfold Path; and C. G. too had to struggle alone, till he found the mandala, an eightfold symbol of wholeness.

He told how, in a Tibetan monastery not far from Sikkim, he had found a mandala on the wall of the temple. There was a very learned man in charge there, with whom he was able to converse because an old Englishman (probably connected with the missionaries) spoke Tibetan and was willing to translate. The lama told him that they did not use the mandala for worship, but to focus the meditation of the monks. They have to contemplate and memorize each element of the mandala and then build it up piece by piece in a mental image, like a solid structure before them. In this way, they make the psychic element substantial, almost concrete. He said they do this according to a given form, while we make real the form that grows from within.

THE ART OF LIVING

+++++++++++++++++++++++++

This interview by an English journalist living in Switzerland, Gordon Young, was published in the *Sunday Times* (London), July 17, 1960, in anticipation of Jung's 85th birthday (July 26), and in abridged form in the *American Weekly* (New York), February 19, 1961. A fuller version appears in the epilogue of Gordon Young's *Doctors Without Drugs* (London, 1962), from which minor changes and several passages not included in the newspaper versions are incorporated here.

Young's career as a newspaperman resembles Knicker-bocker's (see above, p. 115). He was Reuters' chief correspondent in Berlin before the war; throughout the war he was a correspondent in the Middle East and Europe, and for a period he was attached to SHAPE and the American First Army. At the end of the war he made a secret trip to German-occupied Denmark with the Danish underground. At the time of his death in 1964, Young was assistant director of the International Press Institute in Zurich.

What am I planning for my birthday? Why, to keep away from visitors, of course. Especially the highbrows. Most of them haven't the remotest idea what I am talking about. Trouble is, they don't bother to read my books because they're too high-hat. I'm not a bit taken in by intellectuals, you know. After all, I'm one myself.

Do you know, I had an intellectual fellow here the other day—an American. I talked to him for half an hour without his saying one word. Then his eyes suddenly lighted up as though a sun were rising inside him and he told me in astonishment, "Why, Dr. Jung, what you are telling me is just plain common sense."

As I say, the trouble is that some of the people who come

to see me simply don't bother to do their proper reading. They don't even read my books. Do you know who reads my books? Not the academic people, oh no, they think they know everything already. It's ordinary people, often quite poor people. And why do they do it? Because there's a deep need in the world just now for spiritual guidance—almost any sort of spiritual guidance. Look at the popularity of astrology just now. People read about astrology because it offers them one form of mental inspiration, perhaps a form with limitations, but at least it's better than nothing at all.

Do you believe that astrology has any definite value?

The whole subject, of course, is controversial. But you know I once did some statistical research on astrology and my final figures were examined by mathematicians at the University of Chicago. They told me that they found them not without significance. Naturally, when I heard that I pricked up my ears. We are passing out of the period of the Fishes just now and into the sign of Aquarius, which may well bring some new values with it. Some people quite seriously consider that this may be of great significance in the world's imminent development.

Or take alchemy. To most people alchemy simply means a lot of old men who tried to make gold. But that was not the truth at all. If people would only take the trouble to turn up the actual writings of the ancient alchemists, they would find a deep treasure-trove of wisdom, much of which is perfectly applicable to the very events which are happening in the world today. After all, what can possibly be more important than the study of how men's minds work, and have worked in the past? Everything which happens in the world today is the result of what is happening in men's minds. Yet how many people are taking the trouble to consider the minds of, say, Khrushchev or Eisenhower, or the basic psychological reasons for such movements as

Nazism, Communism, or anti-Jewish trends? What would happen to us if one of the present leaders of the world suddenly went mad? Yet how many people are giving any serious consideration to problems such as these? But I must not talk too deeply about such matters or I shall be accused of trying to meddle in politics.

Although people are nowadays living much longer, they are still expected to retire at about sixty. They get forced into inactivity and sometimes loneliness. How do you think elderly people can best come to terms with life?

For a long time I have advocated schools for the adult. After all, we try to equip young people with all the education they need for the building up of a successful social existence. This kind of education is valid for about as far as the middle of life—say, thirty-five to forty years. Man nowadays has a chance to live twice as long, and the second half of life has for many people a structure which is thoroughly different from the first half. But this fact remains just as often unconscious. One does not realize that the rising tide of life carries young people forward to a certain summit of safety, fulfillment, or success. In this period one can forget bad experiences; life is still new and fresh, and every day renews its hope that it may bring the desired things which one has missed hitherto.

It is when you approach the ominous region round the fortieth year that you look back upon the past which has accumulated behind you and the silent questions approach you, stealthily or openly: Where am I standing today? Have my dreams come true? Have I fulfilled my expectations of a happy and successful life as I imagined them twenty years ago? Have I been strong, consistent, active, intelligent, reliable, and enduring enough to seize my oportunities or to make the right choice at the crossroads and produce the proper answer to the problem which fate or fortune put before me? And then the final question comes: What is the chance that I shall fail again in fulfilling that which I obviously have been unable to accomplish in the first forty years?

And then?

Then, with the beginning of your life's second part, inexorably a change imposes itself, subtly at first but with ever-increasing weight. Whatever you have acquired hitherto is no longer the same as you regarded it when it still lay before you—it has lost something of its charm, its splendor and its attractiveness. What was once an adventurous effort has become routine. Even flowers wilt, and it is hard to discover something perennial which will endure. Looking back slowly becomes a habit, no matter how much you detest and try to suppress it. Like the wife of Orpheus emerging from the underworld, who could not resist casting the forbidden look behind her, and consequently had to return from whence she came.

This sort of thing is what you might call the "way of life *à revers*," so characteristic of many people and which at the beginning is adopted quite unawares: to continue in one's accustomed style, if possible more and better—to improve on the past, as if your disposition, which accounts for all your past failures, would be different in the future. But without your being aware of it your energy is no longer attracted to its former objectives in the way it was before: enthusiasm has become routine and zeal a habit. The backwards look will not fail to show you sides and aspects of yourself long forgotten and other ways of life you have missed or avoided before. The more your actual life becomes routine and habit, the less it will be satisfactory.

Soon unconscious fantasies begin to play with other possibilities, and these can become quite troublesome unless they are made conscious in time. They may be mere regressions into childhood, which prove to be most unhelpful when one is confronted with the difficult task of creating a

446

new goal for an aging life. If one has nothing to look forward to except the habitual things, life cannot renew itself any more. It gets stale, it congeals and petrifies, like Lot's wife who could not detach her eyes from the things hitherto valued. Yet these insipid fantasies may also contain germs of real new possibilities or of new goals worthy of attainment. There are always things ahead, and despite all the overwhelming power of the historical pattern they are never quite the same. They are "as good as new," like human beings or even crystals which, notwithstanding their exceedingly simple structure, are never the same.

One might advise old people to live on with the times, and realize that time would provide them with all necessary novelties. But such easy advice takes it for granted that an old individual is capable of perceiving and agreeing with new things, ways, and means. But this is just the trouble: new goals demand new eyes which see them and a new heart which desires them. In all too many cases life is disappointing and even the most cherished illusions do not last forever. It is all too easy to reach the conclusion: *plus ça change, plus ça reste la même chose.* That is a fatal conclusion, however: it blocks the flow of life and causes ever so many troubles of a physical or mental nature. Your pure rationalist, who bases his expectations on statistical verities, is thoroughly perplexed when he has to deal with such cases because he ignores the one important practical fact that life is always an exception, a "statistical random phenomenon." It is so because it is always the life of an individual, who is a distinct, unique, and inimitable being, and not "life in general," since there is no such thing.

Then what do you advise this inimitable being to do once he passes the ominous age of forty?

An ever-deepening self-knowledge is, I'm afraid, indispensable for the continuation of real life in old age, no matter how unpopular self-knowledge may be. Nothing is more ridiculous or inept than elderly people pretending to be young—they even lose their dignity, the one prerogative of age. Looking outwards has got to be turned into looking into oneself. Discovering yourself provides you with all you are, were meant to be, and all you are living from and for. The whole of yourself is certainly an irrational entity, but this is just precisely yourself, which is meant to live as a unique and unrepeatable experience. Thus, whatever you find in your given disposition is a factor of life which must be taken into careful consideration.

If you should find, for instance, an ineradicable tendency to believe in God or immortality, do not allow yourself to be disturbed by the blather of so-called freethinkers. And if you find an equally resistant tendency to deny all religious ideas do not hesitate: deny them and see how that influences your general welfare and your state of mental or spiritual nutrition. But beware of childishness: whether you call the ultimate unknown "God" or "Matter" is equally futile, since we know neither the one nor the other, though we doubtless have experiences of both. But we know nothing beyond them, and we cannot produce either the one or the other.

Then you don't think it is futile for people to place their hopes in the possibility of life after death?

As there is no possibility of proof, it is just as legitimate to believe in life after death as it is to doubt it. We have experiences which point both ways. The only important thing is to find out which of your views agrees better with your general disposition. There are healthy and unhealthy, helpful and obnoxious ideas. Nobody in his senses will eat indigestible food, and corespondingly a sensible person will avoid unsuitable thoughts and opinions. In case of doubt, try to learn from the traditional wisdom of all times and peoples. This gives you ample information about the so-called eternal ideas and values which have been shared by mankind since earliest times. One should not be deterred by the rather silly objection that nobody knows whether these old universal ideas—God, immortality, freedom of the will, and so on—are "true" or not. Truth is the wrong criterion here. One can only ask whether they are helpful or not, whether man is better off and feels his life more complete, more meaningful and more satisfactory with or without them.

Agnosticism is never sufficient when it comes to the question of life as a whole. We need certain general views about things we cannot know in order to sum up our specific life experiences or to satisfy our desire for self-cognition and wholeness. And as nobody knows what the truth is, everybody is free to partake of such ideas or to reject them.

It does make a difference, however, whether your opinions or convictions coincide with traditional and universal wisdom or not, since if you agree, you are swimming in and carried along by the universal current of instinctive mental behavior, and, if you disagree, you have it against you. A negative attitude has its merit too, as it gives you the satisfactory feeling that you are capable of resisting the general temptation to fall in with collective prejudices. Such a resistance may even prepare you in a most efficient way for a later firm conviction of the contrary. The same is true in a reversed sense in the case of one who is carried along by the ideas of his time and milieu without ever questioning himself about their validity.

Young people today are often accused by their elders of being fascinated by a philosophy of despair. Do you agree?

Young people of today, inasmuch as they feel revolutionary, are simply realizing what their parents and educators did not admit openly to themselves, namely disbelief and doubt in religious and moral notions. In the absence of philosophic reflection, their parents based their lives on a positive and practical conviction of an entirely materialistic and rationalistic kind, being supported in this attitude by the enormous influence of the sciences.

One of the most impressive examples is modern physics, which has finally recognized the atom as a cosmic unity. Such a discovery might well have satisfied our desire for unity, oneness, and wholeness, but today we already know of more than thirty smaller particles making up the wholeness of the atom. That is typical of what happens in the science of nature; it never leads to simple oneness and wholeness, but into the multiplicity and segregation of—to use an Eastern term—the "ten thousand things." This is the strict contrary of integration into the oneness and wholeness of the individual as well as of the cosmos.

The older generation of today looks with startled eyes upon their children and their more or less curious behavior. But the children live by preference the unlived unconscious lives of their parents, that which their parents did not know, did not dare, and denied to exist, sometimes against their better knowledge.

Even today education in general has not yet discovered that for pedagogical purposes it would be far more important to know parent- instead of child-psychology. Parents should marvel at nothing except at their own naïveté and ignorance of their own psychology, which is, in turn, the harvest sown by the grandparents—naïveté and ignorance carrying on the curse of unconsciousness into an indefinite future. My answer to this problem is: education of the educator—or schools for adults, who have never been taught about the requirements of human life after forty.

What do you consider to be more or less basic factors making for happiness in the human mind?
1. Good physical and mental health.
2. Good personal and intimate relations, such as those of marriage, the family, and friendships.

3. The faculty for perceiving beauty in art and nature.

4. Reasonable standards of living and satisfactory work.

5. A philosophic or religious point of view capable of coping successfully with the vicissitudes of life.

Both the standard of living the work depend, of course, largely upon the reasonableness of one's expectations and one's responsibility. Extravagances can cause both happiness and unhappiness. And along with a philosophic or religious outlook must go a corresponding practical morality, since without that both philosophy and religion are mere make-believe, without concrete effects.

A list of the factors determining unhappiness would be much longer! What you dislike and fear seems to be just waiting for you, and what you seek and desire seems to be most evasive—and when you find it at last it may easily be not exactly flawless. Nobody can achieve happiness through preconceived ideas, one should rather call it a gift of the gods. It comes and goes, and what has made you happy once does not necessarily do so at another time.

All factors which are generally assumed to make for happiness can, under certain conditions, produce the contrary. No matter how ideal your situation may be, it does not necessarily guarantee happiness. A relatively slight disturbance of your biological or psychological equilibrium may suffice to destroy your happiness. No good health, no favorable financial conditions, no untroubled family relations can protect you, for instance, against unspeakable boredom, a boredom which might make you welcome even the change of circumstances brought about by a not too severe illness.

Yet you are a firm believer in the possibility of happiness in life—even in marriage?

The most elusive of intangibles! Be that as it may, one thing is certain: there are as many nights as days, and the one is just as long as the other in the year's course. Even a happy life cannot be without a measure of darkness, and the word "happy" would lose its meaning if it were not balanced by sadness. Of course it is understandable that we seek happiness and avoid unlucky and disagreeable chances, despite the fact that reason teaches us that such an attitude is not reasonable because it defeats its own ends—the more you deliberately seek happiness the more sure you are not to find it. It is therefore far better to take things as they come along, with patience and equanimity. After all, perhaps once in a while there will be something good, lucky or enjoyable for you in Fortune's bag of relevant and irrelevant gifts.

(Dr. Jung reached down and picked up his hat and his antique malacca walking stick from the grass. I commented on the carving of the cane's heavy silver knob.)

Yes, it's an old Chinese carving. Look, you see it's a dragon, and on his tail is a flower with a precious pearl inside it. It's an allusion to the old alchemists' symbol of the snake biting its tail, but the dragon, of course, is the Chinese symbol of good fortune. He's always chasing after that flower, round and round the stick, but he will never catch it, because it's on his tail. Really, he's rather like those highbrows I was talking about, eh?

✦✦✦✦✦✦✦✦✦✦✦✦✦✦✦✦✦✦✦✦✦✦✦✦✦

Georg Gerster again interviewed Jung on June 7, 1960, at Küsnacht, for broadcast via the Swiss radio network, which also made a present of the tape recording to the University of Basel, where it was placed in an archive of the voices of distinguished Swiss contemporaries. Jung would not consent to being interviewed by anyone but Gerster, who had to be called back from the Sinai Peninsula, where he was photographing for a new book. Sixteen years later, Gerster recalled in a letter to the editor of the present collection: "Dr. Jung refused to name a specific topic for our interview, so I had to go there unprepared. After I had officially closed the conversation by thanking him, Dr. Jung continued to speak, in Swiss dialect, telling me about a dream he had had. Fortunately, the radio technicians outside the house (in the van with the recording equipment) let the tape run on. These last ten minutes—which could not be used as they were recorded without his knowledge—don't add to the subjects that had come up within the official interview, but are a memorable piece of a very earthy C. G. Jung." The interview was first broadcast on July 3, 1960, and several times more until the birthday on July 26. It was rebroadcast on June 5, 1966, in remembrance of Jung's death on June 6, 1961.

Again and again, Professor Jung, I have been struck by the inscription that is carved over the door of your house: "Vocatus atque non vocatus deus aderit"—"Invoked or not invoked the god will be present."—I believe it is an oracle of some kind?

Yes, a saying of the Delphic oracle. When the Lacedae-monians wanted to make war against the Athenians, they consulted the oracle and the oracle answered that the god would be present—*aderit*.

May I ask why just this saying stands over the door of your house?

Well, that is a very complicated story. It has been my experience that these religious phenomena are to be met with everywhere, whether they are intentional or not. It only needs an emergency, a serious emergency, and then these religious utterances burst out again. Thus, when one is greatly astonished or surprised, everyone, even if he doesn't believe in God, says "Oh God" or "By God," and these are involuntary exclamations of a religious nature, because they use the name of God.

Mustn't we define the term "religious" rather more closely, or at least define the way you use it?

Well, we have to take it in a pretty wide sense.

I was only thinking that when you say "God" it could also mean "idol"?

Yes, naturally it can mean all sorts of things, it can also be a mere word. But they still belong to the sphere of re-ligion. All religious phenomena that are not just Church rituals are bound up with emotions. That is why we ob-serve these religious manifestations chiefly—as I have said—in moments of emergency or under very emotional con-ditions.

Doesn't the idea of "meaning" belong to the concept of religion as you now define it? I mean, anything that hap-pens to the ego out of the unconscious—for that is what we are talking about, isn't it?—

Yes.

—must have a meaning, not at the moment perhaps, not within the narrow horizon of the ego, but in a wider sense for the personality as a whole?

Yes, that is so. The concept of the archetype, which we are considering here, is, as we say, "numinous," it has a sort of overwhelming power. It is by its very nature emotional, and so an archetype like the idea of God or of a supernatural power will appear in highly emotional situations. Take a situation, a moment of panic for instance, when a man is at the end of his tether. Maybe a prayer will be forced out of him, he will revert to a view of things he once had, but quite spontaneously, without any kind of reflection. It simply forces itself on him. So whenever something happens that has an overwhelming effect, an answer will arise in us to this overwhelming thing. This shows that situations in which a man feels defeated very often give rise to religious phenomena, that people, without wanting to, suddenly fall back into this form, or rather, this form is simply forced on them without their taking up any kind of intellectual attitude towards it.

May I come back again to the word "religious"? As you are using it now, it really always refers to inner, psychic phenomena, I mean phenomena which we don't need to bother the theologian with, for instance?

No, no, they are perfectly natural phenomena!

Then the rescuing unconscious must stand in a quite special relationship to the ego, that was not known to the earlier psychologists, or even to Freud?

That is quite right. When a man is in a real emergency, instinct will come to his aid, forms of action and behavior, of thinking, feeling, etc., which are termed instinctive. For instance, when you are being attacked, you immediately take up an instinctive posture of defense. You make all the necessary gestures, have all the necessary ideas that fit the situation. Although the situation can develop in a flash, everything is there, everything is at the ready, because from time immemorial human beings have constantly found themselves in such situations. Like every animal, they have instincts that are innate. All animals have their postures of attack, their postures of defense, they behave in a quite specific way that is characteristic of the species—and so does man.

But isn't it a discovery of a quite special kind that this is also true of the psyche?

That's just what "psychic" means! We call it "psychic," you see, when in a moment of danger you say certain things, use certain expressions, certain images. When you begin to swear, for instance, you make use of well-known expressions which you don't have to look for long, they are ready to hand. In the same way the foundation of our conscious psyche is a system of inherited, instinctive modes of behavior, as is the case everywhere, and that is what we mean by an archetype.

You said somewhere that our consciousness floats upon this collective unconscious as upon a sea.[1]

Yes, yes!

In other words, it is in the safe keeping of the unconscious?

Yes, you can say that up to a point unconscious forces come to our aid when the conscious mind is in a situation of being overpowered. But it can also happen that effects emanate from the unconscious which are not a direct reaction to an external emergency, but produce one.

Can you give an example?

Yes. In all critical phases of life, as in early childhood, at puberty, when you marry or take up a career, at the turning point between thirty-six and forty, in women at the change

---

[1] "Psychology and Religion," CW 11, par. 141.

of life, and in men at the climacteric between fifty and sixty, psychic situations can arise whose meaning is overlooked. A young man, for instance, may not yet have sufficient self-knowledge to know exactly how he feels or what kind of career he wants to take up. If it becomes a problem that worries him, dreams may appear, instinctive reactions as I have said, that show him how he really feels or what he really wants to do. When you read biographies you can easily come across these things. The thirty-sixth year is for many men a very critical year, because a great change is taking place of which they know nothing: the sun has started on its downward course and then their attitude can change in a remarkable way. Take the case of Nietzsche, along comes Zarathustra, or of Fechner turning into a mystic philosopher, and so on. I have also experienced it myself, how this second half of life, which is quite unexpected, is ushered in by dreams. Then you often have dreams that are almost like precognitions, they foresee how the future will develop. But that is only a manifestation of our original instinctive makeup. One man, for instance, has a particular idea of life owing to his education, or whatever, and this idea is too narrow and he is not so narrow but doesn't know it, and then he has a dream, perhaps about a much fuller life, and about quite different aspects of the world he has never thought of before, and then it dawns on him: Aha, that is a possibility! I have seen it with myself. For a long time I was in doubts whether I really ought to study archaeology, history, and suchlike, and then I had a vivid dream or two which challenged my scientific interests to the limit, and they decided me in favor of science.

But that is a view of dreams that does not agree at all with Freud's view. I'm thinking of a saying of Schnitzler's, who, probably copying Freud, wrote that "dreams are desires without courage." It is a conception of dreams that starts purely from the past and does not point into the future, like yours.

Yes, in this respect my view naturally differs enormously from Freud's original view, according to which dreams can be traced back mainly to unfulfilled wishes that are ventilated at night. Certainly there are masses of such dreams, which can be explained more or less satisfactorily that way, but that is not the real function of dreams. Dreams are normal functions, they are normal occurrences that are part of human life. Hence all primitives have a great respect for dreams, not always of course for their own, but when the chief dreams, or the witch doctor—that's something else! Because there, under really primitive conditions, dreams still have a social function. Rasmussen, in his book about the Polar Eskimos,[2] describes the case of a shaman who, guided by dreams, led his tribe [from Greenland] over the frozen sea of Baffin Bay to the extreme north of the continent, because there were no seals that year, and there they found the food they needed. But on the journey half the tribe began to doubt and turned back, and they all perished, while the people he led stayed alive.

From this point of view, then, it follows that it is absolutely necessary for the psychotherapist to get his patient, the psychically sick person, into a productive relation with the unconscious?

Yes, precisely. The therapist even steers the patient towards being confronted with a situation which is insoluble, where he is forced to admit that he doesn't know the way out, and the therapist doesn't know the way out either. This brings the situation to a head in a favorable manner, so that the unconscious begins to function. Then comes a dream from which you can infer something that points the way ahead. These are the situations in which religious dreams occur, of far-reaching significance—what the primitives call "big" dreams.

[2] Knud Rasmussen, *Across Arctic America* (New York, 1927), chap. III: "A Wizard and His Household."

Do you think our present civilization needs criticizing in the light of this knowledge?

Well, that is certainly proved by these individual cases. You see, people suffer mostly from too purblind an outlook, too limited a horizon. They don't think at all about the possibilities that also exist, and so it often needs dreams to make them pay attention to what they could still do, or to what they have neglected. This brings a wholly new element into the treatment. For instance, I have often come across highly intellectual men, actively engaged in science shall we say, who get into conflict with their lives because they completely neglect the sphere of feeling, are utterly clueless in this respect, and they are the very ones who have dreams and even visions. I remember one very important man who came to me in a perfect panic and told me he had a vision and it just couldn't be true! I got him to tell me his vision and, remarkably enough, it was a typical vision such as the old alchemists had. So I fetched a four-hundred-year-old book from my shelves and opened it at the picture, held it out to him and said: "Look, there is your vision. You haven't dropped out of human history, you simply don't know that you are human too!"

When I asked you earlier about a critique of our civilization I didn't actually mean these individual cases but was thinking of the problem of our time, as they say. There must have been periods when man's relations with the unconscious through various other channels of communication were infinitely more alive than they are today.

Yes, there is no doubt that it was only the nineteenth century that broke with this tradition and became increasingly intellectual, with the result that a lot of vitally necessary things have become obsolete. Just think of the crisis of Christianity we are passing through today—it simply means that we have lost all sense of its necessity. We no longer know what it is good for. In earlier times people knew, in a way. Naturally they had faith, but this faith was rooted in the feeling that the Christian tradition was "satisfactory," it was something self-evident, part of the picture. Even with scientific books, you need only think of old Scheuchzer,[3] of Zurich, who began his scientific works with the story of Creation!

Do you see any chance for psychology to do something here? I mean, you can't put the clock back.

No, that's impossible.

On the other hand, as a psychologist with these insights, you can't let the world go its own sweet way!

Yes, but what is the voice of a single individual? These things are evidently so difficult to understand that you just can't talk to people about them. It is amazing how little people understand of such matters. They don't think about them at all. Naturally, a very great deal could be said in this respect. But, you see, it concerns the individual so very much that it is far too boring for people! Of course, if I knew a remedy that could be injected into ten thousand people at one go, that would be popular, especially if one didn't have to do anything about it oneself. But the very idea that you should begin with yourself, that is totally out of the question! One must always have something that is good for a hundred thousand, for a million people, but not for the individual, he is far too uninteresting. We have been so convinced by science how nugatory a human life is, and contemporary history has indeed demonstrated before our eyes how human lives count for nothing. And the individual is so utterly convinced of his nothingness that he makes no effort to get anywhere with himself, to develop himself inwardly in any way. It is too hopeless, the individual is nothing, and it is naturally a false view that the individual

[3] Johann Jakob Scheuchzer (1672–1733), physician, polymath, one of the founders of the science of palaeontology, pioneer in the research of Swiss geography.

is nothing. The individual is the vessel of life. Every individual is the bearer of life, and life is borne only by individuals. It does not exist in itself, there is no life of the millions. That is nonsense, but millions of individuals are vessels of life and for each of them the problem of the individual is the whole problem. And then they say: "Yes, but look at So-and-so, that's no vessel of life!" The individual is banalized, you see. Most people get discouraged. The theologians surely ought to be convinced that the individual soul is the vessel of life, and the thing of greatest importance. Yet a theologian told me himself: "We must get through to the masses. If we tried to treat every single individual we would never get anywhere!" I said: "Well, how did Christianity conquer the world in the first place? It always went from individual to individual."

Neurotics naturally think that way too, but they soon change their tune when they see that nothing changes in them if they do not take themselves seriously. But taking yourself seriously is considered improper, you're an eccentric, putting on self-important airs, etc. Everywhere you come up against this depreciation of the human psyche. Of course when you say "the human psyche" everyone thinks it's fine, it is someone else's affair, but I myself and what I do are not considered at all. If nobody bothers about his own psyche, then there is nothing you can do from the psychological angle, you can only say how things are and make yourself unpopular!

TALKS WITH MIGUEL SERRANO:

1961

✦✦✦✦✦✦✦✦✦✦✦✦✦✦✦✦✦✦✦✦✦✦✦✦✦✦

Serrano returned to India, and later in 1959 he completed his stories of the Queen of Sheba, had them all translated into English, and sent a copy of the English typescript to Jung, who responded with a letter on January 14, 1960. Jung permitted Serrano to publish the letter as a foreword to the English translation—*Visits of the Queen of Sheba* (Bombay, 1960; London, 1972).[1]

While in Zurich again in September 1960 (Jung was ill and could not see him) Serrano consulted the *I Ching* to discover whether the time had come for him to leave India. He construed the oracle's answer as yes. (He was later reassigned to Belgrade.) On January 23, 1961, he again visited Jung at Küsnacht.

I am going to leave India. I have consulted the I Ching, *and it has advised me to do so.*

You must do what it says, because that book does not make mistakes. In any case, there is a definite connection between the individual psyche and the world. When I find it difficult for me to classify a patient, I always send him off to have a horoscope made. This horoscope always corresponds to his character, and I interpret it psychologically. So strong is the correspondence between the world and the psyche that it is even possible that inventions and the ideas of three-dimensional time are simply reflections of the mental structure. Thus I was able to predict the last war simply from analyzing my patients' dreams, because Wotan[2]

---

[1] In CW 18, par. 1769. Also see *Letters*, ed. G. Adler, vol. 2, for letters to Serrano of March 31 and Sept. 14, 1960.

[2] Cf. "Wotan," in CW 10.

always used to appear in them. I was not able to predict the first world war, however, because even though I had premonitions myself, I was not analyzing dreams in those days. Altogether, I have analyzed forty-one dreams which forecast grave illness or death.

. . .

I've also come to see Hermann Hesse. He believes that the right road is simply one which is in agreement with nature.

That is also my philosophy. Man should live according to his own nature; he should concentrate on self-knowledge and then live in accordance with the truth about himself. What would you say about a tiger who was a vegetarian? You would say, of course, that he was a bad tiger. Thus everyone must live in accordance with his nature, both individually and collectively. The best example of that method is to be found in India, and the worst, I suppose, is in Russia. Russia is a country with a magnificent organization, but it doesn't function at all, as is obvious in its agricultural failures. The Russians haven't bothered to discover what man really is; they have simply tried to treat him as a wholly rational and mechanical being. Obviously what is necessary for them is not to devise a theory about agriculture, but to devise a theory about man, and to impose that theory or concept. I once knew an old lady who was very aristocratic and noble, and who conducted her life according to the most exquisite ideas of refinement; but at night she would dream about drunkenness, and in those dreams she herself would become hopelessly intoxicated. And so one must be what one is; one must discover one's own individuality, that center of personality, which is equidistant between the conscious and the unconscious; we must aim for that ideal point towards which nature appears to be directing us. Only from that point can one satisfy one's needs.

The Hindus would seem to be saying the same thing when they say that it is better to be partially fulfilled within one's own karma, *than perfectly within a foreign* karma.

Exactly.

Professor Jung, do you believe that your system could function outside of the West, that is, where the psyche is not so divided? For example, there are no neurotics in India, and so far as I know, there are none in Burma, or in Indonesia, Thailand, or China. And I suppose the reason is that the inhabitants of those countries are not persons in the Western Christian sense. As you said, when we first talked in Locarno, the persona *is the product of the sudden imposition of Christianity upon a barbarous Nordic people, with all its resultant inhibitions and uncontrollable drives.*

Yes, and I suppose that very lack of personality is what makes the East able to accept with such ease collective systems like Communism, and religious systems like Buddhism, which aim above all to annihilate the idea of personality.

A little while ago, when I was lunching with Hesse, I asked him how it was that I'd had the good fortune to find myself seated at his table; and he told me that it was no mere accident since only the right guests came there. He spoke of the Hermetic Circle.

That's true; mind attracts mind. Only the *correct* ones come, and we are directed by the unconscious, because the unconscious knows. Once I was on a train, and a General sat down beside me. We talked, and although he did not know who I was, he told me all about his dreams, which is certainly unusual for a man of his position. The General considered that his dreams were absurd, but after listening to him, I told him that one of his dreams had changed his whole life, and that otherwise he would have been an intellectual. The General was startled and looked at me as though I were a witch, or at least a person gifted with second sight.[3] But in reality, it was the unconscious which was knowing and directing. The General had sat down next to me because he was unconsciously searching for an answer. In the same way, I could tell you things about your own life which would startle you. . . .

(*Jung then leaned forward and gazed fixedly into my eyes. In the shadows of the late afternoon, his body seemed to grow larger and larger, and I had the feeling that I was facing an incàrnation of Abraxas.[4] I felt a sudden chill, and then seemed to hear distant voices coming from this powerful being, swirling about us both, like echoes out of the ages.*)

❖

Serrano visited Jung for the last time on May 10, 1961, less than a month before Jung's death. The conversation took place in the study at Küsnacht.

(*Jung was seated beside the window, dressed in a Japanese ceremonial gown, so that in the light of the late afternoon he looked like a magician or a priest of some ancient cult. I gave him the small gift which I had brought him from the East—a turquoise box from Kashmir similar to the one which I had given Hermann Hesse in Montagnola. He took it in his hands, looking at it and feeling it.*)

Turquoise from Kashmir. I never went there; I only saw Bengal and the north-east of India, and Madura in the south. Thank you for this beautiful gift.

[3] Cf. "Analytical Psychology and Education" (1924), CW 17, par. 187, for a different version of this story.

[4] A Gnostic deity, mentioned by Jung in his *Seven Sermons to the Dead* (privately printed 1916; in *Memories, Dreams, Reflections*, 2nd. edn., appendix) and by Hesse in *Demian* (1917).

I have just come from seeing Hermann Hesse, and we talked about death. I asked Hesse whether it was important to know if there was something beyond death. Hesse had said that he thought not, that he thought that death was probably like entering the collective unconscious, falling into it, perhaps.

Your question was badly put. It would be better phrased in this way: Is there any reason to believe that there is life after death?

And is there?

Were it possible for the mind to function at the margin of the brain, it would be incorruptible.

Is such a thing possible?

Parapsychological phenomena suggest that it is. I myself have experienced certain things which also indicate it. Once I was gravely ill, almost in a coma. Everybody thought that I was suffering terribly, but in fact, I was experiencing something extremely pleasant. I seemed to be floating over my body, far above it. Then, after my father died, I saw him several times. Of course that does not mean that he in fact appeared. His appearances may have been entirely subjective phenomena on my part.

But isn't it possible that all these things are in fact external and objective, and not merely something which happens in the mind? Hesse talks about the Collective Unconscious as if it existed externally, and he considers that death may merely be a falling into that state.

During the war, I saw men who had received brain wounds which paralyzed the functions of the cerebral cortex, and thus prevented them from having any sense of time or space. Nevertheless, they were still able to dream, and some of them had important visions. Now if the brain is entirely paralyzed, the question is what organ produces the dream? With what part of his body does a man dream? Is it something physical? Or is it an indication that in fact the mind acts independently of the brain? I don't know, but it's an interesting hypothesis.

There are other phenomena which can support this hypothesis. You know, of course, that a small child has no clearly defined sense of the ego. The child's ego is diffused and dispersed throughout his body. Nevertheless, it has been proven that small children have dreams in which the ego is clearly defined, just as it is in mature people. In these dreams, the child has a clear sense of the *persona*. Now if, from a physiological point of view, the child has no ego, what is it in the child which produces these dreams, dreams which, I may add, affect him for the rest of his life? And another question: If the physical ego disappears at death, does that other ego also disappear, that other which had sent him dreams as a child?

(*As I listened to him, I was once again struck by the magnificent rigor of Jung's mind. On the very threshold of death he was still searching and hoping to believe; but his scientific objectivity prevented him from pronouncing a single word which would not correspond to demonstrable experiences.*)

Today no one pays attention to what lies behind words, to the basic ideas that are there. Yet the idea is the only thing that is truly there. What I have done in my work is simply to give new names to those ideas, to those realities. Consider, for example, the word "unconscious." I have just finished reading a book by a Chinese Zen Buddhist. And it seemed to me that we were talking about the same thing, and that the only difference between us was that we gave different words to the same reality. Thus the use of the word Unconscious doesn't matter; what counts is the idea that lies behind the word.

(*On the small table beside the chair where Jung was sitting was a book called* The Human Phenomenon *by Teilhard de Chardin. I asked Jung whether he had read it.*)

It is a great book.

(I noticed the Gnostic ring on his finger, and asked him what the symbols meant.)

It is Egyptian. Here the serpent is carved, which symbolizes Christ. Above it, the face of a woman; below the number 8, which is a symbol of the Infinite, of the Labyrinth, and of the Road to the Unconscious. I have changed one or two things on the ring so that the symbol will be Christian. All of these symbols are absolutely alive within me, and each one of them creates a reaction within my soul.

I think that in your own being you represent a link with the secrets of the past. You have found the connecting road, the path which was lost with the coming of the European Enlightenment, if not before. Just as the Renaissance found a bond with the external Classic Age, so you, for our own time, seem to have established a link with its internal side. Thus, thanks to you, the essential qualities of man are able to survive. In his own time, Meister Eckhart performed the same role.

What I have tried to do is to show the Christian what the Redeemer really is, and what the resurrection is. Nobody today seems to know, or to remember, but the idea still exists in dreams.

Do you think there is something essentially irrelevant in our discussion of such things? Are our concerns really outdated in this present age of supertechnology and interplanetary travel? I asked Hesse what he thought would happen to introspective people in the future, and he was very pessimistic.

Space flights to other worlds are still a long way off. Sooner or later man will have to return to earth, and to the land from which he comes; that is to say, man will have to return to himself. Space flights are merely an escape, a fleeing away from oneself, because it is easier to go to Mars or to the moon than it is to penetrate one's own being. But what is dangerous about this frantic interest in spatial conquest is that it symbolizes a state of complete anxiety in man. This anxiety would seem to be caused by a fear of the world's population explosion. In a way, space flights seem to be an instinctive reaction to this problem.

(I realized that I had stayed too long. . . . I clasped Jung's hands and bowed and then moved very slowly towards the door. When I reached it I turned back to look at him. He was contemplating me very fixedly, wrapped in the light of the late afternoon which played on his Oriental gown. He raised his hand and made a sign of farewell.)

C. G. Jung died at his home in Küsnacht on 6 June 1961.

INDEX

the Psychology and Pathology of So-Called Occult Phenomena," 6, 260*n*; "Paracelsus as a Spiritual Phenomenon," 227*n*; "The Philosophical Tree," 357*n*; *The Psychogenesis of Mental Disease,* 278*n*; "A Psychological Approach to the Dogma of the Trinity," 156*n*, 187*n*; "Psychological Factors Determining Human Behaviour," 88*n*; *Psychological Types,* 82, 84, 216*n*, 341; "A Psychological View of Conscience," 291*n*, 361*n*; *Psychology and Alchemy,* 87*n*, 227, 322*n*; "Psychology and National Problems," 91; "Psychology and Religion," 296*n*, 318*n*, 456*n*; "The Psychology of Dementia Praecox," 260, 333*n*, 431*n*; "The Psychology of the Transference," 208*n*, 213, 291*n*, 344*n*; *Psychology of the Unconscious,* 55, 56, 173, 177, 254, 261, 322, 339, 433; "Psychophysical Investigations with the Galvanometer and Pneumograph in Normal and Insane Individuals," 330*n*; "Psychotherapy Today," 199–200; "A Radio Talk in Munich," 102*n*; "The Realities of Practical Psychotherapy," 399*n*; "Das Reich des Unbewussten," 38*n*; "Report on America," 13*n*; "A Review of the Complex Theory," 198*n*; "The Role of the Unconscious," 300*n*; *Seven Sermons to the Dead,* 465*n*; "Some Thoughts on Psychology," 8; "The Spirit Mercurius," 141, 355*n*; "The State of Psychotherapy Today," 193*n*; "The Structure of the Psyche," 41*n*; "The

Structure of the Unconscious ("La Structure de l'inconscient"), 340*n*; "Die Struktur der Seele," 40*n*; "Studies in Word Association," 278*n*; "The Symbolic Life," xii, 349*n*; *Symbolik des Geistes,* 187–88; *Symbols of Transformation (Symbole der Wandlung),* 173*n*, 261*n*, 322*n*, 339, 373*n*, 412*n*, 433*n*; "Synchronicity: An Acausal Connecting Principle," 182*n*, 225, 230*n*, 314*n*, 391*n*; "The Tavistock Lectures," xii, 76*n*, 85, 326*n*, 330*n*; "The Theory of Psychoanalysis," 11, 13*n*, 317n; "The Transcendent Function," 325*n*; "Transformation Symbolism in the Mass," 220*n*; *Two Essays on Analytical Psychology,* 213*n*, 294*n*, 297*n*, 302*n*, 341*n*, 342*n*, 345*n*; "Ulysses: A Monologue," 240*n*; "The Visions of Zosimos," 180*n*; *The Visions Seminars,* 50*n*; *Wandlungen und Symbole der Libido,* 55*n*, 173*n*, 261*n*, 433*n*; *Wirklichkeit der Seele,* 80; "Wotan," 196–97, 462*n*; "Zurück zum Urweltglück!" 43*n*

Jung, Carl Gustav, Senior, grandfather of C. G. Jung, 5–6, 271
Jung, Emilie Preiswerk, mother of C. G. Jung, 6, 7, 426–27
Jung, Emma (Mrs. C. G. Jung), 147, 169, 174, 179, 252, 274*n*, 365; Jung's first meeting with her, 266
Jung, Ernst, 2*n*
Jung, Mr. and Mrs. Franz, xviii
Jung, Paul, father of C. G. Jung, 3–7, 160, 417, 426–27, 466

kaivalya, 394

PRINCETON / BOLLINGEN PAPERBACK EDITIONS
FROM THE COLLECTED WORKS OF C. G. JUNG

Aion (CW 9,ii)
Alchemical Studies (CW 13)
Analytical Psychology
Answer to Job
Archetypes and the Collective Unconscious (CW 9,i)
Aspects of the Feminine
Aspects of the Masculine
Basic Writings of C. G. Jung
The Development of Personality (CW 17)
Dreams
Essay on Contemporary Events
Essays on a Science of Mythology
The Essential Jung
Experimental Researches (CW 2)
Flying Saucers
Four Archetypes
Freud and Psychoanalysis (CW 4)
The Gnostic Jung
Mandala Symbolism
Mysterium Coniunctionis (CW 14)
On the Nature of the Psyche
The Practice of Psychotherapy (CW 16)
Psyche and Symbol
Psychiatric Studies (CW 1)
Psychogenesis of Mental Disease (CW 3)
Psychological Types (CW 6)
Psychology and Alchemy (CW 12)
Psychology and the East
Psychology and the Occult
Psychology and Western Religion
The Psychology of the Transference
The Spirit in Man, Art, and Literature (CW 15)
Symbols of Transformation (CW 5)
Synchronicity
Two Essays on Analytical Psychology (CW 7)
The Undiscovered Self

OTHER BOLLINGEN PAPERBACKS DEVOTED TO C. G. JUNG

C. G. Jung Speaking
Complex/Archetype/Symbol in the Psychology of C. G. Jung
Psychological Reflections
Selected Letters
C. G. Jung: Word & Image